Happy 25!!
Charley

4/18.

THE STACEY WEST

A SEASON IN BLOGS

2017/18

First Edition

BY GARY HUTCHINSON AUTHOR

Dad.
—UTI xx

The Stacey West – A Season in Blogs 2017/18

The Stacey West – A Season in Blogs 2017/18

FIRST EDITION

First Published June 2018

Copyright Gary Hutchinson

All rights reserved. No part of this publication may be reproduced, stored in a retrieval system or transmitted in any form, or by means electronic, mechanical, photocopying, recording or otherwise without permission in writing from the publisher

WE ARE IMPS

The Stacey West – A Season in Blogs 2017/18

Bibliography & Acknowledgements

Thanks to the following website and publications which helped with the research of this book.

www.redimps.com

The Lincolnshire Echo

The Imp match day programme

BBC Sports Website

Photographs by Graham Burrell

Massive congratulation to

Ethan Blundell (Bostwick picture)

&

Elizabeth Frankish (Rhead picture)

Who were the winners of our design a cover competition

With years 4, 5 and 6 of Digby Primary School

For Mum

She's always supported me in every way

For Dad

I only ever wanted to make him proud

The Stacey West – A Season in Blogs 2017/18

CONTENTS

Introduction 7

PRE-SEASON 9

August 43

September 65

October 85

November 108

December 131

January 147

February 173

March 193

April 209

May 236

The Players - Keepers 250

The Players – Defenders 252

The Players – Midfield 257

The Players - Forwards 264

5

The Stacey West – A Season in Blogs 2017/18

The people on this page are what it is all about. It is you, blog readers, Imps fans and the lifeblood of the club. I don't know you all personally, not all of you know me either but we're all bound by one thing. Thank you, all of you, for supporting me and supporting the club.

David Ellis, David Ward, Chris Pearson, (Auntie) Jo Pearson, Neil Hanson, Andrea Marshall, Pete Chapman, Andy Chapman, Gavin and Ellie Andrews, Ian Dovey, Pete Summers, Dave Adams, Jimmy Newlin, Sally Blackman, David Reynolds, Paul Bullivant, Harry Bullivant, Charlie Bullivant, Rob Scott, Simon Bullen, Malcolm Froggatt, Lee Chester, Jake Chester, Charlie Carter, Massimo Fabbreschi, Libby White, Bruce Woolfit, Julian Woodhall, Stuart McNeil, Dylan McNeil, Peter Chapman, Andy Chapman, Will Eades, Becca Daubney, Les Daubney, Kerry Milligan, Andrew Bruce, Will Lidbetter, Ben Daniels, Ben Grundy, Dave Martin, Dave Mundin, Kev Barwise, Ian Greaves, John Dexter, Lisa Dexter, Andy Helgesen, James Atkin, Pete Hutchinson, Mo Hutchinson, Shirley Muxlow, Keith Muxlow, Dan Muxlow, Ben Ward, Naomi Spittles, Tony Ackroyd, Ryan Husak, David Brown, Glenys Wilcox, Heidi Langham, Ian King, Alan Long, Ian McCallum, Chris Graham, Darren Speed, Carl Gibson, Lena Harris, Andy Townsend, Sam Yates, Samantha White, Rawiri White, Emma Crellin, Ed Heppenstall, Sinaed Fletcher, Adi Bolger, Jason Robinson, Derek Priestley, Dave Tindall, Mal 'Spike' Froggatt, Dan Thompson, Josh Flowers, Daniel Lambert, Jordan McLaren, Paul Matuszewskyj, Peter Chapman, Peter Wells, Norman Vasey, Michael Thomas, David Wilkinson, Ross Allen, Simon Gray, Rachel Richardson, Ken Wilson, Andy Woodthorpe, Tim Ward, Simon Wells, Graeme Clayton, Nick Oxberry, Ty Corcoran, Ian Dobson, Paul McCrone, Rob Cox, Chris Wray, Glenys Newton, Gary Denton, Simon Gibson, Mike Downs, Doug Robinson, Ben Daniels, Shaun Dixon, Jen Wray, Sarah Skelton, Paul Stallebrass, Matthew Wilson, David Pickwell, Ed Bruntlett, Rob Beezley, Danny Finn, Andy Fisher, Paul Owen, Joe Owen, Steve Jollands, Ben Scott, Sam Ashoo, Rick Keracher, Jon Battersby, Simon Bullen, Ian McCallum, Paul Scott, Graham Jolly, Norman Vasey, Brian Luke, Simon Gray, Richard Godson, Nigel Keal, Andy Cawdron, Stephen Jolly, Andy Bulley, Nick Procter, Charlie Russell, Wayne Raithby, Mandi Slater, Sam Kendall, Richard Smith, Roy Thomson and anyone else who reads, comments and shares my blogs or just supports this bloody ace football club

Lewis Freestone (2006-2014)
Colin Morton RIP
Pete Newton RIP
Jeff Hutchinson RIP

Special thanks to Bubs for his photographs. He supplies me with material not just for my books, but also for the website and he helps bring my words to life.

Thanks as always to my fiancée and life-partner Fe. I suppose she's used to it now.

Introduction

On April 22nd, 2017 Lincoln City achieved promotion from the National League. It had been the darkest spell in the club's history, a six-year exodus from the Football League which marked the longest period in our entire existence.

My book 'A Season in Blogs' covers the 2016/17 succinctly I feel, it is a blow by blow account of one fan's expectations as they sprouted, grew and eventually flowered into the wonderful day of April 22nd. Of course, it wasn't all about the league either, there was the small matter of an FA Cup quarter-final and us being the first non-league team for 115 years to actually get there. It was a historic season indeed.

How could Danny and Nicky follow that? How could our football club develop back in the big time, facing teams such as Morecambe, Yeovil and the dreaded Forest Green, but also mixing it with Luton and Coventry City? What could 2017/18 have in store for us?

The introduction was seemingly all-too brief, after all I'm merely picking up a story where another left off, so I thought we'd cap it off with a brief explanation of who I am, why I'm writing yet another bloody book and then add some kind words from readers of the site.

The Stacey West started as a conduit for my anger and frustration in March 2016, although I'd been writing long before that. My real-life job was a hassle, a protracted process of stress, intimidation and pressure. I came home at night and wrote, then I spent some time signed off sick and wrote some more. Eventually, a spell of severe anxiety side lined me for four months and in that time, the site grew from a couple of articles a week to something updated daily, sometimes hourly.

Once last season finished I was asked if I'd put together a collection of the articles as a memento of the season. Whilst it was all fresh in our minds at the time, eventually it would dull and fade for some, but they wanted the story, through a fan's eyes, as it developed. They wanted it to remind themselves of the stress before Tranmere at home in December, because that rather gets lost when other memories such as winning at Turf Moor are competing for the memory space.

So, I pulled it altogether, raised a modest sum for the Future Imps fund and it's sold a few copies since. I'm not going to trouble the best-seller list anytime soon, nor will I give up my day job, but it's nice that people still ask me about the book now. Some even asked if I was doing one this season, one asked me as we were walking away from Wembley having won our first major cup final in our entire existence. It's hard to say no under those circumstances.

As for giving up my day job, the book might not have allowed it, but my incessant writing has. Recently, I packed in selling building materials and such like and started freelancing for Football League World amongst other sites. I'm not going to retire early, but I get satisfaction from what I do. The last time I released a book I did it in my spare time as a salesman. This one I release in my spare time as a writer. It feels nice.

Something else that feels nice is the warm glow when someone sends me a nice email or compliments the site in some way. To finish off this introduction, I'd like to include a couple of those for you. Enjoy the story of 2017/18, as it unfolded.

"The Stacey West means a lot to me as living overseas in Perth Australia, I'm pretty isolated from the match day atmosphere and the general banter and discussion about all things Imps.

The Blog gives me another avenue to keep my finger on the pulse and the conversational style gives a real feel for the pre and post-game chat down the pub that I'd be having if I lived in Lincoln and was able to attend games regularly.

From Gary's distaste for Steve Evans, to his balanced support for players under pressure, to even his opinion on possible signings, I get a real sense of the rollercoaster from a fan on the front line.... exactly the place I wish I could be!

Having been a diligent reader for some time it was great to meet Gary personally the season before last ahead of the Macc championship clinching game and pass on my compliments personally. Keep up the great work Gary! UTI!" – Jordan

The Stacey West – A Season in Blogs 2017/18

"The Stacey West Stand, named in honour of the two supporters who were tragically killed in the Bradford Fire, is quite rightly part of the fabric of our stadium. In a similar way, Gary's excellent blog, "The Stacey West" has become in a digital age of Tweets, Instagram and Facebook and integral part of the Football Club.

Articles are thought provoking, often controversial, or insightful. Occasionally reflective in nature but always well written and an excellent read. It is little wonder that these blogs from the excellent Gary Hutchinson have been deservedly nominated at National Level, not bad for a blog two year into its existence, featuring what was at the time, an unfashionable and unsuccessful non-league team." – Paul

"Living outside of Lincoln (Nottingham) I have felt in the past a little cut off when it comes to news, views and opinions. I followed as best I could but survived only on gossip and Carling induced offerings on match days. Thin pickings most of the time.

I discovered The Stacey West Blog when I finally gave up my Luddite ways and joined social media. Twitter being my choice although I'm still not sure it will catch on. Anyway, what I found was that most of the posts were gossip and Carling induced opinions, only now not just limited to match days. The one highlight seemed come from some bloke in the Wolds who offered me insight, informed opinion and sometimes an inside view from my club. Suddenly I felt connected again.

The 16/17 season was immense and never to be underestimated or forgotten. In my opinion this last season has been even better, actually matching my rose-tinted forecast by reaching the top seven. Not even I dared dream of winning a Wembley cup final.

The strength of your blogs this last year has matched all that has happened on the pitch. By putting yourself up there, sometimes to be fired at, you have made this exiled fan feel connected once again. Opinions vary but they also matter and whilst you quite obviously live and breathe Lincoln City FC you are not afraid to call out players or staff when you feel it necessary. I look forward to the twitter musings of my fellow Imps laughing and sometimes crying alongside them. However, when I wander in after a long day at the coal face the first thing I do is check my emails for the latest Stacey West Blog, or more often than not, blogs. I agree with some, I disagree with parts of others but I always finish the read, informed and entertained.

In short, The Stacey West Blog is like picking up an old pair of your favourite jeans and finding a tenner stuffed in the back pocket. A delight. So, thank you Gary, please keep the good work and maybe I'll pluck up the courage to say Hi when I spot you at a game." – Andy

"What's special about the Stacey West? Well, it's the bumper blog of fun for Lincoln City fans, that's for sure! It is the only click for on the money views and breaking views about Lincoln City. Match reporting is detailed and insightful; views are balanced and there is a good proportion of objectivity. The writing catches the emotions of match moments, conveying how it all matters to the fans. The interactive stuff is first rate: ......predictions league.... quizzes......opportunity to have your say on Imps past and present. The blog has both quantity and quality. For me, it's a go-to every day. Gary....don't ever stop!" – Dave

"I came across The Stacey West via the News Now site whilst I was searching for up to date information on Lincoln City last season – particularly when there were rumours that Grimsby Town wanted Danny Cowley as their manager. In this age of anonymous, negative 'keyboard warriors' it was refreshing to find a more balanced view with even an optimistic slant. I now regularly read his articles & find that I agree with most of his comments. Living outside Lincoln & not being a season ticket holder, I also rely on the articles for an honest report of any matches I have missed. Having followed Lincoln City since attending my first match in 1971, I may be older than the target demographic market for The Stacey West but I really like the content & at least I remember watching some of the 'older' Imps to whom Gary refers!" – Keith

Thanks guys – best let you get on with the book now!!

PRE-SEASON

The Retained List

May 18, 2017

So earlier I suggested that the retained list might not be out until after the weekend, and four hours later here it is. I also suggested Lee Angol would sign for us permanently in the summer, and today he's signed for Mansfield. Seems like everything I say is wrong, so just for the record we won't win League Two next year.

Any surprises on the retained list? The obvious exclusion of news on Bradley Wood is perhaps the one thing everyone is talking about. Now I've stayed silent on this and I'm going to continue that stance, but here's some advice. We know the situation isn't straight forward, and until either Bradley or the club make a statement, perhaps we should leave it where it is?

The biggest surprise to me was to see Sean Long labelled as a player retained for next season. I know Reading have released him, but there hasn't been any news of him signing a deal for us, has there? Have I missed something? I'm usually quite attentive when it comes to signing players and all that. It has now been revealed though that he has signed a one-year deal, although news of that hasn't broken officially.

There weren't any real shocks on the list, the players who had been part of the promotion party have all been offered deals. Some expressed surprise that Jack Muldoon and Adam Marriott were offered terms, but I think that shows that Danny is a man of his word. He said he would endeavour to reward those who fired us to the title last year, and in the main he has done that. The sentimental part of me is also pleased to see Alan Power has been offered a new deal as well, after six years in the non-league with us I'll be chuffed to see him in the red and white as a Football League player.

At least in offering Callum Howe a deal we know we're not pushed to bring in another centre back in a hurry! In Howe, Waterfall and Raggett we have three quality central defenders. That is if Howe signs the new deal, the same goes for Power, Muldoon, Marriott and Richard Walton. I've read that Jack Muldoon is interesting Fylde, and if he thinks he'll get regular football, would you blame him for leaving?

I notice Terry Hawkridge has been offered a new deal as well. Let's see how that pans out.

I think Lee Beevers being offered a testimonial match is a nice touch. The moment he went to ground against Boreham Wood I wondered if we'd seen the last of him in a City shirt, and sadly it turns out that is the case. Lee had been a revelation in the opening part of this season, and I certainly hope any match we do play for him will be well attended. As for Jamie McCombe, I know he hopes to move into coaching on a permanent basis, but if I'm not mistaken he is based in Harrogate, so maybe it could be a bit far for that role? I hope not, I like Jamie and he's good to have around the club with all his experience and contacts.

For me (and this may come as a surprise) I think news of Adam Marriott being offered a new deal is good news. I've always rated Adam Marriott as a 'proper footballer', and he turned several games he came on in (Ipswich, Tranmere, Guiseley and Torquay). There are question marks over his pace and his fitness, but as a squad player I don't think we could find a better person. When you see him celebrating the goals as a sub, running the length of the pitch to join in, you get a feel for how committed he is. He might not be a 50 game a season man, but he does have the ability to change things when the chips are down.

So that is the retained list, was it worth the wait? I'm not sure there was anything too revealing on there, not given that Farms and Luke Waterfall had already signed deals. There is no guarantee the players who have been offered deals will sign them, so in reality all we've been told is this: all the young players have been released, all the senior players have been offered new deals. So, we'll now sit and wait 'patiently' for news of new signings, shall we?

Welcome to Sincil Bank: Sean Long
May 25, 2017

In the excitement of the retained list being named, it had passed by many that Sean Long had signed a permanent deal with the club. There had been no Facebook live, no news headlines and no real fanfare. The right-back from Reading had quietly slipped through the door with no fuss to become the first of the loan players to join the Cowley revolution.

I wanted to make sure that Sean got a headline or two, so I caught up with him this week to welcome him officially to Sincil Bank.

"Thanks very much I'm delighted to be staying here permanently. Last season was an unbelievable experience. To be part of what the team achieved was brilliant and it's something I'll never forget."

Sean started his career in Ireland with Cherry Orchard and was snapped up by Reading four years ago. In August 2014 he made his Reading debut as a substitute in a 1-0 League Cup win over Scunthorpe, but that turned out to be his only appearance in a Royals shirt.

"Of course, I was disappointed not to nail down my place in Readings first team. I managed to make my debut in a cup game against Scunthorpe but other than that I was only on the bench now and again. There has been a lot of changes over the years which maybe didn't help however I've no bad feelings whatsoever. I met some great people there and learned so much as a player and wish them all the best in the future."

As he wishes Reading well for the future, he now turns his attentions to a full season at Sincil Bank. Despite the move being conducted in a relatively low-key fashion, it was a no-brainer for Sean.

"There was a number of factors which made my mind up to stay here. The club is surrounded by really determined and ambitious people who want to achieve even more great things and I want to be a part of that. Also, the support I witnessed from my time on loan blew me away. Lastly to get the chance to continue working with the Manager and Nick is something I couldn't turn down. I've been with them awhile now they know me well and I feel they get the best out of me. I just want to keep learning."

Sean made his City debut as a late sub at Portman Road as we drew 2-2, he got his first start a week later as we beat Gateshead in the FA Trophy 3-1, and finally he made his home league debut against Dover on January 20th to cap a busy fortnight. Following on from that he started 15 times with a further 4 as substitute as we secured the league title and a historic FA Cup run. It was his home debut that really stood out as a high point.

"A lot of people probably would have mentioned the FA Cup games (as a highlight) however for me my personal highlight of the season was making my home debut in the league against Dover. The Bank was buzzing, and I felt I done quite well in a 2-0 win. Clean sheet was nice as well."

Having now committed to the Imps for next season, Sean is keen to make sure we see the best version of him once we finally kick-off as a Football League team.

"I'll be working hard as I always do in the off season to make sure I report back for preseason in good condition. From a footballing point of view first of all I'm a defender so my main job is to stop the opposition and keep clean sheets. I also want to be able to excite the fans by bombing forward and creating chances. "

He's also certain that hard work will be reflected across the squad, as our ambitious young managers seek another successful campaign.

"As a team we will all come together in pre-season and I'm sure Dan and Nick will continue their hard work to ensure we are ready for what I'm sure will be another memorable season."

Whatever happens it would be incredibly hard to top the twelve months we have just had, and new recruits are going to be very important. There's no Mansfield-style rush needed to drag players in quickly, but Sean represents the first of several new faces who will help shape our future endeavours. We ended our chat with a message from Sean for the fans, and it seems a fitting point to wrap up the article.

"To the fans of Lincoln. Firstly, just to thank you for the support you have shown the team this season you were that 12th man on the pitch. Secondly for making me feel welcomed and part of the club. It was a bit under the radar, but I'm delighted to be able to say I'm a Lincoln player. I hope I can help the team achieve even more success next year and look forward to seeing all of you at the bank next season. WE ARE GOING UP!!!"

Sam is on board for an extra year
May 25, 2017

Great news this evening coming out of Sincil Bank, 'steady seven' Sam has signed an extension to his current contract and pledged his immediate future to City.

Often the pre-season clamour for signings takes precedent, and clubs can be judged on who they bring in rather than what they do to hang on to their key players. Keeping Farms and Waterfall was a great move by the club, and now Sam putting pen to paper really ices that cake.

I've spent all season blowing smoke up the player's arse and I'm sure you're getting tired of it now (at least I don't tag them in social media posts though. Cringe). I don't need to tell you what Sam Habergham offers this side, you've seen it for yourself. He scores free-kicks, something we've never really been good at, he overlaps the wingers but is always first to track back as well. His dead ball delivery is obviously sufficient, he had the third highest amount of assists this season. He's a very good player, more than capable of playing League One football. He also has a wicked left foot, a valuable commodity at any level of the game.

Retaining his services for another year gave me a warm glow, because for me it signals Danny and Nicky's intent to stay with us as well. Sam Habergham is one of their 'generals', along with Alex Woodyard he's been on the journey with them longer than we have. When those two guys sign on for two years, it is safe to assume the intention from the managers is to stay that time as well.

Look, here is a harsh fact: we will lose a player or two this summer. The smart money is on a Sean Raggett move, if someone finally triggers his release clause of course. The other players primed for a move were Sam, Luke Waterfall and Alex Woodyard, but all three have pledged their future to Lincoln City. Don't under estimated the message that sends out to potential suitors.

As fans we only see half of what goes on, the rest we fill in for ourselves. We see Sam is contracted for a year, so we move on to those who are not contracted. However, there will be a lot of League Two and One clubs out there in need of a left back and with a few hundred thousand to spend. The danger of losing Sam was as real as the danger of losing Raggs, but by signing an extension he essentially puts up a 'not for sale' sign and moves on with his pre-season preparation.

Those worried that our current players are signing, but fresh faces are not: don't. The proper season hasn't even ended yet, and teams signing players now are paying over the odds. That is fine if you're Mansfield, but at this level you never know what is around the corner. Being frugal and attentive to the bank balance is common sense, and a player costing £2.5k a week now might be costing £1.5k come the end of June. I trust Danny completely, and I can't ever say I have given any manager 100% trust. I don't believe he will bring filler players to the club, I don't believe he will invest in expensive white elephants but most importantly I don't think he will go into next season under strength.

Getting a player like Sam Habergham to sign an extension is a shrewd bit of business. It is rewarding the player for helping to get us promoted, and it is firing a flare into the sky for our League Two rivals to see. There will be no mass-exodus. We are not a selling club. We are not just back to make up the numbers, we're back to carry on the journey we started twelve months ago.

Now everyone settle back in your chair and be patient for news of new signings, rest assured just because you're not hearing anything doesn't mean challenging work isn't being put in.

When are we going to sign someone?
June 4, 2017

Getting worried now.
Why are we hearing nothing?
All our targets are joining other people.

The joys, and occasional irritation of social media. Giving everyone a voice means everyone uses it, and at the moment the so-called lack of action on the transfer front is causing some real consternation, especially on the banter pages. My question is this: what exactly are you worried about?

Do you think we'll go into the season without enough players? Do you think come the start of August our programme will have a squad of 13 listed on the back and no more? This isn't 1982, this is 2017 and come the big kick off I'd wager our squad will be more or less ready, bar a couple of late loan signings.

Last season Alex Woodyard signed first, and he arrived in mid-June. In the days of Keith Alexander, we often waited until July 1st when a list of the players who'd signed contracts with us would be released. I remember getting an Echo with the names of seven players we'd signed (Keates, Kerr, Cryan and four other who escape me). Back then there was no real panic, no pressing sense of urgency.

In my eyes the 2016/17 season finished last night with the Champions League Final, traditionally the final knockings of football across Europe. With that in mind in baffles me that people are concerned with our situation at present, the season has literally just finished. I know the counter argument will be 'look at Mansfield though, all their business is done'. Granted it is, but at what price?

Danny has a sensible view of the transfer market, he knows that a player's 'value' now will be as high as it can be, and as the days progress and the panic sets in those prices will come down. Let me ask you this: do you think come August 1st there will be a glut of clubs picking from one or two players, or do you think there will be a massive list of footballers without clubs? It will be the latter, and just because one or two are snapped up now does not mean 'all the good ones will be gone'.

What motivates a player signing a deal at this point in the season? Financial security? Getting the inflated wages that their agent has asked for? Almost certainly. Take Terry Hawkridge, and this is no slur on Terry. Has he joined Notts County because he desperately wants to further his career, or has he gone because they've offered really good money for two years? Now flip that over, would we want players who were simply joining for the money and stability, or do we want hungry players desperate to work under a successful management team, not motivated (as much) by pounds and pence?

Look at Angol. I'm led to believe we had a clause to sign him, but I imagine if others joined the race then we'd have to raise our bids accordingly. Angol claimed (allegedly) that he wanted to play football higher than Lincoln, and then signed for Mansfield. Has he signed for Mansfield because he believes they are a great route to better things, certainly stronger than City? Or have they bought his loyalty and commitment? Can you buy loyalty and commitment? I don't think you can. Luke Waterfall signed a deal with us despite intense pressure from other sides, and I'm told much better offers. He's stayed put because he buys into what we want to achieve. I want players like that to sign for our club, and if it means waiting until July then so be it.

Agents are busy behind the scenes, desperate to get their product on the shelf before anyone else, but in two weeks' time prices will creep down. There are players out there like Arnold, Waterfall and Alex Woodyard who are not all about money and immediate security, but they'll be assessing options based as much on footballing merit as anything. There will be players who are still on their holidays, not even thinking about talking to clubs until this season has ended. Just because other clubs are signing good players doesn't mean there will be non left. Remember, one man's trash is another man's treasure as well.

Finally, how do you expect to sign players when Danny is on holiday, possibly Nicky too? Why would you expect them to have their phones turned on all the time when they are getting that precious family time together? If you work in Tesco, would you leave your phone turned on whilst you were on the beach in Spain, or wandering around beautiful Italian cathedrals? No, of course not. Now I know their job is more high profile, but the concept of a holiday remains the same. You might think things are quiet at City, but did you know in May Grimsby don't even open the ground? Everything stops for a few weeks off. Nothing has stopped at Lincoln, it is just happening at a reasonable and considered rate.

In this modern world where everything is immediate, everyone has a voice and life moves quickly, it is easy to get caught up in things, but the truth is our apparent lack of activity is fictional. In years gone by we very rarely had any business sorted by the first week of June, and a lot of the time we didn't by the first week of July. Social media and rich teams clamouring to spend quickly have given us a false impression of the football labour market, and we all just need to calm down and have faith.

I'm fine with the situation, and I'm the most pessimistic person I've ever met. I know we'll be well-equipped come the first game of the season, and I know we'll get better from there. I have no doubt that the players Danny really wants, the ones he has truly targeted, they will still be without a club. There may be the odd one (Angol) that we miss out on but taking a wider view I don't think we'll be losing out left, right and centre. After all, when I read 'another player we've targeted joins someone else', I wonder on what authority people have it we're targeting players? I don't know everything, I speculate whenever I read something on the internet be it on a clickbait site or a proper news source.

I saw a post lamenting the fact Morgan Ferrier had joined Dagenham, but bar a click bait site and some analysis on here six months ago, we've never been officially linked with him. Danny has never come out saying he's interested in the player either, so how have we missed out on an apparent target? It was different when Angol went to Mansfield, but officially nobody really knows who we are or are not after, and therefore we don't actually know if we're being outdone in the transfer market at all. Now if Jordan Williams rocks up at Field Mill...

If you're worried about the squad, so-called lack of signings and lack of news coming out of the club, I have some advice. Open a six pack, pop the cork on your wine bottle, roll a Jamaican woodbine, do whatever you do to chill out. Then, go and actually chill out.

This will come together. If come July 14th we still haven't signed anyone, then (and only then) shall I be concerned about the lack of progress.

Record Season Ticket Sales Herald in New Era
June 11, 2017

Lincoln City have sold more than 5,000 season tickets. Five Thousand.

I'm not sure the enormity of this number is fully appreciated, or what a marked change it represents in the football fans of Lincoln and their relationship with the local club. Last season the club sold 1300, a figure that was slightly up on the year before, and a figure that was seen as reasonable in comparison to previous year's sales. As I'm from a sales background I thought I'd break it down this way: if we were talking about year on year increase, our season ticket sales have increased by 388%.

I am told that once the Junior Imps numbers have been factored into those sales, the base number for league attendances at Lincoln City next season will be 5500. That will be the number of bums on seats before an additional ticket has been sold in anger, before an away fan has squeezed into their part of the ground, and of course before those who do not have £300 lying around to throw at a season ticket. 5500, and counting.

Let me keep going with trying to illustrate the size of what we have achieved as a club and as a base of fans. Looking at last year's average attendances, Cambridge were 8th in League Two with 4737, then in 7th came Grimsby with 5259. We have sold as many season tickets alone, as the average attendance of all but the top seven in League Two. If you throw the Junior Imps numbers into that, Carlisle were 6th with 5305, then Notts County with 5969. Those numbers are attendance averages over the season, including away fans, pay on the day fans, season ticket holders and whatever other incentives those clubs use day to day. Our figure of 5500 is nothing more than a starting point. It also does not include tickets sold through the Fan Players Scheme either, it doesn't consider those who still have to buy. Could we have 5200 by the time the season starts? Very possibly.

Coventry City are seen as a behemoth of a club this season, languishing in League Two when their rightful place is perhaps the Championship or higher. They've got issues of course, and whenever a club free-falls it sheds some of its fan base, but even they have 'only' sold 3200 as of Thursday. Contrast that to our fishy friends down the road, they caught the bus a little late and only went on sale this week, but the last numbers coming out of there were in the low hundreds, but their 'magical' figure, the aspirational figure which will be judged as a massive success is 3000.

It is easy to be a little blasé about the ticket sales, it's easy to put an applauding emoji on social media or for us to lord it over some other clubs as a measure of success, but in truth bragging shouldn't be our first thought. First and foremost, we should be applauding ourselves, the football supporting public of Lincoln City. Despite some opposition fans criticising our fans for being 'bandwaggoners' when we sold 9000 for the Arsenal game, we've proven that Lincoln City Football Club has as much of a reputation in the city than it ever has.

Ever since the club appealed to fans in the 1920's, there has been an ongoing battle between the populous of Lincoln and those sat around the table in the board room. Directors have begged for fans to return, in the 20' when there was a depression on, in the 60's as we plummeted towards oblivion, in the eighties as the GMVC loomed, and then throughout the last two decades as money levels rose in the game but sank drastically at the club. I recall Steff Wright appealing to double the fan base when we were attracting 3500 a week in League Two. So often the people have Lincoln have remained unmoved by such pleas, they come for a game or two, invariably we lose that game and they return to their armchairs, unimpressed with the quality of the product they're being served up.

This season is different. This season they know the product is worth seeing, it was a TV more often than not last season. Those floating fans have seen us beat Burnley, Ipswich and Oldham. They've seen us resilient and exciting, pulling victory from the rabid jaws of defeat against Torquay and Gateshead. They've seen footballers trying to play football, pressing, harassing and working their socks off for the shirt. They've seen a board investing wisely, not over spending but not being frugal to a point where it affects performance. Most of all, most importantly of everything, they've seen a young manager and his assistant talking sense, bucking the trend of bemoaning referees and launching into a blame culture. They've seen two men who genuinely look as if they can lead us not just to the Football League, but beyond. Maybe League One, a level we've occupied once in thirty years? Maybe, just maybe, to the Championship, a level we haven't been at since the early 1960's? Belief is a key part of everything in life. If you believe in something, staunch and unwavering belief, then you can make it happen. Fans are seeing the belief in the players, the management and the staff and we know that it is time for us to believe as well. When Mansfield announce another signing, or when one of our so-called targets rocks up somewhere else, there is only slight indigence, only the odd discerning voice on social media. The nature of supporting a club means there will always be one or two, but in the main there is belief in the manager and staff to get it right. Billy Waters? Jordan Williams? Whatever. We've already made a really important signing this summer, we've signed 5,050 '12th men', 5050 noise making, rabble rousing, passionate and believing fans who showed last season that they are not only the best in the National League, but also the best at Portman Road and at Turf Moor.

So, congratulations to the club, I believe that 5050 is a record, I certainly know we've never sold that many in my lifetime. Twelve months ago, I remarked to my friend Ben Grundy as we entered the ground for the North Ferriby match, that '3000' would be an amazing figure to achieve as an average attendance all season. Now, here we are in real danger of regularly having 7000 fans inside Sincil Bank every single game. We're not just back in the Football League, we're not just back to where we were. This is going to be a very, very different campaign to those final few years in front of dwindling crowds pre-2011.

We're Lincoln City, we're back, and we've brought a hell of a lot of new faces along with us.

No Players? No Panic.
June 13, 2017

There have been some rumblings of discontent on social media platforms recently at Lincoln's lack of activity in the transfer market. Danny Cowley faced questions from BBC Radio Lincolnshire's Rob Makepeace about the situation, and he described making sure we get the right value for money.

However, Imps fans should not be panicking at all. Aside from the fact that twelve months ago we had only made one signing at this stage (Alex Woodyard), there is also the situation at several of our rivals to be considered. Steve Evans might have been a busy man at Field Mill, but over a quarter of the league have yet to make a signing.

Accrington Stanley have not yet brought a player in, and they released six players this summer, including ex-Imp Elliot Parish. Accrington finished 13th in the table last time out, five points outside of the play-off race.

Our friends from Barnet have also not signed anybody up as yet, and they've also released a clutch of players, including Tom Champion. All in all, they've let five go, and haven't strengthened despite finishing 15th last season, 13 points shy of the play-off race.

Carlisle and Exeter both featured in the play-offs, and neither has added to their ranks yet either. Carlisle have lost seven players this summer, ex-Imps Ben Tomlinson and Patrick Brough have been released, whilst Mark Gillespie rejected a new deal, and Jabo Ibehre joined up with Cambridge. The Grecians lost in the play-off final to Blackpool, and they may feel equipped to go again as they have only released three players, including former Imp Bobby Olejnik.

Colchester are another side in our division yet to show their hand in the transfer market, and they do need to add to their ranks. They were just a point short of seventh placed Blackpool, but they've shed eight players, including leading scorer Chris Porter who has defected to Crewe.

Still not convinced? 18th placed Morecambe have released three players, and they've yet to strengthen. Relegated Swindon Town are in a similar place too, only they released 12 players and as yet manager David Flitcroft hasn't signed anybody on. Even Gareth Ainsworth at Wycombe hasn't brought in any new faces, and they finished just one point away from the play-offs as well. Finally, Yeovil have lost nine players, three of which they wanted to keep for next season, and they haven't replaced any either.

Including us, that is ten teams from a field of 24 that haven't signed any new faces as yet. Port Vale and Luton have only signed one each, whilst Notts County, Crawley and Stevenage have drafted in two apiece. In truth only nine teams have signed more than two new faces, and remember we have secured the services of Callum Howe, Luke Waterfall and Paul Farman which gives us more to be happy about than sides such as Yeovil who are losing players they wanted to keep.

Mansfield may have done quick business, and it remains to be seen if that is good business. Fifteen clubs in League Two have signed a total of eight players between them, whilst three (Mansfield, Cambridge and Coventry) have brought in 23 between them. Whilst fans might get worked up at the lack of activity, it isn't unusual at this stage of pre-season.

Why we should NOT boycott the EFL Trophy
June 20, 2017

When you type in EFL on my Samsung phone, the auto-correct changes it to ego. Some might say that is a far more suitable name for our governing body. Retaining the EFL Trophy format showed an immense display of ego, not only from the EFL but also from club chairmen. The real villains were those chairmen who voted against the wishes of the fans they had spoken to.

I'll be very clear with my stance on the competition. I think it has been butchered up into the worst format it has ever taken, introducing under 23 teams from the top two divisions is abhorrent and it makes a mockery of League One and League Two. Effectively member clubs are being told we are considered in some way equal to the reserve squads from 'bigger' teams. The reserves might actually be more of a draw than the kids teams we have to endure next season.

Last season the rules that saw Luton fined for playing a so-called under-strength side were ridiculous, when teams in the lower division need revenue the last thing a governing body should be doing is fining them for squad rotation in the fourth most important competition of four. They should have allowed those teams to play whichever sides they wanted, including youngsters eager to get a taste of first team football.

Firstly, that rule has now changed. The new format stipulates that EFL teams must play 'four qualifying players from ten', meaning four of the outfield players must satisfy certain criteria. They must have either started the previous league fixture, be in the top ten players for league and cup appearances in the season, have made 40 or more first team appearances in their career, or be on loan from a category one academy club or a Premier League club. Just four players need to fit those rather loose guidelines.

That means that last season we could have started an EFL Trophy game with Josh Ginnelly, Alan Power, Adam Marriott and Jack Muldoon, with the rest of the side consisting of young players. Is that so bad? It is basically the FA Trophy of the Football League. It is another competition for the 'Lincoln Lizards', albeit in black shirts this season.

That has allayed my concerns a little, but I still remain convinced it is a lame duck of a tournament in its current format. That doesn't mean we should boycott it. Far from it.

Before I comment on the 617 statement and stance, I'll say why I wouldn't boycott it. Firstly, I don't feel as strongly as they do about the imminent threat of League 3, modern football or under 23 sides. I don't believe for one second that 72 clubs would ever vote unanimously in favour of accepting B teams in the professional ranks. The playing squads of these teams would be too ambiguous, and it would deny smaller clubs healthy competition and identity. If you were to ballot just League One and Two chairmen tomorrow, I virtually guarantee you would have enough votes to not even need to speak to the Championship sides. The threat isn't as real or as imminent as we think because we have people power amongst league clubs. There are chairmen who listen to fans and chairman who would never vote for these ludicrous proposals.

Secondly, our club needs our support. The EFL Trophy does offer financial incentives, a route to Wembley and now a chance to play fringe players in competitive matches in front of crowds, albeit smaller ones. For some young players it will be a debut, for some fans it will be a chance to see loan players and reserves who don't often get a chance to shine. It is another chapter in a season, a proper competitive game that will forever be recorded as such. Like a theatre opening its doors, the lights go on, the staff come in and the show rolls on. All of that costs money.

If I were to boycott these games I would deprive myself of a game of football, I deprive the club of my money and I deprive the players of my support. The 617 will be depriving the players of some of the best support at this level just on their principles, and whilst they are entitled to do that, I think the boycott hurts the clubs much more than the EFL.

Do you really think the EFL give a hoot as to whether Lincoln v Stoke Under 23's gets 400 or 4,000 fans? They talk about falling attendances as if they care, but they don't. They say that to appease chairman and potentially even fans, but they wouldn't care if it was played behind closed doors. They don't make money from the number of our fans at the game, they get it from sponsorship and from the Premier League. Nope, I'm afraid voting with your feet really won't worry Shaun Harvey one little bit. Whoever gets into the final, whatever level of boycott they have amongst the fans, I guarantee you it will sell 15000-30000 tickets depending on who plays. Once again, the EFL won't care one iota if 50 or so ultras sit at home and try not to watch it on TV. Not a bit.

The reason I said earlier chairmen won't vote for a League 3 is because deep down, they do listen to fans concerns, and at Lincoln I imagine they do care if the games are played in front of smaller crowds. Most club owners are driven by success as well as money, and they would never advocate such a move. They listen to their fans on the really serious issues, although perhaps not on the subject of the EFL Trophy. Playing one game against Stoke under 23's isn't a big issue but playing them in the leagues would be. They know it would relegate 'real' teams importance, and if there is one word I suspect makes chairman soil themselves, it is relegate.

I'm not a subscriber to the whole 'sanitation' of fans at games either, I don't believe that has happened at our level to any real extent. All seater stadiums aren't a major problem, and as safe standing debates take place I'd be keen to see a rule change. In the context of Lincoln City, the same sort of people are attending games now as they did in 1970 and 1980. So, we've cleaned up racism, is that bad? Homophobia has gone too, is that bad? I fear that some people look back on the 70's and 80's with a fondness it really doesn't deserve. Besides, the 617 are in their early twenties at best (bar Marcus, obviously), do they really see an issue with modern football that has developed since 1997? I don't think our game has changed at all since 1992, and most of the 617 weren't born then.

Lincoln City have even gone some way to encourage the growth of the 617 and the ultra 'scene', from securing block 7 to a wider tolerance and acceptance of their displays. There have been mental scenes at times from that area this season, and there has been a positive relationship between them and the club, to a degree. If anything, rather than sanitising the fan experience, Lincoln City have tried to cultivate it in the correct way. We now have a fan group renowned for something other than kicking heads in and smashing up pubs. If that is modern football, I'm all for it. In my eyes modern football is defined by the terrace culture, by a movement that still has the nice clobber and Adidas trainers, the same attitudes and identification with a common cause, but instead of throwing bricks and stamping on heads, they're signing, encouraging others to do the same and putting on meaningful and eye-catching displays. That is an aspect of modern football I am not against. Yes, I hate agent's fees, I hate Sky TV, I hate the Premier League, I hate the elite attitude and ghastly sums of money at the top-level. However, I love Lincoln City in 2017, with a nice stadium, good fans and a stadium I can walk away from without getting hit with a bottle or the lace imprint on my face from a size 10 Gazelle. That type of modern football I'm all for.

The 617 have a voice, and although some don't agree with it, they can use that voice how they wish. I respect their decision and, like them, I too am against some modern football. But if you have a voice, why would you not use it? Boycotting the game is missing an opportunity to make yourself heard, surely? The EFL don't read internet forums, and as much as fan power can have a positive effect, it isn't going to change this competition or the EFL's belligerent and obtuse attitude towards it. Staying silent is like not voting in the election and moaning about who won. Boycotting a Lincoln City game has the same effect as farting in your living room and believing that the EFL will smell it in their air-conditioned offices in London, or their hotel suite in Thailand. They don't care about you, your voices or your farts, the only people suffering are the club, and you.

The 617 do excellent displays and great vocals, can't that be channelled into a protest? When you're good at something you should utilise that and make your point doing something you are renowned for. Don't do it by staying quiet on your sofa, do it at a game with banners, songs, walk ins, walk outs, anything. The news won't report on a simple boycott, the club would suffer from invading the pitch and halting the game, but why not find something in the middle? All come dressed as death and chant the death march throughout the game maybe? Do something that gets attention, raises awareness but doesn't hurt the club. Do something that looks like positive action, protesting in the right way but still supporting the club.

Maybe consult with the club about your concern as well and publicise the outcome. Keep this issue in the public eye by being seen and by being vocal, the two things that you really bring to the ground on a Saturday. Don't cut off your nose to spite your face, don't risk missing out on Wembley and a club honour. Teams like us don't get opportunities like that very often, and it would be a crying shame if you had to miss a great occasion, because no matter how crap the competition is, a Wembley final is still what you get into the game for. Don't you doubt this one bit: Danny Cowley will want to win this competition, and if anything is going to scare elven under 23 players from Brighton it is a loud and hostile Sincil Bank crowd.

Make yourselves heard boys, don't be quiet. The Against League 3 movement is great, but it made no impact at all last season. That wasn't because Coventry buckled at the end, staying away did nothing other than give the movement statistics to spout about falling attendances. If the movement had been a success then we wouldn't be faced with a visit from an under 23 side this coming season, would we?

The definition of madness, as described by Albert Einstein, is doing the same thing over and over again and getting the same outcome. Staying away from matches didn't work last season, and it won't work this season either. Try something different, you're the activists and the creators, you're the voice of young fans and you're an eclectic mix of educated and working-class youths. You could think of something far more creative than a boycott, I'm sure of it.

Do what you can, but don't stay away from Lincoln City matches protesting something that won't immediately change, trying to make a point to a body that isn't willing to listen and wouldn't care if it did. You're only hurting the club, something else that the EFL don't really care about.

The fixtures are in, and it's off to Wycombe for our return party
June 21, 2017

As of 9am this morning, our league status was cemented and solidified. The new season fixtures have come out, and our rather underwhelming first league match is away at Wycombe Wanderers on Saturday August 5th.

Uninspiring it might be, but there is a certain irony to have our season opener against the Chairboys. This season marks the 30th anniversary of our promotion from the GM Vauxhall Conference, a promotion that was secured by beating Wycombe Wanderers, 2-0. They're also managed by Gareth Ainsworth, and so we get to see a former Imps legend pit his wits against the most promising young managers on the circuit today.

Our first home match is an equally uninspiring visit by Morecambe a week later, and there's a team we have a good record against. In ten previous meetings we've won five and drawn 3, with just two defeats in the 2009/10 season blotting our copy book. The last time we met them at the Bank an Ashley Grimes double gave us a 2-0 win as we looked to stay in the Football League. We know how that turned out.

Finally, those two clashes are followed by one of the more notable fixtures, a summer trip down to Devon to face Exeter City. It will be nice to get down south for a weekend while the sun is still in the sky for a festival of football. Other than that, it's a low-key start to the new season, two sides from mid-table followed by the beaten play-off finalists. No sign of any of our local rivals in the first four games, our final match of the opening month is Carlisle at home. The first month looks incredibly slimmed down when compared to last year's eight matches.

Where are the other highlights? Licensing laws don't allow me to reproduce the fixtures in full, but here are some of the dates you might want to write on your calendar. The end of September looks really tasty, Mansfield Town visit on 16th, followed by trips to Notts County (23rd) and then Grimsby Town (30th). On October 7th Chesterfield visit, and on the 14th it's Cambridge United. Arguably that is five 'local' derbies on consecutive Saturdays with a cheeky midweek visit from Barnet thrown in for good measure. If we were over-awed at being back amongst football's 'elite', those five weekends will remind us exactly what we've been missing.

We have to travel to Forest Green on a Tuesday night in September as well. Urgh.Our destination on December 23rd, Rodney Parade, Newport. Merry Christmas.

One of the big home games, Coventry City, takes place on Saturday 18th of November, but that is the only real highlight as Christmas approaches. There's very little Christmas cheer in December either, although we have been blessed with a Boxing Day clash at Sincil Bank against Stevenage, and another home game four days later against FGR. New Year's Day see's us take a long trip down to Luton, a game I suspect that won't attract a strong away following.

Mansfield and Notts County come together back to back again in January, and February's highlight is the visit of Swindon Town on the 3rd. Into the third month of 2018 we finally get the 'golden egg', a trip to Coventry and the Ricoh Arena, which is followed quickly by a trip to Chesterfield and finally the first Football League visit of the Cods since November 21st, 2009.

Our final game of the season looks familiar, Yeovil. We've met them on the final day on two occasions already, so this will be the third time we've been in the same division as them, and the third time one of our fixtures has been on the final day. In 2003/04 we lost 3-2 at the Bank, and in

2004/05 we were beaten 3-0 at Huish Park. Hopefully by then, we'll have the league wrapped up anyway!

One or two of the matches are likely to be subject to change if we progress in the different cup competitions. November 6th is FA Cup 1st round day, but obviously we have no game scheduled. Similarly, December 2nd is second round date, again a free weekend for teams at our level. The dates only begin to clash after that, and although it won't be easy, a favourable draw could see us progress to the latter stages again. If so we'd lose the trip to Mansfield on 6th January, and if we were to go further doubts would be cast on Newport at home (Jan 27th, 4th round) and maybe even Crawley away (Feb 17th, 5th round). Just be aware when buying those train tickets in advance.

If we were to get back to back quarter final appearances, in that unlikely event we'd also lose our home clash with the Cods on March 17th. I think we're hoping for a bit too much there!

So, there we have it. The fixtures are now out, the National League is nothing but a sobering memory and a reminder of what awaits us should we ever finish in the bottom two again. It is getting real now, our six-year absence is over and welcoming us back with open arms is Gareth Ainsworth, Dayle Southwell and the Beast Akinfenwa. If any battle defines the Football League more succinctly than Matt Rhead against Akinfenwa, I'd like to see it!

I'll see you all at Wycombe

Alan Power in Kilmarnock switch
June 23, 2017

Imps legend and longest-serving player, Alan Power, has signed for Scottish Premier League side Kilmarnock on a two-year deal.

Power had been offered terms to stay at Lincoln City, but the lure of a longer deal has taken him away from Sincil Bank for the first time in six seasons. There were strong rumours that big-spending Billericay had also offered him a deal, but his future lies north of the border.

The Scottish League has attracted a couple of National League faces, Roarie Deacon left Sutton United for Dundee and last season Craig Clay swapped the bright lights of Grimsby for Motherwell. A move to the side placed 8th in the Scottish top flight last season marks quite a turnaround for Power.

He had fallen out of favour after Danny and Nicky arrived, and early on in the season he had even been linked with a loan move to Boston United. He stayed put and fought barely to get back into the side, a cause helped by the shocking injury to Lee Beevers.

After impressing in the FA Cup games, he still failed to nail down a consistent starting spot, often coming off the bench. He made a brief cameo against Chester City, coming on to help shore up the midfield and being sent off moments later for a rash challenge in the middle of the park.

Up north he joins a side going through a transitional period just like Lincoln. Manager Lee Clark stepped down in February, leaving former Wigan man Lee McCulloch to take the reins. The league is an odd one to compete in, last season Kilmarnock finished 65 points adrift of champions Celtic, but just six points clear of Hamilton in the relegation play-off spot. Hearts finished fifth with 46 points but were closer to bottom placed Inverness (34) than fourth placed St Johnstone (58).

Power will join up with veteran striker Kris Boyd, once of Rangers, but in the main it is a youthful squad at Rugby Park. They have an 18,000-capacity stadium, but at present attracted just over 3,000 on average. He may have swapped the English fourth tier for the Scottish top tier, but in terms of club size there is very little difference.

I would love to have seen Alan Power pull on an Imps shirt in the Football League, because he has been with us throughout out non-league hell. He's been there contesting every ball as we morphed from a bad team of loan players into a bad team of permanent players, and eventually into the Champions of last season. Seeing him in a Lincoln shirt will now, forever, mean non-league, and that is a shame for a player who gave so much to the cause.

I like Alan Power, I always have. He's offered so much during his Imps reign, often looking lost amongst teams with no heart or soul. Somehow, he managed to stay, often pledging his allegiance to the club when it seemed nobody else would. If anyone deserves a crack at top-flight football, albeit in Scotland, then it is Alan Power.

Power's departure means the mantle of 'longest serving' player now passes to Paul Farman, a man who missed out on the first few months of our Blue Square hell, but otherwise has five and a half solid seasons behind him. Having just signed a new two-year deal it looks as if Farms could surpass both Alan Marriott and legendary keeper Dan McPhail for clean sheets and appearances. If one legend has just left us, the other is still here cementing his place in the history books forever.

As for Alan, I wish him best of luck for the future, and I think I speak for every Imps fan when I say you'll always be welcome at Sincil Bank with open arms.

Danny: Don't Panic

June 23, 2017

Losing a long-serving player is never a good thing, and irrespective of your thoughts on Alan Power's ability, losing a committed and passionate player from the ranks is always going to draw certain fans ire. For the record, I think we're losing a very talented midfielder as well as a strong character.

I can understand how some people are getting edgy, but it is completely misplaced. Yes, the new season is closing in rapidly, but traditionally business was normally done later on in the summer anyway. I remember in 2005 when Keith Alexander announced five new faces on July 1st, deals that had been done and dusted for a while but weren't announced until late in the summer. That year we made the play-offs, something we'd all class as a phenomenal success in May 2018.

I also have complete trust in our management team, after all I think they've earned enough credits to be given the benefit of any doubts some of you have. These are intelligent and hard-working men, their preparation for matches is meticulous and exhaustive: what makes anybody think their approach to this pre-season is any different?

I've exchanged messages with Danny tonight, and he has a message for the readers of the Stacey West.

"Tell everyone not to panic. we are about to announce some really great signings! UTI"

It's simple, it's to the point but Danny Cowley has never lied to us. He has never filled us with false hope or empty promises. If he says we're about to unveil great signings, who are we to disbelieve him? Last season we pulled Nathan Arnold and Sean Raggett out of the bag far later in the summer than now, and I have no reason to suspect the next couple of weeks will be any different.

Clive Nates has dropped a teaser tonight as well, tweeting:

"It doesn't happen often but sometimes there are days when it all just comes together."

There are some that say that could be about anything but consider this. Of his last twenty tweets or retweets going back until April, every single one has been about football, and I only stopped there because I got bored counting. Two or three were about Everton, otherwise they were all directly related to goings on at Lincoln City. In truth I have never seen a tweet from him about anything other than football or Lincoln City. It's safe to assume he was talking about our club and tied with Danny's remarks that gives me a massive amount of hope for the next few days.

The club have some 'warm climate' training organised in an as-yet unspecified foreign country. I understand that is due to take place in early July, and as next Saturday is July 1st, we can assume that once this weekend has concluded, we shall be hearing news of players coming in. Will there be an announcement on Saturday? Of that I'm not sure, but I am down at Sincil Bank all day on Monday and I wouldn't mind betting I'll see a new face or three whilst I'm down there.

So, don't panic, enjoy your weekend and stay safe in the knowledge that these guys have got it covered. Last year they were FA Cup quarter finalists and League winners, they know how to manage a football club. We should get back to what we're good at, speculating wildly about who we might be about to sign and drinking the evenings away.

Tomorrow you'll not see too much from me, I'm throwing a party for a few friends and I don't plan on being able to talk coherently by the time the sun goes down, let alone type things you want to read. I suggest you all go out and enjoy the weekend too, because I believe early next week the future of Lincoln City FC is going to start getting even brighter than it is now.

Deep down I'm hoping it's Billy Knott and Harry Anderson. Maybe Josh Ginnelly as well, and I see Matt Green still doesn't have a club either. Go on, you know you want to speculate too.

Ginnelly, Green and Palmer

June 26, 2017

Well, what a day that has been? I spend a whole week sat staring at my computer waiting for news and get nothing. I spend a day down at the ground and we get three signings that I'm the last person to comment on. The fact I was predisposed isn't an issue though, today we've made a real statement of our intent.

I would say something like 'I'm not going to prioritise who is the strongest signing' or something equally as wishy-washy and politically correct, but that's a lie. I'm going to launch straight into the verbal massaging of our brand-new number 10, Matt Green.

The club didn't 'need' a marquee signing, contrary to widely held belief. What we needed were players that DC feels can add value to our League Two squad, and there is no doubt at all that Matt Green does that. The strong rumour is that he could have commanded a six-figure sum just a few months ago, and to see him strutting around in City training gear today re-affirmed any slightly wavering belief I had. I wasn't one of the 'we must sign players' crowd, but I think in landing a so-called name Danny has continued to surprise fans and critics alike.

At the time of his release Matt Green spoke of having offers from the Championship to League Two, and I don't doubt there was a lot of interest in him. One name club he was apparently interesting were Bolton Wanderers, and one year ago Bradford were having significant bids turned down. He scores goals at this level, he is quick and strong too, and at 30 he also brings experience. I blogged before about him not fitting 'the Danny profile', but in truth there is no profile. If you're good enough and can add value, then sod the age or background. Matt Green adds value, no doubt.

I wouldn't be surprised if Notts County fans are watching on with a bit of envy, maybe even our fishy foes as well. Before my best friend Steve Evans joined, Green had scored 8 in 20 games for the Stags. Once Evans was in place that dropped off to 13 in 49, or just five from his remaining 29 outings. If ever a manger arriving had a negative effect on an individual, this was it. Green even commented that he knew his face 'didn't fit' under Evans, speaking to the BBC he said:

"He (Steve Evans) is the new era and unfortunately I wasn't part of his plans; that was obvious. I turned into an unhappy player. It is demoralising for any forward if you have scored the amount of goals I have, and you are not getting the respect you think you deserve."

How tasty does this make Mansfield now? I'm doing my best to underline my own personal distaste for their tubby manager, but now we have a star striker eager to prove what he is worth too. I thought Angol v Green would be an interesting battle next season, I never thought it would be with Green in red and white and Lee Angol in yellow. I'm not going to be a hypocrite and claim I wanted Green all along, I rate Lee Angol and I won't lie about that. However, we have the player who is proven at this level, has bags of experience and a point to prove. Lee Angol liked Lincoln City, had good times here and by September will probably already be disillusioned with his new managers approach.

So, bringing in Green is a statement of intent and hopefully it put a few of those mutterings of dissent to rest. That was followed up very quickly by the arrival of giant striker Ollie Palmer, another former Mansfield player who has also played for Orient.

I was fortunate enough to meet Ollie this morning and let me tell you this: if you spilled his pint you would 100% buy him another one, and probably a bag of crisps too to say sorry properly. He stands almost two metres tall, he has to duck down to walk through a standard door opening and he doesn't need a ladder or chair to change a lightbulb. If there was ever a player who was going to come in and play the 'big man' role in the long-term, it is Ollie Palmer. He's an intimidating presence that is for sure, and he'll frighten an awful lot of defenders next season.

Palmer wasn't a player I had much knowledge of if I'm honest, even though his name has been bandied about social media recently. I lumped my bets on Paul Mullins, instead the big lad has got the nod. He's got Football League experience which is great for us, he's another forward which we desperately need and (to underline in again) he's physically very impressive. Good signing? Everyone is a good signing at this stage of the season, aren't they? He's certainly not underwhelming, and he will add value to the squad which I think is sufficient for now.

I noticed Palmer commented on playing in front of 10,000 fans next season, something I'm sure has been important in selling the club to the new players. Last season our opponents were quick to point out that fans don't win you games, but they do apparently attract players that can win you games.

Finally, we got the news young Josh Ginnelly was coming back for the season. Josh admitted in a press conference this afternoon that he'd made his mind up he wanted to be back at Lincoln before we won the National League, and I think his passion and commitment should be applauded. I'm told he had options to go elsewhere, but he only had eyes for Lincoln City.

I've spoken and written about Josh plenty and I don't want to write stuff twice just as much as you don't want to read it twice. He's quick, he's tricky and I think there is a lot more to come from him. I know we didn't beat York at home last season, but I recall Ginnelly coming on in one of those games and terrifying the full-backs with his direct attacking nature. That won't be any different in League Two, the quality goes up for sure, but there will still be creaking full-backs who will not want this ball of enthusiasm and energy going off like a firework in their face. No, Josh Ginnelly certainly adds something to the squad, he added last season during the run in and he'll do the same from the get go in five weeks' time.

There ended the Lincoln City day of excitement, but you can bet your bottom dollar that's Knott the end of it. I'm led to believe by numerous sources that tomorrow will see the arrival of two more players. How does an attacking midfielder with England youth caps sound? What about a young wide player coming in on the back of scoring 15 goals last season? It's all speculation, and down at Sincil Bank they were very tight-lipped with me snooping around.

Ladies and gentlemen; It's Billy Knott
June 27, 2017

Finally, Lincoln City have announced the arrival of the talented and tenacious attacking midfielder Billy Knott.

Schooled at Chelsea and Sunderland, revered at Bradford and Gillingham. England honours at Under 16, 17 and Under 20 level. Skill, panache, poise and a range of passes that matches that of the great Peter Gain. On paper, Lincoln City have signed player that shouldn't be anywhere near League Two.

Football is a cruel mistress at times, and it hasn't always been kind to young Billy. A rash incident at Chelsea in his youth cost him the chance of emerging at Stamford Bridge, and early promise at Sunderland was cut short when Paulo Di Canio left. The fiery Italian liked Billy though, perhaps he saw something of himself in there.

A loan spell at Woking left an indelible mark on the Cards, their fans got to see glimpses of the sublime player he could be. At Bradford City he got some revenge on Chelsea, he was part of the team that defeated them 4-2, and after the match he received a signed John Terry shirt that he passed on to his father. Despite his talent he lost his first team place and was released against the fans wishes.

So, it was on to Gillingham, closer to home and a chance to rebuild his career under Justin Edinburgh. The former Spurs man described Knott as a 'bright talent' who was also a 'a very creative goal scoring midfielder and a very good dead ball specialist'. Perhaps he was then misused on the left of a diamond formation, but a change of manager early in the season left Knott out of favour once again. That is the path that first led him to Lincoln City.

The lad we first saw lacked a bit of fitness and certainly confidence. He'd gone from representing his country at 19 to the National League at 24. At a time in his career where he could be playing in the Championship he was being asked to travel to Eastleigh and Gateshead. The obvious rumours were of a disruptive player whom teams simply didn't know how to manage.

In fact, that very accusation was levelled at him on Twitter, and several ex-players were quick to defend him, including former City full back John Nutter. He said that Billy is 'one of the most likeable and easy-going team mates I've ever had, and a terrific talent too'. Josh Ginnelly lashed out at the troll saying Billy could 'pass a ball through a letterbox', and Swansea's Oli McBurnie simply offered these words of wisdom; 'He (the troll) couldn't be more wrong Knottdog, keep doing your thing bro you'll be back where you deserve to be in no time'.

Today after a few weeks of speculation and social media chatter, Billy Knott officially became an Imp. He's a talent, perhaps one that has slipped off course, but nonetheless a talent. My own view is that he is the best technical footballer I've seen in a Lincoln shirt since Peter Gain, and like Gain he has the ability to play much higher. Danny Cowley has described him in the past as a 'super talented kid who can be whatever he wants to be'. Billy Knott is a great footballer, and if Matt Green was a marquee signing, Billy Knott's arrival has the same gravity just 24 hours later.

Here's the kicker, here's the icing on the cake. We haven't just got a talented player, but we've got him at a time when I believe we are the very best place he could be playing his football, anywhere in the world. I firmly believe that in Danny Cowley, Knott has the sort of mentor that will handle him exactly as he needs to be handled. He knows the lad, not just from last season but going way back to work experience in DC's previous life. Danny is a renowned man manager, and the one thing Billy needs is someone who understands him.

I don't know Billy, I've never spoken to him, but I imagine him to be a complex person, a lad who has been through an awful lot of different emotions in the game during his short life. As a young lad he was at the very top, Roman Abramovic's Chelsea, one of the first real financial super powers. His fall from grace has been slow but is punctuated by playing highs. For every release he's suffered he has fans believing in his talent. For every manager who has cast him aside he has another who has built up his reputation again. I hate the term 'rollercoaster of a journey', but when you've gone from Chelsea to Lincoln via Sunderland, Bradford and Gillingham then I'd say that's exactly what you have. At 24 he's stood on a threshold looking at two very distinct pathways. One is further decline, more broken promises, poor management and loss of favour.

The other is the one I believe we'll see him take. It involves this diamond of a player, grubby after a couple of years of neglect, being picked up and polished by our own treasure hunters, Danny and Nicky. I see him being given a role at the head of the diamond, never allowed to feel comfortable as Elliott Whitehouse will be there pushing him all the way. He'll feel loved though, not just by the fans who always appreciate a true footballer, but also by the managers who know what a talent he is. I haven't seen them waste a player yet, I haven't seen a lad out of position all the time. Billy Knott is a round peg, and he'll get placed in a round hole for the good of everyone.

Danny is right, Billy Knott can be whatever he wants to be. If he gets twelve months consistent and 'on-method' football under his belt I believe he will become a City favourite. His range of passes and his penchant for the unpredictable is a joy, and the longer he spends with his team mates the more he'll develop an understanding with them He'll be fitter than any point since he started getting first team football, and I genuinely feel this is the true 'big' signing of the summer. Matt Green is a great signing but believe me Billy Knott is every bit as good as that. We might have been made to wait for our new faces, but it was worth it.

Welcome to Sincil Bank Billy, now get out there and prove me right.

Imps sign second keeper as competition for Farman
June 29, 2017

The Imps have unveiled their fifth signing of a hectic week, 21-year old Josh Vickers has signed a two-year deal after being released by Swansea.

Rather unsurprisingly, Vickers is well-known to Danny and Nicky, having spent time on loan at Concord Rangers in their final season there. He's six-foot tall and comes with a good football pedigree.

Vickers began his career in the youth team at Arsenal, spending time out on loan as a scholar at Canvey Island. He played 30 games there before signing his first professional contract at the Emirates. He then spent time out on loan with Danny and Nicky from November 2014 until the end of the 2014/15 season.

In August 2015 following his release from Arsenal, Vickers signed for Swansea City on a two-year deal. With first team opportunities limited he joined Barnet on loan last season, and finally got a break in the Football League. He made 22 appearances for Barnet, giving him regular football but perhaps not always the right defensive cover.

Vickers had a particularly bad week late on in September, conceding 10 in three games. Portsmouth hit Barnet for five, he then kept a clean sheet against Orient before Norwich Under 23s bagged another five. He did find his form though and ended up keeping seven clean sheets from his 22 appearances.

He was released in the summer by Swansea, prompting Danny to move to bring him to Sincil Bank. At just 21-years of age he is a prospect for the future, and he's had a good football upbringing at Arsenal and Swansea. As part of Football League rules, one of the seven players on the bench must be a keeper, and with a season long loan deal in the pipeline for Richard Walton we did need a new face.

Is he here to provide back-up and nothing more? I don't think so. Given where he has come from he'll be hungry to get first team games, and technically he has more experience than Paul Farman in league football. I think come the season opener Paul Farman will be in the sticks, but Josh Vickers will be pushing him all the way.

In terms of 'wow' factor, bringing in a second keeper could be described as a non-event, but that wouldn't do justice to Josh. The announcement might not set pulses racing, but there are interesting elements to the deal. Firstly, another two-year contract being offered up. This suggests to me that any thoughts of Danny and Nicky moving on should be put to the back of your mind. They're clearly planning a season or two in advance and that is cause for excitement in itself.

I also like the fact Josh has a strong background with Arsenal and Swansea. He's clearly highly thought of in football circles, being in goal for Barnet for a majority last season only reinforces the belief he isn't here to meekly sit on the bench. Competition for places is vital, and Paul Farman didn't have that pressure last season. He had a great campaign, and in my mind, Farms is still number one, but with an ambitious and well-schooled player pushing him all the way, he'll need to be on top of his game every week. That pressure and competition will drive us forward as a team.

Welcome to Sincil Bank Josh, you're going to like it here. We're going places.

Woodyard signs new contract
July 6, 2017

If the so-called lack of new signings is concerning to you, it's time to think again. This afternoon Lincoln have secured the services of a £500k rated midfielder, a player instrumental in a championship winning side last season.

The fact he already plays for us is irrelevant in my eyes and given that smaller clubs in higher leagues have been chasing him, its relaxing to know he's pledged his future to City. He's signed his third contract with the club keeping at Sincil Bank until 2019

Scunthorpe made an 'eye-catching' offer for Woodyard last week, but he's pledged his future to City effectively ending speculation over his future. I don't like to say I was right, but I never figured a club like Scunthorpe could just 'buy' a player like Alex Woodyard. He's always struck me as a man who wants to progress the right way, not by having money thrown at him.

This is great news for the club, it isn't a new signing, but it is every bit as good as one. Woodyard is vital to everything the Cowley brothers do, he's integral to the team and cleaning up at the Player of the Year awards proved that.

The contract is clearly a sign of his belief in the management duo, the opportunity to ascend the leagues quickly was in front of him and he refused it. Aside from Scunthorpe he had been tracked by Aston Villa and Bolton according to reports. If that is the situation then it really shows the size of the coup made this afternoon.

I'm really excited about this news, I think Woodyard and Knott will form an effective partnership in midfield, and they're both better than League Two. They are both are clearly influenced heavily by our management duo also, and it is perhaps that point which excites me more than the abilities of the two players.

What is really exciting is the display of trust and loyalty within our club. Alex trusts Danny and Nicky, and they trust him. It isn't something that happens often in football and it is a measure of the culture we have at the club. Billy Knott has dropped down to our league to play for them too, proving that they're offering something special.

You wonder if Raggs might feel the same? Next season we'll have these discussions over Sam Habergham too, will he be the same also? Could the nucleus of our National League winning side form the spine of our club for years to come?

If this is the case, as it clearly is, then why would we worry about players going elsewhere? This side isn't being crafted like Mansfield, throwing handfuls of mud at a wall and hoping some of it sticks. Danny and Nicky are cultivating a team of talented players, players who know each other's game and players who will be on method quickly. The odd striker here and maybe a full back there will help us grow, but there will be a cohesion to our game.

Remember this, when Mansfield cross over the paint on August 5th it is fair to assume the whole 11 players will only have appeared together five or six times in friendlies. When we go head-to-head with Wycombe on the same day, the spine of our team will have played 50 or 60 games together already. If they were National League quality stepping up to League Two then we might have a problem, but they're not. They're players attracting other teams at this level and higher, players other clubs know are good enough to perform a role.

Think about it. Players who played 30 odd games for us last season earned moves to the Scottish Premier or Notts County, players who weren't the first names on the team sheet are believed to be good enough for League Two and the Scottish Premier. When we think about new signings, I'm glad we're doing our business slowly and carefully, because unlike our friends at Field Mill, we don't need a complete rebuild.

It's easy to look at the names of signings and say a team has strengthened, but they've only strengthened personnel. We proved last season you need more than just players, you need the correct training, tactics, sports science, and management. You don't strengthen by just adding names and quality, we've proven that over the years when the likes of Joe Allon and Fortune-West arrived billed as good players.

Fans should not be underestimating our greatest strength of all, the 'Cowley Method'. Alex Woodyard believes in it so as far as I'm concerned, we should all believe in it.

A celebration of football in Lincoln

July 8, 2017

Today may have been the first pre-season friendly, but it was a game where the result is far less significant than the chance to get some minutes under the belt. For Lincoln United it was also a chance to showcase what they have to offer to the people of Lincoln, hoping to catch some of the Imps support when we don't have a game.

I'll come to the match shortly, but first a word about the set up down at the Sunhat Villas stadium, or as we know it Ashby Avenue. I'm going to confess it is the first time I've been there, and I was incredibly impressed. It's a non-league stadium but the facilities were certainly better than North Ferriby, a side that competed in the National League last season.

What really impressed me was the dedication of the volunteers, and their eagerness to show the positive side of their football club. From walking in the gate, through the bar and into the stadium there were smiles everywhere. Perhaps it was the thought of 1700 fans paying into the club's coffers, but I suspect it was simply how they do things.

The food was better than Double M, without a shadow of a doubt, and I came away feeling regret that I hadn't been down before. Had I not been in the process of putting together the Lincoln football magazine I may not have gone today, but after the warm reception we got I won't miss the annual friendly again, and should City not have a game when Lincoln United do, I'll definitely go along to watch the Whites. In that respect Rob Bradley and his team achieved their mission, because if they caught one 'floater' such as me, I'm sure they caught many more. I had the pleasure of chatting to Rob and to Peter Doyle, board member of the Red Imps Trust after the game, and I'll be putting that together in an article for the magazine.

This is a Lincoln City blog though, and I was also there in my capacity as a City fan. Danny didn't mess about, the whole squad got minutes with the exception of Callum Howe who I understand was carrying a knock. There was no Adam Marriott which looks to confirm the rumours he has left the club, although again I understand Danny's philosophy is 'never say never'. It's a shame if that is the case, I think Adam still has a lot to offer the squad, if not the first team. His none appearance at training this week does sound ominous though, and if he doesn't return then he goes with my best wishes, despite being to blame for a broken wrist!

Several trialists did appear for City, James Rowe being the one who most people noticed due to him looking like the love child of Alex Woodyard and Adrian Patulea. Rowe had a decent game in midfield, given it was a low-key friendly on the back of two weeks of high intensity training. The heat was harsh as well, meaning that this wasn't the best indication of the players strengths and weaknesses, but Rowe grabbed himself a goal and zipped around the place with energy which is what Danny likes.

Of all the trial players I was most impressed with Brandon Ormand Otterway who played a majority of the game at left back. We're short in the full back areas having only two recognised wide defenders at the club, and if Brandon's performance is anything to go by he's certainly worth another look. He provided the cross for City's first goal, a teasing a delicate ball that Matt Green gobbled up. All afternoon he worked tirelessly, showing flashes of his obvious quality. He played 49 times for Swindon in League One over the past two seasons and he was schooled at Arsenal, so he has the pedigree to succeed.

The other two fresh faces were both from Norwich City, so I'm told. I really liked the 'big lump' at the back, Michee Efete. He came on for the second half and looked strong and assured, and he had already caught my eye in the pre-match warm up. If indeed it is Efete, he spent a portion of last season with Icelandic side Breidablik, and he's been capped for Democratic Republic of Congo at under 21 level. He had a strong game too, although Lincoln United didn't offer a great amount going forward and his involvement was limited. I certainly think Danny will want to see more of him though, he appeared to have all the ingredients required to add value to the squad.

I believe the final trialist was also from Norwich City, right back Louis Ramsay. He warmed up alongside Efete which seems to confirm they're from the same club, and he too had an assured game when he came on. Both players have played regularly for the Canaries development side, and it is unclear whether they're here with a view to a permanent move, loan move or just for us to run an eye over.

The biggest performance of the signed-on players came from Matt Green in so much as he scored, twice. We've signed Green to score the goals, and a good striker will score in friendlies, in training and in big matches. Green showed his sharpness and his ruthlessness in front of goal to bag two in a short space of time, as City threatened to run riot. If he shows the same sharpness and application in league matches, then we'll not be short of a goal or twenty from him.

I also thought Elliott Whitehouse looked really lively when he appeared in the second half. He has a big twelve months ahead of him, and with the benefit of a 'Cowley' pre-season I think we'll see a new and improved player. He has battled back into the Football League after the disappointment of sliding out at an early age, and he will have a point to prove. It won't be easy as he'll be up against Billy Knott for a starting place, but he has always shown ultimate professionalism and he'll be up for the challenge. He certainly had the air of a senior professional towards the end of the game, directing he younger players with a confidence that belies his own youth.

It was a pre-season friendly, a blisteringly hot day and players were chopped and changed regularly so the game often lacked rhythm or cohesion. I didn't expect a festival of football so early in July, but it was a good chance to get a first look at our Football League team in action. Lincoln United, with the greatest of respect, barely got a kick as Danny approached this game as he approaches them all, to win. I'm not being cruel to Lincoln United, these are two teams at very different levels and the fact they beat us 2-0 last season perhaps shows how different the mentality is these days. When we went 3-0 up after about twenty minutes I really feared for the Whites, but they worked hard to keep us out, and despite not offering much going forward they made sure it wasn't all plain sailing for City.

Towards the end a couple of our youth players came on, and on in particular really stood out for me. Sadly, I don't know his name, and in my eagerness to name the trial players I didn't find out who the kid was (it later turned out to be Ellis Chapman). Whoever he turns out to be he showed some lovely touches and a real burst of pace as well. As you'd expect from a young player at this level he looked raw, but hopefully we can see a couple of the youth players at least get around the first team for the EFL Trophy.

Nathan Arnold wrapped up the afternoon with a fourth before the end, slotting past the giant Lincoln United reserve keeper. By then the result wasn't in doubt and perhaps a sharper and more competitive City could have scored three or four more, but again these games are not so much about the result as the chance to get minutes under their belts, or in City's case their vests. This season the players are sporting GPS vests in pre-season to monitor the work they put in, another innovation unheard of at Lincoln City.

The two clubs part ways now for very different campaigns, City look to League Two and beyond whilst United will be hoping for a play-off push and a money spinning cup run. However, the Whites will be hoping that their brilliant hospitality and warm reception will not go unnoticed and should there be a free weekend or evening for Imps fans, they might choose to head on over to Ashby Avenue to watch the City's second team.

It's JMD
July 10, 2017

I'll confess, I was getting fidgety. After predicting a signing today, it had gotten dangerously close to the end of play without anything happening, I wondered if your favourite Imps blogger was going to be left with egg on his face.

Luckily for me, in more ways than one, we've snared the signature of exciting wide man Jordan Maguire-Drew on a season long loan. As predicted, it's a new face. As predicted, it's a wide man, and true to form it is a player who will add value to the current squad. Immense value.

JMD, as he'll be called from here on in, banged in 15 goals for Dagenham last season, proving he can hack football at a lower level. He's a special talent, he's got the skills to slide down the wing, but the end product to ensure his tricks and pace don't go to waste. He's developed at an excellent rate too, last season he was a lynchpin in the Dagenham assault on the play-off race and the natural step for him was football league.

I'm led to believe we weren't the only ones in for him, we'd be naïve to believe we were, but the player has decided City are a good fit for him and vice versa. Maybe he just fancied a holiday in Portugal!

I've already blogged about JMD here and whatever the delay has been, we've finally got our man. He isn't coming here to sit on the bench and make up the numbers, he'll have his eyes on a first team place. That'll be two Premier League youngsters we have on the flanks now along with Josh Ginnelly, and with Nathan Arnold a sure-fire first team player the competition looks frightening, even more so when you consider Danny will want one more before the big kick off.

Maguire Drew does offer options down the centre as well, you don't score 15 goals if you haven't got a bit of versatility to your game. Last season when we needed a makeshift striker it was often Nathan who shifted into the middle, but I can see JMD being 'that guy' should we need to switch things up in games. However, Danny likes to label players as one or the other (Muldoon being an example) and so it's unlikely we'll see him shifted to and fro from game to game. My feeling is he's here as a wide man, he's here to add pace and end product to the flanks and only in the event of unforeseen circumstance will he be deployed down the middle.

The arrival of JMD has been met with widespread approval already by fans, I've had a private message declaring his arrival is a 'dream', whilst others have commented that he is a 'great signing'. The only word of caution I would offer is that he can be recalled in January, so we could be faced with a 'Harry Anderson' situation where h has significant impact before being dragged back to his parent club kicking and screaming. Of course, his is a minor point, I'd rather have six months of goals and crosses than nothing at all.

Welcome to Sincil Bank Jordan, another piece of the League Two puzzle slots into place.

Marriott Confirms Departure: Reaction
July 14, 2017

Speculation around the future of talented forward Adam Marriott has ended today as he's confirmed he's left Lincoln City.

It had been thought the popular striker was on his way when he failed to turn up to training just under two weeks ago. Danny said he believed Marriott had left, but until he heard otherwise he would 'never say never'.

Marriott turned out for Godmanchester Rovers this week, close to his native Cambridge, and in a statement released tonight he confirmed he has left the club. The statement read:

"After thinking long and hard about what's best for my future, I've decided to leave Lincoln City. I'd like to thank all the staff, my team mates and fans for the unforgettable season last year and the memories we all made. I wish the club all the best for the upcoming season. Looking forward to seeing what's next for me."

Many Imps fans will be disappointed at losing Marriott, we only saw glimpses of the sublime ability he possessed last season. After a promising start he injured his shoulder, and the spell out meant he was always playing catch up with the rest of the squad. After that early injury Danny seemed to hold his player back, with Marriott coming on for cameo roles only.

Over Christmas he came on to fire City to victory against Tranmere, a couple of days later he came on with us losing 1-0 to Guiseley and immediately won the penalty that turned the game. Nobody will ever forget what he did next, the sumptuous pass for Nathan Arnold that beat Ipswich 1-0 in the FA Cup third round replay.

He still found it hard to break into the side, and when he did start he often struggled to make the same impact he had from the bench. He always showed glimpses of his unbelievable quality, and he created one of the enduring images towards the end of the season. His shot created the rebound for Harry Anderson to equalise late into the match with Torquay, and moments later he was fouled for the free kick which led to Sam Habergham's goal.

One thing Marriott did lack was natural pace, and perhaps that has been on his mind since our promotion. In terms of ability I would say he was probably the most technically gifted player we had last season, a Jamie Forrester-style figure who had a penchant for the special passes and out-of-the-ordinary finishes. Unfortunately, he couldn't force his way into the starting eleven, despite us crying out for a player of his ilk when Theo Robinson left.

Adam Marriott is one of my favourite players from last year, he's the sort of forward I admire, tenacious and tricky with a keen eye for goal. I suspect the injuries he's sustained in the past have cost him a yard or two of pace, and doubtless he didn't fancy another season warming the bench and coming on for a few minutes. I believe ten minutes of Adam Marriott at the end of a game has more potential than sixty-five minutes as a starter though, somehow he had a knack of exposing tired legs with a pass or his own movement than he did when the opposition were fresh.

I personally would like to thank Adam for the broken wrist sustained celebrating his winner against Tranmere. Every minute of pain and agony was worth it for that sweet moment when McNulty sunk to his knees knowing that goal would win us the game. Memories like that, you can't buy.

I also had to chuckle when I had my picture taken with him on the pitch after the Macclesfield game. I approached him as he was signing an autograph and I remarked 'don't run away Adam, I'd like a picture in a minute,' to which he replied quick as a flash 'it's not as if I'd get away from you with my pace' and laughed. Witty as well as talented, if only he could still outpace a fat 38-year old man in a flat cap, eh?

I don't think today's news is a surprise to most Imps fans, but it is a sad day nonetheless. He joins Jack Muldoon, Alan Power and Terry Hawkridge in exiting the club with fans best wishes, and I think in all four instances those players would have been on the fringes on the fringe this season. All four have made the right decision for them, and obviously we wish them all the best.

What price on Marriott turning up somewhere like Billericay or Dover next season

The Very Best Time to Be an Imp

July 18, 2017

Being a football fan is all about moments, it's all about taking the rough with the smooth. To make being a football fan justifiable to yourself, you have to place great importance on times such as last season, and not so much on the five years of malaise we endured prior to that.

It's like being in a long-term relationship, eventually you notice all those trivial things about your partner that aren't idea, but you ignore them because the good times make up for it. When you're at work you endure the 40-hour monotonous dredge because once a month you get the kicker, a new pay packet.

Pre-season is a time when all football fans can be optimistic too, a time when the table is reset, the good teams move out of your league and the worst of those about you drop down. It is a time when mid-table obscurity is suddenly viewed as a sound base for a promotion challenge, a time when even fans of relegated teams can console themselves with being in a lower division containing weaker teams. Even if you are inherently crap, you can still glean a bit of hope in July. I've done it, year after year, always believing this is our year. In 2016/17, I was right.

That isn't why I believe now is a good time to be a City fan, nor is it purely because we won the league last season. Firstly though, a word on football fans. I know of nothing else where people can believe so vehemently in one thing but argue so much about the same subject. A glance on social media will tell you all you need to know, people falling out over missing right-backs, over when tickets are available, on whether to boycott games or not. All around me fans are arguing away as if there is no tomorrow, and you know what? I think it's great.

I mean more people than ever care about our club. I never saw any debate like this before, two years ago the 1200 season ticket holders didn't really want to get their tickets, I think they did it out of duty. We weren't in the EFL Trophy to fall out about it either, and nobody cared sufficiently about our players to care whether they stayed or went. All we talked about was the possibility of challenging the top ten in England's fifth tier, a forgotten club lost to the wider world of football and abandoned by all but a few diehard supporters within our own city limits.

That is one of the reasons it is so great to be a fan now, because more and more people care. No longer do you have to walk into your local and scour the room for the one other person who thinks that Welling away is a crucial fixture. No longer do you greet the new person at work excitedly in case he (or she) might harbour the same secret desire for the red and white as you. No longer are you a secret Imp, now you're out. Now you can scream 'We are Imps' randomly in a town centre pub and almost immediately everyone will join in with you. We bided our time, but finally Lincoln City are back in fashion.

We're not just back in fashion now, but we're breaking new ground every single day. I can't recall a transfer policy in the close season that brought the leading scorer from a team who played the season before at a higher level. I can't recall us tempting tenacious Premier League youngsters, not ones who actually have skills to match their status. I can't recall us ever bringing in a player like Billy Knott, skilful and tricky with the sort of pedigree reserved for a higher division. I certainly can't recall our best players being linked with moves away, and then staying put. If you think pre-season itself is cause for optimism, then the actual facts of the situation should feed that even more.

I wonder how many other teams could put on a screening of their season highlights DVD at the Odeon cinema in their City, and need two screens for the demand? That whole event is a testament to how much the club has grown and morphed into something everyone can be proud of. I can't wait, I've had to juggle all sorts of appointments around to take my place on the red carpet, but just like the open top bus ride, that evening is a celebration of the club and the city settling into perfect synchronisation. Lincoln City is loved by fans, but also by the everyday residents of our fine home city. I've never known it, I've never known so many people be proud of the football club.

Financially we're stable, the crowd funder isn't a cry for help but an opportunity to help. The future of the football club is assured, now we are raising money to help build the beast bigger and better. Fund raising isn't always about being on the bread line and paying bills, as Danny Cowley says it's all about adding value to what we already have. If you're proud of this club then it's another opportunity to put cash in. Some don't want to, that fine, that's your prerogative. The fact people are arguing over whether they want to invest in the crowd funder or save their money for other schemes is yet another sign of how far we've come.

A popular football blogging site asked 22 fans of League Two teams who they felt the dark horses were this season, and 10 of them said Lincoln. That's 10 out of 21 (I was asked and couldn't really say Lincoln) other fans recognise what we are building here. They see the buzz and the industrious work around our club, and they're looking in from afar. The tag of 'dark horses' perhaps isn't something we want, sliding under the radar did us nicely last season, thank you very much. What it does show though is that our optimism is founded, that our club is experiencing something unique, something it has not experienced in many years. That isn't disrespectful to previous chairman, managers or boards, they did what they could. No, it is instead a pat on the back for the current regime in achieving a level of togetherness and belief that I have never witness in my thirty-one years following Lincoln City.

So, whenever people wonder why we're football fans, we can tell them about how things feel right now. We're on the cusp of a return to the Football League, bigger, better and stronger than we've been in decades. Nobody has burst that bubble yet, we haven't lost our opening three games, we're not knocked out of the cups yet. Our new signings are still world-beaters, they've not proven to be over-hyped. There's money in the bank, we're well managed and the whole city cares.

It's a great time to be an Imp, it's a great time to be alive.

History

July 20, 2017

What else can we say about this evening's news? History has been made, pure and simple. Never before in the entire life of Lincoln City Football Club has such a double transfer swoop been made. Believe me there are 23 teams in League Two looking at their social media feeds tonight wondering what exactly is happening at Lincoln City.

I'll come to Harry in a bit, his move to City alone is a coup for the club. I can't go a minute longer without typing the following sentence: Michael Bostwick has signed for Lincoln City.

His name might not be 'household', he may not be a Premier League player dropping four divisions but bringing him to the club is the single most audacious coup I have ever known us to pull off. He is a versatile midfield player, comfortable in front of the back four or indeed as part of it. He can sit in at right back, he can even fill in at centre back. He's tough tackling with one setting: intense.

He made his name at Stevenage, helping them to the Conference title in 2010 as well as the FA Trophy the season before. After two seasons with them in League Two he fell onto the radar of Darren Ferguson at Posh and was eventually signed for an 'undisclosed' fee rumoured to be £250k.

He made 39 appearances for them in the Championship and has been virtually ever present over his five seasons at London Road. He's won the hearts of the fans, even this season he was voted their away Player of the Year. He is an established, top-half League One player at worst. I say at worst because when he was transfer listed this summer it alerted a host of clubs. Blackburn were rumoured to be interested, Leeds were rumoured to be interested and Coventry were ruled out by observers for being in League Two.

I'm told the negotiations took well over four hours last night, and although the players have been down at the ground all day, the finer points clearly took some time as well. Just because a player is on the transfer list doesn't mean it is an easy discussion to have, and Barry Fry is better at playing hard ball than anyone else involved in football today. He is the Del Boy of the Football League, a man whom we often love to hate, but today with must begrudgingly respect him for letting these boys move to Lincoln City.

Why was Bostwick transfer listed by Posh? Barry Fry and co have a policy that any player turning down a new deal going into the final year of his contract is put on the list. Maybe it is to keep the club harmony, maybe it is to satisfy Barry's lust for swapping personnel like kids swap stickers in the playground. Whatever it is, Bostwick was made available and a lot of clubs started to weigh up a move for him. Lincoln City was as likely destination for him as Barcelona, he looked almost certain to return to the Championship, or a recently relegated side at the very worst.

That poses the question, how the hell has he ended up holding aloft a Lincoln City shirt this evening? How has a 29-year old midfielder arguably in his prime ended up at our club, 'little' old Lincoln. Maybe it's because we're not 'little' old Lincoln anymore. Maybe, just maybe it is because he sees from the outside things we dare not see here. If anything screams 'this club is going places', it is signing a midfielder far too good for your level. He doesn't even come with a 'Billy Knott' style point to prove either, he's established and proven. He hasn't suffered major injuries, he hasn't had a dip in form, at first glance there is literally nothing at all to suggest he is here for any reason other than our ambition.

Let us not skirt around the elephant in the room either, money. Michael Bostwick will not have come cheap, not in terms of wages nor that undisclosed fee. I wouldn't mind a bet that we broke our record transfer fee paid this evening, and we'll not have a chance to celebrate it. Danny wouldn't want one player to be on a pedestal over the rest of his lads, and rightly so. Hopefully this is the first and last mention we'll have of the fee, because once we've all picked ourselves up off the floor, refreshed our browser in case it was an error, checked the calendar to make sure it is April 1st, then we just move on with Michael Bostwick as another member of our squad. Our bloody good squad.

Matt Green was our marquee signing, leading scorer for a team at our new level last season and coveted by teams in League One and Two. Where does that leave Michael Bostwick? Combined with Harry Anderson we've got enough marquees in our side to host our own festival. At this rate we're going to need more land.

That brings me succinctly on to Harry Anderson, a player whose arrival might get swamped in all of the Michael Bostwick disbelief. I have said all pre-season that if we sign Harry Anderson then we mean business, and now I'm talking about his arrival in tenth paragraph of the blog. Signing Harry Anderson is another coup, and one that will probably be understated over the next 48 hours. The fact he's put his name at the bottom of a three-year deal shows as much about our management team's intent as it does the player. He's here to stay, they're here to stay.

I rate this kid as highly as any of the players he is joining, potentially as highly as Alex Woodyard and Sean Raggett. He oozes class, he has all the attributes needed to be a really special player. I said it earlier, he's direct and powerful but dangerous around the box too. He pushed us through a tough spell last season early doors, and then he returned to give us the extra legs as the season died away. He's a 'Cowley' boy, just like Woodyard and Billy Knott. They know him, they trust him and he feels the same. I'd imagine he could have moved elsewhere too, but he trusts our management team to handle his development correctly.

I wondered exactly how Danny could add value to the squad this summer after the other arrivals. We had a squad of 13 or 14 players that can do a job in League Two, but I wondered how he could bring players in to add value without making them promises about first team games he couldn't keep. How could Danny have justified bringing in James Rowe for instance, knowing he didn't stand a chance of displacing Alex Woodyard? I wasn't worried as such, but I was apprehensive that the rest of the summer dealings may have seemed like filler, players coming in as back up. We are used to it at City are we not? For every Simon Yeo there was a Rory May, for every Scott Kerr, an

Omari Coleman. I just can't see the filler this summer, all I can see are players who are League One quality at least.

I started this blog with the title history, and I truly feel tonight's announcement really is historic for Lincoln City. I've been a fan for over 30 years, and in all of those pre-seasons we've made good signings and bad. Now I do know that these players all have to go out and perform, and names alone do not win you games. I know this, but in Anderson, Knott and Ginnelly we know they can perform in City shirts. In Bostwick and Matt Green we know we have proven players from elsewhere. In Ollie Palmer and Jordan Maguire-Drew we know we have players who threaten great things, and players who have potential that can be reached and breached with the right management.

Anderson, Ginnelly, Knott, Maguire-Drew, Palmer, Green and Bostwick. That, Peter Jackson, really is a Magnificent Seven, and I don't think Danny is done yet.

If you weren't excited about the coming season already, then the time to start being overly optimistic is upon us. Nobody else will say it, nobody wants to heap pressure on the players, but when I look at our carefully crafted squad, the spine from last season's historic win and the new faces with so much experience and talent, I can't help but think we might go through League Two like a dodgy chicken korma.

Football Reacts to Biggest League Two Transfer
July 21, 2017

All across the football world, reaction is coming in on our massive double signing. Perhaps had it just been Harry we'd see a few comments of 'useful signing for Lincoln', or 'he had a decent future at Posh, good move for the Imps', but it is the additional capture of Bostwick that has set the chatter going.

When I say 'football world', I don't mean the Scum newspaper or BBC website or anything like that, I mean those who comment on lower league football, those who make their living from being Football League experts. Those people are shocked at our swoop, and I'm told our odds have reduced again on being automatically promoted. How strange the arrival of one headline payer can cause odds to be slashed, when in truth we're going to have to shuffle the pack around to even fit him in!

When I woke up this morning I have to admit I didn't immediately think of Lincoln City, the fans or the hundreds of comments I've seen across social media. No, what I imagined was Steve Evans sat munching on his third bowl of Coco Pops, refreshing his web browser and suddenly spitting a mix of chocolate, milk and his slather all over the computer screen. I imagined he called his wife through and demanded to know how come he hadn't signed Bostwick. "but we had all tha money, aye?" he probably said, "and if tha boy wanted tae move close tae home we're not tae far away." Then he mops his computer screen using his Teddy Ruxpin bedtime T-shirt and sobs gently into his fourth, now replenished, bowl of chocolate milky death. Once I'd seen that image once in my head I sat down and replayed it again and again, each time increasing the ferocity of the initial expel of Coco Pops. It's the sweetest thing I've seen all month.

I'm not using the single biggest double transfer swoop in our history as an immediate excuse to have a pop at Evans, but I'm underlining the shrewd policy of waiting patiently for the right opening to come along. Steve rushed into the toy shop as soon as it opened and threw all his money at the shop keep in a gluttonous rage, and he got some good players too. I can't mock the quality of his signings, but you wouldn't swap a single one of them for Bostwick.

Danny Cowley, he didn't even go straight in the toy shop, because rather than being handed his money, he'd earned it in the FA Cup. He went for a jog around the block, probably glancing at his watch planning when to go in. No point in going straight in and bidding against Evans, no point in going in once the season has started and picking up the dregs. He waited, he jogged, and he watched. He made a couple of purchases, nothing rash, just the right ones that meant he still had some money left. Now, with money still in his pocket, that limited edition toy, the one that hadn't been released when Evans spent all his money, the one only available only to the big kids, that has now fallen into his price bracket. He's wandering down the street with a wonderful selection of toys, far better than the ones Steve has, isn't he? Oh, how comforting it is to imagine a Coco Pop soaked laptop screen and a red-faced ranting Evans this morning. Cracking. Go on, take a second to picture his rosy red face, Coco Pops dripping off his chin, the ruined laptop and the blind indignation that apparently having more money than everyone isn't sufficient to buy the best players. You have to play the game Steve. The early bird might catch the worm, but the late worm avoids getting eaten by the bird.

There will be accusations of us having a massive budget, of buying up players that are beyond the reach of Carlisle etc, and to a degree that is true. Lincoln will have spent a six-figure sum although I think we'd be wildly off the mark if we assumed it started with a '2'. It is no secret that Posh turned down a bid from Blackburn who were willing to pay around £250k for Bostwick, and Darragh MacAnthony said we paid 'considerably' less than that. Charlton were linked with a swoop as were MK Dons and recently-relegated Rotherham United, all who had significantly bigger budgets than us. This move wasn't about money for Michael, it was about location and family. How refreshing is it that we are finally benefitting from a player moving because of location?

Regarding Harry Anderson, despite tweets to the contrary I haven't seen any indication he signed a new deal at Posh, and if that is the case his fee will be nominal. I wouldn't imagine they cost us an eye-watering sum, even combined. Sure, one will have broken the transfer fee received, but it will always be one of those ambiguous deals where both cost us a combined fee, thus alleviating any individual pressure. We'll never know anyway, most deals are undisclosed these days and whilst it might not please fans, it is sensible from a business point of view.

So, if we had the means to secure the deal, why not use it? We haven't thrown our money around like we're starring in a rap video this summer, we haven't spoken of having any real buying power. When players such as Jordan Williams looked to be costing more than their perceived value, Danny walked away. There's no gross spending here, we're just reaping some of the rewards from reaching last season's FA Cup run. Did Carlisle get to the FA Cup Quarter Final? No. I pick Carlisle because of Keith Curle's comments, he's bound to be getting the 'poor us' rhetoric ready for our August clash at Sincil Bank. Okay so we've spent a bit of cash, but we earned it and in my eyes that is significantly different from throwing a rich owners money at your new toys.

Okay, moving on. The issue now is dropping all of these players into some form of starting eleven. It's a wonderful problem to have though, is it not? Which one of four devastating wingers do we start with, and which pair do we bring on after an hour once the full-backs have been run ragged? Do we play Championship-quality Michael Bostwick in at centre half, or will he drop into right back? If he goes in at centre half, how do we possibly accommodate Raggett and Waterfall? Some have asked if Bostwick will be captain, I'd bet against that. Danny respects his players and he won't remove that from Luke Waterfall after his stellar season at the back. If Raggs stays, which I'm informed is still likely, then he'll partner Luke almost certainly. One thing Danny will want to do is keep the spine of the winning team together, so Farms, Waterfall, Raggs, Habergham, Woodyard, Arnold and possibly Rhead will already be photocopied on the team sheet, and he'll just fill the rest in by hand.

I suspect well start against Wycombe with Farman (GK), Bostwick (RB) Raggett (CB), Waterfall (CB), Habergham (LB), Woodyard (CM), Knott (CM), Arnold (RW), Maguire-Drew (LW), Green (CF), Rhead (CF).

That leaves Ollie Palmer, Elliott Whitehouse, Josh Ginnelly, Harry Anderson, Callum Howe, Sean Long and Josh Vickers to complete the seven-man bench. The squad is still light, but if we could field that squad all season without injuries and suspensions (I know that won't happen), then I think we'd be around the top five.

Where do we go from here in terms of recruitment? I'd imagine it is still going on fervently, and to that initial 17 you could add a couple of the youngsters who will almost certainly be given an EFL Trophy bench spot if nothing else. We saw at Lincoln United there are three or four who might make up the fringes of the first team squad. I suspect that leaves Danny wanting to bring in three more faces at most. He will be prioritising left back cover, and I hear Noah Chesmain could still be on the radar there. If he were to sign we'd be one centre forward away from a very impressive squad, and interest in Ade Azeez recently underlines that we're not done in that department either. Don't expect another marquee signing in that position though, after all there is no more room for marquees at Sincil Bank.

I wouldn't be surprised at a young player released from a Championship club joining up front, or a reserve striker released from a League One side. The days are beginning to disappear as the start of the season looms, and a few players might be beginning to panic that they don't have a club. Danny will be willing to 'take a punt' on a player, someone he sees with potential to add value, but not necessarily straight away. He'll be happy to go with a Green / Palmer or Green / Rhead combo, but I expect he's got the nagging question 'what if Green gets injured' at the back of his mind.

Last year Danny waited until last minute, Sean Raggett and Nathan Arnold fell into his lap, two players that were integral to our impossible season. This year he has done the same, lo and behold he's done it again with Harry Anderson and Michael Bostwick coming to the club. It pays to wait, doesn't it?

Friendly Analysis: Imps 2 Posh 3
July 23, 2017

First of all, to save you the hassle of really reading the blog, there is little weight you can put behind the results or indeed the performances in a friendly. It is nice to do well, it is nice to see the new faces and how they fit in, but the purpose of a friendly is to get match fitness and for new players to integrate with the old hands. Therefore losing 3-2 is irrelevant. However, I write about football and it was definitely football so I'm going to go ahead and talk about it anyway.

I thought it was a decent work out for the lads. We were perhaps a bit naïve in the first fifteen minutes or so, we treated it like a proper pre-season friendly whilst Posh were really fast and vibrant. That isn't to say we started badly, far from it, but when they had the ball they attacked quickly and with purpose.

For most of the first half our stand-out man was Jordan Maguire Drew. He looks a real prospect; his delivery was exemplary and he'll grab a bucket load of assists with the right people on the end of the crosses. He has an air of cockiness when he is on the ball, a confidence that he is about to humiliate a full back, and I like to see that in a winger. His quality was clear for Dagenham last season and I'm sure he'll just pick up where he left off, scoring and creating goals.

Contrary to popular opinion I thought our midfield looked okay in the first half to. I saw some criticism of Billy Knott, and criticism of anyone at this stage is ludicrous. I thought Billy and Alex did the right things the right way, but with Knott in particular, it is harder to turn on that flair in a pre-season game. He'll be a big player this coming campaign, and anyone who feels otherwise is set to be disappointed.

By the time we registered a goal we were two goals down, I think a combination of naivety and lapses in concentration were perhaps at fault. Posh had some really good players, fast creative players that moved the ball forward very quickly whenever they got it. Jack Marriott and Marcus Maddison really impressed me, their movement was so rapid they were out of defence and bearing down on goal in seconds. We controlled possession for long periods without getting any joy, whereas they grabbed the ball and just swept down field to score. Twice.

When we did get a goal, I thought we were a little fortunate. Rheady did well to keep a deep cross in play, too well in fact. I was in the boxes (posh I know) and from our angle the ball looked to go out, and if it hadn't Rheady looked to pull their defender down with him. Before a defender could appeal though, Matt Green did what we hoped he'll do all season and scraped the ball home. The Peterborough players were angry, and I'm not surprised. That is Rheady's game though, he's not about mobility and timed runs, he's all about aerial threats and brute strength.

Danny switched things around at halftime, and it was no surprise at all to see the man of the moment make his first Imps appearance. Michael Bostwick even looks like he's a Championship player, from the hipster beard and flowing hair to the almost arrogant way he moves across the park. We looked to drop into a different formation, and it made an immediate difference, which brings me to my first contentious point of the day.

I've mentioned it before, but in the past Danny has gone 4-2-3-1 with two holding midfielders and an attacking '10' backing up a lone striker. It didn't really work last season because often Rheady was our lone striker, and he is suited to a front two. With Rheady you put the ball anywhere near him and he sucks it in, brings it under control and moves it on. That is great if he has a partner up top, and this coming season Matt Green will fill that role, if we go with two up top. I'm not sure we will.

Michael Bostwick will play this season, I'd wager forty odd games if he stays fit and free of suspension. You don't sign a Championship quality footballer in League Two and sit him on the bench. Alex Woodyard will also play, he's the jewel in our crown, the young player with a big price tag on his head. Again, Lincoln City do not bring talent like him to the table and then not serve him up. Ditto Sean Raggett, if he stays, he plays. I also think Luke Waterfall will play whenever he is fit as well, which immediately prompts a problem with our favoured 4-4-2 from last season. Bostwick and Woodyard both play a more holding role, the pass before the assist as Danny once called it. Bostwick can play centre half, but we won't go three at the back either as it doesn't fit with our intense pressing game. In order to accommodate those four players, we'll have to start with a variation of 4-3-3, and with our vast array of wingers, the only option I can see is 4-2-3-1.

The crucial thing for Imps fans to ponder here is the last digit of that formation, '1'. One up top, and that one has to be mobile and quick as well as strong and bullish. I'm afraid to say that means Matt Green, and our talisman centre forward Mr Rhead may miss out.

We won't play the same formation every week, but on the second half performance I think it will be our preferred starting tactic. I know it won't be popular, I know that some will argue we will just play Bostwick and Woodyard and Knott will miss out, but we won't. Billy Knott will play forty odd games too, barring injuries and suspension. He's more adept at pushing on towards the lone striker, as is Elliott Whitehouse. We haven't stumbled on this either, I'm told Danny has wanted to play this way ever since he arrived, and only now has he been able to build a squad to accommodate it.

Anyway, back to the game. I didn't think it became disjointed as we made numerous changes, and that will please the manager as well. Harry Anderson and Josh Ginnelly came off the bench, and both turned in good performances as Nathan Arnold had when he was on. Elliott Whitehouse did okay when he came on, but again I think Elliott will be fighting hard to have a regular start, especially given the arrival of Bostwick. These are nice problems to have, I just hope Danny can keep everyone happy.

I was pleased to see Josh Ginnelly get a goal as well. He made a real impact when we played Woking at home, his deflected shot giving us the unassailable lead last season, but after that he was all promise and no fulfilment. He's a special talent, just like our other three wingers, but he is the one that has to bring an end product to the table. Nathan led the way with goals from out wide last season, so Josh, JMD and Harry will be eager to replicate that this coming campaign.

Ollie Palmer looked decent when he came on too. He didn't impress me at Lincoln United, but he isn't just a big unit. He was very quick considering he was hauling around far more muscle mass than most of the lads, and he has quick feet too. All the talk of Matt Green and Matt Rhead may be disrespecting Ollie, although I still hold him as our third-choice striker. It is nice to know we have options across the front line though, and before the week is out I wouldn't be surprised at us adding one more.

I thought their winner came against the run of play, but it showed their class as it was once again swift and decisive. It was a little disheartening not to win the game, but it was only a friendly and therefore the result wasn't of massive importance. As long as you don't lose six or seven nil, then maybe it would matter!

The other point to mention was the impact of trialist Matthew Briggs. Sam Habergham hasn't had any pre-season minutes yet, and with just 180 of them left before we go to Wycombe he might be struggling for match fitness. Briggs is the third left back we've seen in recent weeks and I thought he impressed without excelling. He didn't look fit at all, but he did show composure and a touch of the class that once saw him emerge at Fulham as their youngest ever first team player. His career has taken a dive as he tumbled from Fulham, through Millwall and eventually cast off by Colchester, but Danny might be thinking it is a case of necessity. Briggs suffered with injuries last season, something that has blighted his promising career, but he has pedigree which can't be ignored.

It's now July 23rd, and for cover purposes alone I wouldn't be surprised to see a left back brought in on a six-month deal. I'm told Noah Chesmain looked good in Portugal, and although he's long gone I liked Brandon Ormund-Ottiwell too. There is quality out there, quality that still doesn't have a club and before long we're going to have to address the full-back cover question.

I won't delve into the right-back cover question right now, but in the fan's forum I think Danny might have sparked conversations about a very familiar face. I'm not going to write too much more about that out of respect to all parties, especially as I thought Sean Long looked solid against Peterborough.

An early afternoon finish as followed for many by a fan's forum, although I was already on my toes to Ashby Avenue by the time Danny was revealing he was chasing a new centre back. I think we came away having not truly learned anything from the game. We knew Bostwick is a good player, we knew Danny had a selection headache, we knew Peterborough are a decent side and most of all we knew nothing was truly at stake. The amateur pundits such as myself will still write about it, fans will still discuss it but in essence we gleaned nothing but the satisfaction of having seen our team play. Come August 5th we'll start to truly see players credential and be able to assess them accordingly.

I look forward to chewing over the bones of another meaningless but entertaining friendly on Tuesday night.

Imps 4 Forest U23's 3

July 26, 2017

Once again I'm going to stress that you can't read too much into a friendly. If someone has had a bad game or made an error then it is relatively meaningless. That is what friendlies are meant to be isn't it? Meaningless work outs to build fitness and get used to new team mates. Someone should have told Michael Bostwick that.

He thundered into a second half challenge with such ferocity that he could easily have broken his opponent in two. It sparked a short melee, something none of the 1200 crowd expected to see when they paid their entry fee. I was told he was committed when he first joined, and he showed that in abundance. I suspect Mr Bostwick is one of these players that has two settings, 'off' and 'full throttle'.

Whilst that challenge was lively it wasn't the only moment in the game that had fans double-checking they were at a pre-season warm up. Over the course of the 90 minutes both sides put in a few tasty challenges, showing that maybe we can't read too much into the games, but a footballer's desire to win is not diminished just because there is nothing at stake.

The game started much the same as Saturday's clash with Peterborough. City had some possession, a half chance or two before conceding two quick fire goals to incredibly good opponents. This Forest side might have been a late substitute for Oxford, but they showed no signs of just going through the motions. Tyler Walker really caught my eye with his speed and movement, and I've already seen calls on social media for us to sign him on loan. The rumour is he is heading to Blunder Park, and if he does Grimsby will have quite striker on their hands. I'm not sure his Dad Des was amongst the 36 travelling Forest fans, but he would have been pleased with what he saw if he was.

From a City perspective we conceded two weak goals, the second was especially poor. I'm not going to judge as this is pre-season and the time for throwing criticism about is not after ten minutes of a mid-July friendly. Thus far we have conceded six goals at home in two matches, and I'll leave it to Danny to discuss that with his players. Given how we performed last season that isn't normal, you know it and so do I. If that had been a Checkatrade Trophy cup match I doubt very much we would have been 2-0 down so quickly.

A fish could count the number of times Luke Waterfall delivered a short back-pass last season on its tail, and so he was probably due an uncharacteristic error. It might not have been punished in a full match either, but there aren't many former Portugal internationals waiting to pounce in League Two.

I thought the similarities with Saturday were striking though, City had more of the ball but impressive breaks from quick and talented opposition gave them a strong lead. In competitive games it is us that starts with intensity and vibrance, and I'm not concerned with what I saw despite the goals. I thought we stuck to the plan admirably considering we went 2-0 down, and as the minute ticked by we looked a composed side applying ourselves in the right manner.

There is going to be a lot of emphasis on delivery into the box, and if Bostwick's first half header is anything to go by we'll have success. He headed it harder than I've ever kicked a ball, and he was desperately unlucky not to make it 2-1. Our delivery was incessant, time and again we broke out wide and put the ball into the danger area. The Forest keeper had a nightmare, he just couldn't deal with what was essentially our reserve wingers constant barrage of crosses.

Eventually it wasn't one of the new faces that got us a goal back, but Elliott Whitehouse. He picked the ball up on the right, cut towards goal and fired a decent shot into the Forest net. Being objective, the keeper should never have been beaten at his near post, but Elliott did well to angle his left footed shot past young Bossin.

The more the game went on the better City looked. I thought Bostwick showed his class, and the runs by either wide player were often picked out with smart cross field balls. When the proper competition starts I can see us being able to move from left to right very quickly, and that will stretch opposition defenders. It will be an effective ploy that will tire opponents out quickly and we look to do it effectively.

Ollie Palmer showed flashes of what he might be capable of, but at times he was a lone striker, although occasionally Elliott was up with him. It did occasionally look a disjointed pairing, but Palmer covered a lot of ground and showed some nice close control.

Minutes after the restart it was more poor defending that allowed Forest a third they barely warranted. It was Lica and Tyler Walker again, this time the former found the latter in acres of space on the left side of the area. If I'm being incredibly picky I'd ask where the trialist Bob Harris was, he'd had a quiet first half and I wondered if he'd even come out for the second. Walker had time to control the ball, light a cigarette and smoke it before slotting past Josh Vickers. At 3-1 the game looked gone, but in our executive box (yeah I know, lifestyles of the rich and infamous) a bet was offered up immediately. Lincoln to win 4-3, a trust me there wasn't many takers.

After that City turned the heat up a notch, and to be fair to former Bristol Rovers full-back Harris, he redeemed himself very well. Of all the left backs we've seen this pre-season he perhaps had the most eye-catching 42 minutes, we shall have to wait and see if the quiet 48 count against him.

Bostwick's challenge came with City 3-1 down, and many of his team mates were quickly alongside him diffusing an ugly situation. He simply walked away, the referee didn't even have a word, so perhaps my poor eyesight misjudged his clattering challenge to be unfair. For a second I thought he would be withdrawn, but even when Danny did make changes, Bostwick remained on the field.

It is easy to say the changes drastically altered the game, perhaps the truth is we simply had players on the pitch who knew how to play with each other. Nathan Arnold, Alex Woodyard, Sean Raggett, and Matt Rhead all came one, the nucleus off our title-winning team. Matt Green also came on, a man who can score on demand. The complexion of the game altered immediately. Anybody writing Matt Rhead off had better have the tippex ready, because in truth his physical presence was one of the key factors in reviving the game.

Forest knocked the ball around quickly when they had possession, but in the second half they rarely troubled the goal directly in front of me in the boxes. I think I counted three attacks, one of which they scored from. It wasn't that they were bad, far from it, but in the end City wanted it a whole lot more. I also suspect one or two of their lads saw that Bostwick challenge and decided against lingering on the ball too long.

Josh Ginnelly has had an eye-catching pre-season, and of all four wingers he is perhaps furthest down the pecking order. Given his performances I'm sure he knows he has to force himself into the side, time and again he roasted his full-back to get clear, and he even found a couple of good crosses as well. It was one of his mazy runs that led to the second goal, his lovely cut-back caught the defence out and Matt Green doesn't need a second invitation to put the ball in the back of the net.

Rheady then had an effort cleared off the line as Lincoln took full control of a game in which they'd always been better. Nathan's fresh legs caused issues and in the middle of the park Bostwick and Woodyard cleaned up any loose balls. I've predicted they'll start together in the opening match, and there won't be a better midfield pairing in League Two.

The equaliser came as it had threatened to, but it was a far from conventional strike. Michael Bostwick had already announced his arrival with the challenge and an all-round commanding display, but just in case that wasn't enough he produced a world-class overhead kick that even a decent keeper couldn't have kept out. Nonchalantly walking back to the centre circle, I imagine he was thinking 'job done'. For him maybe, but for City there was one more twist.

Bob Harris was the provider, not content with fizzing an effort over in the second half he was still full of running as the clock wound down. He slipped a superb pass through to Nathan Arnold, and we all know what Nathan Arnold does when he receives a good pass. He strode confidently towards goal, and right on cue blasted the Imps fourth past the hapless Bossin. It may not have been Ipswich in the FA Cup, but in case you needed reminding Nathan Arnold is still an Imp, and he has a massive part to play this coming season.

So that was that, the game that never-was until Oxford bottled it ended up being a meaningless classic. Seven goals, at times a confident display from City, at times a little fragile too. Forest's kids were by no means a push over, they played with pace and direction but in the end, the men beat the boys.

You win nothing in pre-season, some players who don't look the business only come alive when there is something to win. If I was being critical I'd say Luke Waterfall looks much more accomplished when Sean Raggett is on the pitch, but then again they did play nigh on sixty games together last season so it stands to reason. Given the left-back situation I think the defence will always look a little more fragile that the last campaign too, any cover we get needs to get into our pattern of play. Bob Harris certainly has the ability to get up and down the line which DC likes, and with Sam Habergham sat watching in the box next to us we do need to bring someone in soon.

Going forward it is clear to see we are going to be all about getting balls into the box, and both Harry and Josh looked to cause issues all evening. With JMD's delivery on Saturday catching the eye, and Nathan with his 14 assists last season, we are going to cause many problems for opponents. Matt Green will thrive on that supply, and we know what Rheady can do. Ollie Palmer has a point to prove, but as he gets himself aligned with our patterns of play we'll see much more from him I'm sure. One thing to mention is that despite his stature he isn't the stereotypical target man, I think there is more to his game than what he has from the neck up. Fans shouldn't judge a big striker on his heading ability alone, and certainly not when they've seen him for 60 minutes in a friendly.

On to Walsall on Saturday and having seen 13 goals in 180 minutes I wouldn't advise missing it! Another piece of advice from me would be aimed at the Walsall players: don't hang around on the ball too long otherwise Michael Bostwick will snap you in half, and if you're not sure which one he is, he played 'The Hound' in Game of Thrones.

Lee Beevers: Thank you

July 28, 2017

Tomorrow will see Walsall visit Sincil Bank for the testimonial match of defender Lee Beevers. It will be an emotionally charged affair for Lee who suffered that awful injury last season, and it is the perfect chance for Imps fans to say thank you to a great servant of Lincoln City.

Lee has made 229 starts for City, appearing a further 16 times as a sub in competitive matches. Over the years he has proven himself to be a committed and consistent player. He first caught the eye whilst playing for county rivals Boston United. He arrived there after starting out at Ipswich as a youth player, but it was at York Street where he got his break, his first consistent run of starts. His impressive performances convinced a promotion-chasing Keith Alexander to spend an 'undisclosed amount' to bring him to Sincil Bank, something of a coup at the time. Over the years Lincoln have often underlined county superiority by cherry-picking Boston's players, and Lee (along with Paul Casey and Dany N'Guessan) was a classic example of this. Although primarily a right back Lee found himself employed all across the defence, regularly appearing in the left back position. He remained at Lincoln after Keith left, through the highs and lows of John Schofield's brief reign and into that of

Peter Jackson. He perhaps played his very best football under Jackson, a consistent and experienced head in a team that was slowly falling apart at the seams.

It was only a matter of time before he rolled the dice and tried to step up a level. He opted to sign for League One Colchester, which represented a climb up the football ladder for him. His spell at Layer Road was injury-hit, a damaged shoulder ruled him out soon after joining and he made just 23 appearances for Colchester before he moved on to tomorrow's opponents, Walsall. He appeared 35 times at the Bescot before moving on to Mansfield Town, where in three years he helped them to the Conference title and an FA Cup tie with Liverpool, at Lincoln's expense.

Following his release by the Stags in May of 2015 Lee signed a 2-year deal with City. He dropped in at left-back during the difficult 2015/16 campaign and although he performed adequately, it did look like his last season at National League level.

The arrival of Danny and Nicky Cowley changed all that, and at the start of the 2016/17 season he began to show the sort of form he had exhibited the very first time he played for Lincoln. He slotted in at his preferred right back and was a revelation, prompting many fans to favour keeping Player of the Year Bradley Wood in midfield to allow Beevers a run in the team. Indeed, when he was dropped and Tom Champion came into the side, the Imps went on a losing run. When Lee was restored to the team we went on yet another unbeaten run.

As we now know Lee suffered a ruptured patella tendon during our home win against Boreham Wood in October 2016, an injury that ruled him out for the remainder of the season. He remained a popular figure around the ground as he recovered slowly, and he looked to forge a new career in punditry with a series of TV appearances during our cup run.

Tomorrow is the perfect chance for fans young and old to say thank you to a superb servant of our football club, a family-orientated man now looking to his future outside the game. I hope for a big crowd and a massive send off for Lee, and of course we hope to see him one last time in the red and white of Lincoln City.

Personally, I can't be there, I'm truly gutted I can't thank a man who has served my football club so well. Hopefully I can say it with this small article, and maybe buying him a beer if I ever bump into him again. Thanks Lee.

The following passage was taken from my book, Who's who of Lincoln City 1993-2016, and was written by football commentator and Imps fan Oscar Chamberlain. It sums up Lee Beevers the person far more succinctly than one of my own stories.

"When I started my Sports Journalism degree back in 2008, one of the first assignments given to me was to interview a professional athlete. It was quite a daunting task because I had never done anything like that before and I didn't know any professional athletes or how to go about contacting them.

After a few failed attempts to find a suitable interviewee, a friend of mine offered to contact Lee Beevers and ask him if he'd be willing to help. Much to my surprise, Lee called me the next day and we arranged to meet at Sincil Bank later that week so that I could speak to him.

I remember being extremely concerned about asking the wrong question or making a fool of myself. After all, this was a professional footballer who had been interviewed by 'real' journalists and now he was speaking to a clueless student who was struggling to get his Dictaphone to work properly.

I needn't have worried. Lee wasn't at all bothered by the fact that I wasn't a proper journalist and he was happy to talk about his career to date, his ambitions for the future and Lincoln City in general.

It was a genuine pleasure speaking to him and he certainly compares favourably to some of the footballers I have spoken to since. He was easy-going, humble and seemed to be genuinely interested in the course I was doing and my ambition to work as a commentator.

When I left he said that he'd been impressed by the way I'd conducted the interview (I'm sure he wasn't, but it was a nice thing for him to say!), wished me luck for the future and even offered to give me a lift back to the University.

I spent no more than 30-40 minutes with him and he probably never gave it another thought but as far as I was concerned it was the start of my career in the media, even if it was just a bit of course work.

I'll always be grateful to Lee for taking the time to speak to me when he didn't have to. It says a lot about the kind of person he is and I imagine that he is a great influence on the younger players now that he is back at the club again.

He is probably one of the more versatile players that I've seen at Sincil Bank since I started watching the Imps in 2002. Capable of playing across the back four, he was named 'player of the season' playing predominantly at right-back in 2007 and was described as the 'best left-back in League Two' by Peter Jackson a little over a year later. John Ward even used him as a holding midfielder during his spell at Colchester in 2010 while Danny Cowley called him 'irreplaceable' and compared him to an iPhone 6.

He's played in League One for Colchester and Walsall and at international level for the Welsh U21s but I believe he could have achieved even more had he not suffered big injuries at crucial times in his career. It is a real shame that he may miss the rest of the current campaign because he deserves the chance to be part of a successful Lincoln side after so many years of great service."

A Case for The Defence
July 30, 2017

We're now less than a week away from the big kick off, the pre-season posturing and predictions will be left by the wayside as we look to our first opening day fixture in the Football League since August 2010.

The summer has not been without its ups and downs, on the whole I think we've had a strong month or two. Our transfer dealings have seemed very astute, bar one or two players I think we've added strength and value throughout the squad. Where Hawkridge, Power and Muldoon have departed, Maguire-Drew, Bostwick and Matt Green have come in. We've retained the spine of a successful team and built around that. Performances have been good albeit not an indication of how we'll do in the league, but we've almost every reason to be confident.

One area I believe that is still in the balance is the back four, and Danny's revelation that he expects 'one in and one out' this week goes to show that he is still not happy. We're short in both wide positions and whilst I wouldn't call it disarray, I'm fairly certain we would like to have another week or so before the big kick off. Please note this isn't pessimism or me being negative, there are teams in far worse positions than ours, but being objective there is still work to be done. To put it into perspective last year at this time we'd only just signed Nathan Arnold and Sean Raggett was still a Dover player.

Sean Raggett, for me there is perhaps one of the most important cogs in the machine that there still may be a question mark over. I have this nagging fear that as the transfer deadline approaches a team from the Championship or League One might panic and start throwing money at their own defensive problem, and as we know it will only take a certain set amount to prise our star defender away from Sincil Bank. That would be a severe set-back in no uncertain terms.

Raggett has it all, pace and power along with that 'don't give a shit' attitude that elevates an average defender to a good one. He works well with Waterfall by virtue of the fact they played so many games together, and that was obvious against Forest in the week. Callum Howe didn't have a bad game, but we looked much more solid when Raggett replaced him. I feel a little for Callum, I think he is a decent defender and Danny must feel the same otherwise he would have left the club. However, he's 23 as is Sean and yet he's being farmed out on loan and someone else is being brought into his place. It isn't exactly a vote of confidence is it? I expect DC sees Callum as an investment, hoping that a season of National League football will bring him on as a player.

Whoever the new face is, I still believe our first-choice pairing at centre half is Raggett and Waterfall, although knowing Danny there could be a surprise this week. Whoever it is he'll have his work cut out displacing either of those two, unless of course Raggett does end up with a deadline day panic move. We saw it with Southend and Theo Robinson in January, and with Scunthorpe and Johnny Margetts in August. Both players were the subject of last-minute panic buys, Southend even paid a fee for a non-contract player because they'd failed elsewhere in the window.

The next 'interesting' aspect to our defence is the full-back situation. Sean Long was in and out of the National League winning side, and he is currently the only player we have signed on who can play right back. Sam Habergham is consistent and able to play at League One level in my opinion, but his spell on the side lines has taken longer than we expected. He won't be fit for next weekend and without a pre-season I don't think we'll see the best of him until mid-September. With less than a week to go that means we have just one fit and recognised full-back.

It isn't all doom and gloom though. The quality of trialist we've seen has really impressed me, Bob Harris looked competent against Forest, I liked Brandon Ormund-Ottiwell against Lincoln United and I heard good things about Noah Chesmain as well. The fact they haven't signed shows Danny is being cautious and careful even when looking for cover. The truth is we're not in this situation because of poor planning, we're actually here because Danny wants to add the right players, not just fill the positions.

I does look as if he may attempt to bring Neal Eardley and Matthew Briggs to the Bank, I would speculate that one might be offered a one-year deal and the other a shorter-term contract. The fact these players have even been in a Lincoln shirt does fill me with hope because both have superb pedigree but have suffered from injuries.

Firstly, Matthew Briggs. This is a player that represented England from under 16 right the way through to under 21. He became the youngest ever Premier League player at Fulham, and by 2010 the world looked to be very much at his feet. Some players get the all the luck though, some do not and Briggs sadly did not. In December 2010 he started Fulham's match against Chelsea but was injured after just 28 minutes, that resulted in an operation and a spell in the stands. A series of loan moves didn't bring him joy, and eventually his seven years at Fulham ended with just 30 appearances in league and cup.

His move to Millwall brought no joy either as Ian Holloway chopped and changed his side, and then two seasons at Colchester were injury hit too. In just a few years he has gone from being a Premier League 'wonder kid' to a hopeful trialist at Lincoln City. That fall from grace isn't due to a lack of ability nor a bad attitude, it is pure and simple bad luck. His bad luck might just be our good fortune though

I didn't see him but I liked the look of him against Posh and he wouldn't be back if Danny wasn't interested. A 26 years of age he still has a chance to rescue his once-promising career, and despite his recent troubles he still has ability as well. You don't represent your country at all those youth levels without having something to offer, and I firmly believe he's worth a punt at left back on a short-term deal. I'd like to see him handed six months in which he can prove his fitness and offer vital cover for Sam. It would give both parties a chance to assess each and be mutually beneficial. He'd get regular game time as Sam recovered and we would have that cover and eventually competition for places.

Neal Eardley came out of nowhere to start at right-back, and again by all accounts he had a good game. Surely he was always going to though, after all he was a full Welsh international and he has also played regular football at a good level. He was last called up to the Welsh squad in 2013 but withdrew due to injury. His recent descent of the leagues has also been due to injury problems. In six seasons he made 248 appearances, firstly at Oldham in League One and latterly at Blackpool where he enjoyed Premier League football. In the last five seasons he has made just 34 senior appearances, ten of which came last year. It was the spell at Birmingham which really did for him, a ruptured medial ligament and a dislocated shoulder restricted him to just 21 games over a three-year period.

Like Briggs his quality is still there though, he offers more experience than his fellow trialist but less top-flight pedigree. From what I have been told he looked to have the sort of class that could push Sean Long all the way for a first team berth should he be offered a deal, and I think Danny would like to add some experience to his defence. The quality between National League and League Two may not be all that different, but over a full campaign it would not hurt to have some real Football League experience in the back four. Michael Bostwick will almost certainly play in midfield and I can see Danny looking to add generals to each area of the field. I would like to see Neal Eardley offered a one-year deal if at all possible, especially as he can operate on either flank as well.

Both players must be chomping at the bit for an opportunity to show what they can do, and the fact they have been on trial proves the tactic of sitting tight in the transfer market pays dividends.

Here we are with six days to go before we kick off and we're trialling a former Welsh international and a one-time Premier League wonder kid, both the right side of 30 and both with plenty still to offer. With the season drawing ever closer I'd imagine a deal that is favourable for the club will be much easier to strike that it might have been in late May.

Despite the questions still being posed in the defence I'm not overly concerned. The basic errors in the two friendlies were frustrating, but there is no doubt Danny and Nicky will be working feverishly to correct them. I'm certainly not worried about the full back positions, the quality of trialist has convinced me that we'll be covered properly in those areas. If one of the two is to sign I would expect it to be Eardley due to the versatility, he would be a 'Lee Beevers' style utility man offering cover in both positions.

The biggest factor in our pre-season being judged as a massive success will be hanging on to Sean Raggett. It may only have been a friendly but his goal underlined the impact he has at both ends of the pitch, and keeping him is really important if we're to launch a second promotion challenge. I'm not going to say it is critical to our success, if he is the subject of a late bid I would imagine (at worst) Callum would be recalled and whoever the new face is will partner Luke. The reason I'm would be apprehensive at first is that I have seen many terrible defences at Lincoln over the past few seasons, and I've seen many good players (Josh Gowling) be made to look poor due to incompatibility with team mates, never having a consistent partner and a range of other factors. All the best teams have a steady central defensive pair that know each other's game and it was the bedrock of our success last year. If we have the same solid foundations once again then there's no reason we shouldn't challenge for promotion, but if Sean moves on it has the potential to set us back a month or two.

August

Welcome to Sincil Bank: Rob Dickie

August 1, 2017

The Imps have unveiled the latest addition to this season's playing squad by bringing Reading defender Rob Dickie in on a season-long loan.

Dickie (21) has previously had spells at Basingstoke and Cheltenham, and it is with the Whaddon Road club that he has caught the eye. In his first spell there he scored on his debut against Barrow and helped them to the National League title, making 27 appearances. He even managed a hat trick in the FA Trophy against Chelmsford Town. After suffering an injury, he returned to Reading but was back helping the Robins in the final day victory over us. He even managed to squeeze in 45 Championship minutes the following week for Reading away at Blackburn.

He was back with the Robins the following season, again on the score sheet on his debut in a 2-0 win against Crewe. He went on to make another 26 appearances as they finished fourth from bottom of League Two. He didn't have a settled campaign though as James Young of Gloucestershire live explained to www.getreading.co.uk:

"The manager (Gary Johnson) has struggled to get him in to a position and the team is still trying to settle down. But Rob has looked solid and has done well. He started as a right back then a wing back and he has also played at right-back in a back four. He played in central midfield in one game as well."

It seems this season that Reading fancy a change of scenery for the player, perhaps hoping for a solid run in one position. Having loaned us Sean Long last campaign they are entrusting us with Rob Dickie.

Dickie becomes the fourth recognised centre back at the club, five if the versatile Michael Bostwick is included. However, Callum Howe is almost certain to now head out on loan. There is some discussion as to why we need to bring a player in and immediately loan one out in the same position. I've chatted to a source at the club, and they've revealed that Callum's lack of game time last season was seen as a hinderance to his progress. Dickie and Howe would both be fighting for a first team spot with our usual pairing of Luke Waterfall and Sean Raggett, but whilst Dickie has two full seasons behind him, Howe does not. Therefore, it is important for Callum's development that he goes out and gets 30 games under his belt, possibly in the National League where he excelled with Southport.

Dickie has England under 18 and under 19 caps and is highly rated by Jaap Stam at the Madejski Stadium. After the disruption of last season, they're doubtless looking for him to get some consistency this time around, although his apparent versatility could be an option if we find ourselves down to the bare bones.

The Imps in 2017/18 – Stacey West Predicts

August 4, 2017.

I think last season has given lots of people immense confidence in what we are able to achieve, and although the official line is to not get carried away, I think there is much cause for optimism amongst City fans.

I can understand Danny's rhetoric playing down our chances, and it is refreshing from a fans perspective to hear it. In hispress conference he said if we were in the top 12 by Christmas then we would be in a strong position as we'll get better as the season progresses. He called it last year too, but we got better and more fatigued as the games went on. There's no reason to suggest we shouldn't improve as this season goes on, but then again there's no reason why we shouldn't be on our game nice and early either. The crux of the squad has remained the same, many of the new signings are already familiar to the club and those that are not are (in the main) thoroughly experienced professional footballers.

Let's look at the three reasons that we might not succeed first. The main thing I've seen is that our strategy, described by some as 'moon ball', is one-dimensional and easy to predict. The arrival of Ollie Palmer has suggested to the rest of the league that we're a side that goes long all the time, looking for the big 'un and then getting pace around him to pick up the scraps. Unfortunately, aside from a season under John Schofield we've been labelled as a long ball side, but in this instance I'm afraid that is way off the mark.

If sides come with a view to doubling up on Rheady and stifling our only outlet then I'm afraid they're going to be surprised at what happens to them. I'm going to come to positives shortly, but it is a fallacy to believe that we are a long ball side. We can go long, I won't deny it is an option we look to utilise at times, the equalising goal against Forest Green at home is proof of that, but we also break at pace on the floor, the opening goal away at Forest Green is proof of that. Yes, we take advantage of set pieces, but who wouldn't? We have players that can deliver a fantastic ball for this level of football and whipping in a corner or a free kick does not make you a long-ball side. It means you take the opportunities that arise and that is just good football.

I've seen some 'expert' pundits suggesting that Danny and Nicky will need to alter their style for the Football League, my question is why? In ten seasons or thereabouts Danny has always managed a team challenging at the top of a table, and invariably he's experienced success. The definition of madness is doing the same thing over and over again and expecting a different outcome, so surely (by definition) if you do the same thing over and over again successfully you'll get the same outcome. Anyone claiming that inexperience at this level will be detrimental ought to look at their first season with Braintree to see how stepping up a level is not an issue. Football League clubs believe that League Two is a different world to the National League, but outside the top ten I don't think we'll see a serious gap in quality at all.

One aspect that has concerned some fans is the defence. With you-know-who not in the squad from last season, Sam out injured and Sean Raggett's future uncertain, many are saying we might be susceptible at the back. Luke Waterfall had a great season last time out, but in pre-season he hasn't quite looked as sharp as he could, and many question Sean Long's ability to succeed at this level.

If Sean Raggett goes then we have to deal with that. He's a superb footballer and to keep him in League Two is akin to locking the Mona Lisa in a basement where people can't truly appreciate it. He will play Championship football, he may play Premiership football and frankly he is good enough to do both. We've been lucky to have him pass through our football club, and if he stays then great. If he doesn't then it is with our best wishes that he progresses.

Luke is still a great centre half and a couple of low-key outings against Peterborough and Forest do not change that. I think Rob Dickie is a good player too, and it may take him a little time to settle but he knows all about football at this level. I had to chuckle in yesterday's press conference when someone asked if it would phase a young player like him coming into the squad: the boy has had almost two seasons with Cheltenham, winning the National League in one of them and banging 20-odd league appearances out in the other. He has more Football League experience than Sean Raggett, I don't think he'll be too worried about his performance levels.

Yes, full back is a concern, but not in the way people suspect. Sean Long is a competent right back who will only get better with games. He's different to Brad, perhaps not as aggressive or as gung-ho but arguably possessing better distribution. In an ideal world we would have both scrapping for a spot in the side, but for now we will see Sean given a run of games in which he'll settle down and I believe become Mr Consistent. On the left Sam's injury is temporary, his class is permanent and if you remember him being one of our stand-out players last season, you'll also remember him missing most of pre-season. In the interim period we have to 'make do' with Neal Eardley, a former Welsh international who has played all of his football higher than League Two, and a player that is still only 28-years old. It's a tough life, isn't it?

It may take some time for the back four to settle down, but the longevity is there and if Sean does go then it's almost certain we'll see someone come in to replace him. If that happens expect Dickie and Waterfall to form a partnership at the back and see if you can spot the difference.

The Stacey West – A Season in Blogs 2017/18

The final concern for some people is up front. I've heard whispers that Ollie Palmer isn't impressing, Matt Rhead isn't mobile enough and we're hoping for too much from Matt Green. We're going into the season light up top by Danny's own admission, but you and I know that won't be the case come September 1st. Therefore, we only have to struggle through August with three forwards before a fourth arrives pre-transfer deadline.

Any criticism of Ollie Palmer is ridiculous at this stage. He's had a couple of outings in friendlies, we've not see him in competitive action and that will be when we should judge him. He's new to the squad and hasn't been a regular elsewhere so he needs time to get 'on method' and perhaps needs a run of games to sharpen up. He's an option and an experienced one at that, you don't spend time on loan at Luton and Grimsby if you're not a half-decent striker.

As for worrying about Rheady, best to let him prove us wrong. He isn't mobile, nobody is claiming he is, but he is incredibly skilful and composed. He's a massive asset in more ways than one, and there won't be a team in League Two that isn't plotting a way to stop him. Whilst they're doing that they may be ignoring other aspects of our side.

So, they're the things that might hold us back, but what reasons do we have to be positive? We did win the National League last season, and the spine of that team know each other's game inside out. There's a cohesion there right from the 'B' of the bang, and that will be a sharp contrast to big-spending Mansfield Town for instance. I keep rattling on about consistency being king, but I believe in that mantra. A good side that stays together will very rarely lose that understanding of each other's game, and when they're winners as we are it can only mean good things.

Where we have added, we've done it really well. I'll boldly predict there isn't a better midfield in League Two, assuming we start with Bostwick, Woodyard and Billy Knott. The first two players are generals of the highest order, our Player of the Year and Peterborough's too. I've talked about Bostwick for the last three weeks, but Alex Woodyard staying was as good as any new signing. We know his potential and endeavour is an asset but perhaps he'll be overlooked now he has the mammoth alongside him in midfield. Seriously who is going to dominate those two, the brawn and the brains, endeavour and strength, industry and brute force. I believe this is the best midfield pairing in my lifetime, and with Billy Knott oozing potential ahead of them Imps should be excited. Billy has a lot to prove this season, and with Elliott Whitehouse snapping at his heels he will have to reach that potential we all believe he has. In terms of technical ability there isn't a better player in our squad, and if he reaches the levels Danny expects then we will have the best midfield in League Two.

We also have the best selection of wide players too. Nathan Arnold weighed in with goals and assists last season, and he will thrive at the higher level, and he'll have to Ginnelly, Anderson and Jordan Maguire-Drew all vying for a first team place. I spoke of Ginnelly being the 'fourth' winger, but his pre-season has been scintillating and he's looked a cut above the player we saw last season. He's so direct and aggressive with his runs, and we're seeing some proper end product which is really exciting. Crucially he is happy here as well, I think he took the club to heart last season and he always has a smile on his face around the ground, Happy players are good players, and Josh is a really good player.

Jordan Maguire-Drew was the 'Nathan Arnold' of Dagenham last season, and his delivery from the left is extraordinary. He has a whipped cross the like of which we haven't seen here for a long while, and delivery into the box is going to be key. we know Rheady, Luke Waterfall, Raggs and Bozzie will all thrive on good balls in, as will Matt Green the natural predator. JMD doesn't just bring the delivery though, he's keen in front of goal too and anyone concerned that we're placing too much weigh on Matt Green's shoulders need only look at Nathan and JMD's tally from last season to realise we have goals covered.

I've done two paragraphs about wingers and not mentioned Harry Anderson, the first Imps signing in almost two decades to be given a three-year deal when he first joins. I've waxed lyrical about Harry ever since he first arrived, he's got it all at such a tender age, he's quick and direct but powerful and another who has a keen eye for goal. Potentially he could go on and play much higher, and the length of the deal is testament to the promise he has. I was shocked we managed to bring him in permanently, with Bozzie arriving on the same day it got played down, but he is a massive signing for the club.

Four wingers, two wings on which to play and even the most basic of mathematician knows that isn't going to work. Imagine though, sixty minutes into a hard-fought game against Mansfield it's 0-0. Arnold and Maguire-Drew have run the full backs into the ground, but they're pace is dropping off slightly. The board goes up, off go number 28 and number 14 to the relief of all the yellow shirts. Then the board flashes up number 7 and number 26, Harry Anderson and Josh Ginnelly take up their positions….. potential carnage.

There is my assessment of the playing squad, and off the pitch we'll be as structured and methodical as ever. I've read some articles saying Danny's 'marginal gains' approach isn't new, and they're right. It isn't new, and I would imagine many teams in our league look to exploit any little thing they can. I just believe we do it extremely well, I don't imagine Steve Evans is often at Field Mill at 11pm watching videos, or that he's up at 5.00am reading blogs and articles online before heading into the ground. Danny, Nicky and everyone behind the scenes operate the one-club philosophy and whilst there will always be ups and downs I don't believe we've been as together as a club since the days of Keith and the 2003 play-off final. That year we achieved something remarkable with a set of players we have heard described as 'greater than the sum of its parts'.

Imagine if this squad achieves something 'greater than the sum of its parts', adding up Bostwick, Woodyard, Ginnelly, Green, Waterfall and all of them and getting something greater. How much can they achieve?

I know Danny has played down expectation, I know most fans are happy with top ten and just like last season nobody is heaping pressure on the players. Danny puts the most pressure on himself, he admits that freely. You know what I don't think he would ever admit freely? I think that as the light goes out at Castle Cowley at 1am, sometime before he falls asleep waiting for the 5am alarm, he affords himself a wry and knowing smile. I think Danny Cowley believes this team, his team, are good enough to reach the play-offs. You know what?

I do too.

Stacey West prediction for Lincoln City: 6th

Away Days: On the road to High Wycombe

August 6, 2017

After a late finish last night and a well-earned lie in this morning, I can bring you the story of our first away day of the season, a testing trip to Buckinghamshire to face Gareth Ainsworth's Wycombe Wanderers.

We (my Dad and I) booked onto one of Warren Ward's coaches, we've travelled with him before and they're always well-run and fan-friendly. The usual meeting place is the Ritz, today was a 9am departure allowing time for a full English breakfast. The pub wasn't busy as it was for trips to Ipswich or Arsenal, but there was a covering of Imps in. I got asked in the toilet by one patron who we were playing today, and my only thought was 'what the hell are you doing with your life to be in a Weatherspoon's before 9am if you're not going to football'. Obviously I didn't say that, I said 'Wycombe' and kept my scathing thoughts on his social life to myself.

We were joined by my mate Ben Grundy whom many of you will know. He had gotten himself into a bit of a pickle, waking up too late to get his pre-booked us spot elsewhere. He had rushed to the Ritz with no phone, no money and no bank card, but he had a match ticket and in his own words 'I'm not missing this game'. Fair play, as we boarded the bus it turned out he wasn't the only one, another lad turned up with a back full of beers explaining he should have been on the 617 coach that had set off about eight days earlier or something.

It did mean on our smooth journey down the A46 and latterly M40 we got a running commentary of where the core group were heading. I had to laugh when he said they were planning to go to a strip bar. It cast me back to the days when I used to be young and carefree, when the alarm on Saturday morning meant beer, mates and whatever else we could find to amuse ourselves. As I sipped on my tepid can of Carling (provided by my old man at great annoyance to him) I smiled wryly picturing the mass of 617 boys converging on a den of iniquity in the middle of High Wycombe.

Aside from a bit of traffic coming past Bicester we arrived in really good time, and our driver found a decent looking pub on the main drag in. One of the great things about travelling on a coach is that the planning is done for you, no worries about where to drink or where to park, that is all down to the driver. All we needed to concentrate on was warm beer and football chatter. The bus pulled up and we disembarked, once again invaders of a Football League town, reppin' LN5 with red, white and attitude. Last time I went to a Football League ground I was 31 (I didn't go away under Tilson, I sat at home stabbing infected hypodermic needles into my testicles as it was slightly more bearable) but here I was at 38 sporting my colours, wiser than last time and with a few more wrinkles.

The pub did have a menacing air, we couldn't see anybody on the windows and the huge chunk of bouncer on the door was accompanied by two policemen. He looked like Akinfenwa's shorter, butcher brother and I made a mental note not to say anything untoward. As we approached the door he put his hand up to stop us.

"Right boys, here's the rules," (ominous) "On the left as you go in is a bar. there's a pool table, some football on and you can get a drink just as normal," (nice, that sounds about right), "There's a beer garden out the back," (check I've got my cigars. Boom, ticked two boxes of two). "On the right as you go in…." (slight pause from Adebayo 2, what is on the right? What could possibly be in a football pub other than the things already mentioned) "On the right there are some nice girls dancing on tables." (hahaha, good one Akinfenwa), "They'll do private dances if you want, but even if you watch they'll be passing around a pint glass. Make sure you put a pound in it. In you go."

For a second I had to do a double take. This respectable looking pub was half sports bar, half strip bar. Indeed, as you went in, the left-hand side was a well-lit pub with a pool table and seats, the right-hand side was a poorly lit area featuring almost naked women gyrating on a table to the amusement of increasingly drunken football fans. I've been in menacing pubs on away days, friendly pubs and pubs where there seems to be no rules, but I've never been into one that was half-strip bar. I felt for those on our bus that had children under 18, but no doubt they found a Wacky Warehouse or something.

Not long after the 617 arrived as did a couple of coach loads of other very familiar Lincoln City 'faces'. There was a great atmosphere, although as my Dad and I sat in the well-lit bar area it became apparent most fans were happy either in the dark or in the beer garden. It didn't bother me, it meant when I went to the (constantly busy) toilet I didn't lose my seat.

After an hour and a half drinking some of the worst lager I've ever tasted we were ready to roll. That pub may have known how to put women on tables or turn a blind eye to the more salacious behaviour of the modern-day football fan, but their Foster had less life in it than road kill. I actually stuck my finger in my fourth pint and wiggled it around to try and get some fizz, but all I got was a wet finger, not something you want to boast about on the way out of a strip bar.

It was soon back on the bus and off to Adams Park. Oddly having had a few spare seats on the journey down we suddenly had people standing in the aisles as stranded Imps who didn't fancy a 25-minute walk piled on for a free lift. We're all Imps, aren't we?

Once we had negated the single lane running up to the ground we found ourselves in the 'fan zone', a new phenomenon to Imps fans but a staple of the Football League. These are tented areas where travelling fans can get a bit of food, a plastic bottle of Fosters and mix safely with a few other fans. We didn't have long until kick off which was a shame as there were a lot of people I would have liked to chat to, but the one I did have ten minutes with was Colin Murphy's son and his pal, both who lived away. They're blog readers and top blokes too, and I even got a free flag to take away. I was particularly interested in his shirt, a match-worn number 14 from the GMVC days. We discussed who might have worn it, and for the record it would have been one of Willie Gamble, Shane Nicholson, Mark Sertori, Les Hunter, Dave Clarke or Andy Moore. In case you're reading.

Adams Park isn't a bad ground at all, despite my Dad's proclamation of 'shit hole' as we walked through the turnstiles. He says that pretty much everywhere we go, including Burnley, so I take it with a pinch of salt. It might be on an industrial estate but it is surrounded by greenery and hills and I always consider it to be one of the better grounds we visit. Aside from the flooded toilets which caused me concern for my red and yellow Munchen, everything seemed to be in order. The whole 'sit in your own seat' mantra that I spouted last week went out of the window when Dad and I realised we weren't sat together, so we positioned right at the back of the stand in a cordoned off area. We're Lincoln City, we sit where we're told (unless I don't like it, then we move). What can I say, I'm a self-confessed hypocrite at times?

I was disappointed with the away following to a degree. Given this was our first game back in the Football League I thought 2,000 was a real possibility, even if half of the season ticket holders travelled we would have filled the stand. Talking to a few faces it appears that the clubs message of just 23 tickets being left in the week put many off travelling. Dad would have brought his partner Mo for instance, but they believed the club rhetoric that we were almost sold out. I spoke to four or five people that said the same thing, and I can't help but think that the miscommunication on the club's part led to us having a reduced number of fans travel to the games. I'm not going to start demanding explanations or getting indignant like many on social media, but it is perplexing to say the least.

That said 1433 isn't a bad number to take away on your first game of the season, and with the 617 boys grouped together the atmosphere had a little nudge when it was required. The moment he lads came out was wonderful though, to a neutral onlooker it was just two teams coming out for a football match, but for Imps fans it was so much more. This was redemption, the holy grail that we have been chasing for six years. Paul Farman visibly had the biggest smile, he's been on the journey longer than many fans and being in the Football League has always meant so much to him. Inwardly I would imagine both Danny and Nicky had the largest grins. By his own admission in the press conference both he and Nicky had wanted to be professional footballers but had 'come up a little short' of what was required. Now, after almost a decade managing in the non-league scene, they got to walk across the paint as Football League managers. I can't think of two nicer blokes for that to happen to.

The away end was noisy without being given any real reason to be on the pitch. The opening was scrappy, a series of long Wycombe balls towards Akinfenwa resulted in fouls against our defenders, whereas the same in reverse resulted in fouls against Matt Rhead. The exchanges on the floor were limited to a few passes but nothing for the fans to cheer. Then, against the run of play, came Matt Green's opener and the roof lifted slightly. A well-worked ball from Nathan Arnold across goal was always going to be gobbled up by a predator like Green, and I've seen enough of him to be convinced we have a 20-goal striker on our hands. I'm sure Green noted that his 'replacement' Lee Angol endured a miserable start to his Stags career, taken off and (allegedly) having a little paddy when he was. Oh dear.

Wycombe scored two quick-fire goals to change it all around very quickly. One was a free header inside the area, the other a 'Sam Habergham' style free kick that cut the grass as it beat Paul Farman. Both were disappointing to concede and I'm sure a Cowley shaped boot was connecting with arses during the half time period. The half-time whistle came at the right time, the Imps had looked devoid of ideas and Wycombe had begun to look dominant. They're very one dimensional, lots of play is focused around hitting the lump up top and getting around him for the pieces. It's a shame because in spells they look like a really good footballing team, but they insist on playing the longer ball. Gareth Ainsworth is an Imps legend, but he was raised in football by John Beck and although he has refined the art you can see elements of his master's tactics in there.

City had looked decent in flashes without ever really ascending to the heights of which we know they're capable, but within minutes of the restart we were level. It was arguably the pick of the afternoon's goals, a super Alex Woodyard ball found Josh Ginnelly, and his first goal in Imps colours. Ginnelly looked a threat all afternoon, he's so pacey and he sprinted away from the defence to lift the ball into the goal right in front of the home support. 2-2 and at that point I thought perhaps only one winner.

Wycombe weren't at the races in the second half, their balls to Akinfenwa became more erratic and he isn't one to go chasing anything not within two feet of him. Our balls to Rheady became less frequent, instead we looked to get wide and attack from the flanks. Neal Eardley had a solid game at left-back, and I suspect when Sam is fit Sean Long may have a real battle on his hands to keep his place. On the right we struggled against a really good left-back, Nathan got little change out of Joe

Jacobson who won the home team Man of the Match and my own unofficial Wycombe man of the match too.

Despite a couple of late corners Wycombe never truly threatened us, and despite the odd chance we had nothing clear cut either. I got the impression after around 70 minutes both teams decided a point was a solid enough to start to the 2017/18 season and settled for that, more disappointing from Wycombe's perspective than ours. The final ten played out with an air of inevitability which convinced me to take down my flag and go to the loo before the whistle went to facilitate a quick exit. I needn't have bothered; my old man doesn't have my incredible foresight and so all I managed was to stand around outside the ground waiting for him.

Before that though the players came an applauded the fans, Sean Raggett notably coming over alone before disappearing quickly down the tunnel. Much was made of this, it could be his last game for the club, Stoke were watching him and he's just saying goodbye etc. Let's just see how the week pans out.

Gareth Ainsworth came over and took some applause too which was a nice touch. Afterwards he spoke highly of Danny and Nicky and thanked the Imps fans for their support as he always gave us his all. Ainsworth is a City legend and he's still unique as a football manager. How much did he look like a rock star in his casually opened shirt and long hair? This isn't a festival though, it is the Football League and if his Wycombe side are a barometer of how good you need to be to enter the top ten, Lincoln City are laughing.

Finally, we were away, last into the coach park always means first out and so we were on the road by 5.30pm, back in Lincoln by 9pm and for me finally through the door of my Wolds cottage at just after 10pm. City had managed a draw in a tough opening game, a match that we perhaps should have won. Aside from five crazy minutes defensively we really deserved to come away with all three points. We were nowhere near the levels we will reach as the season progresses, and we still drew away at play-off chasing Wycombe. There were plenty of positives to take away from the game, the performances of Ginnelly, Eardley and Green amongst those. We did look fragile across the back at times, but not throughout. We did look one-dimensional at times trying to hit Rheady, but not throughout. On the other hand, we moved the ball swiftly across the park on the floor, but not throughout. One thing we did not do was exert enough of a threat in the final third, something that will come as our exciting attacking players get more used to each other.

Welcome to our new CEO
August 7, 2017

This morning sees the arrival of brand new Chief Executive, Liam Scully. On behalf of the Stacey West I'd like to wish him the very best of luck in his new role. Although the club is in great shape, Liam will have an awful lot on his plate as he contemplates how to ensure the club continues to become 'EFL ready'.

I am a pro-club writer as you know and I will always try to promote the Imps as best I can. I am also an independent writer however, and I am not going to pretend that everything is rosy behind the scenes. The club has operated on a skeleton staff for an awfully long time, and through the summer many of the staff have been besieged and beleaguered as we attempt to enter the all-new EFL structure with an incredibly low head-count. Today, Liam Scully enters a club that desperately needs his experience and direction. That isn't a criticism of anybody currently working for the club, they've done a great job under extreme pressure.

The first thing I'm sure he will be looking at is communication. Overall this summer has brought many new challenges, not least the new ticketing system. On the whole it has gone very well, but there are still issues as we saw with conflicting reports at the Wycombe game. Many fans missed out on our return to the Football League as the message from the club seemed to be we had sold out. Just hours later that message changed, but it wasn't made entirely clear. That resulted in a couple of hundred people not attempting to buy tickets when they would like to have travelled. I'm not one for demanding explanations or pulling the club down needlessly, but I hope the crossed communication wires will be addressed.

I would imagine one of the main topics he'll be addressing is the potential for a fan zone at the club too. It seems to be a staple of Football League clubs now, and with the number of fans coming to games it would be crazy to rely on the TP Suite alone. It would seem the only option for such a zone is at the South Park end of the ground, and if it served BBQ food such as is already available in the bar, and plastic bottles of beer as we've seen elsewhere, I'm sure it would be a roaring success. Towards the end of last season many fans came to the ground with money in their pocket to spend, but demand far outstripped supply. I often use the phrase 'make hay while the sun shines', and despite the rainy summer the sun is shining on Lincoln City right now. Make hay.

Many staff will no doubt be hoping to get back to doing what they are meant to do. There are a lot of really good people at the club, people who have worked long hours in fields unfamiliar to them in order to make things work. With a Club Secretary to arrive shortly as well it frees up people to get back to their proper jobs. The EFL isn't the same beast we fell out of in 2011. Licensing is different, social media is different, media is different also. Press conferences are beamed live to your computer, and everyone now has a mobile phone in their pocket. Trademarks are far more important and I wager we'll see a stop to these unofficial products being hawked about by opportunist entrepreneurs very soon. When the club have time to deal with these things, they will. Did you know by broadcasting live on Facebook in the ground, you're breaking EFL rules? Even by filming a goal and putting it on Facebook you're contravening broadcasting rights, and if the club don't act on it they could be punished by the EFL. That needs policing, and to police it needs people with time.

It would be wrong to pretend everything is perfect at the club, it isn't. When a business grows it takes on new people, and Lincoln City have gone from 1300 season ticket holders to nearly 6000. That is around a 300% rise, if that brings a 300% increase in workload then it stands to reason that more bodies are needed to make things run smoothly, and Liam's arrival is a big step towards us addressing the issue. We must remain on the club's side whilst the teething problems are ironed out, we must be patient with the small ticketing issues, or the double-booked training days. Our business has grown at a rate nobody could have expected or predicted, even the most optimistic of fans. Lincoln City Football Club isn't just about the first-team, it is about a business from the very top through to the very bottom. The first-team is the saleable product, and whilst they are winning games we must ensure the support structure for the business is in place to both maximise the income from fans, but to also ensure fans are treated with respect, kept well-informed and continue to feel part of the wonderful ethos the club built up last season.

Welcome Liam, I look forward to the impact you can have on our great football club.

The Curse Goes On – Rotherham 2-1 Imps

August 9, 2017

City were eliminated from the League Cup tonight, although far from crashing out they were eased gently aside after stubbornly refusing to lie down for League One side Rotherham.

The game was much a tale of two halves as Saturday was at Wycombe, but for me the similarities ended there. Instead of strip bars and bus journeys, I enjoyed a far more sedate pre-match routine. My friend Pete lives close to the Rotherham ground, so I took a leisurely drive (in the rain) to his, enjoyed his Mum's home-made steak and ale pie with kale before getting driven to within spitting distance of the ground. No jovial bus journey, no full English breakfast and certainly no ladies with their tops off. There was some rain though, and as is traditional a chance for a pre-match pint and cigar. We chose the Cutlers Arms because it was next to the car park and frankly I didn't fancy getting any wetter than we already were. If I hadn't have known better I would have wagered that a bloke with a long beard is bashing a load of four by two together somewhere and planning on taking the all the animals on it, two by two.

I wanted to have a good look at the Rotherham ground so we walked there early (in the rain) to have a nose around and critique it as a possible blueprint for our own. I liked some of it, there was lots of room around outside for lounging around in the warm August sun rain had we so desired, and behind the stands there was ample toileting and feeding facilities too. I would suggest a wider concourse though, it all got a bit crowded and the queues were just as long as at Sincil Bank despite there being numerous places for a pie. I'm informed the food was okay, I wouldn't know because I don't trust food bought inside grounds these days and Pete's Mum steak and ale pie had filled a gap nicely. I might be a rotund man, but I am not a gluttonous one.

Inside the ground was acceptable, I'm not a fan of the large stand one side and the smaller one the other but that could just be me. It as tidy enough but I wouldn't want us to base our ideas on it entirely, something just didn't feel right. They've tried to add some soul, but I didn't find the design practical, the aisles were still far too narrow and there wasn't a clock to be seen anywhere in the ground. I appreciate that everyone has the time on their phone these days but given that we were two to a seat as people sheltered from the rain, I didn't fancy pulling my phone out every five minutes.

On with the game, and if I'm honest I thought we were no more than okay in the first half. Rotherham played the ball about nicely, but I didn't think there looked to be two leagues difference between us. Sure, they had neat patterns of play they liked to operate, but more often than not those patterns were interrupted by Alex Woodyard or Michael Bostwick. It wasn't all one way, we did find ourselves attacking from time to time, but Matt Green cut a lonely figure up top (in the rain). Everyone worked hard, they had to as Rotherham were a Championship team last season.

I'm going to confess, I missed their goal. Mindful of the queues and desperate to spend some time not awkwardly apologising every five minutes to the giggling teenage girls who had decided that seat 125 was mine and theirs, I had retired to the toilet. When the cheer went up I thought it was City who had scored, the Millers fans had been on mute all night. Then we got a crescendo of terrible music to accompany the goal and I realised the home side had scored and they were 'atmosphere generating'. That was soon drowned out by the Imps fans singing (in the rain). If our support is as good all season as it has been for the first two games then we're in for a treat.

The goal sparked us into life and moments later we could have been level through the head of Sean Raggett. I hope Raggett stays even if it means losing him on a free in the summer. He looks better every game and he was bossing the back line. Rob Dickie looks excellent too, but that might be because I keep mixing them up! Seriously though, Sean Raggett is class, he was a monster all evening and I think another year of his services will be more beneficial than £350k split between us and Dover. Part of me doesn't want Dover to get anything either, I still bloody hate that lot.

For me the only real issue in the first half was our inability to stretch the game. Jordan Maguire Drew played on the right, Harry Anderson on the left meaning if they did get the ball they were cutting in rather than going out wide. I wonder if this was to fit the 4-2-3-1 formation, bringing the attack to a point rather than spreading it in the final third. I'm not sure it played entirely to our strengths, and often our attacks consisted of winning the ball and trying to pick out Matt Green in the channels. He worked tremendously hard, but aside from a couple of half chances he didn't get a sniff of goal, as we know if he does get a sight, he will score.

Another reason we might have been looking to come inside is the strength of our midfield two of Woodyard and Bostwick. Both were working incredibly hard, and considering it is only their second game together I don't think they're doing a bad job of understanding each other's game. Perhaps Danny felt that by bringing our wide players inside it gave us the option of winning a turnover should they lose the ball.

On reflection I don't think 1-0 was unfair at half-time. We had played well without looking too dangerous, and we'd contained Rotherham well when they threatened to break free. They had a few decent strikes at goal, but Josh Vickers looked calm and assured at all times. That would continue through the whole 90 minutes, and on tonight's showing him and Farman are going to have a colossal tussle for the starting spot. It was a cautious display from City, but aside from (what I'm told) was a good strike there wasn't much between us.

Immediately after the restart (in the rain) City looked a different side, just as we had on Saturday. Billy Knott hadn't had a great first half, but once we emerged for the second half he looked a different player. We endeavoured to keep the ball on the deck and play our way through the centre as well as out wide, and I could see it was beginning to stretch Rotherham. Long and Eardley began to find the overlap more often, Long in particular looked really lively after the restart. Raggs again got forward and tested the keeper with a header, and it seemed only a matter of time before we got something for our constant probing.

Just after the hour Matt Green came off for Ollie Palmer, and around me there was a collective groan. Ollie hadn't looked great in pre-season, but his introduction injected fresh impetus into our attacking play. Within thirty seconds of being on, he influenced the game. I've heard his heading ability criticised, but Matt Rhead would have been proud of that flick on. Rotherham panicked, and Billy Knott capitalised. Now, it might have been an error but Knott's finish was excellent, a lovely placed shot from a tight angle. It was no less than City deserved, and you didn't need piped music or a shouty compere to generate false atmosphere in the away end. At that point I genuinely thought we'd go on and win the game (in the rain).

Palmer was immense from the second he came on, he did pick up a booking though after contesting one of a string of bizarre calls from the linesman. The Rotherham full back dribbled the ball out under pressure, and yet won the throw in himself. All six-foot five of the imposing Ollie Palmer remonstrated with the lino, and it meant a yellow card for him. I did wonder if Danny might get in trouble as he immediately made for the fourth official and spent several minutes politely explaining what a fucking awful decision it was, and how it wasn't the only decision that could be described as such that had gone against us. I like Danny Cowley, but I would not want to cross him when he's in game mode.

With ten minutes to go Rotherham grabbed the winner. It wasn't against the run of play as such, they always had a toe in the game even when we had spells of pressure. They're a good side, they were Championship and they're hoping to be challenging again this season. It wasn't a defensive lapse, there was no blame to attribute it was just a well-worked goal from a decent football team. Josh Vickers had made a couple of good saves prior to them scoring, and he couldn't be blamed either. Sometimes you just have to hold up your hands and accept it, and this was one of those times. City didn't think the game was over though, and (in the rain) it never felt as though we were beaten. Harry Anderson fired over when perhaps a square ball to sub Nathan Arnold would have yielded a goal, Ollie Palmer's persistence created a chance for himself that he struck tamely, and that was shame as his endeavour deserved a reward. Of course, Sean Raggett was looking to head anything he could towards goal, and a late nod across goal from him almost gave Harry a glorious chance. There wasn't panic in the Millers defence, but City did look like getting back into it at any point.

I can't state this next sentence enough: Ollie Palmer was superb. I've put a question mark over him after I first saw him at Lincoln United, but if he plays like that every week then Matt Rhead and Matt Green have a fight on their hands for a starting place. He's strong but incredibly mobile for a big unit, and although he needs to work on some aspects of his game, he really impressed me. If anything, his arrival on the hour mark swung the pendulum City's way, and had it been a league game where the opponents don't have the little bit of class like Rotherham do, then I think we would have gone on to win by a couple of goals. Nathan coming on changed the dynamic too, he looked to use the width and Sean Long thrived on that.

What is frustrating me at the minute is every time I see City I change my idea of our best set up. I did like 4-2-3-1, but after the second half display I think 4-4-2 looks more threatening. I did think Matt Green was the only player who can play alone up top, but now I think Ollie Palmer can too. I thought Arnold and Ginnelly was our best wide pairing, but Harry Anderson had an eye-catching second half. Every time I think I've settled on our 'best XI', something changes. I can't imagine how tough it must be for Danny, but how long has it been since we've had genuine competition for places all over the field? Even Josh Vickers put a nagging doubt in my mind about his role this season.

Unfortunately, the intriguing second half had to come to an end, but not before an ovation for Lee Frecklington from Imps fans. It will be nice against Morecambe on Saturday not to find myself cheering for their manager or midfielder or some other ex-Imp. In fact, I'm looking forward to Carlisle at home so I can roll out some of the good old-fashioned Stacey West vitriol aimed at the opposition, because after two games all we seem to be making is friends. Rotherham fans were gracious, the stewarding was sensible and any potential issues well-managed. Much like Wycombe on Saturday I have come away with nothing but good things to say about the experience. That's unlike me, I'll have to glance down my fixture list and see when we play Mansfield.

On our way out of the stadium (in the rain) I had a listen to some of the Millers fan's conversations, and the overall consensus from them was that we'd be okay. One guy I heard stated that he thought we matched them in most areas, and that we should be more than competitive in League Two. He's not wrong, there's no shame in going out of a competition to a side that were Championship just a few months ago, not when we were non-league during the same period. Tonight, two teams on different trajectories clashed, and I'm not sure whether we were good which made Rotherham look average, or whether they were average which made us look good. The fact is that a neutral would have had a tough time picking which side were from a higher division, and that in itself is a massive compliment to Danny and the boys.

Man of the match for me was Alex Woodyard. How he hasn't attracted the same level of interest as Raggs I don't know, he's so good it's frightening. He's tenacious, hard-working and oozes endeavour. Video footage of him over 90 minutes should be shown to kids wanting to be footballers, and they should be told 'this is how much you need to run, this is how you should act when you lose the ball'. He will be as crucial this season as he was last, and now he has the big hairy beast alongside him we should dominate midfield battles all season. Both Raggs and Dickie were excellent too, I can't see us conceding goals through the centre if they settle as our central defenders, any team that comes and tries to compact play is going to find themselves struggling.

Josh Vickers wasn't far behind that though, he had more saves to make in these 90 minutes than Farms did in seven or eight games at the end of last season, and he looked calm and collected whenever he was called into action. Farms is still my number one, but for the first time in years I think we have two very good keepers on our books.

I've never come away from a 2-1 defeat as positive as I have tonight, but genuinely all I see is good things for Lincoln City. We might have crashed out of the Carabao Cup, but we've got all the components of a side looking to gate-crash the play-offs.

It's now 1.59am in Withcall near Louth, and I got out of my bed this morning at 9am. In that time there hasn't been a single minute where it hasn't been raining, and not just drizzle but an almost apocalyptic downpour. When we got back to the car this evening I felt like I'd just climbed out of the bath although I smelled much worse. I hope Pete's car seats don't smell too much of wet cigars and ginger.

The most one-sided draw ever – Imps 1-1 Morecambe

August 12 2017

The first Football League game at Sincil Bank in over six years certainly didn't disappoint, aside from the fact we didn't win it.

I'm not sure I saw such a complete display from City all last season, we controlled the game from start to finish and had more possession, more efforts at goal and more to be hopeful for in the future.

Pre-match there was a real buzz about the place, a continuation of last season's good feeling. My magazine 'A City United' sold out around the ground, 120 copies gone just like that. If you missed it, there are several outlets you can still get it from in town, check out my earlier post.

The Lancaster flying over was a nice touch. I remember seeing people laughing at suggestions it could happen on social media, and when it did I felt a bit emotional. I'm not sure why, but the roar of those engines invokes images of a staunch togetherness across the nation in the face of adversity, and for them to fly over our ground on our day, that was something else. I'm a man though so I swallowed it down, pretend I'd got some dust in my eye and carried on hawking my wares to anyone with three quid to spare.

I'm not sure what the fuss was all about with tickets, I didn't try to get in the ground until 2.45pm but I was in my seat by 2.49pm and that was after a quick comfort break. I was pleased to see the new system still needs the men in their red cages though, I get nostalgic about these things and another season of someone being paid to scan our tickets made me feel comfortable that things aren't changing too fast!

Lots of people around me got choked up to see us running out for our first Football League match in six years, but oddly I didn't. It didn't feel all that different to matches last season, packed home end, packed main stand, handful of hardy but vocal away supporters and an away team wearing yellow. All that had changed was the writing on the Stacey West stand and Poacher has turned up now we're back in the league. By the time the game kicked off it felt like we'd never been away, apart from the film premiere, open topped-bus tour, championship parade and numerous renditions of Sweet-bloody-Caroline.

Firstly, the opposition. Morecambe are a side I have a bit of time for, despite the fact they've got Kevin Ellison playing for them. They're compact, tough and their fans were vocal throughout. I'd like to say they'll be fine this season, but on that showing I'm not entirely sure they will.

From the first minute we brought that energy and zest that we started most games in the first half of last season with. After around 10 minutes we'd already had efforts from Bostwick, Maguire-Drew and Matt Green, and that just set the scene for a woefully one-sided first half. When Morecambe did try to get out it seemed to spring from their right back Aaron Magowan. Vadaine Oliver had a bit of running in him, but nothing compared to every single red and white shirt. City were completely dominant.

From back to front we controlled the game, utilising our usual tactic of direct balls through to Rheady, or breaking at pace down the flanks. I thought against Rotherham we suffered from having JMD on the right and Arnold on the left as it forced us inside, but today we switched it around again, immediately opening up the flanks. Sean Long and Neal Eardley were excellent too, overlapping whenever they could. What really struck me though was Matt Green.

He's the player we didn't have last season, the centre forward not just getting around Rheady, but also running the channels. At times Morecambe didn't know which runner to pick up, the winger or the centre forward making parallel runs to each other. It gave our midfielders options whenever they had the ball, and if they didn't pick either run then they spread the play and stretched the defenders. Once they'd done that, the ball could come back to where it had originally been with more space. It left the yellow shirts all at sea, and ensured we broke through time and again.

There were periods in the first half when I thought we looked infinitely better than the National League winning side of last season. Sean Long is growing by the day as a player, and he showed lots of nice close control in the final third. He worked hard to get back whenever he had to, but as we poured forward the width he gave in particular was vital.

On 16 minutes Morecambe keeper Barry Roche set the tone for the rest of the afternoon by tipping a JMD effort onto the bar, and at that point the result seemed inevitable. Every time we swept forward it looked as if someone would score. Arnold hit the side netting, Green dragged a shot wide but time still ticked away.

There was the odd scare, Sean Raggett cleared a rare Morecambe attempt off the line, and McGowan hit a shot from nowhere that clipped the bar, but they were rare chinks of light in a dark first half for the beleaguered Shrimpers. City had moved across the pitch fluidly and organically, as if those eleven men were one single living organism trying to penetrate a porous back four. Somehow, 45 minutes elapsed and the opponents had held on.

Universally around me the consensus was City would win the game with ease. There wasn't a pessimist in the house, not even the numpty one row in front of me who returned for another year of calling Woodyard clueless whenever he got the ball. Oh, the joys of keeping your seat from last season.

Less than ten minutes after the restart Morecambe had what they never looked like getting, the opening goal. Danny will tell you it was lazy from a City throw in, and then the cross should have been stopped, and he's the expert so I'll go with that. We did seem to dally a little in a rare showing of uncertainty, and in fairness to Aaron Wildig he caught the loose ball sweetly to beat Farman from twenty yards. The Morecambe fans celebrated for a minute, it may have been longer but after the initial stunned silence the nigh-on 8,000 Imps fans broke out into song. Every time I've seen us concede this season the fans have responded louder than the opposition celebrations, and today at a ratio of something like 80 Imps to every 1 Shrimper, it wasn't difficult.

The goal broke City's stride, but not for long. Normal service was soon resumed, and this time we had another outlet as Sean Raggett discovered that Morecambe were so certain we'd play the ball out of defence, they didn't challenge his runs. He made it to the edge of the eighteen-yard box on one occasion, and when Morecambe reacted the next time he simply played a pass to take another man out of the game. If the goal knocked us off method it was for minutes and no more, and when we did go close again it was Raggs with the header which was cleared off the line.

With just 20 minutes to go the constant pressure finally paid dividends after a superb Nathan Arnold pass found Matt Green. He had missed easier chances but not this one, holding his defender off before turning and slotting home from close range. It was no less than he deserved for a performance packed full of endeavour. Behind me someone remarked he was doing the job Theo Robinson did last year. They're half right, the difference is Matt Green stays onside and he turns up for league games. I was a big fan of Lee Angol, but any manager that thinks Green is worth discarding in favour of the former Posh striker is deluded.

Kevin Ellison was withdrawn to a round of boos, and not long after Vadaine Oliver got the same treatment. Neither were bad players for our club and both have only gotten their reputation as villains based on performances against us since, and you know what that means; both are decent players that play to their strengths. Neither would get anywhere near our first team.

Barry Roche still had a couple of champagne moments for him to tell the kids about, the pick of the bunch a superb double save to keep out Matt Rhead and Nathan Arnold. The new signings might have caught the eye, but Nathan looks leaner and meaner than last year, and he had a positive afternoon. As for Rheady, well my Dad thinks he's a fat lazy something-or-other, and by the end of the game he was applauding everything he did. "I was wrong about Rheady" he said, for the millionth time in two years.

Ollie Palmer came on Tuesday night and changed the game, today he came on and didn't. The game didn't fizzle out as such, another fifteen minutes of play we'd either score three or would have been hit on the break. Morecambe weren't so bad they offered no threat, they broke quickly and as well as McGowan on the right they had Patrick Brough on the left, a lad we had on loan once. They offered pace and width, and to be fair when they did get numbers forward there was a suggestion they might have a threat of some sort, somewhere. Maybe on their own ground they're more positive, but when the opponents are wasting time with forty-odd minutes to go you know they've come for a draw.

The match finished 1-1, not the result that we hoped for but undoubtedly a performance that overshadowed the actual score line. I remember a decade or so ago losing 3-2 to MK Dons and leaving the ground happy because we had turned in the sort of display to be proud of, and I haven't felt that way since leaving a game we didn't win. Today, that changed. I came away from the ground brimming with confidence despite only drawing. There was plenty to be positive about, if we play that way every week we'll be in the top ten at least come May. We were at times rampant, and as Danny says missing chances isn't a major problem (unless it continues), but not creating chances is. We're unbeaten after two league games, more than Forest Green and Grimsby can claim. We've matched all the teams we've played, including Rotherham, and today we overran an established League Two side. It's early days, but I've seen nothing to suggest my prediction of a top seven finish won't be close.

The other thing we can be thankful for is that we won't get that bloody referee for a few games now. After fifteen minutes I said to my mate Dave that I thought he was having a good game. 'Don't talk too soon' was the reply, and after ninety minutes I felt like reminding him he wasn't officiating a WWE wrestling match. I know the club shop are short of Imps shirts, but at least ask Rheady to take it off before you try putting it on. Shirt pulling goes on, I wouldn't want to see it punished all the time, but in the area and blatantly in front of the official? Come on. Also, since when has it not been an offence to climb over an opponent and roll down the other side like he's a slide in a children's play area? I know the big man attracts that sort of climb, but whether that is the case or not it is still a foul. When it is done in the area, it is a penalty. The rules are not ambiguous, so why interpret them as such?

Did the referee stop us winning the game? Of course not, we had enough chances to win our next three games and most of September's too. We're creating chances, and although we were wasteful it wasn't a woeful waste. They efforts went just wide or just over, never too wild or uncontrolled. No, the man in the middle didn't lose us the game, he didn't spoil it either, he was just bad at his job. Like Danny said we don't want to be the victims, nobody likes a victim. The referee interpreted the game as he saw fit, it wasn't always to our liking, it wasn't always right but he did do the best he could. I've seen bad referees, really bad, and this one wasn't really bad. He was just crap.

I'm sure the message from Danny will be 'keep doing that, but score the goals', and Matt Green won't need asking too many times. He's scored two in two league games and we're talking about his profligacy in front of goal? Not a bad position to be in is it? Nathan banged in double figures last season, he won't be missing as many chances as he did today either. Ditto Matt Rhead, JMD was a whisker away too and that's before we've even mentioned the midfield. If we keep doing what we did today, goals will come. If that is the case there's no reason why we can't still count ourselves as play-off contenders. We're unbeaten, and in truth we've never looked out of our depth at all, not even against Rotherham. We're only going to get better, and I'm not sure the same can be said for Morecambe, no matter how much of a gentleman Jim Bentley is.

Raggett is a Canary

August 18, 2017

After months of intense speculation and debate, Sean Raggett has signed for Championship side Norwich City, but he returns to Lincoln for an immediate loan spell until January.

As the weeks have rumbled on it always looked as if one of our best players from last season was on the move, and today it has been confirmed. Norwich have been suitors all pre-season, and despite interest from the likes of West Brom and Sunderland, Norfolk did seem like a sensible destination for Raggs. The fee, as ever, is undisclosed. Dover are due a 25% cut of it, but we are also due the same from any future move Sean Raggett makes.

This is the bit where a newspaper tells you who he signed from and what he's done for us. You know all of that, so I won't bother. What I will say is Sean's actions in the last couple of weeks have been superb, and top-flight players might want to take a leaf out of his book.

He was advised ahead of the season not to play for Lincoln. The reason? By turning out in the red and white it meant a club could not sign him and loan him anywhere else. Perhaps Sunderland would have liked to buy him and send him to Bury for instance, but FA rules state you can only play for two professional clubs in a single season. By turning out for City Sean ensured that if he did move then the only place he could come back is Sincil Bank. I'm sure he didn't do it with that in mind though, he played because he is a good, honest man who has shown the same respect to us as a club that we have shown to him.

This is how transfers should be conducted, this is how players should conduct themselves and for Lincoln City this is perhaps the best we could have hoped for. Sean Raggett, in my opinion, will be in the Norwich first team come March of this season, and could well emulate Gareth McAuley in playing Premier League football after making his Football League debut with Lincoln City. He is that good, and whoever negotiated the return on loan as well as a fee deserves a slap on the back.

I hope the loan has cost us a little too, because in essence that would erode Dover's cut, and the nasty element in me doesn't want them to get as much after we were stitched up at the tribunal. However, they did raise Sean in footballing terms and they do deserve some further recompense from us for that. I may not like Jim Parmenter, but the youth set up and Dover nurtured Raggs and they don't deserve to miss out on some of the crumbs from the deal.

Danny can now add to his kitty for the 'silly-season' of transfers, but also plan for the next six months with our brightest centre half committed to Lincoln City. The Sean Raggett saga might be over, but that six-figure boost means the rumours, recommendations and motorway miles will not end for another 12 days at least.

Still searching for the first win - Exeter 1 Imps 0

August 19, 2017

Defeat down in Exeter this afternoon means the Imps are still looking for the first win of the season, and doubtless many will be looking at two points from nine with a degree of trepidation for the coming weeks.

City have had a tough start to the season, Exeter were play-off finalists last season, Wycombe Wanderers were on the edge of the top seven and the next two opponents, Luton and Carlisle, were the other sides in the top seven that were not promoted. However, we've been touted as potential play-off material ourselves and therefore we need to be winning games against our rivals. At this present moment, a win of any sort would be nice.

Perhaps the more reactive fans will already be critical, but we have to remain positive that things will get turned around. In the grand scheme of things very few teams will come and win at Exeter. This isn't time for fans to panic, but I imagine Danny and Nicky will be wanting to put some real work in over the next week.

The issue today was City simply not creating chances. Arguably it was an even game in terms of possession and play, but Reuben Reid scored and Lincoln City did not. We didn't dominate, this wasn't Morecambe all over again, but relatives of mine (Exeter fans) messaged at half time to say how well we were playing. That means very little if we don't create chances, after last week Danny said he can live with missing chances if we're creating them. This afternoon we did not, and with respect I'm not sure this Exeter side will trouble the top seven this season.

I wasn't at the game so I'm not in a position to dissect the finer details, I'm pulling this together from conversations I've had through the game. I think today was a bad day at the office, but in context it isn't a debacle. City did still have an even amount of the play, we defended well in the main. We might only have two points from nine, but we haven't played badly in any of our games. Neal Eardley had a good game today, and with Sam to come back soon I suspect our offering from out wide will get better. Remember, our captain only returns today too, it is early days for this fledgling side and nobody ever said it would be easy!

I still believe in this squad and in our management duo and I'm sure everyone will feel the same. It isn't nice looking at the league table and seeing us ensconced in the bottom three, but we won't be there at the end of the season. Those that thought we'd go straight through the league will perhaps be thinking again, I suspect the level of opposition has taken some fans by surprise. I'll hold my hands up, I thought the quality between National League and League Two was minimal, but I think we've seen that there is a significant difference. On the whole today much of the play resembled some of our matches last season, but that little bit of class from Reid is the difference.

Three games gone, there is no need to panic as yet. and I really hope that the general consensus is to remain positive. I also hope we don't see lots of calls for us to splash the cash on a top striker; we have a top striker. Matt Green has two in three and has every attribute needed for a centre forward. Where work will be put in is the quality of the ball we are delivering. I know we created a lot of chances last season, but perhaps the quality from out wide hasn't quite been there. Certainly, if we'd had 26 efforts today as we did last week I think we would have beaten Exeter, their keeper was no Barry Roche and as the game wore on they tired much quicker than City.

The patterns of play are right, the work rate is spot on and we do have quality throughout the side. Another area we have quality is on the terraces, 316 hardy souls traveling down to Devon is no mean feat. On the radio they were in fine voice, and that carried on despite the result. Fans don't win points or games, but that support is superb and I'm sure it will continue as fervently over the next two tough games. Similarly, if we keep doing the right things next week against Carlisle in a loud and packed Sincil Bank then the win will come, and once we rediscover how to win games we'll be fine.

Danny Cowley wasn't hiding from the fact the Imps are struggling, but as usual there's no excuses.: "We're disappointed to lose. I'm not interested in being a 'nearly' man and at the moment we look like a nearly team."

"We dominated the first half in terms of possession, we were pleased with the performance up until then. Their keeper has made an incredible save from Matt Green, but they're the harsh realities at this level."

"We did enough territorially and got in enough good areas to score, but we have a no-excuse mentality. We're winners, we like winning, we're used to winning and we're incredibly disappointed not to do so."

Whilst it hasn't been the sort of start that was in keeping with our rampant championship last season, it is a big step up for everyone at the club. Danny and Nicky will be aching for their first win as Football League managers, and whatever the next few months hold they know they are safe and comfortable to develop the team as they see fit, even if the results are not there straight off. Nobody ever won a division or got relegated in August, and once we've got the next two games out of the way I believe there will be a clear pathway to a mid-table surge.

There will be no rash purchases, Danny said that poor decisions are made when emotion is brought into football, alluding to the fact he won't let the three-game winless start to the season cloud his judgement on player recruitment. He. like me, argued that another striker isn't urgent purely because of how we've done over three games, I reiterated Matt Green has already scored twice this season.

Keep the faith, it could be worse. We could be Tranmere still stuck in the National League, and like Hartlepool we may have two points, but they're third from bottom of the National League and we're a League Two club with a bright future.

League Two standard: An Apology

August 26, 2017

Time for me to retract a statement that I made several times last season, and again heading in to this campaign. I openly stated that the quality between most of League Two and the National League wasn't that far apart. I was wrong.

I think many have been surprised by the quality shown, certainly by the likes of Morecambe who were amongst the favourites to go down. Instead of steaming into this division, all guns blazing with seven points from nine, I think we've found it challenging. Danny wasn't under any illusions, but I was.

Many of you were too, and I've heard lots of people stating they knew it would be difficult. Surprisingly I didn't hear too many people saying it when we won the league last year. The underlying feeling then was that we were capable of going straight through League Two. A pair of draws and a defeat so far are testament to the fact it isn't all going our way.

That said, we're not playing badly. I've watched Imps teams start the season with a similar record, but they've been limp wristed and devoid of ideas too. I've seen worse Imps teams get off to winning starts, managing to snatch opening day wins over poor Barnet sides. This team, the squad as a whole even, are competitive, organised and focused. We're not without a win through lack of trying, lack of ability or a lack of hope. If the rub of the green had gone our way we should certainly have done Morecambe four or five one, and on a better day we could have snatched the Wycombe game. If we're being objective I think a draw at Exeter would have been a fair result.

We're creating chances, our players look match fit and sharp for ninety minutes and our patterns of play are developing too. Michael Bostwick and Alex Woodyard are working well together, Matt Green looks really lively and we have superb combinations of players out wide.

Here's the issue; I'm not sure we'll be out of the bottom five come the start of October. This may seem incredibly negative but having looked at the fixtures I can see a few hard-fought draws coming our way. Mansfield at home, Luton at home, Notts County away and Grimsby away are all going to be tight games in which a point would (arguably) be a decent result. We could be playing well, doing the right things and still be in the bottom five come the end of September.

I am confident though that nothing would change. Danny and Nicky believe in their approach, and as yet I've seen nothing to suggest it isn't the right approach. Exeter and Wycombe were either in the play-offs or knocking on the door last season, and we matched both. Today's opponents were beaten semi-finalists too, and I think we'll take something from the game. Even if we're still swimming against the tide in a month's time there will be no rash boardroom decisions, no panic buying of goalkeepers or ostracising of players for missing chances. We will continue to be professional, believe in ourselves and apply ourselves correctly. Other teams may lose their heads in that situation, but not Lincoln City, not this Lincoln City.

If we do struggle for results as we acclimatise to League Two then I hope the fans will remain on the club's side. I'm not just looking at the returning fans here either; many were quick to get on Chris Moyses' back when things didn't go so well despite us moving forward. It isn't always those so-called new or returning fans that are likely to start the negative stuff, it is everyone. We're all one now, looking back at sub 2,000 attendances fondly is a folly and will only open divides amongst a fan base that we need to be united. If everyone could see training sessions, if everyone could get half an hour with Liam Scully, or watch the players interacting, then you'd know there is nothing at this club that suggests we won't be competitive once we find our feet properly.

I was around the club when Jacko was in charge, Tilson, Sutton and even (to a degree) John Schofield. Often they said the right things when the chips were down, Jacko in particular always had an answer, an excuse or a media-friendly soundbite. Those managers said the right things in the face of adversity, and Danny Cowley does the same. The distinct difference is that Danny Cowley also does the right things as well, in the way he sets up his team, the way he treats his players and the way he conducts himself. The smiley face in the press conference isn't a façade, the talk of tactics and thorough approaches isn't just bluster and showmanship. He talks the talk, but also walks the walk.

I know 99% of you reading this won't need asking to stay behind the lads if come September the good ship Lincoln City sails into choppy waters. We have more of an advantage at Sincil Bank this season than we've had since the early eighties. Packed stands, vocal fans and an intimidating atmosphere for visiting supporters. That is a safety net for our players when things are tough, we're there to help turn those matches around. When Morecambe scored two weeks ago the loudest cheer came from our supporters for our team. If September is hard going then the lads will need that backing even when things are tough, and come October, November and December I think we'll see any faith we've had to show repaid twice over. Danny Cowley's teams only get stronger as the season goes on, and I firmly believe that will be the case this season as well.

No matter what happens today, keep the faith, and don't bother looking at a League Table until Halloween.

Off the mark in style: Imps 4-1 Carlisle

August 26, 2017

2359 days ago, I walked away from Sincil Bank having witnessed us beat Southend United 2-1. It never crossed my mind I would have to wait so long for the Imps next Football League win at home, but finally we got what we have been waiting for today as we soundly thumped Carlisle by four goals to one.

I'm not going to come out with some corny line about it being worth the wait because no result is worth waiting that long for, but that doesn't take away from what was a superb win. I'd like to personally congratulate Danny and Nicky on their first ever win in the Football League. I could tell in his interview Danny wanted to say, 'it is our first win', but quickly changed it to 'back in the league' so it encompassed the whole team. Let's not forget for us it's nice to be back, for the men that got us here it's all new territory. Not that you'd guess because they handled the game superbly from a tactical point of view.

Firstly, Carlisle. I was impressed with them, they were organised and got from back to front quickly, or to use another phrase, they played long ball. I had taken Keith Curle's comments about us playing direct a little too personally, and very soon it became clear the reason he understands our game so well is because he employs it himself. The outcome is different, rather than looking for a flick on into the channel they look to bring it down and play it across the 18-yard area trying to tease an opening, but the route they use to get there is pretty much the same. They, like us, showed an ability to mix it when they needed to as well. It might pain some fans, but they're very much like us, apart from we've got a rich vein of class running through our team, and they perhaps lack one or two vital components.

The Stacey West – A Season in Blogs 2017/18

I was especially impressed with their front two, Ritchie Bennett and Hallam Hope, certainly in the first half. They worked tirelessly to penetrate our back lines and were it not for some staunch defending from Raggs and Luke we could have found ourselves trailing. I also liked the look of their central midfielder, Mike Jones. He had composure on the ball and was involved in anything they chose to put through the middle of the park.

Anyway, this isn't a Carlisle blog so that is enough about them. The next figure from today I'd like to discuss is experienced referee Eddie Ilderton and his linesman Michael D'Aguilar. In the first half I thought both had absolute stinkers, my case point being the 100% stonewall penalty on Matt Green as Mark Ellis hauled him down in the area. I've seen marginal penalty shouts turned down recently, but there was nothing marginal about this. He was dragged to the floor and both officials missed it. The linesman compounded the agony by flagging Rhead every time the ball went near him. Officials need to realise Matt Rhead is a human being, it hurts his feelings when he is clearly fouled and nothing is given. He might be big and bad but he can be fouled, he is regularly fouled and as yet I've not seen a sympathetic referee. They didn't influence the result, and in the second half their performance was better, but even though the standard of football is significantly different in League Two, the standard of officials is not.

On to the Imps, and a fairly complete display against a side far better than the Morecambe team we failed to beat. I thought we went about things the right way, utilising the pace and awareness of Matt Green excellently with the power of Matt Rhead. It isn't one dimensional which is what Danny alluded to in his press conference, and occasionally we looked to build down the flanks as well. Carlisle doubled up on Rheady for a while, but in the second half they seemed to change their approach to his threat, and he started getting much more joy. For a team that did their homework and boasted about it in the media, I didn't think they did enough to combat our multiple routes to goal.

Our first goal came the same way many of our goals will come this season, from the tenacity and determination of Matt Green. He refused to give up the ball even when it wasn't entirely under his control, and when Alex strode towards it you have expected row Z to duck in avoidance. Instead he placed a beautiful effort past the despairing keeper. In his post-match interview Alex said he's been working on his finishing, and his measured shot showed all the hallmarks of a well-practised technique.

After the goal we looked to slow the game down a little. The full backs were having good games, Eardley in particular stood out. He misplaced on or two passes, but on the whole his class is really showing through. He's composed on the ball and as Farms said on Thursday he has cultured feet. He switches from left foot to right comfortably and uses that to beat opponents. He has a wicked burst of pace too, and his crossing was dangerous throughout the match. On the other flank Sean Long put in a solid ninety minutes, but I fear he'll have to fight hard when Sam comes back.

The game threatened to boil over a couple of times, not least because of the apparent inconsistent officiating when it came to blocking the keeper's kicks. Matt Green appeared to impede their keeper without being punished, whilst Ritchie Bennett did the same to Farman and got a booking. My interpretation was that Green didn't step across their keeper as he kicked the ball, whereas Bennett stepped right in front of Farman as he released the ball. It was harsh and if I'd been in the blue end of the ground I would have been riled. I'm not sure whether I would have been riled enough to later throw a smoke bomb over the stand and into the ground though.

I'm not sure anyone thought at half time the score would remain 1-0, it hadn't been nip and tuck by any stretch of the imagination. It had been a competitive and engrossing game of football. There was always going to be more goals.

Quite what Alex Woodyard had for breakfast this morning I don't know, but he was the unlikely scorer of our second as well. this time it was Matt Rhead the creator, threading a fine pass through for Woodyard who found himself in an unusually advanced position. He never broke stride as he collected the pass, powered into the area and fired the ball past Jack Bonham. 2-0 and you would have thought it would be game over.

On 68 minutes it was, and once again it was Matt Green causing the issues. He works the channels so well, and he's tenacious in possession. I lost count of how many times he seemed to bulldoze his way through players and still retain possession, and on this occasion their defender got beaten for pace. He hauled Green down and gave the ref no option but to award a penalty and give Tom Parkes a second yellow. Both his fouls were bookings, there can be no complaints at all. The main complaint came from Alex Woodyard who wanted the penalty, but Matt Rhead wanted his first Football League goal since March 2015, and he wasn't going to be dissuaded. I confess I always fear when Rheady takes a penalty, but he made no mistake. At 3-0 you knew we'd secured all three points, especially as they had ten men. Keith Curle threw on three subs, and we settled down to close the game out.

It didn't feel like that was the end of it though, I remarked to Dave (the lad I sit with) that I felt there was goals in the game, possibly at both ends. Our wait for a clean sheet goes on after an innocuous looking run from Reggie Lambe resulted in a smart finish from a tight angle. Farms looked at his defence, they looked back and you just knew the video replay was already being uploaded to Danny's phone so the players could take collective responsibility on Monday morning. One blot on the copy book, but still not the end of the scoring I felt.

The game opened up in the final 15 minutes, Carlisle poured forward hoping for some sort of an unlikely comeback, and we in turn surged forward looking to wrap up our win. Billy Knott had come on before the second goal and looked every inch the class act he is, but when Harry joined him on 73 minutes we had two very exciting players fresh and eager to impress. Anderson caused all sorts of issues for the hapless Danny Grainger at left back, whilst Knott made his passes look effortless but cultured. As gaps appeared we had more than one chance to push the envelope, and when we did wrap up the game it was a real corker. Anderson had created panic with a surge forward, and we looked to seep through the holes in their defence. Green's mere presence caused panic, and Billy Knott was the beneficiary. It took him a second bite of the cherry, but after it found him in space a second time he didn't need asking again. It was perhaps the pick of the finishes, another placed effort much like Alex's first goal past the stranded keeper. You could see what it meant to Billy as well, he ran up to the block seven area and saluted the fans. He didn't need to say anything, his actions said it all. That is what he is capable of, and he is desperate for a chance to do it every week.

That was that, ninety pulsating minutes of football, a score line that perhaps flattered us in terms of margin, but a game we absolutely deserved to win. Nobody is getting carried away, I stick by the whole 'judge them in October' rhetoric from this morning, but it is bloody nice to be here writing about a Football League win. I imagine somewhere in Essex now there are two very happy brothers silently toasting their achievement. It's never about them, always about the team. It's never about where they're going, always where the team is going. Tonight though, two very special brothers have won the first of many Football League matches they will triumph in over the next twenty years or so. I hope they afford themselves a little glass of wine and a moment to enjoy their evening, because that's exactly what I'll be doing thanks to them and the fourteen red and white shirted players from this afternoon.

Now we really are back, we're up, running and ready to pit our wits against the very best. With Luton to visit next week, we won't have to wait long.

You prioritise competitions, we'll prioritise winning games: Mansfield 1-3 Imps

August 30, 2017

The 3-1 Checkatrade Trophy win might be in a so-called underwhelming competition, but it brings with it another small piece of history, something else to help build the positivity and morale around the club.

I accept that a win in the league would be far better, but a team should play every game to win. Danny Cowley doesn't give any competition so much priority that he'll risk being eliminated, and tonight he fielded the same sort of side that faced Rotherham in the Carabao Cup. There were no young players such as Ellis Chapman, not even a start for keeper Josh Vickers. Danny went to win the game, using his squad, and win it he did.

I don't subscribe to the theory teams in our league are happy to earmark certain games as low priority. It doesn't matter if a fan has paid £10 or £50 to watch their team, they want to see them win and managers should respect that. Danny always offers the value for money, giving the paying fan belief that he is going to win the game, and that it is winning games at all costs and any level that motivates Lincoln City. Winning games is catching, it lubricates the wheels of an effective and confident set of players, building the players belief and confidence.

I don't think you could tell Ollie Palmer (pictured top) that it was a low-priority game, allegedly barracked by the home fans tonight and responding with a goal. I don't think you could tell Matt Green that either, applauded by fans of the club he was frozen out of, and later scoring against the manager that pushed him out. I don't think you could tell Mansfield's bench it was low-priority by the way they ungraciously refused to shake Nicky Cowley's hand after the game. Despite the 617 boycott, you couldn't tell the remaining 900 fans that travelled the victory meant nothing. After all, we're back in our familiar position at the top of the league, albeit the group stages of the Football League Trophy.

What about Elliott Whitehouse? I'm sure it was a priority for him, aching to get a kick after a limited start to the season. He fell down the pecking order significantly this summer with the arrival of Bostwick and Knott, I'm pretty sure he attached a lot of importance to his well-taken goal. Sam Habergham, returning after a torrid summer, will also have prioritised the match.

I'm labouring on a point here. In professional football there is no such thing as 'not prioritising' a match, nor is there any dignity to be restored by claiming you only put your reserve squad out. That is like a five-year-old losing at a computer game and claiming he 'wasn't really trying' to win the game afterwards. Those so-called Mansfield Town reserves are players not released in the summer or brought in over the summer. It matters not they've played less football than some others, they should still be a capable and able team. Elliott Whitehouse hasn't had much football; Luke Waterfall didn't start the season and Rob Dickie isn't in the side at present. Ollie Palmer is on the fringes, Harry Anderson is effectively a reserve at the moment, and Sam hasn't kicked a football competitively since April. So, your reserve squad couldn't beat our fringe players and a few first teamers? There is no comfort to take from that, nor is there a great amount of truth.

Mansfield played well for half an hour tonight, a third of the game. My man at the ground tells me Alfie Potter looked dangerous, as did Jimmy Spencer, and Omari Sterling-James looked a handful too. However, Lincoln upped the tempo with some of the fringe players seizing their chance. Harry Anderson caused all sorts of trouble; Ollie Palmer gave a committed display up front and Billy Knott oozed class in the middle of the park. You know how many games those three players have started in the league this season? None. In fact, five of our starting eleven tonight have not started a league game for City. Five. Of Mansfield's team, seven hadn't started a game. Of Lincoln's non-starters, two did start our League Cup game, as did two of Mansfield's. Not exactly reserves versus first team, is it?

Tonight was the first Football League Trophy game Lincoln City have won since November 2003, when Gary Taylor Fletcher scored an extra time winner against Chesterfield to wrap up a thrilling game 4-3. For 14 years we've suffered the indignity of a 5-2 defeat at home to Hartlepool, 1-0 defeat away at Conference side Halifax, penalty defeats against Grimsby and Leicester after 0-0 draws, and even a defeat that cost a manager his job, 1-0 at Darlington. Peter Jackson was fired the day after that match, despite giving Sam Clucas his only Imps start. This might be a Mickey Mouse competition, but when we last won in it I was 25, and I'm now staring down the barrel of 40.

I'm not claiming this is a result to change our season or anything like that, obviously I'd rather we lost here and won in the league, but what's to say that this 'winning games' habit can't become a habit like last season? Who's to dampen down a fine victory over local rivals in front of vocal support, just because the actual competition is badly organised, clumsy and laced with ill-feeling and ominous under-current? Not me, we just beat Mansfield 3-1. I'd be happy if it was the under-15's that had won, or our fans team.

The second half was a clinical and organised performance from City, and contrary to some people the Mansfield side were tough and disciplined opposition. City though controlled play, perhaps the weakest player in the pitch was Jordan Maguire-Drew. He's drawing some criticism from the fans at present, and I wouldn't be surprised to see him have a spell on the bench, just to alleviate some of the pressure. I wouldn't want to see another Tom Champion situation, and like To,. Jordan is keeping a fan favourite out of the side. Champion pushed Lee Beevers on to the bench and the irked some fans, and now JMD is keeping Harry Anderson on the side lines. I wonder if it might be that Harry starts against Luton to give JMD a chance to impress from the bench and regain confidence.

It was also interesting to see Woodyard and Bostwick operating in the holding role with both Knott and Whitehouse accommodated. Knott is an insane talent, full of tricks and vision. He offers something different to anyone else in this squad, maybe even in League Two. As for Elliott, he's labelled as a midfield man at city, but I think he has more of the centre forward in him. His aerial ability is probably better than Ollie Palmer and he's a few inches shorter. The game gave Danny a chance to look at different patterns and approaches, and it is fair to say at 3-1 they paid off.

Of course, he had to conduct most of it from the stands but trust me he will have even gotten some value out of that. He'll see more up there than he can on the touchline, and I bet he's already one step ahead of watching the match back on tape.

So, the curtain closes on another one of those annoying 'first win since' statistics. We see the end of round one of 'the great Checkatrade trophy' debate too, although I'm sure we'll have plenty more as the season progresses. I've tipped City to at least get to the semi-finals this season, given Danny's desire to win matches, and with an attendance of just over 2400 it was the night's best attended game, with the 890 visitors the highest number of travelling fans by some distance. For some that will be a source of shame, for others a source of pride.

I don't care, we won 3-1 and I didn't mention you-know-who by name at all. Tonight wasn't about him, it was about us. It was about Lincoln City winning another game. That's two in a row, now bring on the Hatters and let's see where we really are as a team.

The Ballad of Danny and Steve

August 30, 2017

It isn't an obsession, although I'm sure a psychiatrist would seriously question that. Here, for the final time this week, is an article mentioning my favourite Scottish football manager. This isn't a tale of his previous crimes though, this is a story that is bang up to date.

Last night our own paragon of virtue, Danny Cowley was sent to the stands in apparent disgrace after something occurred on the side of the pitch. The post-match analysis shone little light on the subject, Danny was as mystified as anyone as to what had happened. Steve didn't help matter by refusing to shake Nicky's hand after the game. What heinous crime had our otherwise picture-perfect boss committed? We know he likes the odd expletive when he's 'on duty', but surely he wasn't sent to the stands for swearing?

Here, probably for the first time, is the truth of the situation as revealed by a trusted source earlier today.

Steve had apparently been aggressive from the outset, eclipsing his issues on Saturday with Luton Town manager Nathan Jones. Rumour has it the two had a bit of a coming together in the tunnel following on from Jones' comments in local media about sharing 'chicken nuggets' with the Mansfield boss. Evans was outraged his side failed to win the battle of the big-spenders, especially after he outrageously labelled Luton as the money bags team.

Perhaps Evans was still riled by that, perhaps he felt we'd cheated somehow by naming Alex Woodyard and Sean Long in the side when he graciously played his reserves. Maybe Mrs Evans hadn't stocked up on his favourite chocolatey breakfast treat the night before. Whatever the issue was, Evans was in Danny and Nicky's ears and they're not going to take that.

The incident came to a head when Paul Digby deliberately impeded Paul Farman as the keeper went to release the ball. He picked up a booking for doing so, but over on the touch-line trouble was brewing. Steve had taken exception to something Danny said, and he was making his way towards the Lincoln dugout with fire (amongst lots of other things) in his belly. My sources claim he uttered the 'C' word a couple of times in the direction of Danny Cowley. Danny might be a few weight divisions below Steve, but he won't shy away from confrontation and he also moved towards the man-mountain, waving around his hands. In one of those hands was a water bottle.

I'm told Steve then complained to the fourth official that Danny had deliberately flicked water at him, and the officials took the word of Evans over Danny, and our manager was sent to the stands. My source tells me that Danny's hand did have a water bottle in it, and at no point was it aimed at Steve Evans, nor did it spill water in his direction. You know Steve though, he's prone to being economical with the truth (£750k for Bostwick? £100 a week for Mike Marsh, etc).

A friend of a friend knows a referee's assessor, and he's told The Stacey West that Danny and Nicky are no angels. They won't openly criticise an official and they're respected for that, but they're happy to express an opinion whenever they can on the touch-line. Football is passionate and you would expect nothing more. The exact description I got was that Danny and Nicky can be a nuisance on the bench but compared to Steve Evans they're Mother Teresa.

Steve Evans is a canny man, he believes that by creating tension and ill-feeling it will introduce emotion into games which may cloud judgement. With a massive clash between the two sides on the 16th he will want to play the victim with the Stags fans, try to create a bit of the siege mentality. After all, even with just six games under his belt, the pressure is on.

Some of their fans are not happy with progress, and he's already castigating players that he himself has signed. After all, only four of the side that played last night have not be signed by Evans, and he's already saying players are 'not ready' to step in when he needs them. Pressure manifests itself in many ways, but false claims of water throwing is a new one on me, if that is indeed the case.

That is it now, I promise no more Steve Evans articles for at least a week or so. I promise.

Pos	Team	Pld	W	D	L	GF	GA	GD	Pts
1	Exeter City	4	3	1	0	7	4	3	10
2	Newport County	4	2	2	0	9	5	4	8
3	Stevenage	4	2	2	0	8	5	3	8
4	Crewe Alexandra	4	2	2	0	5	3	2	8
5	Luton Town	4	2	1	1	13	5	8	7
6	Accrington Stanley	4	2	1	1	9	7	2	7
7	Notts County	4	2	1	1	8	7	1	7
8	Wycombe Wanderers	4	2	1	1	10	10	0	7
9	Swindon Town	4	2	1	1	4	5	-1	7
10	Coventry City	4	2	0	2	5	3	2	6
11	Carlisle United	4	2	0	2	7	7	0	6
12	Yeovil Town	4	2	0	2	10	14	-4	6
13	Lincoln City	4	1	2	1	7	5	2	5
14	Mansfield Town	4	1	2	1	7	6	1	5
15	Morecambe	4	1	2	1	3	3	0	5
16	Colchester United	4	1	1	2	7	8	-1	4
17	Barnet	4	1	1	2	3	4	-1	4
18	Cambridge United	4	1	1	2	2	3	-1	4
19	Forest Green Rovers	4	1	1	2	7	12	-5	4
20	Crawley Town	4	1	0	3	4	5	-1	3
21	Port Vale	4	1	0	3	5	7	-2	3
22	Grimsby Town	4	1	0	3	6	9	-3	3
23	Cheltenham Town	4	1	0	3	5	9	-4	3
24	Chesterfield	4	1	0	3	4	9	-5	3

September

Will we ever welcome Simeon Akinola?
September 1, 2017

It's taken a year longer than some might have imagined, and thus far it's taken 24 hours longer than almost every Imps fan imagined. Is Simeon Akinola going to become a Lincoln City player?

He's been seen at training and around the ground today. Barnet clearly didn't fancy him up top and have willingly let him go, and yet still we await news. As recently as half an hour ago Leicester unveiled a new signing, is it just that the FA haven't had time to rake through all of the paperwork? I understand when you have a workload, but this isn't like trying to sell 9,000 Arsenal tickets from two terminals in an overworked office is it? This is the FA, and surely it's just a matter of stamping a fax and saying yes or no to us?

Simeon Akinola was one of Danny's 'Class of 2016', a member of the part-time Braintree side that had no right to storm the play-offs given the teams they kept out of the frame. He's quick, strong and does have an eye for goal, and Danny rates him incredibly highly. In 2016 he described him in the Sky Sports: "Simeon has Championship pace and agility, he's unbelievably quick and another player who doesn't give defenders a moment of rest. He can change a game in a minute and one of his best strengths is he's a great counter-attacking player, who can sit on the shoulder of the last defender but he can also play wide. He loves cutting in from the left onto his right foot. He's intelligent off the pitch as well... he's got a first-class degree in economics."

According to Wikipedia Danny it is actually Systems Engineering, but then according to Wikipedia he was a Lincoln player at 11pm last night.

He's not prolific, but he does have a penchant for the outlandish. Last season he won the Barnet 'Goal of the Season' award for an audacious overhead kick, but in truth he had a rough time at Barnet. After Danny left Braintree he scored six times before a £40k move to Barnet, but he hasn't had the best of times with the Bees. He did score twice, but this season he's been restricted to coming off the bench, and with them securing Maidenhead striker Dave Tarpey he became surplus to requirements.

As we understand a deal for an 'unnamed striker' was agreed at 10.50pm, the paperwork sent off at 10.59pm...... and the wait was on. The wait is still on. Once again a deadline day saga kept us glued to our screens, but for once it was incoming and not departing, as was the case last August (Margetts) and last January (Robinson). This year the 11pm deadline passed, but club sources were keeping the mystery alive asking people to stay awake. Those that did were awake until morning, and I imagine the live press conference broke viewing records for the Imps feed! Now it's getting a bit like the TV series Lost... people are wondering if sticking with the saga was worth it. Let's hope it is.

What can we expect from Akinola, should we get the go-ahead from the FA? Well, he is certainly quick and he appears to offer options out wide as well as up front. He isn't the dedicated centre forward many have suggested we needed, but as I've said all along I didn't feel we needed that role. We needed pace, a direct player who could cover a couple of positions if needed. Danny will try to utilise him down the middle I feel, but with Josh Ginnelly offering a similar option it does give us some real variety.

I think we may be getting an unpolished diamond, a rough gem ready to be fashioned into one of our crown jewels. Of course, Simeon is going to be raw, he's only played a couple of months of full-time football in his career. He is only 25 though, he has bags of potential and despite his time at Barnet I think Danny and Nicky are the key to unlocking it. I believe he went to Barnet with them hoping for instant impact in the starting eleven, and I'm not sure Sim was in a position to offer that. He's now had six months full-time football in his career, and although I still don't see him as a starter at the moment, he could bring an added dimension to the squad. If the fax arrived in time.

This move, should it occur, proves Danny is a rational and measured man. I said if he brought anyone in on deadline day then it would be someone he knew, someone on whom he had conducted the due diligence and research. Ultimately, how could it be anyone other than Akinola? How could anyone have possibly signed for Lincoln City at last-minute if Danny didn't already know them inside out, from how quickly they run the 100m to which bedtime stories they prefer?

Simeon Akinola (could, maybe) almost bring us to the position Danny wanted us to be in when he set out his transfer policy way back in June. One for each position he said, and aside from a full-back we have one for each position. This year we are looking more fluid as a squad, more players can cover different positions than last time out. This season we have Neal Eardley, Michael Bostwick, Josh Ginnelly, Sim Akinola (possibly) and Elliott who can all switch positions if needed. Maybe that is a symptom of the Football League, maybe it is just an evolving squad.

I can't wait to see Simeon Akinola in a Lincoln shirt, 12 months and 1 day later than I imagined he might be.

Now, let's hit F5 on the browser, refresh Twitter and stick the kettle on. Again. It could be a long night. Again.

Imps pass Hatters test: Imps 0-0 Luton Town
September 3, 2017

My apologies for the lateness of today's blog, last night I hit the red wine with friends, this morning I've been off watching the Shakespeare Imps and Saxilby in the Sunday League. Anyway, better late than never, here's my views on the game.

As always, I'll start with the opposition, this time the fans. There was clearly a big police presence in town pre-empting any trouble, but as far as I'm aware there wasn't any. I did witness one unsavoury incident, two Lincoln 'fans' walking to the ground behind two Luton fans. The Imps fans were clearly the worse for wear and (without sounding elitist) 'not all there'. They were hurling abuse at the two fearful looking Luton fans, both wearing shirts and scarves. The police and match day security were on them like a wasp on an open coke can, and I suspect they didn't see any match action. Good.

I thought Luton were a properly supported club, passionate about their own team, humorous with their chants and ultimately good-natured. The funniest chant you'll hear all season came when they clocked sight of Sid. 'It's coming for you, it's coming for you, Diabetes, it's coming for you'. It might not be what Sid wants to hear, but it was bloody funny. All in all they played their part in making this a proper Football League encounter, the type of occasion we've missed so badly over the past six years.

As for their side, they were very good. We were fortunate to see Collins go off early, both him and that odious Hylton creature looked really sharp, but with him coming off I thought they lost a bit of bite. I expected a bit more from Luke Berry in the centre of the park, but as he settles they'll only get better. I'm sick of hearing 'if you finish above Luton, you'll be promoted', but it is correct. If you are above them after 46 games you will be a League One side next season. I can see how they've torn apart teams such as Yeovil, and they will do again this season. Here's my prediction; they'll not feature in another 0-0 draw this campaign. In 'him' (I'm not saying his name again) they have a really talented striker, despised by opposition and loved by his own. Think 'Matt Rhead', but with a lack of class off the pitch and on it. Rheady winds up opposition, celebrates in front of fans and all of that, but off the pitch you don't get him on Twitter bad-mouthing opposition or 'fishing' for people to hate him.

That's enough of Luton, I didn't go to watch them. The game was by far the most entertaining 0-0 draw I have seen at Sincil Bank, to a man we were excellent. We harried, we harassed and we chased everything we needed to. Yes, we went long for parts of the game, but nobody gives us credit when we do play it about. We got down the flanks plenty with the ball on the deck, Neal Eardley and Sean Long both had excellent games. I've got to call them out equally too, they carried out their tasks to perfection. I'm wondering how Danny is going to set up when Sam is back to full fitness, because I think Eardley has been one of our best players this season, and Sean Long has improved with every second he's had on the pitch. Often Dan Potts had time to move forward for Luton from left back, and the crowd were on our lads backs for not closing him down. I think Danny was happy to let them have possession in the middle third if it was out wide. We seemed happy to make the game quite narrow, possibly crowding out 'him' and their creative midfield players. It was interesting to hear Danny say how Luton used all of the park; I think our game plan was not to be drawn into stretching the game.

The one exception to that was Billy Knott (pictured top). It was interesting to see Knott out wide as he isn't really a winger, and he tended to drift inside, thus narrowing the play. I'm not sure that was by accident, I'm not sure anything we do on the pitch tactically is by accident. However, he ran everything down, chased every ball but didn't really get the success his endeavour deserved. He had a decent game though, flashed a good effort wide of goal too. He's such a talented player, Danny's current predicament has to be fitting him into the system.

I thought Alex Woodyard was the best player on the pitch, we won the midfield battle hands down. He's live wire, literally covering every blade of grass and rarely putting a foot wrong. It might be that Michael Bostwick has allowed him more freedom, but we must be careful not to reinvent the wheel. Alex was our Player of the Year last time out, he has far more pace than Bostwick and after a man beats him, he can get back and still win the ball. Bozzie, in my opinion, can't do that. I'm not being critical but at present I haven't seen this League One quality from Bostwick we thought we had gotten when we signed him. I'm sure it's adjusting to our style, but of the two players it is Woodyard who looks more like the former Championship player.

Much was said of the back four and central midfield duo yesterday, but very few people mentioned the running of Matt Green. I've seen all-but two of City's games so far this season, and I'm in a position to make a bold statement I feel. Matt Green is the best centre forward I have ever seen play for Lincoln City. He works harder than Taylor-Fletcher, he has more contribution outside the box than Simon Yeo, he's stronger than Jason Lee.... I can't think of a City player post-1987 that I think is better than Matt Green. His 'for' column will start with a two in May if he stays injury free too. To have him leading our line this year isn't just exciting, it is an honour. If Steve Evans thinks Lee Angol is a better player, he needs to lay off the funny-fags.

Something we noticed in the game, and I'm sure Danny did too, was Paul Farman's kicking. On at least on occasion he bounced the ball before booting it forward, and although the referee didn't pick up on that, it's an indirect free kick as far as I'm aware. Something to watch Farms. That said, his harassing of their lad when we contrived to gift them an effort was excellent, and he got back into position too. We had some nervy moments, against Luton Town you expect nothing less, but I feel confident when a team attacks that we have a keeper capable of stopping a good portion of efforts at his goal.

We were very compact yesterday, and with Rheady playing the link role between Green and the midfield we often had a huge gap in front of Bozzie and Alex. That may have been intentional, Luton can't hurt us for seventy yards up the pitch, so maybe the plan was to let them have control of that area but remain solid further back. Again, some fans got on the players backs for not chasing down, but as soon as you start chasing Luton they hurt you. They poured into empty space like sand falling in an egg timer, they key to our success was to block the space. In the end they resorted to balls over the top for 'him', and that suited us. The comments afterwards from 'him' were that we were a rugby side, humping the ball forward. Oddly he was the only one to attempt a try by grabbing the ball and getting it on the turf, and he was dominated in the air by our on-loan defender Sean Raggett. Nobody can deny we play long ball, but not for ninety minutes and we're not the only ones to do it.

We could have wrapped the game up, it might not have been a fair reflection of an even game, but we could have won it. The break I refer to was on 89 minutes, Nathan strode away with two in support and two defenders to beat. Their lad cynically clipped him, a challenge from behind with no attempt to get the ball. Was it a red card? I'm afraid not. If one of our lads had done it we'd take the yellow and comment on a 'sensible' foul. It wasn't sensible for Nathan, it looked like it bloody hurt, and it wasn't even close to be fair or sporting. This is professional football though, you play to win and teams like Luton don't finish in the top five or six by playing 'fair' all the time; they have 'him' up front for heaven's sake. The only way that is a red is if the referee deems it a tackle from behind, which I'm sure many will argue it was. If the shirts were the other way around we'd be screaming how he wasn't the last man, and we'd be right.

I thought the ref had a decent game, he could have flashed an early card, made a rod for his own back and ended up sending a couple off, but he let a combative game flow and it was a better spectacle for it. He didn't give us everything we wanted, but he called it fairly and consistently.

When you put everything aside and take the emotion out of the game, when you look at this result objectively, we were bloody excellent. We've held the title favourites 0-0, a team featuring at least two six-figure players in Collins and Berry, and we've come out with a point. Either side could have won it, neither side deserved too, but how much of a compliment is it that big-spending Luton Town, 8-2 winners on the opening day, were happy with a draw at Lincoln after about 70 minutes? What does that tell you about where we are? A damn sight more than a league table can after five or six games, that is for sure.

There's no denying it, Lincoln City are back and, in my opinion, we're as good as we've been at any point in my thirty years of watching the Imps. To end, ask yourself this. How many times under Big Keith did you come away feeling we hadn't competed? They were magical times, but how often did you leave disappointed with the product served up? Ditto Colin Murphy? Both great managers whom I am not attempting to tarnish in any way, but they had teams of fighters, often uncomplicated fighters that just battled and fought, sometimes playing football, other times leaving you wishing you still had you entrance money in your pocket and the option of not going.

Now, how many times have you truly come away from a Lincoln City match managed by Danny Cowley and felt you've not had your money's worth? How many times during his tenure have a side come to Sincil Bank, National League, League Two, even Championship, and truly outclassed us? How many times have you been disappointed with the performances or efforts of the players? I bet you can count those times on the horns of your rainbow-coloured unicorn.

Akinola Deal Collapses

September 5, 2017

The deal agreed for forward Simeon Akinola has collapsed this afternoon, with the player now on his way back to Barnet to resume training with them.

It's been the transfer saga of the season, the one / off move for the former Braintree man has had Imps refreshing their browsers for a whole weekend. Firstly, we waited on Thursday for news, then it emerged we might have got him anyway and refreshed all Friday too. By Saturday pictures of Simeon training with us came out, and we awaited the news. Sunday, we waited. Monday, we waited. Tuesday came, and Tuesday has brought the worst news.

I imagine the club statement will be a sanitised piece explaining how the deal has collapsed due to a technicality, and that all parties are extremely disappointed. I imagine not long after that irate fans will be venting their frustration on all our favourite social media platforms, screaming we shouldn't leave the deal so late and all the other ill-informed opinion which is so prevalent these days.

Firstly, the time scale is purely down to the selling club and the transfer window itself. I'm sure Danny would have liked to have Simeon Akinola in the squad as we journeyed down to Wycombe, in fact I know he would. Back in January perhaps £40k was a bit rich, but now he's deemed surplus to requirements at Barnet I imagine a fee in the region of £25k was far more appealing. However, that would not have been the case had we gone in before the season started. We may even have enquired, but at that point Akinola was not for sale.

His availability hinged on Barnet signing Maidenhead's Dave Tarpey. Once he signed that deal with Barnet then Akinola would become available, but thanks to the agent involved this wasn't ever going to happen until the deadline had counted down. The excellent Bleacher Report did this short video on Sheffield United's transfer deadline day, to show exactly how clubs have to operate, receiving late demands. Instead of Chris Wilder picture Danny Cowley, sitting by the phone waiting for news of Tarpey joining Barnet. Now imagine the same over at Barnet, but instead what if Dave Tarpey's agent suddenly called up at 10pm and insisted the deal cost another £5k fee to get over the line? What then happens to us in the chain?

The Stacey West – A Season in Blogs 2017/18

It is my understanding that this isn't far from the truth. I occasionally chat to someone who knows someone, I'm sure you know that (I did call our interest in Akinola on Wednesday which was even before Danny and the player knew. That's knowledge for you). Danny has been actively chasing Simeon for a while, but unfortunately the deal wasn't possible until Thursday as agents hold all the cards. No agent, certainly not Dave Tarpey's, was going to move his player on early when he knows by waiting and pushing late for more cash he might panic a club. That is why so much happens on deadline day. There isn't a club in the Football League that likes being held ransom with an hour to go, but it is the situation the window has created.

On the other hand, you have Simeon, a player who was not represented by an agent looking to maximise the deal, rather he was being looked after by an agent who had his player's interest at heart. Simeon Akinola wanted to play some football, he wanted to work with Danny and Nicky and his agent wanted to get him that deal. I understand that there were no late shenanigans on their behalf, both agent and player were on the ball, prepared for a move and ready to progress well before the 11pm deadline. As this was our only bit of business of the day, it is safe to say the paperwork was completed and ready to go on time at our end. I wasn't the one who pressed the button, but we were not late with our paperwork, I state that as fact, not conjecture.

We weren't late, the player and his agent were not late, my only deduction is that Barnet were late. The Non-League Paper had a story this week about the deal, saying how Peter Griffin (seriously), the Maidenhead Chairman, was playing five a side football with his phone was on silent. This caused a delay in that deal, and even after it was finally agreed they struggled to get paperwork done. The Barnet fax machine would not work and the e mail system was down.

They had to register Dave Tarpey incoming at the same time as Simeon Akinola outgoing, but anyone with any tech savvy knows that you can't send two emails simultaneously. You can't press send at the same time on two faxes either, and that is after you get them working properly. If you're Barnet do you process the sale of Akinola first, or the purchase of Tarpey? If Dave Tarpey goes through at 10.50pm or thereabouts, and the files are 40mb of contract and agreement, you can wager the next email couldn't go until 10.55pm. If it is a fax machine I suppose there is a similar timeframe once the data is in the air. What if the Tarpey paperwork was sent at 10.55pm, or 10.57pm? In that instance it is Simeon Akinola and Lincoln City that miss out

Lincoln City won't tell you this though, and even if you want to scream for complete transparency you'll never get it and rightly so. This is business, if we came out with a statement claiming in was Barnet's fault, do you think we'd have any chance of a good deal on the same player in January? Do you think we'd have a chance of any deal with them ever again if our statement read 'Barnet messed up and now we're all suffering because of it'? Of course, we wouldn't, it would be goodbye for good to Akinola and probably for any relationship we have with Barnet.

This may be a football deal, something closely monitored by fans and observers alike, but it is also a business deal, a deal I imagine we hope to resurrect in six months' time with another business that we will be dealing with again and again. Imagine if we blasted them in the press, and then they visit here later in the month. That would be an awfully frosty boardroom wouldn't it? We had enough of those whenever the repugnant Jim Parmenter rolled his Dover roadshow into town. Lincoln City want to make friends, not enemies and in the Football League (not that Jim knows) we conduct ourselves in the right manner. No, Lincoln City will remain stoic and balanced in whatever they put out to the press in the interests of good relations. After all, Barnet haven't intentionally collapsed the deal have they? Their wage bill is now higher than they'd like for six months and they have a decent player and a nice guy who won't be getting much game time. Not ideal for anyone involved at all.

There will be those who will say 'so what if the Barnet paperwork was ten minutes late, the FA should show some leniency'. I've got that covered too. Last day of the season at home to Yeovil, Akinola scores the winner that earns us a play-off spot at Mansfield's expense, do you think they'd take it lightly? Or do you think they'd rake up the fact he shouldn't be playing for us? The FA have rules that must be adhered too, and however much we don't like them, they're there for a reason. If you bend the rules for one, you have to be consistent and soon the deadline day is even more farcical than it is now.

I imagine there are a lot of unhappy people at Sincil Bank right now, and a few at the Hive. I pity the person who sent the transmission at just gone 11pm who has spent the last few days desperately pleading for leniency. I pity everyone at Lincoln City who, upon hearing that Simeon was available, stopped pursuing the other lines of enquiry and concentrated on the player. This is normal, and even if we'd kept chasing other targets what good would it be? We thought we gotten Akinola over the line, other irons in the fire would have been wasted.

I mostly feel sorry for Simeon though, as his career is almost on hold for six months. He's now at a club that doesn't want him, rotting away in the reserves without much chance of first team football. As well as Tarpey they signed Mars from Chelsea, they've got Akinde to come back from injury as well as two or three other forwards. Simeon Akinola is a victim of the awful situation deadline day puts clubs in, created not only by it coming during the season but also greedy agents holding clubs to ransom. Most of all, he's probably a victim of Barnet having a slow fax machine or internet connection.

Resilient, determined and dogged: Stevenage 1-2 Imps
September 9, 2017

City have recorded a fine 2-1 win this afternoon, not by domination nor by superior skill, but purely by character and attitude. Danny Cowley's side never knows when they're beaten, they never give up fighting and more often than not, that pays dividends. There are no easy games in League Two, and this afternoon proved that.

Stevenage started the day in second place, unbeaten in the League with the wind of momentum behind them. They've ended it in fifth, beaten at home by a side that scored twice with a numerical disadvantage. From controlling the early exchanges against a lacklustre City, half time brought about a complete change. City came out hungry, fired up and not even the dismissal knocked us off our stride.

The Imps team selection was interesting, despite a decent draw against Luton last week Nathan Arnold found himself on the bench with fan-favourite Harry Anderson brought into the fold. Billy Knott continued out wide in the absence of Josh Ginnelly, but Josh did appear on the bench as he looks to return from injury.

The first half was tepid from City at best, Stevenage looked like a side playing with confidence. They scored a decent goal and could have had a couple more as they poured forward. City didn't lack desire, but they were facing a side in good form on their own turf. That's the Football League for you, the level is consistent and much higher than we've been used to. It was slightly ironic that the goal was scored by Matty Godden, a player mentioned by fans as one they'd like to see at City. Meanwhile up front for City Rhead looked to be struggling, and despite his hard work Matt Green didn't get rewards for his hard work.

We know Lincoln City don't give up though, and half time gave Danny a chance to get in his side's ears. Matt Green might have been too enthusiastic as he encroached twice prior to the kick off, referee Anthony Backhouse producing a yellow card. To the letter of the law, it is a booking, but the Stevenage player was feigning taking the kick and drawing Matt into the centre circle. Green had made a rod for his own back though, and just seven minutes later he was sent off. Again, to the letter of the law, the referee made the correct decision. Green was clearly fouled and he showed his frustration by kicking the ball away, and immediately you could see he regretted it. Last week we saw a Luton player do the same, and the referee let it go. This weekend, no such leniency. City 1-0 down and reduced to ten men too: it looked like being a long afternoon.

Danny needed to act and he did just that. Ollie Palmer came on, a player that hasn't truly won over the Imps fans, with Matt Rhead heading off. Rhead wouldn't be suitable to lead the line on his own, and Palmer seemed the sensible option. He immediately changed the look of the attack, and within minutes City were level. After wasting most corners in the first half, a near post delivery was met by Sean Raggett with a resounding header. The keeper had no chance, and immediately the 1200 travelling fans erupted.

Michael Bostwick, another player I feel hasn't hit the heights he threatens, suddenly moved up the gears as well. He started throwing himself around in midfield, and I wonder if he's like the Incredible Hulk in that he only really moves into top gear when he's angry. One challenge in particular was rousing, it was his 'Braveheart' moment. They might take our striker, they might take the lead, but they'll never take…… OUR THREE POINTS.

City looked a completely different side with ten men, and if anyone was going to win the game it was us. With fifteen minutes left our endeavour finally got a just reward. Chris Whelpdale inexplicably handled in the area under no pressure at all, gifting City a chance to take the lead. In the absence of Matt Rhead the question of who would take it arose, but Ollie Palmer stepped up and made no mistake. Sometimes a player needs one performance or moment to truly arrive as a player at a new club, and if anyone was still doubting Ollie's value then this was it. The penalty was calmly slotted home, but the composure he showed was typical of a Lincoln City player of late. At 2-1 there was still a chance the eleven men of Stevenage could get back into the game, but Whelpdale would not be involved, he was taken off moments after the goal.

The game threatened to boil over, and Luke Wilkinson did level things with ten minutes left, but not the score line. His cynical stamp on Alex Woodyard brought the red card out of Anthony Backhouse's pocket once again, absolutely the correct decision. As he trudged off the pitch, he took with him Stevenage's chance of getting anything from the game. Even if they were plotting a way back, Paul Farman ensured they barely had time to do it as he ate up minutes as the game ran down. He took a yellow card for his troubles, but nobody will be complaining about that.

Our other County sides took thrashings today, Gainsborough lost 4-0, Boston lost 5-2 and Lincoln United lost 3-0. At 1-0 down with ten men, Lincoln could have joined them, but we have a team full of leaders, players that won't give up, won't let their heads drop and will never be beaten for desire, application and commitment. Michael Bostwick was superb, Sean Raggett led from the back and Billy Knott had a super second 45 minutes. Ollie Palmer came on at a tough time and ran himself into the ground. We believed we were going to win the game when we came out in the second half, and nothing was going to stop that. I'll take a season of lukewarm first forty-five minutes if we perform like we did in the second half every time.

Danny Cowley acknowledged the first half was not good enough. Talking to Michael Hortin after the game he said:

"We were really disappointed with ourselves at half time, it's not often we get out-run or out-fought but I thought we did in the first half. We had a lot to ponder at half time. I'm not going to come on here and start singing their praises because they've only given half a performance today."

It might have been a poor first half, but the gaffer was delighted with the response.

"Second half they showed me the determination, desire and resilience that we know they have. We showed huge fight to be 1-0 down with ten men to win the game, but we have to question why we got ourselves into that position in the first fifty minutes of the game."

Danny sounded angry, he spoke faster than usual as he discussed the referee performance, something he tries not to get drawn into.

"I think he (Matt) was frustrated. I don't want to talk about referees but I've never seen anyone booked from a kick off, particularly when their player is feigning to take a quick one on three occasions. I'm not going to be critical of individuals in the media. What I will say is Matt will win us lots of games of football this season. He's hell of a player, he'll be disappointed with himself today."

It wasn't just the red card for Matt Green that had pulses racing though, a first half challenge on Sean Long left the player facing six weeks out. When Michael said, 'five yellows and a red today, it didn't feel like that sort of game', Danny was firm and concise.

"No, it didn't did it? I thought it was a competitive game. Sean Long has stud marks about half way up his leg and that wasn't even given as a free kick…."

He paused, contemplating his words carefully. Clearly Danny had thoughts on the officiating he wasn't going to share, or perhaps he wanted to ensure he articulated them in a manner which was consistent with his usual rhetoric of respecting referees.

"It's not easy, I appreciate it's two teams going at it on the front foot, but I was surprised with the application of some of the laws today. Once Sean took his sock off, there's no way he can carry on, it's horrific. Ten years ago, that was just a good challenge, but the rules have changes, rightly or wrongly. Now, you are not allowed to use excessive force, and that was excessive force and it was really high. That's player safety. If that's not even a foul, you have to question it."

Danny was clearly angry despite the win, but on the terraces the travelling faithful were delighted. Pre-match reports of potential heavy-handed stewarding were way wide of the mark, most fans report laid back match day staff, willing to let our huge following enjoy the game, even when it got heated on the field in the second half.

All in all, no matter how Danny sees it from the inside, this was a massive result for City. To fight back after a poor first half showed all the qualities of the side that won the National League last season, albeit with a better group of players. Michael Bostwick and Neal Eardley bring a certain experience which is going to be vital, and whilst the personnel are different in parts, the outcome is the same. We do not cave in, we do not stop fighting and we do not give games away cheaply. We have Mansfield up next Saturday, and you'd hope we could go into that match with a win against Forest Green under our belts too. One thing is for certain, whatever happens at the New Lawn you know we'll go there and compete, at least for the second forty-five minutes.

City a different class, in more ways than one: FGR 0-1 Imps
September 12, 2017

Okay I admit it: for the next few minutes you're going to be listening to a bit of over-enthusiasm from a writer slightly drunk on success. Victory tonight has got me thinking that perhaps, just perhaps, we are going to be challenging for the top seven.

Firstly, the game. City were efficient, infinitely better in all aspects of the match and just lacked the killer touch or lucky ball. It is clear one side promoted last season have acquitted themselves well, and the others are rudderless. FGR didn't have a clue what to do to break us down, there wasn't really one dangerous effort at goal, and they lacked any discernible plan or approach. They played as eleven average individuals thrown together by fate. Amusingly their sole approach towards the end was 'lump it to the big man', something Cooperman was berating us for back in May. I'll tell you something, Mark Cooper is a sitting duck, he's in the sights of Dale Vince and Vince is ready to pull the trigger (humanely one assumes, probably a tranquiliser dart before Cooperman is released safely into the wild. You know these vegans....).

I suspect he wants to desperately wants build FGR's reputation within the football community and he doesn't want to go firing the manager that promoted them as it'd be received negatively by the media. It must be a nightmare for Vince, he'll know Cooper should have gone last year, but thanks to Tranmere's capitulation he got to cling on. Now the question is when does he fire him and not come out of it with bad press? Soon I'd wager.

Harry Anderson's start is a good thing for Imps fans too. Anderson is a superb wide player, he's so quick and direct, and he didn't come here to sit on the bench. Danny has been coy with starting him so far this season, but tonight we saw the qualities that earned him such a strong reputation last season. His goal was opportunistic, made by his own tenacity and finished with aplomb. Remember, this boy is on a three-year deal, but I suspect with a run in the team he'll be attracting Sean Raggett-style attention before too long.

I wondered if Rheady (pictured top) starting on the bench was the ultimate managing of small margins by Danny. He'd know which way FGR like to kick at the start of the game, most teams have an 'end' they usually attack first. Supposing he gets to the ground and realises that they'll be kicking with the wind behind them in the first half. He tells Alex Woodyard that if we win the toss, we kick into the wind. If they win the toss likelihood is they'll kick off, and thus we'll be kicking into the wind.

He then drops Matt Rhead, knowing that for the first half the long ball is not going to be effective. He goes with the smaller, more mobile players knowing there will be a lot of running to do battling against the elements. In the second half, with the wind behind us, we bring on the big man. FGR will have set up for us not playing Rheady, and with the wind behind us the long balls will land on his head. They'll have to readjust during the game, possibly they'll become a little disorganised. Far-fetched? Maybe, but this is Danny Cowley. Maybe it was just to freshen things up, but given that it was Billy Knott moved into the centre and Nathan Arnold returned to the side, were things really that fresh? Both those players have played most of the opening matches.

Anyway, we won. It was a game deep down we all expected to win, and the sort of game any side in the top seven will be expected to win. What we did was efficiently carry out the task and bring home the points, just like we did last season. It was routine, doing what was expected and that is exactly why I am getting excited.

The Lincoln City I've known and loved for the last 30-odd years don't do the things expected of them. If there's a big match that they need to win, they usually lose. If there's a promotion we look as if we're going to make, we usually fail at the last hurdle. We were the masters of creating hope and dashing it, even when we were at our best. Southend 2005? Almost avoiding relegation in 1999? Missing out on the play-offs by two goals in 1992? Failing to pick up enough points in eleven games to avoid the drop? We get so close to achieving our goals, but rarely do. It's rarely us celebrating in the streets, we more likely skulk off into the horizon muttering something about 'next year'.

Last season we got everything right. We won all of the 'you have to win against these if you're going to challenge' games. We won all the top of the table clashes. We won most of the routine home matches, the bread and butter games that fill up a season without being noteworthy. When it came down to it, we performed whenever we needed to in league and cup. It was a unique experience for an Imps fan, and I didn't think we'd get there again.

Losing at Exeter made me suspect we could be looking at mid-table this year. They're a decent side, and I wasn't sure we had what it took to compete with anyone better than them in the league. It was my 'Dagenham' moment of last season, the moment when sobriety kicks in and you realise you're not as good as you think you are. Then we started getting results, and I took another swig from the hope bottle.

The results since Exeter have been building my hope-meter ever since. Drawing with Luton was pivotal, it proved we're as good as the best in this division. Winning against Carlisle and Stevenage eradicated my doubts we couldn't kill teams off even if we played well. Morecambe had been an eye opener, but since then we've proven we can score goals.

I'm now looking at the top three, Notts County, Exeter and Accrington and wondering if any of them are really better than us, significantly? Exeter beat us but on another day we could have won the game. We weren't outclassed, and as for Notts County, Terry Hawkridge starts every game and was essentially deemed not good enough for our first team. Accrington have had a decent start, but the struggling Cods beat them tonight.

Are we in with a shout here? Come May will we still be involved in the chase for promotion, or even better will we be promoted? Is this side good enough, and can it continue to develop into a side worthy of League One football? (Told you I was optimistic).

So far all I have seen from Lincoln are positive signs. The squad is superb, a little light on numbers but packed out with real quality. Our managers are the best in the business at this level, their man-management is like no other and they have the reputation in the industry to attract players. Tactically they're spot on, they rarely get it wrong and when they do, they hold their hands up. They are hungry and eager and they want to achieve things with our football club.

Financially we're comfortable, the FA Cup run not only kept the wolves from the door, but it has financed a sensibly assembled squad good enough to compete. There's clearly still money in the kitty after the Akinola deal fell down, and we'll be active when we get the chance. There's no off-field turmoil to speak of, no growing issues that will eventually derail the campaign. Everyone is on the same wavelength, pulling in the same direction.

Then you have the fans. With Coventry's pitiful attendance this evening (pitiful by their standard), City will have the highest average of anyone in League Two. When you consider we have Grimsby, Coventry, Port Vale, Swindon and Notts County in our division, that is some feat. If we're battling up the top all season, you can guarantee we'd sell out of season tickets again. It will be the longest I have seen such strong attendances sustain at Sincil Bank.

Is this the best time to be a Lincoln City fan since I've been watching the club? Have we ever had so many factors all coming together in this manner? Promotion last season, looking more than competitive this season, and all of those other factors I've already mentioned. I can't think of a time when it has ever been this positive. I appreciate its early days, but if the film is as good as the trailer then we're in for another epic season.

We now need some luck on our side. With just three full backs we must ensure we remain as injury free as possible. Much relies on some of our players being able to cover in different positions, and a couple of injuries could spell trouble. What if Alex got injured and Bozzie suspended? Or if Sean Long is still out and Neal Eardley gets sent off? The management of the squad will have to be spot on, and we'll need that little bit of luck. If January comes and we need to buy in cover players then we can, but from now until then we just need some good fortune in remaining as injury free as possible.

This Lincoln City is a different class, and when speaking of class, it is notable what little Forest Green actually have. They may be seen as the fashionable club, the eco-conscious eco-friendly boys from the country, but that is far from the truth. The spitting incident at full-time is disgusting, and it'll be interesting to see how they react to that. I'm also told our 350 or so travelling fans were made to stand in the rain whilst a covered stand remained empty. What sort of club would not look to move the soaked visitors? Apparently they want the covered areas behind the goal filled with home fans to increase the atmosphere. Less than 1500 for a home game? They need to fill one end before getting ideas of filling the other. Not that the fans are motivated to turn up, given that the club captain basically called them embarrassing on the radio. Ouch couldn't happen to a nicer bunch. Danny even joked that he made more noise than the Forest Green fans. Double ouch.

We may have both come up last season, but there is a gulf in class between us and tonight's opponents, and by the end of the season I suspect there will be a hell of a lot of points between us as well.

Evans up to his tricks as below par City edged out: Imps 0-1 Mansfield

September 17, 2017

It was a case of the match never living up to the billing, the clash of two fancied sides in League Two never got out of second gear as the combination of well organised defences and lacklustre forwards meant the odious Steve Evans got the win he so desperately craved.

For the course of this article my self-imposed ban on being mean to him is lifted because he simply gave me so much material I'd be fearful not to mention him. I'll strive to cover the game first before I move on to the morbidly obese ball of anger and his nasty little sidekick.

It was nice to see yet another packed Sincil Bank, and although the away end was full it didn't create the sort of noise Luton had the week before. Mansfield don't have a great repertoire of songs unfortunately, whilst we had one for most of our outfield players they just kept singing for Danny Rose, despite him being on the bench. Perhaps that was just prophetic, but if the noise level was anything to go by, City had the upper hand.

I sat in the Selenity Stand for the first time this season, and it is the first time I've seen block seven all bouncing together. Fourth tier of English football? That's second tier support at worst. The Coop stand is an awesome sight when it is full, and I'm almost jealous I don't sit across the other side all the time. I got a cushion on my seat and the people next to me were not practically sat in my lap, so the Selenity Silence stand does have its good points.

There was some pre-match interest surrounding the team sheet which few seemed to have really picked up on. The ongoing discussions around Matt Rhead seem to have distracted fans from the fact captain Luke Waterfall has been dropped. On Tuesday it was to 'freshen' things up, but this game? There's no doubt Rob Dickie is good player, I think he brings more in terms of ability to the side then Luke. Luke is a 'blood and thunder' defender, whereas it appears Rob is more defined and cautious. Has the old order shifted now?

Nathan Arnold is still struggling to, I believe it is a knock-on effect of the tackle against Luton but I may be wrong. There have been mutterings of a potential broken bone in his foot, but

I've had nothing confirmed. I do think he is a loss, and had he been available I suspect we'd have seen another change to the starting line-up.

I'm not being down on Matt Rhead when I kept predicting him dropping to the bench, I'm being honest. I think Matt has loads to offer the team, but he might be more effective in the final fifteen minutes as opposed to the first half hour. He spent most of the game frustrated, being fouled and Mansfield getting away with it, or flicking the ball on and then being unable to catch up with play sufficiently to have an impact. I suspect this was the situation Matt was in a couple of years ago when Mansfield came up, and by his determination and application he dropped down to the National League and earned himself the right to be here again. However, I strongly feel that number 10 role is destined for someone else, someone of such sublime talent who we have only really seen ten per cent of at present.

Billy Knott obviously. I assume you knew that? Did you know that as a youngster Billy was at Real Madrid, and that the Spaniards even paid for a house over there for his parents? No, me neither. How good must he be once we get him firing on all cylinders?

Anyway, we had best of the opening exchanges, man-on-a-mission Matt Green created a chance for Billy Knott, but his effort was blocked. Mansfield hadn't settled at all, and of the two sides you'd suspect it was the ones in red and white that were paying their centre forwards £2.5k a week. Man-on-a-mission Lee Angol, one recipient of the abhorrent wages, looked a frustrated figure, nothing like the energetic player we had last season. If I were a betting man I'd say his body language and work rate suggests a move motivated simply by pound coins and not a desire to succeed.

It was Angol that was brought down 25-yards from goal around the 30-minute mark, and the stocky little midfielder Alex MacDonald's fired wide of Farman's post. They were tentative exchanges at best, the closest either side came in a tense match of few openings and few neat passages of play.

I thought the likeliest to score would be Lincoln, and as half time approached we seemed in the ascendancy. One City effort was saved spectacularly, not by keeper Conrad Logan, but by Stags defender David Mirfin. I know we're not a team to bemoan hard luck, but when your hands are raised to you face and the ball hits them, it's a penalty. Still the Stags held firm and as the rain subsided, the half ended without a goal.

The expensively-assembled Mansfield forward line of Kane Hemmings and Lee Angol was looking completely ineffective. Sean Raggett had his usual commanding game at centre half, and eventually Hemmings was replaced by Danny Rose, much to the joy of the travelling fans. Now, finally their favourite player was on the pitch, and sadly it was him that got the only goal of the game shortly after.

Early in the passage of play a foul on Alex Woodyard was ignored, and the ball eventually found its way out to the right-hand side. Hayden White showed great pace down the line, the sort of pace that left Sam Habergham in his wake. Fully fit Sam might have stopped the cross, 95% Sam did not. The ball went across the six-yard box, waiting for a keeper to claim it maybe, but instead Danny Rose rose highest to nod the visitors into an undeserved lead.

It was less than Mansfield deserved, but in truth it was the only truly clear-cut chance of the game. After that we pressed hard, but at 0-0 the Stags were running out of ideas, at 1-0 they had a simple plan: defend the lead. Despite an introduction of pace in Josh Ginnelly and the arrival of Ollie Palmer (who that Stags also have a song for), City simply didn't open up the resolute defence. At the end of the whistle Evans bounded onto the pitch as if he'd won the FA Cup, omitting the obligatory handshake and celebrating in front of his fans. How satisfying it must be to finally get a win over Lincoln too.

That's the match action over with, my summary would be two teams cancelled each other out, one assembled at great cost but with no real plan other than 'get up and at them', the other Lincoln. We lacked finesse in the final third, but it isn't a case of 'not having a goal scorer' or even 'lacking goals from all angles'. If I'm brutally honest I think it's a case of playing with 10.5 men rather than eleven, because if Rheady is involved in an early passage of play, he struggles to enter the later phase too. It isn't a criticism of him, I hope this doesn't have people commenting 'yeah, he's done', because he isn't. He's still a good player, he's still an option but he needs to be the plan b. I suspect

Simeon Akinola would have been plan a, but we all know what happened there. I also suspect if Ollie Palmer was better in the air, he might partner Matt Green, but he isn't and so he won't.

I was lucky enough to be in the VIP bar afterwards for the presentations of Man of the Match and Young Imps awards. Billy Knott got the main award and he trudged in looking like someone had just burned his favourite childhood teddy bear. The cameras came up and to his credit he forced a smile, then as soon as the flashes stopped he was morose again. He said what we all thought, there had been a clear-cut penalty in the first half and he was disappointed. Later on, Matt Green came up to, similarly as disappointed. This result hurt the players, and whilst I suspect many fans have walked away thinking 'one point from the play-offs', the players thought no such thing. One by one they trudged into the SRP Player Lounge and sat, ashen-faced, as the sponsors and VIP's slowly dispersed. I was with Paul Smith, and he told me stories about Paul Raynor I can't repeat. Paul was a right back to Raynor's left winger slot for a while.

Onto the antics of Steve Evans. All afternoon him and his ridiculously angry assistant Raynor were in the referee's ear, the whole time they were berating the Lincoln bench, arguing and niggling. I sat just a row behind them, and I picked up on every word. He's a foul-mouthed man, angry to the extreme and will claim anything at all. Even the most blatant of free kicks he contested, I have no doubt the foul on Woodyard in the build up to the goal was ignored because of him and his bodyguard. It was right in front of his dugout and he'd been in the ear of the linesman all afternoon. At one point, stood right by Evans, the linesman gave a throw-in the opposite way to the referee. I think the ref was correct, but he changed his decision and went with the linesman. I'm not sure about pantomime villains, they're more like Bond villains.

I understand we're not always a nice side and I wouldn't expect anything less of Mansfield either, but what we have is good grace before and after the game. Danny approached the Mansfield dugout before the game to shake hands, but at the end of the game there was no chance. Evans had thundered across the pitch (measuring 2.7 on the Richter scale I'm told) leaving just henchman Raynor to shake hands. Danny (or Nicky, I can't recall) approached with his hands out for a shake, but Raynor launched into a foul-mouthed tirade, pointing aggressively into the face of our official and screaming abuse. To what end? What was the point? He'd won the game, the curtain had come down on the Steve and Paul pantomime of hate, why carry it on? At this point a proper manager would have shook hands, thanked us for the points and moved on. Is it the fact that this isn't a pantomime, that Evans and Raynor are just thoroughly unpleasant and none of it is a show at all?

I hear even before the game there was issues with the meeting between managers and officials in the ground, but I can't comment on the nature of those. I know that in the tunnel after the game they were still arguing something, swearing loudly and getting physical whilst kids and families were within earshot. There's no need, the game had been played in a competitive but fair spirit, a couple of fouls went unpunished on both sides, but surely we were the aggrieved party if any. Even Jimmy Walker had a go on Twitter, saying "go to shake hands after we beat them and get told to f*ck off. Go to shake hands after we get beat- same result #wonthappenagain #classless #c*nt" Harsh words, but fair. Evans gets a lot of stick but you know what? Paul Raynor is just as bad. The pair of them are a stain on football.

So, we push on to the next game. Danny was disappointed later in the evening at our pre-arranged dinner date, perhaps not as disappointed as I was to discover I'd picked up a stomach bug and had to leave early. I think it was just one of those games you hold your hands up and admit, we didn't win it. Luton could have scored their golden chance to leave us defeated in that game, and we could have scored six against Morecambe on another day. Sometimes in football your endeavour is not rewarded, and sometimes your lack of endeavour is. For us it was the former was true, for Mansfield the latter.

On that showing I'm afraid I can't see the Stags finishing in the top three, because they offered far less than Luton, Stevenage or even Wycombe Wanderers. All that for a couple of million quid, well done Steve. Now get booked in at your doctors and get booked in for an ECG because I'm worried about you. Kind of.

The Stacey West – A Season in Blogs 2017/18

Incandescent with anger: Notts County 4-1 Imps
September 24, 2017

Notts County away should have been such a good away trip, they've got a great set-up there with good players and welcoming stewards. We were travelling in our numbers too, eager to match them on the pitch in a clash between two really good League Two teams. I should be sat writing a celebratory blog or one lamenting our own poor finishing over County's clinical strikers. I'm not though, in truth you're not even going to read about the day. Maybe later, but now I have to get something off my chest.

I'm angry, and it isn't just a little bit angry either, it is a full-on raging anger that could, had I encountered Seb Stockbridge, caused me a real problem. I didn't, I won't and instead I came home seething with fury. I sat down briefly to write last night, but I felt perhaps the excitement of the day was too fresh to write anything of value. I've slept on it now, and unsurprisingly my anger hasn't abated one bit.

For 30 minutes, we were involved in a game of football befitting the two teams on show. I'm taking nothing away from Notts County, they were a really good side playing a sweeping, passing game that was easy on the eye. In Jorge Grant they have an insanely talented midfielder destined for the Forest first team, and up-front Jon Stead showed an awareness that you'd expect from a top-flight forward. For the first thirty minutes though Lincoln City were on top, Harry Anderson was causing all sorts of problems down the flank, and Matt Green had put a decent effort wide when it looked easier to score.

I was a happy fan, I felt perhaps we'd end up with a draw, but in front of 11,000 fans (4100 of our own) anything could have happened. It was panning out as one of the days we live for, the football days that we missed for six long years. Then some officiating of Sunday League standard stole the whole day away from us in one swoop. That isn't even fair to Sunday League referees to be honest.

In real-time, my first instinct was Billy Knott had been fouled. He appeared to have flicked the ball on, turned to go and been clattered from the side. I had a decent view, and when the red card came out, I cheered. I genuinely thought their lad had been sent off, until someone told me it was Billy. It wasn't long before the video came up on the internet and I've now viewed it 100 times. It wasn't a red card, in my opinion it wasn't even a foul, and the referee ruined a great game right there.

I spent the next hour arguing with my Dad that nothing after that point mattered. I couldn't see that we were poor after the red card, because as far as I'm concerned if you go down to ten men against Notts County you'll always look poor. Their game uses the whole pitch, it's all about space and freedom and nothing affords you space and freedom like an extra man. Had we not gone down to ten men we could have matched that able County side and produced a game of football befitting of 11,000 fans in such a fine stadium. Instead we witnessed a proper Shakespearian comedy where the joker in green conducted farcical scenes of a one-sided battle, robbing the assembled masses of a good game of football. I'm sure County won't mind being 4-1 winners, but well over 4,000 fans we rewarded for turning out in their numbers by an ineffective and inept match official. One day it has to stop.

After that there was only ever going to be one winner I'm afraid. With ten men we looked lost for a short period, and Jon Stead showed what an accomplished finisher can do with the opening goal. Could Farms have done better? Perhaps. It's easy to find a scapegoat when things aren't going well and as we know one of Farms' weaknesses is command of his area. However, before the ball gets whipped into the box there are several points where the attack can be stopped but it wasn't. It is easy to blame the keeper when things aren't going well and that is two weeks in a row now he's come under fire. I wouldn't be surprised to see him rested for the Barnet game, if only to take a bit of pressure off. I don't mean rested like Luke Waterfall has been either, I mean rested for a game and then brought back in. Paul Farman is still our number one in my eyes, and even if he was at fault for the first goal we didn't lose 1-0 did we?

I took a moment towards the end of the first half to relieve myself of some anger by going to the front of the stand and shouting a lot of foul-mouthed abuse at the referee. It might surprise you to know that I'm not always articulate and fancy-free with my words, sometimes I believe a good old fashion cuss or two will do the trick. A female steward came across smiling and asked me to return to my seat, and we exchanged some friendly banter as I carried on shouting at the referee. The steward was friendly, warm and almost understanding of my anger and her attitude placated me somewhat. After one more burst of questioning his parentage and suggesting he enjoys manipulating himself I returned to my seat. Fine stewarding, well done.

Halftime gave me another lesson in how Lincoln City should look to accommodate fans moving forward. The doors behind the concourse were opened and the smokers were allowed into the street for a cigar, fag or whatever they chose to give themselves a shorter life with. It was roped off of course much like a night club, but it was another good example of how the fan experience is enhanced at some grounds. Notts County have been the most accommodating and friendly of the away games I've been to this season, and little touches like not demonizing smokers underline that fact.

I was still poisoning my lungs when an almighty roar went up to signal we'd scored. A surge of lingering Imps made it up the stairs to celebrate and briefly there was hope. Perhaps if we'd scored on 70 minutes to make it 1-1 we'd have had a good chance of protecting the lead, but our goal was a consolation, nothing more.

From there a ruthlessly efficient County took us apart with an expansive passing game that tired our players out. They moved the ball from left to right which opened up gaps naturally and having Matt Green so isolated up top meant there wasn't a chance of a breakaway goal either. County had some very good players and against ten men they looked the best side I'd seen all season. It would have been a different story if Billy hadn't been (wrongly) sent off, but he was and they made us pay. I was particularly impressed with Jorge Grant, he's got a tremendous career ahead of him.

Terry had a decent game too, but I found the hero-worship a bit sickly if I'm honest. He was niggling our players and I'm sure I saw him kick out at Anderson, but he was still cheered louder than some of our own boys. I know some booed and that wasn't entirely acceptable, but some cheered when he scored and that is also just plain daft. It was nice to see him not celebrate, I wonder if that would have been the same had he scored a winner in the last-minute? Our fans need to start getting behind our own players, not so-called legends that put in 30-odd appearances in last season's 60-game haul. I know that might sound harsh but aside from his goals against Macc, Terry was a bit-part player last season. Let's not go building a statue of him just yet, eh?

Could we have done better with ten men? It was one of our forward players sent off, so surely across the back we should have put in the same performance? There is an argument for that, but I think Danny still wanted to win the game and we took a few risks. He didn't want to shut up shop at 1-1 and that meant leaving gaps to exploit. If it had been an away day at Crawley and we'd got two hundred fans in the stands might it have been different? Maybe, maybe not. We went for a win by bringing on Palmer and Whitehouse, and then after their third we went back to a back four and brought on Sean Long. The red card knocked us and despite getting the goal back we never got on method and a good side killed us off efficiently.

I've just watched the incident again and I won't be swayed into even agreeing it is a yellow. As far as I'm concerned there is no similarity between Sadio Mane's raised foot for Liverpool and Billy's, because I don't think Billy's foot was raised. He had control of the ball, the play was with him. Their player has stooped in, and the official reason is that Billy was endangering their lad. Where do we draw the line? If Raggs dived in, head-first, at the feet of Terry Hawkridge, could Hawkridge be sent off for endangering the player?

Also, if that was a red card, how was their lad not sent off in the second half? How was their first goal allowed when their player had his feet at the same height as Billy's when he connected with the ball? How can we still allow this wonderful game to be spoiled by such a poor level of officiating? Seb Stockbridge might get a dressing down for this, but we'll never know will we? Referees are protected beyond belief, never having to justify their actions nor be held accountable for the terrible decisions they make. What makes this even worse is that we probably won't get it rescinded because the boys club at the FA will rally around their inept, unaccountable officials and close the doors on the Football League newcomers.

Only turning up for 45 minutes IS enough: Imps 2-1 Barnet
September 27, 2017

On a night where the Imps took great strides off the field with the introduction of the new Fan Zone, on the field they spent the first half giving their opponents a master class in complete and utter domination of a game. Once they'd amassed a lead they thought they were playing cricket, declared, and waited for the Barnet onslaught.

There's so much to try to pick through that I couldn't do it justice last night. Firstly, the new fan zone. It may not look much, a couple of branded tents with tables in the corner, but it represented so much more I think. Winning the league last season was not just about achieving our goal after beating Macclesfield, there is a whole other battle to win now. Fan experience is paramount to our ongoing success, and the fledgling fan zone represents another large step forward.

Often, Imps fans have felt marginalised when the club have made decisions. There's never really been consultation and certainly from 2006 (ish) to 2011 we were barely considered. Caterers were changed in the ground, stands were opened and closed and generally we were the afterthought. What those few tents and tables showed last night is a focus on our experience as customers and fans. We pay our money to watch Lincoln City, and whilst the quality of football can never be guaranteed, the quality of our experience can be. I saw a few faces in the fan zone that usually spend their time ambling up the High Street with a 2.45pm arrival time at the ground (on a Saturday before the jokes). Build it and they will come.

It was also nice to see Roger Bates taking former Imps Trevor Swinburne, Paul Mayo and Warren Ward around meeting people and mingling. I understand that may be an ongoing feature too, maybe with a few pre-match questions and a bit of interaction. It all bodes well and I doubt many club's initial thoughts after their first foray into fan zone were: 'we're gonna need more tents'.

All this is well and good if your team are playing well and for forty-five minutes Lincoln City played as well as at any time under Danny Cowley. I'll hold my hands up; I was fearful when I saw Ollie Palmer (pictured top) starting. Up until last night I haven't 'got' Ollie Palmer. He's a big man who can't jump? How does that work? Surely at six-foot twenty or whatever he is he can't run quick either? We'll come to him shortly.

Josh Vickers got the nod too, not entirely unexpected given the criticism Farms has come under recently. I fully expected this before the County clash as I think I said before. It isn't even that Paul Farman has played badly, but Josh Vickers is a keeper that has come to play football and he needs games here and there. Paul won't be dropped in the light of one mistake, what message would that send to the other players? No, Danny planned to bring Josh in as far back as Mansfield or even earlier I'd wager.

Other than that, as predicted, it was business as usual for Lincoln. I say 'business as usual', there was nothing usual about our performance in those opening exchanges. We were absolutely brilliant, I'm not one to over enthuse about our displays either, but we played a free-flowing and expansive game of football that a terrible Barnet just couldn't get to grips with. As early as the 2nd minute we could have taken the lead when Josh headed over, but City looked rampant.

There were seven minutes on the clock when I ate my words about Ollie Palmer. He capped a great opening period by collecting on the edge of the area and smartly curling in from 20-yards. Cue much mickey-taking from those I'd been knocking Palmer to before the game. I'm always happy to hold my hands up when I'm wrong and Ollie Palmer proved throughout the game that I had indeed be wrong about his ability to play in the ten role. Billy Knott, watching from just above me in the gantry, must have been a little bitter knowing the ten shirt had been his. Many more outings like that from Palmer and Billy will have to settle for a sport out wide again.

To a man we were excellent throughout the first period. Simeon Akinola started for Barnet which I found interesting. What does it say about a manager when he's willing to sell a player one week as surplus to requirements, but the next he's starting matches? It might say he's a forward-thinking manager that gives everyone a chance, or it might say he isn't sure what his best side is and he's winging it day-to-day.

Harry Anderson and Josh Ginnelly were causing havoc when they ran at their respective full backs, and Neal Eardley put in the sort of display that earned him top-flight football once. We need to think about tying Neal up for the rest of the season at least otherwise we could have another Theo situation on our hands in January. He was one of the signings of the pre-season in my eyes, a calming influence at the back who understands football perfectly. He can speed play up with direct running, he can slow it down by cutting back inside or stepping on the ball and pausing a run, he really does have a footballer brain.

Bozzie had his best game in an Imps shirt too, and I noticed something very subtle about his play. He refuses to step too far from the front of defence, even if it means the opponents get time on the ball in the first third of the half. He refuses to move away from the back four and creates pockets of space. In the Football League there are so many quick and able-bodied forwards that any space will be exploited and his experience is showing. It can be frustrating to the fans in the stands as it looks as though he isn't pushing up or coming to meet the player, but in truth it is astute and measured positional play that underlines his usual level of football. He never looks to break a sweat either, he effortlessly moves across the pitch, coming forward only when the defence does or when the man he is marking does. I thought he'd advanced at one stage to disprove my theory but Pete who I sat with noted 'only because Akpo has dropped deeper'. Follow his man when marking, sit tight when not. To recognise his immense contribution is to fully understand the players doing the so-called 'dirty work'.

It should have been 4-0 at half time, Josh had his stinging drive tipped over and Raggett's header from the corner goes in 99 times out of 100. As his head connected with the ball I imagine it felt routine, exactly what he's worked on after training for a year, how it went wide I'll never know. When Harry's smart finish added the much-needed gloss to the score line it looked as though we'd be coming out at half-time and ending up with five or six. 'Barnet will tire' I told my old man at half time 'and we'll bring on JMD to punish that'. It seems as though after my Palmer predictions I was on a roll.

In the second half we looked like a completely different side. Barnet had a zest about their play and a desire to break us down, but one or two of our players just could not get going. I'm a massive Alex Woodyard fan but he just could not get a break. His chasing was excellent and he covered every blade of grass again, but it looked as though he'd never had a football at his feet. His passes were going astray and some others followed suit. Dickie and Raggs defended superbly, but their long punts clear often just fell at the feet of Barnet to launch another raid. In the first half our forward players had moved so well for each other, after the break they looked like strangers. The application levels didn't fall off but technically we looked a side far-removed from the first half.

We did get forward which was more than the Bees managed in the first half. Raggs had a header cleared off the line and had it gone to 3-0 I'm absolutely certain we would have found our groove again and pushed out another couple of goals. Their heads would have dropped and our players would have lost the nerves they played with as the game went on. I think there was such a desperation to get a win, such an urge to put the two back-to-back defeats behind us that we actually created pressure for ourselves. The crowd didn't do it but perhaps the players did.

Barnet's goal had been coming a while and when it did I thought it was poor defending that allowed them into the game. Coulthirst had looked potentially threatening all match, but he had enough space in the box to park a double-decker bus. It was no surprise to see him rattle the back of the net with a well-taken volley. A deathly silence descended Sincil Bank for just a second, then we got that 'go again' attitude and the noise levels lifted. On the pitch we began to fight for our lives.

Danny brought on Maguire-Drew and Whitehouse to give us movement up front, and after the game he praised them for doing what he asked. I'm not usually one to disagree with Danny, but I thought Maguire-Drew had another poor game. At one point Neal Eardley was tracking two defenders, his winger was fifty yards away jogging back like a centre forward. The frustration around me was evident, especially as we were so close to the win. Eventually he won the tackle and one of the centre halves came across to help him out. Now Raggs doesn't have his head-piece on I'm not entirely sure which one it was.

The Stacey West – A Season in Blogs 2017/18

Josh faded too but his contribution had been there for all to see. I'm a big Ginnelly fan and this comes after I called him as our 'fourth winger' in pre-season. His all-round game has come on immensely since last season, he's so quick it is frightening and I'm at a loss as to how last night's opening goal was the first we'd scored in the opening 30 minutes all season. We have such direct players that bring pace and skill to the game that we should be far more effective form the B of the bang. Eventually he came off to a proper round of applause, although his award of man of the match later was baffling. He had a decent game but was he a Bozzie, Neal Eardley or Harry Anderson? No. Ollie Palmer had a legitimate shout to be named MoM too and given our nervy second-half I think the fact so many players were in with a shout really shows how we can mix up play. Harry and Ollie were superb in the first half, but in the second the dirty work of Bozzie and Neal Eardley really paid dividends. Overall I think Bozzie just edged out Neal Eardley as the best player on the park last night.

I don't like to criticise players on here but also I say what I see and I can't see Maguire-Drew doing the dirty work Danny praised him for doing. Football managers see a different game though and I desperately want to see him hit his potential. He is a special player young Jordan, matter not what we've already seen from him. However, last night was not an example of that. He did have a two-minute spell where he got a shot away and launched a counter attack shortly afterwards, but there's still so much to come from him. You'll see.

I wasn't sure Elliott took his chance either. He got a bit of the ball, but one run down the left saw the ball just go away from him and run out of play. We really needed to eat up a few seconds, create and chance, do anything other than give possession away cheaply. Elliott has his fans and many felt he might start instead of Ollie (me included), but on last night's brief showing Danny made the right call with the starting line-up. He didn't want to come out and call his two subs on the radio though did he? He doesn't do that and I suspect he saw two players low on confidence drop into a potentially damaging atmosphere. We needed to freshen up on 65 minutes but who could we turn to? Sending on Ellis Chapman could have ruined the young lad's confidence if they'd scored, Luke doesn't add pace which we needed and neither does big Matt Rhead. I think those last twenty minutes were an indication of how frail our squad really is, even if Nathan had been fit it would have been an out ball. Instead the game narrowed and that played right into Barnet's hands.

As normal time tip-toed into six minutes of additional time we were hanging on for dear life. Bringing on Luke was a predictable plan and of course if there's one thing our captain does well it is kick the ball away or head the ball away. I settled a tiny bit seeing him coming on, he might be out of favour at present but he's still a hard bastard committed to throwing everything on the line for City. I don't think there was a dry armpit in the house when the final whistle went, such was the worry of us losing that precious lead. It went, we won and all that Barnet play in the second half won't ever show in the history books. All that will show is a 2-1 win and all I'll remember is the domineering and swash-buckling first 45 minutes.

I think the 7320 fans can be more than happy with what they saw last night. It was a tough game played in a good spirit, much the same as the first thirty minutes of Saturday. I was on 'raised boot' watch and by my reckoning there could have been four red cards inside the first forty minutes or so. The reason the game flowed so well and thoroughly entertained both sets of supporters, was Trevor Kettle.

He's been a Football League referee for fifteen years now and I think that showed last night. He was sensible with his bookings, Alex Woodyard could easily have been booked in the first half for a late challenge but the cards stayed away. One of their lads could have had the same shortly after, again Kettle took the players to one side and had a word. He was assured and anonymous bar the odd call. When he overruled the linesman to correctly give us a corner when the flag suggested goal kick he showed the confidence in his own decisions. We didn't get every decision but I was confident every decision was fair.

It was vitally important to get back to winning ways and suddenly the league table is starting to open up a bit. I always say don't bother looking until the end of September but I'll comment on it now we're ten games in. Between us in 12th and Barnet in 15th there is now a four-point gap, whereas that gap represents the different between 12th and 4th going the other way. There is a definite split emerging and we're on the right side of it. Furthermore, of those in the top 12 we've already played six, including the top two away from home. I think that highlights not only the tough start we've had, but the impressive nature of still being tucked in after ten games. There's still an awful lot of promise in this season and if we reach the levels of the first forty-five minutes on a regular basis then the only way, for Lincoln City, is up.

Derby Day Draw: Grimsby 0-0 Imps

September 30, 2017

I imagine one set of supporters are very happy this evening, having avoided a firm hammering from their county rivals. The other, Lincoln City, will perhaps be a little annoyed that their endeavour and dominance didn't reap a three-point haul.

Clean sheets are a bonus, not least for Josh Vickers in his second league start of his City career. From my viewpoint on the Isles of Scilly it isn't easy to offer any of the normal match analysis, despite having been able to listen to the game.

It did sound as though Nathan Arnold had a great game, and one wonders if he'd have been applauded by the Cods as Terry was last week? He's clearly held in high esteem in codland and rightly so. Talk of his demise recently has been premature in the extreme, he is still one of our key players and dropping immediately back into the first team reflects that. Danny knows Nathan is a special footballer and he has an important role to play in any top ten finish.

The preferred wing pairing is Arnold and Anderson I feel, and once again it was Harry that looked the most likely creator on the pitch. I've spoken glowingly of Harry on many occasions, and my Premier League supporting friend Pete has proclaimed he looks the most likely of all our squad, including Sean Raggett, to have top-flight potential. We may be goal-shy at present but once we have those two starting on the flanks regularly I think that will change.

Not from today, obviously, but "wo-oo, we've got Alex Woodyard" was being sung on the far flung reaches of Bryher today.

I'm also noticing a game on game improvement in Michael Bostwick. I suspect it has taken a little adjusting to life in League Two for him, but he's becoming stronger with each outing. He poses a goal threat, especially in the air and as training on set pieces continues we'll see him amongst the goals. It won't be long before we see Matt Green amongst the goals either, and when we do I suspect he'll grab a glut of them.

There may be no bragging rights as such but gone are the days of them collecting six points from us, or even walloping us up there and shutting up shop at our place. The official match reports will say they're happier than us, I'll argue against that all-day long. Do you know why? Because we are the better side with better players. Remember, we're still a work in progress, we're still a couple of players away from a full squad. They will be delighted not to have been beaten, and in the context of a full season I suspect it will be a good result for them.

Near 1900 fans were in Blunder Park with another 522 at the Bank to enjoy the game. I'd say our support never fails to amaze me, but in truth it is what we come to expect now. Lincoln City are a well-supported club, the big question is how long that will remain. I feel we've lived in the shadow of the Cods since records began, in fairness they've always had more fans and always had the upper hand, bar the odd battle. Now, in 2017, it is us with bigger attendances, us with a better side and us with the bigger prospects. They showed in the 1990's that a small team from 'out in the sticks' Lincolnshire can hold their own in the Championship, and now as we move towards the second decade of the 21st century, I believe it is us that can be that team.

All the talk of plastics, new fans, who'll stay when we lose a few games etc is all irrelevant as far as I'm concerned. Our city has thrived over the last ten years or so and the club has never been in a position to capitalise on that. Now we are, attracting 522 to watch a game on a big screen is testament to the popularity we are getting in our own city. Today, we went to Blunder Park not as underdogs, but expecting a result. My understanding from this coastal cottage is that we perhaps deserved a result too. It isn't the small battle that is important though, it is the trajectory of the two clubs. In their first season back in the league Grimsby sacked managers and suffered discord and disharmony. We have none of that, we're continuing to push forward.

We're in the ascendency here, and the expectations of the two fans today reflected that. This season we'll win games, draw games and lose a couple too, but we're on a journey and we're moving in the right direction. Anyone can see that, even from nigh on 400 miles away.

The Stacey West – A Season in Blogs 2017/18

Pos	Team	Pld	W	D	L	GF	GA	GD	Pts
1	Notts County	11	8	1	2	21	11	10	25
2	Exeter City	11	8	1	2	20	12	8	25
3	Accrington Stanley	11	7	2	2	21	13	8	23
4	Coventry City	11	7	1	3	14	6	8	22
5	Luton Town	11	6	3	2	21	10	11	21
6	Stevenage	11	6	3	2	19	12	7	21
7	Wycombe Wanderers	11	6	3	2	22	17	5	21
8	Mansfield Town	11	5	4	2	18	13	5	19
9	Swindon Town	11	6	1	4	16	14	2	19
10	Newport County	11	5	3	3	15	12	3	18
11	Lincoln City	11	4	4	3	13	12	1	16
12	Cambridge United	11	5	1	5	11	11	0	16
13	Cheltenham Town	11	4	2	5	14	13	1	14
14	Carlisle United	11	4	2	5	15	16	-1	14
15	Grimsby Town	11	4	2	5	14	18	-4	14
16	Colchester United	11	3	3	5	16	18	-2	12
17	Yeovil Town	11	3	3	5	17	24	-7	12
18	Barnet	11	3	2	6	15	16	-1	11
19	Crewe Alexandra	11	3	2	6	12	18	-6	11
20	Crawley Town	11	3	1	7	11	14	-3	10
21	Morecambe	11	2	4	5	10	16	-6	10
22	Port Vale	11	1	2	8	8	17	-9	5
23	Chesterfield	11	1	2	8	9	23	-14	5
24	Forest Green Rovers	11	1	2	8	10	26	-16	5

October

Two Months In: The Imps Analysis
October 2, 2017

We're now two months into the new season, our National League hell is well and truly behind us as we embark on our journey into the unknown. Lincoln City are in the finest shape of my lifetime and our destination isn't clear. There's plenty along for the ride though, record numbers in fact, but what have the first two months brought for us?

I think the fairest words would be 'realisation' and 'consolidation'. For the fans, realisation that the level of League Two football is considerably higher than some of us thought. That isn't generalising of course, plenty of your will say you knew it'd be tough. I'll hold my hands up, I didn't think the standard would be as high as it is. I got lulled into a false sense of security by wins against Oldham and Brighton. Danny and Nicky didn't though, otherwise we'd be much lower than 11th at present.

I think that realisation is balanced somewhat though. Whilst Morecambe and Barnet have proven to us that the lower teams aren't as bad as we hoped, matches against Luton and Mansfield have suggested the so-called fancied teams are also not as far ahead as we thought. Exeter and Notts County lead the way, two sides we matched in terms of skill and ability. Exeter were more streetwise of course and we didn't get a fair assessment of our progress once the referee intervened against County, but overall we've acquitted ourselves nicely. Don't be fooled, our opening two months have been tough but other sides have had similar opening sequences too. I'm not one to bleat about bad luck (not a couple of weeks afterwards) and these things even out over the season.

The other word I used to describe our opening was consolidation, and I think that was what everyone wanted for the season. Danny knew the challenges that lay ahead and he said prior to the season that staying tucked in around tenth place would give us a springboard going into the second half of the season. we're some way off Christmas but in terms of staying in touch, we're there. There is enough of a gap between us and those clearly struggling to say we're comfortable, but there is enough of a gap between us and the top three to suggest we are going to be in that middle pack.

I've seen plenty of comment about where we're short and what we need and one issue I can't argue with is being light up front. It isn't a desperate situation though, is it? We're not four points adrift of everyone else and short on goals. We're missing chances, but as Danny would tell you that means we're creating chances. Often Matt Green looks isolated up front, but we did manage to secure Matt Green in the first instance. If ever a player had 'Cowley's type' stamped on him it is Green, and despite his lack of goals I've perhaps been impressed with him as much as anyone. His work rate is immense, but he needs someone up there with him that can create an attack but also stay up with that phase of play to support Green. It breaks my heart to see Matt Rhead on the bench but I think we know that he just isn't mobile enough to be that guy.

Sure, we missed out on Akinola and perhaps a couple of other players too, but anyone that thinks Danny pinned his hopes on one last-minute signing is living in a dream land. Ollie Palmer has the ability to be effective up top, he's bagged a few already this season and against Barnet he was outstanding. Billy Knott is desperate to get a chance to play the '10' role too and once his suspension expires I think we'll see him back there. Cambridge will need to watch out because Billy is technically gifted and he'll be like a wounded animal on his return.

Our squad is evolving and changing with each game which is a sure indication that we'll never rest on our laurels. Josh Vickers coming in shows how much of a squad game we're playing, ditto Luke Waterfall. I can see Luke spending much more time on the bench then we anticipated at the beginning of the season, Rob Dickie is another 'Cowley' type of player. That isn't to say Luke isn't, but it's clear DC likes his loan defender.

Last season in September we were looking at the side commenting on how Danny was planning for League Two. The players he brought in were not National League quality, they were Football league quality. Now he's looking at League One quality and that is surely of comfort to Imps fans. He isn't filling the squad with dross, nor with players that have little or no first team role to play. It might be leaving us short at times, that was evident when looking at the bench against Barnet, but that will switch in January significantly.

Last year Danny was planning for promotion to the Football League and (in my opinion) he believed he could get that promotion. Pre-season saw a ruthless cull of those players disguised as amiable contract discussions, but it also saw an influx of players on two-year deals. You know why? Because our League Two promotion journey is a two-year plan. Danny is building a coherent squad to stay around the top half this season and be right up there next season. If you need an indication of whether this works or not, look at Exeter City who have done the same thing.

We do need to be patient as fans, Danny and Nicky have managed eleven Football League games and they're learning just as quickly as anyone. With the power of hindsight do you think they'd perhaps up the offer for a striker earlier in the window? Maybe. Would they have tried to tie up Akinola or whoever else ahead of the final day? I doubt there would be anything they could change there. The transfer window moves so fast, one minute you've got a player ready to sign, the next he scores a hat trick in a friendly and Preston move for him. With our strict policy of references and recruitment criteria we were never just going to get filler, no could we react as quickly when some deals fell through.

I think our players, in the main, have done well since stepping up. Alex Woodyard has picked up where he left off, certainly up until the last game or so. He's adjusted his game slightly too, Bozzie has dropped into Alex's role of last season meaning Alex has had to advance a little. That led to his two-goal haul against Carlisle but it is adding an additional facet to his game as well. He'll be learning from Bozzie and becoming even more of a rounded player. Other National League heroes that have stepped up with ease include Raggs (obviously), Harry Anderson and Nathan Arnold. Nathan's return is massive for us, anyone who doubts his ability to step up only needs to remember that late run against Luton, the dying embers of the game and he was still swift, alert and ready to attack. It's him and Anderson on the flanks for me with Ginnelly coming off the bench for impact.

Harry Anderson (pictured top) is a real prospect too, a player whom will eventually play at the very highest level. If he remains fit then that direct running and raw power can only keep bringing us goals. He'll be an Imps hero of 'Gareth Ainsworth' magnitude, not least because of his down to earth and unassuming persona away from the pitch. He can be devastating when he runs at players and as he gets games under his belt nobody will dislodge him from the first team.

Of the new signings, after Matt Green, Neal Eardley has impressed me the most. He's a monster of a full back, he reads the game superbly and has such a subtle and succinct touch. His arrival has allowed us to go into the season a full-back short and keeping him fit is crucial over the next couple of months. Sam is still regaining his match sharpness and Neal offers cover across the two full back positions. I'm told he's close to triggering an extension in his deal and that will be more great news for the Imps.

Jordan Maguire Drew has yet to win over the fans, but he will. As those days turn into months we're going to rely on depth in the squad and he's an able boy with a lot to prove. I'd expect him to start against Everton U21's at the end of October and that could be the kick start he needs to push on. We shouldn't be writing any player off at this stage, aside from Tom Champion I haven't seen Danny bring in a flop which is incredibly considering even great managers such as Keith and Murph missed as often as they hit.

All in I'm delighted with our start in a tough league. Danny is up front enough to admit we don't want to be nearly men and we know as fans we're still a body or two short of where we want to be, but in truth this is a two-year plan with just two months elapsed so far. The signs are there that we're not pushovers, we're not set for a return through the trap door and we've got enough, on our day, to trouble anyone in the league. Over the next two months hopefully we'll remain consistent, and when Billy returns we'll discover the method that doesn't involve the big ball up front. If we do, one or two teams might get a bit of a surprise when 'misfiring' Lincoln City come to town. Once Matt Green gets one, he'll get a bag full, and when he is properly on form we're going to be a real prospect.

It's a win, that is the important thing: Imps 2-1 Chesterfield
October 7, 2017

A win is a win, they all count whether it is a free flowing ninety minutes of samba soccer or a hard-fought narrow victory against well-matched opposition. This afternoon was neither but the end result was the same. A below-par City racked up their seventh point from nine against a visibly down-trodden Chesterfield side.

As always I'll start with the opposition, and it is clear to me Jack Lester has a big job on his hands. His side looked, in the main, clueless as to how to approach the game this afternoon. It was their dismal first half showing that made our average display look good, and even with a late goal and their fans energised they never truly troubled Josh Vickers. In very small patches they played football in nice patterns, that could be the early influence of their former centre-forward rubbing off, but he has a mammoth task picking them up off the floor. Two weeks ago, Barnet looked awful first half but showed in the second why they're a decent side, and lowly Morecambe had spells in our early season encounter. I can't find the positive in our opponents this afternoon, everything that Chesterfield created was of our own doing, giving away silly free kicks, or the referee gifting the odd dubious decision also.

The penalty, and it was a penalty I'm afraid, was just reward for them never giving up, but their efforts on goal were often incredibly poor (and that was the good ones). They had two free kicks on the edge of the area in the first half, the second of which Josh Vickers did pull off a world-class save, but that was the total outcome of their endeavours. Sure, they harried and harassed and looked like a team that wanted to do well, but they're seriously lacking in quality. Chris O'Grady was an embarrassment up front, petulant and niggly without an end product to match. We've seen players of his ilk at Luton (Danny Hylton) and in our own ranks (Matt Rhead) but to carry it off you need to have some sort of input with the ball and he had none. In order to avoid a long season of relegation torment Jack needs to keep them tighter than he did today and hope Forest are generous with loaning young talent in January.

A word on the Chesterfield fans though, they're proper football fans. They sang loud for most of the game, swinging from eternally-hopeful to self-deprecation and back again. They're fans that know, in a nutshell, their team is awful but they still turn out in their numbers to support them. I applaud them for that and I genuinely wish them well for the rest of the season. There are at least ten teams I'd rather see relegated than the Spireites and hopefully now we have three points they'll pick up a bit because those fans deserve it.

On to us, I'm afraid to say I thought we were average throughout. I'm going to have to be harsh on one or two players in the blog, please don't start screaming 'negativity' and all that rubbish. I write what I see whether we have won or not, you wouldn't expect any different. I know we got three points but that was down to eight or nine, not the full eleven.

Jordan Maguire-Drew. He's a player with bags of skill, a few tricks and a wicked left foot. Today, out wide on the right, he looked like a little boy who had lost his Mum in a supermarket. The game plan may have been for the wingers to come inside and the full backs to overlap, it looked that way over on the other side of the pitch, but Neal Eardley ploughed a lone furrow up and down the right whilst JMD did what I term to be a 'Kevin Gall'. He was full of running, often away from the ball, and he looks like a player low on confidence. Granted, this blog won't help pick him up if he reads it, but my honest assessment was he had his worst game in a Lincoln shirt.

One passage of play suggested to me the player we signed is trying to burst out, in the first half he jinxed past the same full back three times in succession, going back to beat him again before whipping a cross into the area. That is what he has come to do, but on the right-hand side he didn't look at all comfortable. On the way home, during his BBC Radio Lincolnshire interview, Alex Woodyard (rather amusingly) said that the Imps fans were like 'the eleventh man'. I chuckled suggesting he misspoke and Pete, driving me home, said "no, Maguire-Drew was playing, so effectively we only had ten." Cruel, but not an afternoon he'll be keeping the newspaper reports from in my opinion.

A player that worked harder but to similar none-effect was Ollie Palmer. I get it, he's a big man who has more ability with the ball in front of him than in the air, but surely he can get a few feet off the ground to win a header, can't he? It is telling that Matt Green looked as isolated up front today as he did when he was partnered by the big man Matt Rhead, and apparently Rhead doesn't have enough mobility to create a phase of play and then join in with it too. I actually thought the latter stages of today were custom-made for Matt Rhead, maybe I've been playing too much Football Manager.

So that is the critical stuff out-of-the-way. I thought we started brightly against a really poor side, and at 2-0 we threatened to run away with it. Harry was superb early doors, a couple of really wicked crosses after good link up play led to the goals. I don't buy this 'they scored for us' malarkey either, own goals come about by applying pressure and attacking the right areas. The cross from Harry for the second was textbook, pull it across goal at pace when players are running in and it could go anywhere. It was Harry that scored that goal, no matter who got the final touch, by virtue of his excellent delivery. As for the first, it might have taken a couple of deflections but Bozzie got a shot off, on target, with enough pace to ricochet off a player but not be cleared with ease. I think the dubious goals panel might just have a look at it though, but they all count. Bozzie will bag a couple from that position this season, mark my words.

Chesterfield might have been poor up front but they were dealt with professionally by our solid back four. It is a shame Sean Raggett is out next week especially as Jabo Ibhere is up top for Cambridge, because that would have been a quality match-up. Instead it'll be Dickie and former Captain Marvel, Luke Waterfall which will give us yet another permutation across the back. The key to a strong back four is continuity and with Eardley, Habergham, Dickie and Raggett we're beginning to get that. Sam looked back to the levels he ended last season on and he combined well with Harry when the opportunity arose. Over on the other side Neal Eardley is simply a cut above this level, he's composed and reads the game like a child's book. He looked alone at times as I've touched on and towards the end he got caught once or twice but on the whole he was, once again, superb.

Josh had a good game in goal too, those suicidal balls back to him will lose us a goal one day, I'm sure of it, but he was steady enough. His save from the free kick was top drawer and he'll be pleased with the form he is showing since stepping into the first team. I've never been comfortable when the so-called second choice keeper gets a regular run out, not under Mazza nor prior to that. I always feel a second-choice keeper is prone to an error and usually ends up back on the bench, but Josh has ended that irrational belief in their inferiority with a couple of confident and composed outings.

Matt Green still hasn't got a goal, but if there was a 'leading effort' chart that tracked centre forward's running and work rate I have little doubt he'd be way out in front of anyone else in our league. Some people around me today had a little moan when he failed to chase a punt forward in the 93rd minute, seemingly oblivious to the fact he had chased everything for the preceding hour and a half. If Ollie Palmer had the foresight to move the ball on early in the first half instead of twisting and creating a weak half-effort for himself, Green would have easily bagged a confidence building goal. I'm not one of these players that solely judges a striker on his goal ratio though, and as yet I haven't seen a centre forward playing for one of our opponents I'd rather have than Matt Green.

Man of the match (and by some distance for my money) was Alex Woodyard. I thought he sat deeper today and Bozzie played the slightly more advanced role, if that was the case Alex certainly looked more comfortable. Alex epitomizes the perfect midfielder, he works tirelessly, constantly harried and harassed their players and started attacks whenever possible. He rarely gives the ball away (twice against Barnet which I know as after he read my blog he messaged me to ensure I was aware!) and his partnership with Bozzie is getting better by the game. I did wonder if perhaps the reason the two wingers played on their unfamiliar sides was to force our play inside to those two because there's no doubt they're our prized assets.

In the end, we deserved the win as we did play better than our opponents. However, we weren't at our best at all no matter what Danny said in the interview at the end of the game. I didn't envisage him coming out and being critical of a third match unbeaten and rightly so, he can leave that to me. It doesn't actually matter how we go the result, we beat Chesterfield and picked up three points to stay tucked in just outside the play-off race. We had a tough start to the season, but on the eve of the Barnet game I called it as the time to start winning games and building a run: we did that today. Alex hinted in his interview though that they now have a week to look at the negatives from today and plan for Cambridge. I think there will be a few things covered on the back of today's match video, but it'll go on behind closed doors.

Last season as the games came thick and fast in April we looked far from our best, but we won games and racked up points. It's slightly different now, we're carrying a few injuries and of course Billy's suspension, and it does show a little in how we approach certain games. The end result is the same though, we grind out results and keep the points pouring in. Remember, in the last three games we've got more points than Chesterfield have all season, ditto Port Vale, ditto Forest Green. I've been critical of one or two performances, but we're still on track and we're still bringing home the bacon every weekend. With Billy back next week, expect him to drop back into the ten role and for our focus to shift slightly to more balls into feet. It might work, it might not, but rest assured we'll still be fighting hard whether the game plan looks pretty or not, and we'll still be competitive whether we're on method or not. Those are two traits all successful teams have.

If we can get seven points from nine but only truly play well in one half of those three games (Barnet first half), imagine what we'll be able to do when we're on method for ninety minutes at a time, week in, week out.

Are we really still non-league off the pitch?
October 16, 2017

One thing I noted from Danny's post-match comments was his insistence that off the pitch Lincoln City are still a non-league club. I'm not one for disagreeing with Danny, far from it. That man has delivered my football club back to me, hosed down, polished up and fit for the Football League.

However, I can't help but feel that his comments are exclusively aimed at the training facilities and perhaps, just perhaps, they don't do justice to the strides the club have taken over the past few months. I'd also have to ask exactly how 'non-league' we were off the pitch when we were actually in the non-league. Had we not been down to skeleton staff to save the pennies, did we really erode away to a non-league club?

I get how important the training ground is, I understand now we have a management team and coaching staff that will add significant value to the current squad by spending increasing amounts time with them. The squad themselves work tirelessly too, I'm told Billy Knott is often out there on his own practising free-kicks and he is by no means the only one putting the extra hours in. He needs to by the way, our free kicks have been terrible this season. That aside though there is a real desire to get better and our training facilities are hampering that effort.

By describing us as 'non-league' though I think perhaps there was a sweeping generalisation that we're not up to scratch in many ways and aside from the training ground and staff numbers I'm not sure we were ever truly 'non-league' in our set-up. Anyone who queued for tickets last season or anyone who waited for away shirts to come into stock this season might disagree, but in my eyes being non-league involves situations such as your local Post Office selling your match day tickets or your games being called off every week because your pitch is essentially a quagmire, or your club shop being a portakabin or shipping container lit up by industrial building site lights.

Have you looked at the Sincil Bank surface recently compared to years ago? I know we used to suffer from having the Ladies play on the pitch and having to train on there, and I know the facilities available such as covers has improved, but we had the best playing surface in the division last season and that was the case right up until the final day. I don't care what Mark Cooper said about it after our 3-1 win in March, our pitch is Football League quality.

Every game sees our fan experience improving too. Speaking to Liam he feels we're making small steps, but at present they're little cosmetic changes that improve the experience but not significantly. I firmly disagree, each little step has a major impact on fan's enjoyment of the matches, and the willingness to listen and develop is refreshing also. The need for focus on fan experience wasn't as pressing when we had 2,200 turning up at just gone 2.50pm each week, but we're a booming business now and I'm noticing a change every game that makes Sincil Bank a better place to be. This week there were several, firstly Ribs n Bibs in the fan zone. It has long been the desire of fans to be able to grab some different food outside the ground, no slur on Double M nor on the excellent catering in the TP Suite, but the more options you have the more likely you are to please a larger portion of people.

Music in the fan zone too, such a small step and I would imagine inconsequential to many, but it is just another little tweak that adds something. Like Danny loaning some cover in midfield or training Josh Ginnelly as a striker as well as a winger, it is something small that helps to develop the overall value. I didn't get to hear too much of it (a by-product of the new fan zone is I'm not allowed to sell A City United in there) but it did improve the atmosphere. The warm October weather helped, but Saturday felt like a carnival and remember, it was just a run-of-the-mill home game against Cambridge. I noticed away fans mingled with home fans too, that isn't particularly new but I'm sure our set up left those away supporters with a better view of our club, plus we took those notes out of their pocket and put them in our bank account. FA Cup run or not last season, profits still need maximising and that is happening.

Another change made came at the back of the Stacey West stand. It sounds very obvious, but the gate the cars exit from was moved from one part of the car park to another. This meant that fans leaving the game and walking behind the stand were not mingling with moving traffic, nor were they crossing in front of cars exiting the car park either. Foot flow was improved, safety was significantly improved and everything just worked a little bit better. Last home game that barrier at the rear of the South Park stand got opened, removing that bottleneck that has plagued us for seasons. These are all small steps, things that maybe those in charge see as obvious tweaks, but with each one I feel we take a step forward.

I know there are other things being addressed, larger changes being investigated that hopefully will allow lower tier fans to buy a beer or smokers to poison their lungs at half-time for example, but all things take time. Three matches ago an area was roped off and a few tables and gazebos set up outside the ground and every match since then large numbers have congregated and enjoyed their pre-match beer at the ground. Sure, they're small steps and everyone must recognise that it is all work in progress, but this isn't the thinking of a non-league club, not one bit.

The only aspect I feel is non-league is the lack of training ground. How much damage did Goal 2010 really do? I don't know the politics and background to our mothballed training ground, but it breaks my heart to know we had exactly what Danny wanted right there in the palm of our hand, and now we don't. It might not have been exactly what he needed, but there was a purpose-built facility that was simply wasted. I do know hard work is being put in to move us forward but I hope for our sake that it continues to progress quickly. I believe a site has been identified and plans are being laid but I don't know specifics. It won't happen overnight but progress does need to accelerate. Danny Cowley isn't a man to place blame anywhere, not at the feet of individual players, not at conditions and certainly not directly at the lack of training ground, but he is clearly frustrated with having to travel up the barracks every day. The guys involved in getting that facility useable deserve much credit, having it last season helped the pitch no doubt and the players, but we have now outgrown it.

Danny hasn't moaned once about his budget, unlike almost every manager from Gary Simpson right the way back to John Beck. He doesn't hang players out to dry, they're fit and the effort is never questioned. The one thing he refers to constantly though is the training ground and how much it is holding us back. Holding us back? We're tenth in League Two, three points outside the play-offs and unbeaten in four games. If we're being held back, what might be achievable when he gets what he needs? Promotion? The Championship? It might sound ridiculous, but where can this club go when things do finally fall into place?

I feel in every aspect other than training facilities we're a Football League club. We're learning and adapting but in truth we never were a non-league club off the pitch. We mothballed a training ground, never to be used again, and we cut down on staff which essentially mothballed much of our set up behind the scenes too. We were always fit for purpose but we didn't have the staff to carry out the things we needed doing. Now, a few bits need replacing here and there, things need tweaking and re-introducing, but Lincoln City were always a Football League club in waiting.

We're not (for instance) Forest Green Rovers, throwing money away on players and arrogantly proclaiming that we're in an easy league. We think Football League, on the pitch we look Football League and our fans are Championship standard. Once those pitches and facilities appear for day-to-day training I see no reason why we can't achieve Goal 2010, maybe a decade later but without the fanfare, big promises and empty gestures.

Clean sheet the positive: Imps 0-0 Cambridge:
October 14, 2017

All the way home from the game I've been pushing the positives. I've written a positive headline, we're 10th just three points outside the play-offs and we're unbeaten in four games also. As far as form, position and defending goes I think we're in a good place.

So, allow me to start with a couple of negatives would you? It won't be all the way through the blog, nor am I one who is just going to write something innately inaccurate and general like 'Green is crap', because Green is not crap. Green is low on confidence in front of goal, but he's a very good, hard-working footballer.

Gripe One: Billy Knott is, for want of a better pun, Knott a winger. He's a talented boy but he isn't a wide player. I believe that we have some fine wide players at the club, we've got four from a squad of twenty players which is 20%. However, one of those fine wingers is not Billy. It is frustrating to watch us play our game with wingers that are not offering width. You know when we did offer width today? When Nathan came on. He didn't have time to make an impact, but as soon as he came on Sam advanced and the link up play started. Maybe Nathan has been carrying a knock which may be why he didn't get the nod from the off, but we must utilise the width more effectively. Obviously having Harry injured isn't ideal, with a small squad we need our best players fit.

Gripe Two: Ollie Palmer and Matt Green can't play as a front pairing. I believe, judging by the work rate, that Matt was playing the number nine, up front working the channels and looking for openings, whereas Palmer was meant to be playing behind him looking for flick-ons? Or was Palmer meant to be playing alongside Green? I may see a different game to many but in Matt Green I see a hard-working player low on confidence in front of goal but not letting it affect him too much. In Ollie Palmer I see a player looking to cement his run in the first team with a goal whatever the cost. If that means getting his head down and running at goal without a moment's thought for who is around him, so be it. I've seen social media comments tonight suggesting Woodyard and Bostwick, two of the best players on the park today, can't play together. Rubbish, look further up the field for a perfect example of two similar players unable to form a partnership.

When did we look best today? When Matt Rhead came on and Nathan Arnold also. It might be mean us being more direct than we'd like, but Rheady wins headers in the ten role for players to feed off. I could feel Matt Green's smile as the big man took up a position just in front of him. Rheady has been written off by many, maybe I've even had him down as no more than an impact sub, but after today maybe that is premature. He came on, he won headers up front and at the back and he lifted the crowd. If Palmer and Green can't play together then maybe Rheady and Green can. If you think dropping Matt Green is the answer then you've been watching very different games to me and you understand how football works in a very different way to me also.

I don't like to pull my team down but I do want to call it as I see it. I alluded to Woodyard and Bozzie being two of the best players on the park and I stick by that. There's this guy that sits in front of me, face as red as a beetroot from all of the hating he does, vein pumped out across his forehead and over his skull. He's about 60 and I swear he'll drop dead one day with all the hate he saves for Alex. I wonder if he's blind as well as angry and red, because he started with the anti-Woodyard bile this afternoon. I've said it before and I'll say it again next week; Alex Woodyard was the best player on the pitch today. He dictates our play, he controls the ball and the pace of play superbly. He always looks to switch from side to side where possible, something that midfielders from 1986 until 2016 were berated for not doing in Imps colours. I love the little drop of the shoulder he gives when receiving the ball, opponents don't know which way to go and his brain is quick enough to ensure he's one step ahead of their thinking.

Along with Bozzie we have a really solid heart to our team, the grizzly bugger doesn't do anything fancy but he mops up any mess. If there is a tackle to be made and Alex can't do it by buzzing around like an angry blue-bottle, Big Daddy Hair steps forward and makes that challenge for him. Bozzie didn't lose a header today, he barely missed a tackle and if he gets the ball, he lays it off to someone in space. It might be simple but it does contribute heavily to clean sheets. Can we play with two so-called defensive midfielders in the side? Obviously, we're tenth in the table and three points from the play-offs. We've got creativity in the team, we've got players ahead of them to score goals we just need to find the method of doing so.

Luke had a superb game, especially given his time out 'resting'. I actually thought we looked more of a threat from diagonal set-pieces than we do when Raggs is in the side, that isn't a criticism of anyone either. Luke showed great application and attitude today and Danny has a big headache on Tuesday. For my money, Luke did enough to stay in the team, but how could you drop Dickie? Aside from the odd stray pass he's been as good as any of our centre backs last season. If DC leaves Raggs on the bench it might encourage Norwich to take him back in January, what would you do? I think Luke will have to bide his time until Christmas and see what happens, but he spent time in the stands under Chris Moyses and he returned to captain an FA Cup Quarter-Final side. He's not done, not by a long way.

Neal Eardley was outstanding once again, a cool head and a player whom is incredibly important to the side. Someone questioned how I called a full-back as one of our five most important players, it's his versatility as well as his individual performance. He's like two players, providing cover but also turning in great performances. Across the back we were solid today, Neal Eardley is a vital component of that. Cambridge had big lumps up top, if balls came in regularly they'd score eventually. The full backs had to cut off at source, Neal did that extremely well. Sam wasn't terrible, Danny didn't mention him when talking about our good performers today which I thought was a tiny bit harsh on him. Both full-backs struggled from their wingers not being on their game, Neal just reacted better to it than Sam. When Nathan came on it brought something out in Sam that Josh had been unable to do.

Josh Ginnelly ran until his legs would let him run anymore, but so does Mo Farah and it isn't enough in itself to be effective. Josh is learning all the time though, but today wasn't his day. As I mentioned Billy isn't a winger, his inclination is to come inside and until he's in the ten role we won't see the best of him. He wasn't today but he was a bit sloppy, he played at least two balls blind and gave possession away.

Josh Vickers did what he needed to do when asked. Jordan Maguire-Drew came on too. We've yet to see what he can do. I promise you I haven't copied and pasted that from every other blog I've done this season. I'm not convinced the blond kid Brighton have sent us is the same one that turned out for Dagenham last season. Maybe if he had a chance on the left flank, being left footed, we'd see the best of him.

Look, this might not have been an inspiring home victory but you must remember scenes like last season, the sort that actually warrant Sweet Caroline, do not happen every week. We've lost once at home in a year, I remember when we used to lose once at home whenever we played at home. In a 46-game season there is grind, there are matches which test the patience of the fans and there are performances that do not do justice to the players on the field. Sometimes I've watched players that barely seem to recognise each other play for Lincoln, players whom I wouldn't fear if I came up against them in a pub five-a-side. That isn't our squad of today, that isn't what we have now. The reason it is easy to be critical is because the bar was set so high last season and because the quality in our squad makes the fans believe we are capable of so much more. Yes, we need a striker, you think Danny doesn't know that? He tried to sign Simeon Akinola (scored today for Barnet) and if rumour is to be believed Ollie Hawkins (scored twice for Portsmouth today). Those players would not just fill the bench, they wouldn't just provide cover, they'd add value to the side. Anyone Danny brings in must add value and make us better, those exacting standards are what has us just outside the play-offs in League Two, and even if they've meant we have a squad of 20 and not 23, they've clearly done us well so far.

Yes, I've been negative about some aspects of today, that is the nature of post-match analysis. However, you will not find me criticising anything as a whole, certainly nothing that Danny

Cowley has done or will do. I want a manager that gets value for money, I want a club that is both frugal and progressive. I want a team that is competing at the right end of the table, looking to catch teams above in order to progress not to save our skins. I understand there will be matches that I walk away from thinking 'that was turgid', and if those matches form part of a four-match unbeaten run then that's not a bad place to be in, is it? The nature of the football fan is to be critical when matches are not won, the nature of Lincoln City in 2017 is to get better, one game at a time. I hate these 'last season' comparisons, but this weekend last season we drew 0-0 with Guiseley in the FA Cup 4th Qualifying Round, and the weekend after we drew 0-0 with Eastleigh in front of just over 3,000 people, believing that was a great result. How is that for 12 months progress?

The small changes off the pitch are beginning to pile up too, aren't they? Music in the Fan Zone for instance, such tiny little thing but something the adds to the atmosphere. Also, behind the Stacey West the cars were using a different gate meaning foot traffic and motor traffic was separated. It seems so simple, 'open another gate', but it has taken best part of six years to figure out. It just proves that a different pair of eyes looking at a situation will spot things that are blindingly obvious to anyone that hasn't spent the last six years looking at them.

Cambridge? Big lumps, decent side but if I'm honest mid-table fodder nothing more. I was worried about Ibehre but he seemed to only be effective if we let the ball bounce three times so he could hold our players off. He was lucky too, by the letter of the law he could have been sent off for his little movement towards a fan at the end, however justified it was. I did like Piero Mingola, he had a stinging effort saved and looked quite lively, and I thought Medy Elito was quite effective too. The forwards were kept quiet all game by our defenders, but Ikpeazu would be a really good addition to our side with his physicality and a bit of mobility too. Outside of that nobody stood out as brilliant, they played alright, no better than say, Carlisle or even Morecambe.

Finally, and this isn't an attack on Casey, but Sweet Caroline after a 0-0 draw with Cambridge? Really? Singing in the stands to celebrate a mid-season draw against a mid-table team? I might just be a bit grouchy but the shine is being taken off the song by playing it all the time. I used to associate it with those magical days of April this year, topping the table and heading for success. I don't remember it being played after the 0-0 draw with Eastleigh though, I'm beginning to wonder if maybe we've had all the other CD's pinched? Pre-match, post-match I'm surprised it isn't piped into the toilets and the bar areas, I'm surprised we're not required to change our ringtones to it and then ring each other at half time so we can all sing along in a never-ending state of Neil Diamond inspired insanity. I feel forever doomed to have someone I don't know sing the words 'so good, so good' (words Neil doesn't even sing in the song) at me even when we've lost 1-0 to Mansfield, forever finding my Facebook feed clogged up by someone who has heard one of the most played songs ever somewhere, anywhere and then felt the bloody need to tell the world all about it, 24 hours a day 7 days a week……. Guess what I just heard in the supermarket, on holiday, in a bar, on the radio of a house I walked past, in the background on a TV show, on my dog's vet's receptionist's radio, anywhere, everywhere, Neil Diamond everywhere…… everywhere….. 'so good, so good'……

JUST STOP IT NOW

Are we really still non-league off the pitch?
October 16, 2017

One thing I noted from Danny's post-match comments was his insistence that off the pitch Lincoln City are still a non-league club. I'm not one for disagreeing with Danny, far from it. That man has delivered my football club back to me, hosed down, polished up and fit for the Football League.

However, I can't help but feel that his comments are exclusively aimed at the training facilities and perhaps, just perhaps, they don't do justice to the strides the club have taken over the past few months. I'd also have to ask exactly how 'non-league' we were off the pitch when we were actually in the non-league. Had we not been down to skeleton staff to save the pennies, did we really erode away to a non-league club?

I get how important the training ground is, I understand now we have a management team and coaching staff that will add significant value to the current squad by spending increasing amounts time with them. The squad themselves work tirelessly too, I'm told Billy Knott is often out there on his own practising free-kicks and he is by no means the only one putting the extra hours in. He needs to by the way, our free kicks have been terrible this season. That aside though there is a real desire to get better and our training facilities are hampering that effort.

By describing us as 'non-league' though I think perhaps there was a sweeping generalisation that we're not up to scratch in many ways and aside from the training ground and staff numbers I'm not sure we were ever truly 'non-league' in our set-up. Anyone who queued for tickets last season or anyone who waited for away shirts to come into stock this season might disagree, but in my eyes being non-league involves situations such as your local Post Office selling your match day tickets or your games being called off every week because your pitch is essentially a quagmire, or your club shop being a portakabin or shipping container lit up by industrial building site lights.

Have you looked at the Sincil Bank surface recently compared to years ago? I know we used to suffer from having the Ladies play on the pitch and having to train on there, and I know the facilities available such as covers has improved, but we had the best playing surface in the division last season and that was the case right up until the final day. I don't care what Mark Cooper said about it after our 3-1 win in March, our pitch is Football League quality.

Every game sees our fan experience improving too. Speaking to Liam he feels we're making small steps, but at present they're little cosmetic changes that improve the experience but not significantly. I firmly disagree, each little step has a major impact on fan's enjoyment of the matches, and the willingness to listen and develop is refreshing also. The need for focus on fan experience wasn't as pressing when we had 2,200 turning up at just gone 2.50pm each week, but we're a booming business now and I'm noticing a change every game that makes Sincil Bank a better place to be. This week there were several, firstly Ribs n Bibs in the fan zone. It has long been the desire of fans to be able to grab some different food outside the ground, no slur on Double M nor on the excellent catering in the TP Suite, but the more options you have the more likely you are to please a larger portion of people.

Music in the fan zone too, such a small step and I would imagine inconsequential to many, but it is just another little tweak that adds something. Like Danny loaning some cover in midfield or training Josh Ginnelly as a striker as well as a winger, it is something small that helps to develop the overall value. I didn't get to hear too much of it (a by-product of the new fan zone is I'm not allowed to sell A City United in there) but it did improve the atmosphere. The warm October weather helped, but Saturday felt like a carnival and remember, it was just a run-of-the-mill home game against Cambridge. I noticed away fans mingled with home fans too, that isn't particularly new but I'm sure our set up left those away supporters with a better view of our club, plus we took those notes out of their pocket and put them in our bank account. FA Cup run or not last season, profits still need maximising and that is happening.

Another change made came at the back of the Stacey West stand. It sounds very obvious, but the gate the cars exit from was moved from one part of the car park to another. This meant that fans leaving the game and walking behind the stand were not mingling with moving traffic, nor were they crossing in front of cars exiting the car park either. Foot flow was improved, safety was significantly improved and everything just worked a little bit better. Last home game that barrier at the rear of the South Park stand got opened, removing that bottleneck that has plagued us for seasons. These are all small steps, things that maybe those in charge see as obvious tweaks, but with each one I feel we take a step forward.

I know there are other things being addressed, larger changes being investigated that hopefully will allow lower tier fans to buy a beer or smokers to poison their lungs at half-time for example, but all things take time. Three matches ago an area was roped off and a few tables and gazebos set up outside the ground and every match since then large numbers have congregated and enjoyed their pre-match beer at the ground. Sure, they're small steps and everyone must recognise that it is all work in progress, but this isn't the thinking of a non-league club, not one bit.

The only aspect I feel is non-league is the lack of training ground. How much damage did Goal 2010 really do? I don't know the politics and background to our mothballed training ground, but it breaks my heart to know we had exactly what Danny wanted right there in the palm of our hand, and now we don't. It might not have been exactly what he needed, but there was a purpose-built facility that was simply wasted. I do know hard work is being put in to move us forward but I hope for our sake that it continues to progress quickly. I believe a site has been identified and plans are being laid but I don't know specifics. It won't happen overnight but progress does need to accelerate. Danny Cowley isn't a man to place blame anywhere, not at the feet of individual players, not at conditions and certainly not directly at the lack of training ground, but he is clearly frustrated with having to travel up the barracks every day. The guys involved in getting that facility useable deserve much credit, having it last season helped the pitch no doubt and the players, but we have now outgrown it.

Danny hasn't moaned once about his budget, unlike almost every manager from Gary Simpson right the way back to John Beck. He doesn't hang players out to dry, they're fit and the effort is never questioned. The one thing he refers to constantly though is the training ground and how much it is holding us back. Holding us back? We're tenth in League Two, three points outside the play-offs and unbeaten in four games. If we're being held back, what might be achievable when he gets what he needs? Promotion? The Championship? It might sound ridiculous, but where can this club go when things do finally fall into place?

I feel in every aspect other than training facilities we're a Football League club. We're learning and adapting but in truth we never were a non-league club off the pitch. We mothballed a training ground, never to be used again, and we cut down on staff which essentially mothballed much of our set up behind the scenes too. We were always fit for purpose but we didn't have the staff to carry out the things we needed doing. Now, a few bits need replacing here and there, things need tweaking and re-introducing, but Lincoln City were always a Football League club in waiting. We're not (for instance) Forest Green Rovers, throwing money away on players and arrogantly proclaiming that we're in an easy league. We think Football League, on the pitch we look Football League and our fans are Championship standard. Once those pitches and facilities appear for day-to-day training I see no reason why we can't achieve Goal 2010, maybe a decade later but without the fan fare, big promises and empty gestures.

Missed Call: Danny Cowley

October 17, 2017

I don't suppose that is something you see every day on your mobile phone, but every so often I have the pleasure of chewing the fat with our manager on a range of issues. Yesterday, in the wake of my blog about us not being a 'non-league' club, or manager decided to call me up and have a chat to put his views across.

I've heard stories of Peter Jackson hunting a certain former blogger down in the Centre Spot Bar after an unfavourable review, Leigh Curtis talks of bust-ups with a certain manager over his articles and in some instances clubs now ban reporters from the ground. In the age of social media and instant news in is often easier for a club to whitewash their own news feed and keep out the rabble. Not Lincoln City, not Danny Cowley.

Firstly, this was initially an 'off the record' chat. Danny is very open and honest about a number of issues, if you've dined with him or spoken face to face you'll know this. There is an unwritten code, an understanding that what he shares isn't all social media friendly or to be written about. However, at the end of our conversation I asked if I could put an article together covering the conversation and the message he wanted to get across to me and he was happy for that to happen. This is why there are no specific comments, I don't record my phone conversations nor keep notes when chatting to people.

Danny wanted to talk about how I'd understood his comments after the game on Saturday. You might remember that he had said the club was still very much 'non-league' when competing against sides such as Cambridge or Notts County. I had pointed out whilst he was correct regarding training facilities, the rest of the club was taking great strides. Danny actually agrees very much with that.

He went to great lengths to make sure that I knew the bar and catering guys, the ticket office girls and the general infrastructure of the club was very good, Football League all day long. Those involved with the fan experience do a great job and people such as Liam joining the club were further steps forward. His comments hadn't been negative, nor had they been aimed purely at the training ground. This wasn't a frustrated manager trying to hold the club to ransom after a 'disappointing' result, not one bit. A draw with Cambridge at home shouldn't even be classed as a disappointing result, so there was certainly no reason for him to lash out. His comments had been factual and should have been taken as more complimentary to Cambridge than derogatory to Lincoln.

Cambridge are basically Lincoln in three years' time, something I alluded to in my programme notes. They're a team that have invested their cup money carefully and over a period of time. I'm not talking about cover for disabled fans or more bars in the ground here, I'm talking about bodies behind the scenes. They've got a Head of Recruitment for example, Alex Fraser. They've got a First Team Analyst as well as a Head of Performance. We're championing our new CEO (and rightly so), they got a CEO, a Head of Football Operations, a Chief Operating Officer and a Head of Strategic Development.

I could go on. Our excellent Academy, growing all the time, currently has an Academy Manager listed as well as a Professional Development Lead Coach and a Head Scout. Cambridge has an Academy Manager, Academy Operations Manager, Head of Academy Coaching, Professional Development Phase Lead Coach, Youth Development Phase Lead Coach, Foundation Phase Lead Coach, Senior Academy Physiotherapist, Lead Sport Scientist, Head of Academy Recruitment, Head of Internal Recruitment, Head of Education and Performance Analyst. That isn't me saying our academy isn't up to scratch, absolutely not. It is saying we're growing quickly and getting the right people in the right places takes time. It does colour in some of the blank picture Danny's comments left though, does it not?

Now this is very important so listen up and listen up good: Danny isn't unhappy about the situation we're in, he's excited to be a part of it. If he had the interview back, doubtless he'd clarify the point but he's in full view of the media glare, so often something may be interpreted wrong. He underlined to me the excitement at being central to this development and a key figure in the club regaining its place at the Football League table, not just to dine on the scraps but to be a central figure.

All these things are happening and taking time to fall into place. Every week there is another development, another person joining the back-room staff or another role being proposed and filled. It isn't a case of getting anyone in to do these jobs with fancy titles either, people need to be selected properly and with due diligence. Just like our recruitment on the field, the proper people are being found for roles off the field.

Danny's fear, and I'm sure he won't mind me sharing this part of our conversation, is losing something we have that these teams do not. One thing Cambridge do not have, Coventry do not have and Luton don't have, is you. Our fans, this season, are the best in League Two. We travel in greater numbers, we have the highest home attendance which, frankly, is ridiculous when you look at who is in our league, and we're vocal in our support. A 0-0 draw with Cambridge might keep a few quiet or set a couple off moaning on the internet, but 9,000 fans every week? Seriously? This is the fourth tier of the English Football League and we get more fans than all but six of the clubs in the league above us. Cambridge, a side that have all the structure and people in place that a modern-day Football League club need, they get 4,500.

Last season the change was instant, City were under achieving and our management were able to effect quick action to make us successful. Building a legacy, creating the sort of club that can thrive, not here but in League One or (dare I say it) higher, that will not happen overnight. The fear is the great support that we have begins to dwindle away if we stay tucked in the middle of the pack. I hope not, I'm sure it won't but I think that is what our manager fears. If we go on a four-match streak without a win, will some stop turning out for games? Will that wave of optimism and hope we rode all the way to the title last year break on a beach of indifference and dispassion?

There is a difference between being critical and managing expectation, people calling Matt Green or the tactics we use are just being critical, there's no benefit in that for the club or manager. We shouldn't be apathetic, shrugging our shoulders at a 0-0 draw because 'we were non-league last year', but at the same time we shouldn't be pulling the club down for the exact same reason. We were non-league last year and Chesterfield were in League One. The FA Cup draw could have paired us together as it did with Oldham and we would have had the situation of being giant-killers in November but disappointed we'd 'only' won 2-1 ten months later in the league. Football fans, me included, are always judging matches on current form, current league place and things that are happening right now. I suppose sometimes we all need a little perspective, me included.

Last season we often needed to score three goals to make sure we won a game, this season we're far less likely to concede and therefore should only need one or two goals to win a game. Yes, we're more defensive but that is paying dividends is it not? We can't massacre a side in the last twenty minutes in this division like we could last season because fitness levels are far higher. Our game has changed because it has needed to, it is tighter and at times it is a slower pace and perhaps a little less pleasing on the eye. We're still within touching distance of the play-offs though aren't we? We're currently in our highest October position since John Schofield and John Deehan were in charge eleven years ago. Think on that.

Danny ended by saying 'you can quote me on this' and then promptly gave me something quotable that I didn't write down or record. Look, when Danny speaks football you listen, occasionally dropping something in that lets him know you're understanding his point of view or (more importantly) you know what you're talking about. His quotable caught me without a pen, but he underlined his commitment to keeping fans on board, informed as much as protocol would allow, and entertained wherever possible. He is committed to building a legacy here and excited to be part of the journey and to helping shape to future of this great football club.

This is a journey and we're not even half way to our destination. It isn't straight forward, there are some roads we're going down that might be bumpy or seem to be out of the way to where we're going but stay with the club. We must keep Sincil Bank full, big crowds won't win you every game, but you never know which one we will make a difference in.

After our conversation I thought about what he'd said. Imagine, we're a team without proper training facilities and several steps behind almost all of the clubs we're going to face in the league. We still drew 0-0 with Cambridge and in truth we still felt we should have beaten them. Yes, we're a couple of players short and many have put that down to planning on Danny's part. That isn't true, we missed out on players in the summer for a host of reasons. I'm led to believe (not by Danny) that one or two asked to see our training facilities when being shown around Sincil Bank, you can imagine how that conversation went. Danny himself would admit we missed out on one or two because he won't pay a player something he isn't worth, nor will he pay a club more than his own valuation of a player. Off the field our CEO started after the start of the season, we're still in the middle of bringing in a club secretary and we are still a 'work in progress'. We have a threadbare squad of talent, proper talent, and as a squad we're working well and holding our own. Bob Dorrian has already spoken of budgets in January, let's not shout that about too much though, eh? We don't want the clubs we intend to buy from to start bumping up transfer fees even more, do we? The FA Cup effect has doubtless also cost us players, clubs think we'll pay more because we've got a bit of cash, clubs that obviously don't know how good Danny is with money.

Cheers Danny for the chat, hopefully I've put our conversation across in a fair and accurate manner. I look forward to the next time one of my blogs causes you to pick up the phone, because there is no sweeter sight on my mobile phone than the words 'Missed Call: Danny Cowley'.

Swindon 0-1 Imps: The run continues
October 17, 2017

Remember earlier when I said we only need to score one or two to win a game? Well, once again, a solitary goal has been enough to give Lincoln all three points on their travels.

It was a dogged performance from the Imps, not the prettiest but always committed and resolute. The goal came from Sean Raggett (pictured) with a late header, and City had the clearest chances against a disappointing Swindon side. For all their possession the Robins really didn't impress me, the result means we now leapfrog them into ninth position.

I thought for long spells the game had 0-0 written all over it, we had chances in the first fifteen but neither side really threatened in the middle section of the game. Swindon edged possession but did nothing significant with it, not for the want of trying though. City were excellent without the ball, defending in numbers and always there with a tackle or a block. Luke Waterfall might have been unlucky to be back on the bench, but the two centre halves were immense and unfortunately for Luke nothing is going to split up the Dickie / Raggett partnership until January.

Some Imps fans have muttered that the defensive approach to games is nullifying our attack, but this result absolutely justifies the current tactics. It isn't necessarily negative, we won 1-0 and had the better chances. It isn't boring either, it is an effective way of playing that only works if players are committed and organised. Swindon have capability to hurt you, but we allowed them very little time on the ball. In the final few minutes they started throwing long balls into the box, looking for the chink of light that would get them back into the game. They didn't find it, everything they had was matched and countered by City. We defended brilliantly and closed Swindon time whenever they had the ball.

I thought we looked better going forward when Ollie Palmer came on. Early doors we had a few chances but after that Billy Knott drifted out of the game. It wasn't a game for panache and style on the ball though, it was a dog fight, a battle of strength and application. Ollie Palmer gave us a physical presence which just changed the focus of our attack. I haven't been a fan of Palmer so far this season, but he did have an effect.

I also thought Josh Ginnelly had a good game, so much so that he was roundly booed by the home fans as he left the field. That is always telling, if a player is roundly booed he must have had an effect, although how he didn't score after Nathan hit the post I'll never know. From the angle I saw it looked like a super block. Minutes after that I thought he was fouled in the area also, he was a thorn in the side of Swindon and he's a player I'd love to see reach his potential.

I was delighted to see Nathan start the game. He gives us something on the flank, a know-how and experience that the other wide players do not. Early on in the game I thought Arnold made a real difference, he delivers a great ball from out wide and he almost teed up Billy for a goal too. If Nathan is back on it and fully fit that can only be positive going forward towards Christmas because he is one of our key players.

Ultimately though, whenever you go away in midweek to a side such as Swindon, everyone has to be on their game if you want a result, and everyone was. Sean Long did superbly after coming back into the side in the absence of Sam Habergham, Rob Dickie was outstanding again and, as usual, Alex Woodyard was excellent. As early as 29 minutes he was making crucial challenge in the penalty area. Sean Raggett not only got the goal but was also excellent. There wasn't a player that could be picked out that had a poor game. The lads have every right to be extremely proud of the result. Even Jordan Maguire-Drew can be happy, on as a late sub it was his delivery that Raggs nodded into the back of the net. JMD has had a torrid start to the season but hopefully an assist will give him the confidence he needs to kick on.

As I've mentioned there has been some negativity around social media, but City are unbeaten in five and a solitary point outside of the play-offs. Imagine, we're not fully on method and we're still battling just outside the top seven. What can be achieved when we get to add a couple of bodies and get our injured players back? They say if you win your home games and draw the away games then you'll be there or thereabouts, well the last five games we've played three at home and two away, we've won three and drawn two. Textbook. We've also kept three clean sheets in five, another superb achievement. Swindon failed to score tonight, the same Swindon that smashed three away at Mansfield on Saturday. Make no mistake, this result is brilliant.

Also, as much as we shouldn't get carried away, that 'refuse to lose' attitude is evident again, the same attitude that served us so well last season. We've lost three in the league this season, the same as second placed Notts County and third placed Exeter City. In the last twelve league and cup matches we've lost just two, one of those against County which may have been different had we had eleven men on the field. There is a long way to go and the threadbare squad will be tested to the maximum, but the signs are there that we can compete with anyone in this league. Luton, top of the table now and I suspect for the next seven months, couldn't beat us at Sincil Bank.

Danny Cowley won't be getting carried away, the players can enjoy this superb win on the way home and then focus on Cheltenham on Saturday. The fans though, we'll enjoy this right up until Saturday at 3pm. Winning away at Swindon Town is a big achievement, last season two divisions separated these sides but tonight we just wrote another paragraph in the wonderful story of The Cowley's Lincoln City adventure.

Cheltenham 1-0 Imps: Just one of those days
October 21, 2017

One of the set-backs with the modern world is the desperate clamour for stories, the need for an angle to every little occurrence. You see it in the top flight where a West Brom v Stoke clash is billed as 'Super Sunday'.

You see it on my site sometimes when rumours of Matty Fryatt being at the ground are explored and discussed. Tonight, you've maybe heard it on BBC Radio Lincolnshire where James Williams quizzed Steve Thompson about the Imps lack of goals, asking how Danny goes about solving the problem. There has to be an angle, no longer can a match just be chalked off and moved on from. There has to be analysis, reports and dissection. People will discuss it on social media and if I didn't blog about it I'd be accused of being a club stooge, happy to build up the positives but glossing over the negatives. However, what do you really glean from a match like today?

Danny admits himself we don't score enough from open play, but is it a problem, a real bona-fide problem? A problem, by definition, is a matter or situation regarded as harmful and needing to be dealt with and overcome. Is the lack of open play goals directly harmful? Well, we're tenth and just two points off the play-offs. If this was May then maybe it could be perceived as such, but I'm not aware of anyone missing out on the play-offs in October. Okay, if we scored more from open play we might be a bit higher, but is it directly harmful? Is sitting tenth after 15 games a situation that needs rectifying? No, not given the fact the twelve months ago we'd just played Eastleigh and had Guiseley and Southport on the fixture list.

I appreciate we all need subjects to discuss, I'm usually happy to talk about things that I think need to be tweaked and changed, but the situation we find ourselves in isn't straightforward. We can't just go out and get a new player thanks to the League rules, we have to make do with what is in our squad. If we'd drawn 0-0 today we'd be six unbeaten, would there have been questions asked over the lack of goals in that instance?

In every press conference, every post-match interview and doubtless every casual conversation he has, Danny Cowley is asked if we're looking to bring someone in to address the problem. He could almost have a card in his pocket he pulls out whenever asked with the words 'we're always looking' written on it. In truth, what can he do? How many good quality, fully fit professional footballer's do you think are out there just waiting to be picked up?

For whatever reason we missed out on targets in the summer. We made some really good signings, the talent in our squad is as good as it has been for many years, but we're a work in progress. We've only been a Football League club for fifteen games, we've only known we were returning to the league for six months. The whole club has to be adjusted, tweaking and improved, from top to bottom. Change doesn't happen overnight and unfortunately we're going to come up short at certain times. The last six matches prove we're not far away and yet we still have so much work to do throughout the club. The new CEO coming in was the start of the revolution, he is identifying problems and issues and sorting them out. Rome wasn't built in a day, nor was Lincoln City Football Club. We've been building for at least five years now; my suspicion is we'll be building for some time yet.

There's little point in lamenting the defeat today although I appreciate that won't be much comfort to those who travelled. I did call this as a game we were likely to struggle in, the conditions accentuated that somewhat and whilst they're the same for both teams they do make planning a strategy very hard. Listening to Elliott Whitehouse's interview I couldn't help but feel sorry for him, he gets his first team chance on a day where the weather makes it very hard for midfielders to have any impact on the game. It really was the stereotypical 'game of two halves', they throw everything at us in the first forty-five and we reciprocate in the second period. By all accounts their keeper has pulled off a word-class save to deny Jordan Maguire-Drew, a player that seems to be growing in confidence (pictured top against Chesterfield). That is football, you win some you should lose and you lose some you should win. Today we lost one perhaps we could have drawn. Let's take a positive, if JMD comes home with a little more confidence and self-belief that has to be a god thing. There's a cracking player in our squad that we've barely seen a glimpse of at present.

The key thing is for everyone sat in front of their keyboards tonight is to retain some perspective. Any perceived problems with the current squad are not detrimental to everything we are trying to achieve, they're not bringing the very future of the club into question, nor our ability to move forward. Even with a threadbare squad, even without lots of goals from open play, we're competing at the right end of the table. Nobody, not Luton, Exeter nor Cheltenham, have outplayed us. Nobody has looked a cut-above when we've been 11 v 11 and maybe as a fan base we need to retain some perspective and perhaps manage our own expectations a bit.

So far I've only seen one idiotic comment, something along the lines of 'sort it out Danny', which is heartening. There isn't a lot to be angry about, days like today do not need lots of analysis or opinion. It was a game of football in which everything went out of the window; form, preparation and tactical approach. The conditions dictated the style and quality and both teams did what they could to manage. Cheltenham did it better than us but there's no need to panic, criticise nor get down-hearted. I hate the phrase 'we go again', but that is exactly what happens. Some of us will be there to watch Elliott, Matt Rhead and Jordan Maguire-Drew start on Tuesday night and hopefully stake a place for a first-team return, others will prefer to wait until next Saturday due to their politics. Whichever you choose to do, neither is right and neither is wrong.

What would be wrong is losing sight of the bigger picture after a 1-0 defeat at Cheltenham, falling for the angle the media choose to put on the result, they have to do something with it otherwise what would they broadcast and report? This type of shoulder-shrugging blog is fine on an indie football site like mine, but it won't wash with the BBC or Trinity Mirror, they need clicks and listeners.

There isn't a wholesale issue to address nor is there a crisis that needs averting. If the players keep doing what they're doing, applying themselves in the right manner and staying on method then the goals will come, these players are good enough to make sure that happens.

The lads just have to dust themselves down and glean whatever developmental points they can from the performance. We, fans and pundits alike, would be best advised to simply chalk this one-off as a bad day at the office and look ahead to the real newsworthy stories, which I confidently predict will be either boycotts or awful stewarding. Those are subjects that we can get our teeth into, certainly ones worthier of angry keyboard tapping than today's game.

Welcome to Sincil Bank Cameron Stewart

October 24, 2017

City have unveiled the signing of Cameron Stewart, a winger released by Ipswich last summer. Stewart has been with Port Vale and we've been waiting for confirmation from the FA that his appearance in a reserve game for them against Walsall did not constitutes having a club before the window closed. It does not and he becomes the latest member of Danny's threadbare squad.

Stewart has had a few clubs and is one of those players looking for somewhere he can thrive. He began his career with Manchester United, representing England at under-17, under-19 and under-20 level. He had loan spells with Yeovil Town and Hull City in the first half of the 2010–11 season, before he joined Hull permanently for an undisclosed fee.

He fell out of favour at Hull and ended up spending short terms on loan at various clubs including Leeds United. He was due to join Leeds permanently at the end of his Hull contract in July 2014, but the transfer was cancelled and he instead joined Ipswich Town. He never settled at Portman Road, but he did have a successful loan spell with Doncaster which was his last meaningful football. He can score a goal or two, he grabbed a last-minute winner for Doncaster against Crewe during his loan spell there, scoring four times in total.

I know some will be running their eye over this signing saying 'not another winger', but it is worth noting that Danny feels we haven't had the right penetration from the wings as we did last season. I still maintain Matt Green will score goals and honestly, I can't wait when he does to quieten a few people down. The key to him scoring is good service, something we've struggled with. The 4-2-3-1 that Danny favours relies heavily on wide players getting at a full back and providing bullets, so I suspect Danny's thinking is he needs to strengthen where he can.

Look, centre forwards are not in plentiful supply, almost all are contracted to clubs. We do not necessarily need a 'proven' goal scorer, we have one in Matt Green. What we need is to find the formula that gives Matt the sort of service he can thrive on, and Cameron Stewart might be able to do just that.

He brings experience, he brings potential and he's another player with something to prove after a stuttering career. At 26-years old he still has an awful lot to offer and I firmly believe if Danny didn't think he had the ability to turn his career around, he wouldn't have signed him. At this stage of the season, with no players allowed in contracted to clubs currently, Cameron Stewart is a very good find.

He's been training with the club for a while so it is odd that the news hasn't broken sooner. I do know we hoped to have it tied up ahead of today's game but the finer details were being checked with the FA. He is now available for tonight's match and I'd wager he gets a run out from the bench, if not a starting role.

Checkatrade Trophy win, for those who care: Imps 2-1 Everton U21

October 24, 2017

There was very much a friendly feel to last night's game, a general chatter rather than constantchanting, an unfamiliar tactics coupled with fresh faces and even different coloured training kit in the dugout. It felt very much like an LDV Vans game of old, or an Autoglass Windscreens Shield.

Predictably City gave a run-out to some 'fringe' players if it is possible to have such a thing with our squad. Ollie Palmer started up front in a 4-3-3 formation, Billy Knott and Elliott Whitehouse played in midfield with Michael Bostwick sitting deeper. Josh Ginnelly and Jordan Maguire-Drew provided width, or rather in a 4-3-3 provided support. Luke Waterfall got a start as did Farms, familiar players that have fallen down the pecking order.

I have to say, we started the game with the sort of intensity that was more recognisable last season. It may have been the switch from two holding midfielders to one, it may have been a conscious thing knowing the opposition and the fact it is a cup competition, whatever the facts we came out of the blogs like a team possessed. Maguire-Drew opening the scoring after a couple of minutes, Josh Ginnelly got free on the left-hand flank, perhaps should have scored but his shot cannoned back off the post to the feet of JMD. He reacted quickly and slotted the ball home. 1-0, a judging by his celebration I'd say he was fairly happy with his goal.

Whilst the young Everton plays passed and moved well, fluid and in nice patterns, they lacked something you expect a youth team to lack, physicality. One or two of their boys looked strong and none looked half-hearted, but I didn't see one of them that looked comfortable being asked to challenge Michael Bostwick in the air. I overheard someone jokingly refer to it as 'men against boys'. How apt.

The second goal came for a dead-ball situation, something not often seen at Sincil Bank. Amusingly after the foul it appeared as though Ollie Palmer wanted the free-kick. Billy had the ball in his hands, Ollie turned to him and Billy threw it over his head to JMD. Momentarily Ollie didn't look happy and it appeared as though he wanted to wrestle the ball from JMD. That clearly wasn't going to happen, we've heard the youngster has a nice free-kick and he wanted to make sure we saw it.

Boy, am I glad he hung on to the ball. There was no run up as such, no procrastinating or shimmy, nothing at all to suggest he was going to do anything other than score. He took three steps max and curled a delicious ball over the wall and into the goal. It wasn't even top corner, it was just sublime. Up and over the wall and back down to a height the keeper couldn't get in the flick of his boot. Stefan Oakes was once billed as being able to peel carrots with his left foot, I'm pretty sure JMD could peel, slice and cook potatoes. He certainly roasted their keeper.

His emotional celebration underlined how much criticism on social media must get to players. He urged the crowd for more noise, whether for him or the team it was certainly passionate. Fair play, I've said for a long while we have a special player and I really hope we see that come to the fore over the next few weeks.

After that the game began to match the atmosphere. I'll be dealing with the whole boycott impact in another blog later (and it will be the last I do), but the game continued in the vein of a friendly. Their lads were good footballers and they had numerous efforts at goal, not good efforts but nonetheless they attacked well. Farms didn't have too many saves to make, not in the first half.

Jordan Maguire-Drew controlled the show on his flank, cutting in to offer support wherever he could. He wasn't greedy whilst looking for his hat trick either. On the other hand, Ollie Palmer, ploughing a loan furrow up front, did just that. When Ollie gets his head down to run, it doesn't come back up and on two or three occasions he ran himself into danger last night.

At half time I grabbed a coke in the rain (that wet rain, you know the stuff) and the queues were very Football League. I'd sat in the Coop Lower for a different experience, one I won't be having again. The lower is not the place for me I'm afraid.

Everton came out in the second half with a bit more panache and composure about their play. We did too, we introduced the new boy Cameron Stewart for Josh Ginnelly. At 2-0 up and playing against boys I thought the game lost a bit of its intensity, certainly for us. However, it was promising to note Stewart's ability on the ball, assured to the point of being cocky and full of little flicks and smart passes. What he did well was cut inside and provide link up with the midfielders behind Ollie Palmer. One of the criticisms of our front players has been a lack of goals, another thing the wingers have received negative comments for is their cutting inside and playing on the opposite flank. Last night, did we get a glimpse of the actual master plan? Does Danny put a left footer and the right and vice versa, because they are meant to be cutting inside and playing neat passes with the ten, allowing the main centre forward time to find space? Cameron Stewart certainly had that in abundance, He linked up well with Billy Knott in particular.

We also saw the arrival of Ellis Chapman, the youngster that we've heard so much about and, as yet, seen nothing. The beauty of this competition is it allows us to blood these youngsters, especially as we were playing boys. He was an age group where he wouldn't be out muscled every time he got on the ball. He had a good start; the boy clearly has bags of technique playing one of two lovely balls through. He's 16, he's going to be raw and have a long way to go, but if you have natural technique and a good attitude, you'll go a long way. Sure, he has to bulk up, but you name me a young player that looked physically ready for the man's game at 16? When I was 16 there was more meat in a Double M's burger than on my frame, I got knocked off a football if someone within ten feet of me. Ellis scrapped when he needed to, energetically and with commitment. I hear the boy is special, let's hope we progress in this competition so we can see some more of him.

Eventually Everton did get a goal, the city back line had played very well, Luke especially. against boys you expect those strong players to have a real impact, there's no doubt Everton came more into the game once Bozzie went off. Luke headed well, tackled well and was vocal throughout. I really like Luke and it was great to see him with the armband on again, if only for one night. I really like Farms to and he had a good night, although I'm sure he would have liked a clean sheet.

Their goal was a bit scrappy, it set up a nervous final ten minutes, then the referee found five minutes injury time in a game where nobody really wanted it to carry on that long. Everton probed but didn't look like levelling, we just kicked it away whenever they came near and eventually the man in the middle ended the game.

Overall, a good night of football. It was a competitive friendly, one booking perhaps but no real nasty challenges. We're in a great position to progress to the next round now meaning at least two more games in the competition, two more matches where we'll argue until we're black and blue, call each other names and debate the intricacies of the boycott, but ultimately two more games where players like JMD gain confidence or players like Ellis Chapman gain minutes. Let us not lose sight of the benefits in footballing terms here, whatever the politics.

Another blank afternoon: Imps 0-0 Crawley
October 28, 2017

Football isn't always about last-minute free-kicks winning games, it isn't always controversial cup tie against youth sides either. Sometimes, football is a Saturday afternoon spent wondering what on earth you're doing with your time, knowing that when someone asks in two weeks what game you attended, you'll have to rack your brains to remember anything positive about it at all.

Today, as you'll probably already know, was one of those days. City looked laboured, devoid of ideas in the final third and often out-muscled by a strong and organised Crawley. Let's not give the visitors too much respect, they are to League Two what Burnley are to the Premier League. They sit tight, bully and battle and hope you gift them an opportunity, or to put it another way, they do what we do away. We did our best in the second half to play gracious hosts, creating more for them than we created for ourselves.

I'm not blind and I'm not ignorant, we have an issue up front. I maintain things will come good but at present, we're firing blanks. Even the blanks we're firing are missing the target. We're not always getting the breaks, we had a couple of half chances and one Rhead header that rattled the bar, but for all the possession we had, we didn't ever look like breaking down the Crawley back line. It's pointless pointing to exactly what is wrong too, because every week it seems a different player or approach is at fault.

For what it is worth I thought we looked better with Rheady to aim at, but he does make us much more one-dimensional. With twenty minutes left we brought off both wingers, meaning from a squad of 21 not one of our five wide players were involved in the action. There will have been a plan behind it, but I thought Crawley tired in the final ten and we didn't have any width to expose them. Maybe it was the conditions that made crosses relatively ineffective, but it seemed an odd move to make. The centre of the park looked congested and cramped, suiting Crawley's game-plan of getting a draw more than ours.

There's not an awful lot to analyse is there? Jordan Maguire-Drew had a great free kick on Tuesday night and scored, but the one we got this afternoon we obviously felt was more suited to Neal Eardley's right foot. It wasn't. Then Maguire-Drew went off and Ollie Palmer got his chance to have a go; hopefully that will stop him asking for the ball at every set piece. That said, Palmer was perhaps the most direct of our players after he came on, if we did look dangerous at any point it was from his surging runs down the left flank. He cut a lovely ball back with about ten minutes left that was begging for Matt Green to get on the end of, but he wasn't there. At present Matt Green's running sees him cover every blade of grass bar the blade the ball falls loose on in the eighteen-yard area. That isn't a criticism of Matt, it is just fact.

He had a peach of a volley early doors from a Rheady knock-down and he was pulled down in the second half but tried to stay on his feet and missed out on the penalty. Other than that, he worked tremendously hard, but it just isn't going for him. For an awful moment this afternoon the names of Joe Allon, Tommy Tynan and Leo Fortune-West began to enter my mind. Surely that curse isn't going to strike again, is it?

We're proud of the clean sheet and rightly so, but again I felt we were trying our hardest to create something for them. Usually our back four looks assured and comfortable, not so today. We were solid facing their players but contrived to scare our own fans with suicidal back passes, dodgy headers and clearances. That isn't to say we played badly, just a bit sloppy.

I really don't know what else to write. Danny knows we don't have a route to goal at the moment, the player's body language showed we don't and we're in a situation where some players are just not reaching their levels. Sam was well below his steady seven, Billy was ineffective when he came on and Nathan struggled to get into the game. The front two worked hard but got nowhere,

Ollie did the same when he came on also. I noted Rob Dickie got the MoM award, he played well but I thought either Eardley or Vickers deserved it.

We do miss Harry Anderson but we must not become a one-man team. Our wingers are not getting into games, they're not as effective as last season and we're all the worse for it. That said, we didn't get beaten, we didn't concede and we're still in touching distance of the play-offs. The only frustration is we could be doing better, but there's nothing to be overly concerned about, yet.

As for Crawley, they're a well-oiled unit, they know their jobs and they weren't going to get bullied anywhere on the field. Their centre halves were massive, they made us look like midgets and they approached the game correctly. They came here not to get beat and against a side that put not getting beaten first, as we do, there was only ever going to be one outcome. 8038 fans watched the sort of game that 2500 spent a majority of the 1990's and 2000's avoiding. However, don't let this blog be one to bring you down, nor let it reflect my overall thoughts on where we are as a team.

Imagine this; there's two fans talking to each other. One says his team have lost once in eight games, have kept four clean sheets in seven matches and are three points outside the play offs. The other says his side have failed to win in the last two league matches and have only scored three in the last six league encounters, one of which was an own goal. Both are fair assessments of Lincoln City at present, but one is the glass half-full response and one the glass half-empty. If we were conceding goals and losing games there would be a lot to worry about, but all good teams start solid at the back and build from there. We've conceded twice in the league in October, but only scored three. Apart from last season, Sincil Bank never was a place for thrills and spills, but good honest endeavour will win out. Our players are organised, apply themselves well and work incredibly hard to make things happen. Attitude is so important and we have that even if we're not always as effective as we'd like. If this is our sticky spell, three points off the play-offs and conceding twice in a month in league action, I think we're in a good place.

I'm not trying to gloss over a turgid game of football, it's not the first this month and it won't be the last before Christmas, but football is a game that often flatters to deceive. 2016/17 was a special season but this is the daily grind, this is league football. Even the best of mid-table sides stutter from draw to defeat before stringing a few wins together, it happens. I'm not complacent, I'm not a club stooge trying to say the right things, I'm a realist. We could be rock bottom now, we're not. We could be losing games regularly, we're not. We could look clueless all over the field. We do not. We can't score, fans know it, players know it and Danny knows it. He'll work to find the formula, in the mean time we need to be patient, acknowledge the positives and keep supporting the team as best we can.

I do hope the booing I heard at the final whistle was aimed at the fans perception of the referee, I know he was picky and inconsistent this afternoon and passed over two decent penalty shouts too. If it was aimed at our players in any way then I'd be extremely disappointed. It is prudent to note though that immediately calling those fans plastic is short-sighted. I hate that term anyway, but there's no evidence to say those booing wasn't the same ones boing us off when Keith's side drew as we battled to the play-offs. To claim it is the new or returning fans is a brash assumption and as sensationalist and dividing as a Sun newspaper headline about immigrants and Muslims.

One thing I will say, I was in Running Imp's box today (cheers Chris) and the foot-long hot dog was absolutely superb. In fact, the whole service was exemplary, from the service in the boxes to the quality of food and drink. We might be looking shot shy on the pitch, but we're definitely on target behind the scenes.

I'm not going to fall into the 'we go again' trap, the lads just have to knuckle down and find a formula that works. As for me, I'm going out to watch Dave Mallet's band in Louth, doing my absolutely best to avoid some of the more outlandish criticism that social media is likely to provide tonight. I might be able to absorb the poor match of football I've just seen and still be content, but I just can't have an evening of reading 'Matt Green is crap' or 'we should bring back Jack Muldoon', because I think I'd end up smashing my computer screen.

Brilliant Fans? Now Is the Time to Prove It.

October 30, 2017

The Stacey West – A Season in Blogs 2017/18

Like all football fans, I think my club is special. I'm sure they feel the same at Grimsby, Mansfield or wherever else they happen to have a football club, but I think Lincoln City is a unique place to be. This past eighteen months who could argue?

Having reached the FA Cup Quarter Finals, the FA Trophy Semi-Finals and of course winning the National League, fans came flooding back. This season we're outnumbering every single one of our League Two rivals, something I haven't experienced in my thirty-odd years following Lincoln. The volume of people coming into the Bank is unprecedented, those chants of 'where were you when you were shit', they're jealous chants. It's amusing, we'd sing the same, but Luton Town and Coventry City do not want to average less home fans than Lincoln City.

When things are going well, being a football fan is easy. Last season, even when things didn't go well we had plenty to cheer, Torquay at home was a typical case point, despite going 1-0 down the fans sang their hearts out and fulfilled the 'twelfth man' cliché absolutely. We were top though, we'd seen how much fitter and stronger the lads were and momentum was with us. It's easy to be a football fan when things are going well.

Yeah, we out-sung Burnley, Arsenal and Ipswich, we were the underdogs with nothing to lose, riding a wave of achievement that we never thought possible. When you're used to losing at home to Welling and suddenly you're beating Premier League teams in their own back garden, it is easy to be up at 5am driving across the country. Sure, the noise was deafening and the atmosphere often bettered only by the week after, but unbridled joy motivates you. They say we had the best fans in the non-league last season and I don't doubt it.

With numbers comes a weight of responsibility though and this is the tougher side of being a football fan. You see, sometimes it isn't all rose and sweetness, it isn't all Habergham free-kicks or Nathan Arnold volleys. Sometimes the goals are hard to come by, sometimes the games are less entertaining than the turgid Mrs Brown's Boys. When you enter November struggling for goals it can seem like a grind, those heady days of hammering two or three goals a game are long gone and all that we can see looking forward is 0-0 draws and mid-table obscurity. In my eyes, that is brilliant, mid-table obscurity in League Two is better than top of the National League, and clean sheets are the bedrock upon which great teams are built. However, now is the time that brilliant fans stand up and be counted.

The team is not finding it easy at the moment, certainly not in front of goal. We're in a great position by the way, exceeding what the pundits expected and leaving many to criticise us as being one-dimensional and predictable to cover up their own misplaced pessimism over our chances. The problems we perceive ourselves having are there, but in the grand scheme of things they're not as big as some make them out to be. I know Danny Cowley (pictured top) will sort it out, I know plans are afoot, players are being stalked and our lack of goals is right at the top of the Cowley 'to do' list. Unfortunately, thanks to bizarre Football League rules, we're unable to make significant moves in the transfer market until January 1st, in 61 days' time.

The transfer window is creeping up all the time, when it arrives I have a gut-feeling Lincoln City will be amongst the biggest movers and shakers. Unfounded rumours of deals already being agreed for advanced midfielders and a striker have already reached me. Danny has openly stated he's in net profit for the season, the board have announced there is money to spend and we'll have a club secretary in place alongside a CEO. In January we'll be in a much better position to lure players to the club than we were in pre-season. We might even be able to show them plans and progress on the training ground.

May I be so bold as to say if we're three points outside the top seven when 2018 arrives, I firmly believe we'll be in it come May. The crucial point of the season from the fans perspective is now, our input today, tomorrow and right up until New Year's Eve is absolutely crucial. it saddens me to hear Danny mention getting a slating on social media, to see Neal Eardley believe the booing was aimed at the players and for JMD to react angrily to someone shouting at the referee. Our actions in the stand have an impact on players mentally and I would hate to think some of the mindless negativity reflects on us all.

Now is the time to get right behind the team, travel up and down the country and sing all the way through poor matches. I won't hide from the fact we didn't entertain on Saturday, I did see it described as the 'worst match seen at Sincil Bank for years' though. That made me howl with laughter so much I almost wet myself. A 0-0 Football League draw with Crawley where City hit the bar is worse than watching us lose 3-2 at home to Dover last January, or 1-0 at home to Bromley in October 2015? Come on, get some perspective here. We didn't trouble their goal much but we were resolute, solid and only looked threatened when we made defensive errors. Anyway, this isn't an analysis of the game, it's a rallying cry.

I'm going to Wimbledon on Saturday, usually I'm not one to shout about ticket uptake but we should surely be looking at selling out our 1500 allocation shouldn't we? It would be a tad embarrassing for the club if we negotiate double the amount of tickets expected, only to see half of them unsold, wouldn't it? If transport is a problem three people can get in our minibus, there's a start. The week after against Crewe, why not look into that? I appreciate not everyone can go all the time, I'm not laying into anyone here, but we took 9,000 to Arsenal and 5,000 to Ipswich. If we get a result on Saturday another cup run is a possibility, if you missed out on any of the big games last season then you need to be on board from the get go this time around. If we do progress there will be priority for any big draw at I'd wager attendance of the Wimbledon match will be a must.

Again, I'm not talking down to anyone but we absolutely need to get behind the team now and for the next 60 days at least. Sitting behind a computer screen tapping away about strikers being rubbish or tactics being negative or whatever else is being written at present won't help. We can't sign anyone decent right now, Cameron Stewart was a one-off I'm afraid. The current squad, threadbare as it is, are what we have and they need our support through thick and thin. We've had the euphoria, we've had the Sweet Caroline moments and the dancing in the street. Now we need to show ourselves as fans, we need to stand up and be counted and back the team through the tough spell. If we can emerge having consolidated our current position in January we might be welcoming in the great times again, but we owe it to our football club to stand together for the next two months, loud and proud.

If you're wondering whether to get Wimbledon tickets or indeed Crewe tickets, stop wondering, log into Eventbrite and I'll see you there. We are Imps, and right now the players need our wholehearted support more than ever.

The Stacey West – A Season in Blogs 2017/18

Pos	Team	Pld	W	D	L	GF	GA	GD	Pts
1	Notts County	16	10	3	3	28	16	12	33
2	Accrington Stanley	16	10	2	4	30	19	11	32
3	Luton Town	16	9	4	3	34	15	19	31
4	Exeter City	16	9	3	4	23	18	5	30
5	Swindon Town	16	9	1	6	24	18	6	28
6	Coventry City	16	8	3	5	17	8	9	27
7	Wycombe Wanderers	16	7	6	3	31	25	6	27
8	Newport County	16	7	4	5	23	18	5	25
9	Lincoln City	16	6	6	4	16	14	2	24
10	Cambridge United	16	7	3	6	16	16	0	24
11	Stevenage	16	7	3	6	24	27	-3	24
12	Grimsby Town	16	6	5	5	19	21	-2	23
13	Colchester United	16	6	4	6	23	21	2	22
14	Mansfield Town	16	5	7	4	22	21	1	22
15	Cheltenham Town	16	6	3	7	23	23	0	21
16	Carlisle United	16	5	5	6	22	23	-1	20
17	Yeovil Town	16	5	4	7	24	29	-5	19
18	Crewe Alexandra	16	5	2	9	16	25	-9	17
19	Crawley Town	16	4	4	8	12	16	-4	16
20	Forest Green Rovers	16	4	3	9	16	32	-16	15
21	Barnet	16	3	5	8	19	24	-5	14
22	Port Vale	16	4	2	10	16	23	-7	14
23	Morecambe	16	3	5	8	12	22	-10	14
24	Chesterfield	16	2	3	11	15	31	-16	9

November

Checkatrade Trophy Update
November 1, 2017

#	Team	Pl	W	D	L	F	A	GD	Pts
1	Lincoln City	2	2	0	0	5	2	3	6
2	Mansfield Town	3	2	0	1	4	4	0	6
3	Notts County	2	1	0	1	3	3	0	3
4	Everton U21	3	0	0	3	2	5	-3	0

The penultimate game in our Checkatrade Trophy group took place last night, with Everton U21's (erroneously reported as U23's by Mansfield Town) lost 1-0 at Field Mill.

Steve Evans, the same manager who played down the defeat of his side by City in our group game, hailed the result as an achievement against a very good set of Everton players. It seems winning against Notts County and Everton has reignited his love for the competition.

Anyhow, that means with one game to play we are top of Group F with Notts County set to visit Sincil Bank next Tuesday. Only a sound thrashing at the hands of the Magpies would now see us eliminated.

In fact, for us to be eliminated Notts County would have to beat us by four clear goals. A repeat of the 4-1 defeat at Meadow Lane would wipe out our goal difference, but we'd still qualify ahead of Mansfield Town by virtue of our victory against them. The only team to beat Danny Cowley's side by four clear goals during his tenure are Arsenal.

There wasn't a side that beat Braintree by four clear goals during their tenure either. You have to go back to 20th March 2014 for a Danny Cowley side to be beaten so heavily, Boreham Wood inflicting a 4-0 defeat on Concord Rangers. Rather ironically, Lee Angol played for Boreham Wood that day, a player likely to suffer if Mansfield are eliminated as he plays for Mansfield Reserves at present!

So, City look like they may progress to the next round of the much-maligned trophy, bringing Wembley on step closer. I'm not getting into debate on its merits now, but the lure of finally playing at the home of football is enticing, I imagine if we were to progress further then Danny would begin to slip a few more of his established stars into the side. After all, Michael Bostwick started the Everton game proving Danny s 'in it to win it'.

The last time we got past the first stage of the competition was 2003/04, a first round win against Telford United looked set to give us a cup run of sorts. Francis Green, Marcus Richardson and Mark Bailey scored, either underlining Keith's belief it was a cup worth winning or highlighting our small squad! In the next round we despatched Chesterfield 4-3, but just as we were dreaming of Wembley non-league Halifax beat us 1-0 thanks to a Kevin Sandwith goal. Keith liked what he saw from Sandwith and signed him six months later. Niall McNamara, Richard Liburd and Dene Cropper started that match, maybe suggesting that the league had taken priority!

West Ham youths are proving to be a real handful in their group, six points from two games and on course to reach the next round

The main controversy around the competition this year is the inclusion of top academy sides, but the old adage 'boys against men' has proven to be true with very few of the top-flight sides looking as though they'll progress. In Northern Group B, Middlesbrough are already eliminated, in E West Brom have already gone and both Everton and Sunderland have suffered the same fate. Manchester City, Newcastle, Stoke and Leicester all sit outside the top two in their groups going into the final game.

It is a different picture down south. The West Ham youths are proving to be a real handful in their group, six points from two games and on course to reach the next round. Swansea have already qualified also, they won all three group games against Forest Green, Newport and Cheltenham. Spurs kids are out, Chelsea face an uphill battle to progress and it's in the balance for Fulham, Brighton and Southampton. Even Reading U21's, with one point from two games, could still make the next round.

The trophy's integrity has been brought into question and that debate will rage on (not on these pages though). The big question hangs over whether one of the youth teams will progress to a Wembley final, if that was the case then the competition would lose any shred of dignity it held within the Football League community. However, that looks highly unlikely in the Northern Section.

What price on a Lincoln v West Ham U21's final, with Danny Cowley's West Ham allegiance the main talking point in traditional media? It's entirely possible at this stage.

Just as long as we don't have a ridiculous red card against Notts County that changes the game, I'll be happy.

Raggett: D-Day Approaches

November 3, 2017

I tuned in late to yesterday's press conference, but I'm informed one of the earliest questions was surrounding the immediate position of defender Sean Raggett.

Raggs is on loan from Norwich you'll remember, he signed a deal ahead of the season that saw him return here for until January. With an FA Cup date looming, we're about to get an indication as to Norwich's intentions when it comes to recalling our star defender. Danny was asked if he'd play on Saturday, to which he replied, 'you'll find out at 1.30'. He wasn't being obstinate in any way, why would he reveal an aspect of his line-up ahead of kick off? After all, Raggs delivered in the FA Cup last year, he's a key player and a threat in both boxes.

The permutations are obvious. If he is picked to start tomorrow it is relatively safe to assume that Norwich will be allowing him to stay here for the rest of the season. It isn't nailed on by any means, but the early rounds of the FA Cup can be a chance to blood younger players for a bigger side, look at Brighton last season. Promotion to the Premier League is crucial for Norwich and a cup run can be a distraction.

If he is not allowed to play tomorrow that suggests that Norwich are looking to feature him in the FA Cup themselves and therefore he'll probably be going back there in 2018. It wouldn't be a surprise at all, nor is it certain him missing our cup game means he won't be coming back. Norwich may want to have him back, stick him in the FA Cup 3rd round (depending on their draw) and then send him back to us. They may just want to keep their options open.

This is all well and good, discussing what Norwich want and how it might pan out, but I've heard nobody consider what Raggs wants. Take emotion out of it for a while, just picture the scene. A 23-year old gets the move of a lifetime, the big break that could take his career to the next level, even the level above that. He's worked towards it his whole life but, respectful and appreciative of those that helped him get there, he agrees to give a further six months to his present employer. He gets the odd taste of the high life, trains with the Premier League standard club a couple of times but gives his all to the Fourth Division club who have sold him. Finally, January arrives. What would you want to do? Now, imagine you're not a Lincoln fan, imagine it is your future and your development. What would you want to do now?

The harsh reality is that Sean Raggett is not our player and after agreeing to this six-month stint he doesn't owe us anything either. We're in profit on our transfers, no mean feat considering we've paid out for Michael Bostwick and Harry Anderson. Our defence is one of the best in League Two and it could be argued we've quickly established ourselves as outsiders for the play-offs. We're in a good place, isn't it better for all concerned if we handle this break-up sensibly? Raggs goes off to his new club to start his exciting journey and we bring in a replacement quickly. That way, if we don't make the play-offs, we're not starting next season with one or even two brand new faces at centre half?

I'm not trying to get rid of Sean Raggett, not a chance, if he does decide to stay I'll be delighted, but I can see the benefits for all if he goes back. It'll hurt us in the short-term, but if we do have a small chest to use in January then I'm sure Danny knows of a centre half or two he can pick up for a good price. Rob Dickie looks a real talent, maybe he'll make his move permanent. We've got Luke Waterfall and Michael Bostwick who play there to, another couple of grand might pull a decent defender from the National League, one we own outright.

Ultimately the decision rests with Norwich, but they're currently in 9th place. If they miss out on promotion it might be safer for Raggs to remain here until May, but if they go up to the Premier League, it could have severe repercussions for him. He's likely to break into a Championship side, but without the last six months of this season to impress them, how likely is he to get into a top-flight side?

As Danny said, we'll know much more by about Norwich's intentions by 1.30 tomorrow and whilst exclusion from our FA Cup journey won't mean he's definitely going, it will at least show Norwich are keeping their options open. Whatever happens in January I hope it is the best thing for Sean Raggett because the lad deserves every chance of success.

Plenty to be optimistic about: Wimbledon 1-0 Imps

November 4, 2017

Well, we're out of the FA Cup, no more talk of Burnley, Arsenal or Ipswich. I daren't look at social media first-hand at the moment, I fear it will be full of comments about a lack goals and desperate first round elimination.

I'm in a minibus writing this and I can hear the negative stuff that has been said. Maybe I'm alone, but I'm actually not that gutted. In fact, I'm quite positive.

This afternoon we matched a League One side for eighty minutes and once Matt Rhead came on we looked dangerous. The facts don't lie, we didn't score a goal, but I felt for the first time in several games we actually might.

I'll start with the obvious negative, their goal. It was atrocious defending, the sort of slip you cannot make against the likes of Lyle Taylor. He finished with aplomb and for a few moments everything felt very negative. 1-0 down at Wimbledon after seven minutes with both Taylor and Cody McDonald looking dangerous as anything. I feared a ride home full of despondency and disappointment.

Then, we started to play. It wasn't scintillating, it wasn't penetrating, but it was us giving it a good go. Michael Bostwick, the undoubted man of the match, bossed the midfield. Nathan looked dangerous when we did get him on the ball. We had two chances, perhaps half chances, but we looked as though we might claw our way back into the game.

Yes, we were toothless when it dropped in the final third, but the other two thirds of the pitch belonged to us. At half time most of the people around me identified the problem and they all agreed on what it was.

Ollie Palmer and Matt Green play virtually independent of each other. Green was often asked to track back and help defend whilst Palmer wandered around up front looking to win headers against defenders considerably shorter than him. More often than not, he failed.

Also, Billy Knott couldn't get into the game. Since his dismissal at Meadow Lane he hasn't captured his early season promise, despite his desperation to do well. We huffed, we puffed but we didn't blow their defence down. After Lyle Taylor went off, they stopped knocking on our door too.

The second half was completely different, we came out full of purpose and energy, looking for the opening that might get us back into the game. Sean Long and Neal Eardley pushed on well, Wimbledon began to sit off us and it looked as though the chances might come.

The golden opportunity fell to Billy Knott and unfortunately he fluffed his lines. Their keeper, dodgy at the best of times, found himself in no-man's land. He came onto the ball with a gaping goal, a Billy full of confidence would have buried it. Instead, he took a touch, slipped and the chance was gone. It felt as though that was it, that was our one opportunity to get back into the game. It was the best chance we had, but not the last.

Everything changed when the big man came on. Rheady has something more than the average player, he has a presence and attitude that sparks belief. From the moment he entered the fray we looked as though we might get a goal.

He dropped into the hole allowing Matt Green to get forward and in doing so we suddenly looked to have a viable route to goal. It resulted in a shot on target for Green, not the goal we needed but a chance to get ahead. Green was then hauled down in the box, a clear penalty all day long but one that wasn't given. Maybe he should have gone down quicker, maybe he is too honest, but for whatever reason it wasn't given. Again, there was another chance.

I felt we remained undeterred, stoic in our method and invigorated with the arrival of Rhead. If we could deliver a decent corner into the box we might have bagged a goal or two, but it wasn't to be. Despite dominating the second half, genuinely controlling the play in my eyes, we couldn't find the breakthrough. However, I didn't feel it was just 'more of the same' from the Crawley game. We created half-chances and more than matched a League One side.

I had to address the negativity I know is circulating on social media. Remember, Lincoln City has never really been about FA Cup quarter finals, it's barely been about second round matches in my time. Usually a draw pitching us away at a League One club would result in gutless elimination, no brave battle and no matching them all over the park. Okay, the outcome is ultimately the same, but it is difficult to be too down-hearted after our display.

Yes, there is work to do. Yes, we need to start scoring, but unlike last Saturday I felt we created a couple of chances and gave Wimbledon a scare. It's on to Crewe next weekend where a performance similar to today will see us grab all three points. I just hope Danny gets the team sheet out now, right now, and writes the name 'Matt Rhead' next to 'Matt Green', because we look far better with the big man on than not.

City Progress In FLT: Imps 2-1 Notts County

November 8, 2017

It took a Josh Ginnelly wonder-goal to separate the two sides in an engrossing but low-key affair at Sincil Bank, but the real benefits may not be evident until the lads run out on Saturday.

The Checkatrade Trophy has proved a divisive competition and last night's game was relatively well-attended but lacking severely in atmosphere. Despite this, one or two players managed to put in eye-catching performances whilst one or two others might be running out of lives when it comes to first team selection.

A crowd of just over 3,000 was good compared to other teams but poor when looked at in context of our usual attendances. It was a wet, drizzly night though, with little at stake. Only a 4-0 defeat would have seen City eliminated, whereas Notts County had to win in order to progress. A draw would have brought a penalty shoot-out, the least important that has ever involved City. Had it gone to penalties it wouldn't have mattered who won or lost, City would have gone through. Luckily we were spared that ridiculous scenario.

County opened the scoring with a really poor goal from City's point of view. Ollie Palmer 'won' a header which actually landed at the feet of a County player. He played a simple ball through to Jonathon Forte who charged through on Vickers, rounded him easily and slotted the ball home. It wasn't a fair reflection of play, City had retained possession well up until then, but it won't surprise anyone to know we hadn't really threatened the goal.

I don't think I'm being unfair when I describe a majority of the remaining first-half minutes as turgid. The game had a 'friendly' feel to it and although both sides clearly wanted to win, it lacked the ferocity and intensity of a league match. Elliott Whitehouse did stand out though, he was energetic and eager to get on the ball in the middle of the park. He needed a big performance, his is certainly a fringe player and in order to change that status he has to take his chances. Thus far this season he hasn't managed to do that, but he did catch the eye in a relatively dour first half.

Cameron Stewart got his first start for City and he looked rusty but promising. On the other flank Josh Ginnelly was full of running also, but often the ball didn't find its way out to the flanks. Nine minutes after County took the lead it was a foul out wide on Josh that gave us a route back into the game.

The resulting free-kick was whipped in by Stewart and the unfortunate Pierce Bird turned it in with Ollie Palmer lurking behind him. Whether we would have got a significant touch is another issue, we have been a little shot-shy, but a goal is a goal no matter how it goes in. The cross was excellent and if that is a brief glimpse of what Cameron Stewart can do then we may have found ourselves another diamond.

1-1 seemed a fair score at half time and whilst the players went in for a chat and a biscuit with Danny, I was left in block seven surveying the scene. I've never been in the home of the 617 on a match day, I got my ticket there out of curiosity rather than anything. Predictably it was full of wannabe kids who really should have been at home with their parents. The youngest must have been seven or eight, clambering over seats and leading chants. It was amusing at first, but at half time it began to get tiresome, especially as the older lads with them (12-14 maybe) were more interested in throwing hats and messing about. Stewards had to chat to them on numerous occasions, even when they clearly broke a seat and started messing with the 617 banner, they still got a telling off. I understand it is a 'damned if you do, damned if you don't' situation for the stewards, but they ended up really getting on my wick.

To top it off a shady group of track-suited sorts behind us were clearly smoking too. I'm not a prude or anything but it just hacked me off because I knew I wouldn't have the balls to spark one up and I really wanted a cigar.

In the second half luckily the game improved which distracted me from the kids for a while. Their antics gradually got worse until I was convinced they didn't even realise there was a match on, they seemed happier just climbing over seats, throwing caps into the lower tier and generally being little bastards. Frankly, I'd be ashamed if they were my kids. I told my mate Dave that too, only to discover their 'guardians' were sat behind us, probably smoking.

Anyway, City came back out with a purpose and intent as Danny always says. It looked as if the formation altered slightly, Billy dropped back alongside Alex Woodyard leaving Elliott as the tip of the midfield. Elliott was constantly on the ball, looking to create something. Neal Eardley was getting forward too, he had another excellent game. I'm convinced if he really wanted to, he could play on the wing He made their full-back look a mug on more than one occasion and delivered some great balls into the six-yard area.

Up front we had Ollie Palmer. I'm beginning to think I might be looking for the negative stuff with Ollie, but I just didn't see what he brought to the game. Aside from his partial assist of their goal he looked lost, barely winning a header at all. When he did win one it went askew, anywhere but an area where a red shirt waited. When the ball came into his feet he lost it, when the crosses came in he was always behind the first defender and (in my opinion) he offered very little threat at all. My fear is I'm deliberately not seeing what he contributes because I've conditioned myself not to like him as a player.

One moment summed up two player's fortunes in one brief move. Ollie found a ball at his feet about ten yards out, but he couldn't get anything decent on it and scuffed a weak effort into a defender who cleared. It fell to Billy Knott on the edge of the area and he smashed a first time shot that looked as though it had been hit with a cricket bat. It sailed wide, closer to the corner flag than the keeper. Two players low on confidence, two players I'd be surprised to see amongst the starting eleven on Saturday.

Despite this we controlled much of the play in the second half, County offered very little even after Jorge Grant came on. Grant had their only real effort of the second half though, Josh

Vickers forced to make a good save to keep the score at 1-1. Harry Anderson came on for City, getting one of the loudest cheers of the evening. Everyone knows Harry is a cracking player, one that we've missed in recent weeks and it was great to see him back on the pitch.

City were working the flanks really well and getting plenty of balls into the area, something we haven't been doing much recently. The wide players were right in the game, the full backs both overlapped and did their bit too. Sean Long loves to bomb forward and he crossed for Palmer but the striker couldn't get on the end of the cross.

With five minutes left on the clock it was time for Billy to make a telling contribution. He launched a great ball into the area for Raggs who rose high and headed at goal, only to see his effort skim the crossbar. It roused the crowd though; the players had been pouring forward and a goal seemed only a matter of minutes away. First though, young Ellis Chapman came on for his second appearance.

When the winning goal came it was a 'I was there' moment. The FLT has thrown a couple of those up now, Jordan Maguire-Drew's free kick against Everton was special, but Josh's strike was even better. After a couple of neat passes on the left flank it looked as though we were building for a cross. Josh cut inside and glanced up, a good twenty-two yards out on the angle. Instead of the predictable cross he curled an absolute peach of an effort over the keeper and into the net. It was a demonstration of his latent talent, a sighting of the potential he possesses to pull off the spectacular. He didn't seem to want to celebrate particularly, but the crowd certainly did. It had been 333 minutes since a City player last scored a goal, Maguire Drew's free-kick against Everton after 23 minutes the last one we'd witnessed. I'd say it was almost worth the wait.

In the final minutes a late County effort could have unfairly levelled things, but Josh Vickers again produced a fine save to earn us the victory. From a staunch Paul Farman fan such as myself this is tough to say, but Josh Vickers is an excellent keeper and has earned the right to remain our first-choice number one.

The game ended 2-1, we go through whilst County are eliminated and their fans will, of course, say they don't care. 178 of them cared enough to make the journey, but it is an easy way out of elimination to say you weren't bothered. Sure, many might not be but winning is a habit and we need to rediscover that habit.

I had a brief chat with Alex Woodyard after the game, he said it was a game to take confidence and build upon. That's exactly what it is, we've got a couple of goals in the bag, we've produced another decent performance which was the case on Saturday and we're finding a route to goal. We looked dangerous from out wide and with Matt Green in the area on the end of crosses I'm sure we'll start scoring in the league again soon. Low-key it might have been, but you tell that to Josh, Elliott, Ellis or even Sean Long. These are players that maybe needed to catch the eye or just wanted some time on the pitch. The politics of the FLT Trophy are one thing, but ninety minutes on a football pitch is bread and butter for the players and they've taken a big step this evening in grabbing two goals.

I feel I have to comment on the conduct of people prior to the game on the topic of boycotting. Those who choose to do so were not vocal at all, I didn't see any of them baiting people, criticising those going to the game or pushing their agenda at all. Unfortunately, the same couldn't be said for some in attendance who are still intent on trying to provoke a response. Now we're progressing I expect more snide comments about 'bet you'll go to Wembley' and the like, aimed at the boycotters. They won't, that is a fact.

We switch our attention to Saturday now, Crewe away which is a traditional eighties fixture but one that hasn't been played much in recent years. Gresty Road is a classic old ground, they're a decent side and we're 277 minutes without a league goal. However, if we can expose the flanks as we did tonight then we'll have ample opportunity to put that right and, if all else is failing, we can only hope that Josh Ginnelly has got a taste for the extraordinary and can produce it on command!

Crewe Alexandra: We meet again, old friend.

November 10, 2017

Those with enough years of supporting City behind them will be familiar with Crewe Alexandra. Whilst the last decade or two our paths have only crossed briefly, before the Dario Gradi revolution Crewe were struggling Fourth Division side, much like ourselves. We met them more often than not, swapping hammerings but never escaping each other's attentions for long.

We did play them during our last season in the Football League, Paul Green struck in the 47th minute of our April clash in a game we needed to win to assure safety. Clayton Donaldson shattered our survival hopes with a late penalty, but I remember feeling positive that we were one point closer to survival. It was the last point we were to win in the Football League for more than six years.

As a child Crewe were, in my mind, the whipping boys. They were the Joker to Lincoln City's Batman, the Tom to our Jerry. The first time I saw them play was the FA Cup First Round in 1987, us a GMVC side and them in the Football League. We won 2-0, John McGinley and Bob Cumming giving us a two-goal lead. They pulled one back in the 87th minute but we progressed on a historic day. The St Andrews Stand, now the Selenity Stand, was open to supporters for the first time. Sincil Bank as we know it had started to take shape and Crewe had simply played their role. I barely noted their midfielder David Platt, although three years later both Dad and I were cheering as he volleyed past Prued'homme in the Belgium goal to push us forward in Italia '90.

I already had them down as an easy team to beat though. In 1986 I had been given a copy of the 1985 Football League Yearbook, and I studied it religiously until it was well out of date. I was fascinated by the record wins of various teams, and after reading we had beaten Crewe 11-1 I scoured the pages to find other teams that had hammered them. Spurs record win is also against Crewe, 13-2 in the FA Cup. When I looked at Crewe and saw their record win was a measly 8-0, I was convinced they would never beat us.

That 11-1 win for City was remarkable at the time. One can be fooled into thinking hammerings of that nature were common place, but that isn't entirely true. On the same day as our record goal haul, Mansfield Town beat Bradford Park Avenue 1-0, Grimsby won 2-1 at Carlisle and Liverpool won 2-0 at home to Derby. Okay, Wolves won 7-1 at Huddersfield but these results were not the norm, certainly not double figure thrashings. Andy Graver scored six that day and was called up to the England B squad at the end of the season, a remarkable achievement for a Division Three North player. Injury kept him out of the game, but it was still a real feather in his cap. You can read more on our record win here, if it tickles your fancy.

I fully expected to be revelling in the glory of Lincoln City winning as my 12th birthday approached. Saturday 17th November 1990 was once again FA Cup First Round day, and Crewe were the hopefully hapless visitors. They'd been promoted to the division above but I still felt a win was on the cards, after all this was Crewe Alexandra. I sat in the St Andrews Stand for the very first time, eager to have my last pre-teen birthday anointed with the regulation whipping of the Railwaymen.

Midfielder Aaron Callaghan gave them an early lead, but my hero 'Stormer Lormor' grabbed a 33rd minute equaliser to send us in level at the break. Allan Clarke was in charge at the time, but not for much longer. An awful second half, devoid of any direction, saw City hammered 4-1. Mark Gardiner, David McKearney and Scott Ward wrapped up the win for them. Clarke was sacked not long afterwards. Crewe had future England right-back Rob Jones playing for them, Craig Hignett, Neil Lennon on the bench and Kenny Swain at centre half.

Allan Clarke, who signed Phil Stant on loan just days later without having seen him play, said "We played as well as a Third Division side in the first half, we conceded two bad goals after which we were unable to get back and our performance deteriorated." He's not wrong, I didn't get a City shirt for my birthday and after watching that I was delighted.

We've only met five further times since 1994, drawing all four league games and winning our 2005 League Cup tie 5-1. Maheta Molango scored for the Imps that evening, as did Gary Birch, Marvin Robinson and Lee Beevers. Crewe, then a Championship side, took their keeper off at half time with City 2-0 up. That worked well for them. We did play them in a friendly, one of the first under Danny Cowley, where Jack Muldoon grabbed a goal (pictured above). Friendlies don't really count though, do they?

It isn't a great time to be a Crewe fan at the moment, they're struggling in 18th place. They've won just three in the last thirteen competitive games, losing ten of those. A fine FA Cup win over Rotherham was immediately let down by a 4-2 defeat at the hands of Port Vale.

Jordan Bowery, son of former Imps player Bert, has been one positive for them though, he grabbed a 90th minute winner against Stevenage amongst other strikes. Chris Porter and Chris Dagnall have also been amongst the goals, but a fragile defence has been their Achilles heel. It will need to be though, the shot-shy Imps have scored as many in a month as Crewe have in the last 180 minutes of football.

In an unusual turn of events, your truly is heading to a second consecutive away match, something rarely seen. Hopefully the 12-year old in me will see some sort of justice served for his ruined birthday, something that has burned long and hard for many years.

World War One Imps
November 11, 2017

Remembrance Day may have been and gone, but the time to honour our fallen heroes isn't restricted to one day or one year. I'd been working on an article covering the Lincoln City players we lost in the First World War and today I found a site that had an extensive list.

For nothing more than to remember their sacrifice almost a century later, here are the Imps that fell in the First World War.

Arthur Hulme

Arthur Hulme, often erroneously referred to as Joseph, started his career at City in 1897. City were a Division Two side and Hulme had a keen eye for goal. He scored 12 times in 29 games. He missed just one match as City finished 14th from 16. He scored as we beat Luton 4-2 at Sincil Bank, only to score again 12 days later as they hammered us 9-3 at Kenilworth Road. He scored a brace as we beat Burton Swifts 3-0 and grabbed his final goal in a fine 2-1 win against third placed Manchester City.

Despite playing regularly, Hulme was released at the end of the season to join Gravesend along with Imps goalkeeper William Wilkinson. Their time at Gravesend was not a success, it is reported that the club's committee was keen to dispense with the services of "the men with drinking reputations, who proved such failures last season". There is no indication at all that Hulme was a drinker.

He ended up at Brighton where he became something of a star, making 159 appearances over the course of seven seasons. He contributed to them reaching the last 32 of the 1905/06 FA Cup and helped them rise to the First Division. In recognition of his five years' service to the club, he became the first Brighton player to be awarded a benefit match, a Western League fixture against Southampton.

Upon leaving Brighton he returned to his native Leek where he was trainer of local team Leek United. Corporal G/4581 Hulme enlisted in the Royal Sussex Regiment. He was serving as a corporal in the 7th Battalion at the time of his death in action in October 1916 at Gueudecourt, in the Somme department of France

Thomas Asnip

Thomas Asnip made just one appearance for City, in 1904/05 he played away at Manchester United as we lost 2-0. He was a local lad, recruited from the Lincoln League after representing St Catherines and later Adelaide Park.

He was a Lance Sergeant in the North Staffordshire regiment and was also killed in action at Flanders. He died on 24th July 1918.

James Comrie

James 'Jimmy' Comrie made just 12 appearances for City, scoring once. He began his career at Third Lanark, appearing in a Scottish Cup final in consecutive seasons. He later moved to Reading and garnered a reputation for turning up late or even missing training. He was obviously a talented player though, given the number of appearances he made for the Royals. After a spell at Glossop, a 'substantial' sum was splashed out by Bradford City for his services. He left Valley Parade for City in November 1910.

The move wasn't a success. The 1910/11 side struggled against relegation, a fight they ultimately lost. Comrie scored once, earning us our final win of a dismal season, 1-0 away at Birmingham City. He made only 12 appearances for the Imps in total, a part-time player who worked as an attendant at Bracebridge Asylum. He was placed on the transfer list for £100 at the end of the season, a sum that got reduced to £20 on appeal.

After leaving City he worked as Assistant Manager at Boston Swifts, before joining the army. Private 4064 Comrie enlisted in the 1/7th Battalion of the Northumberland Fusiliers, a territorial unit that had crossed the English Channel to France on 20 April 1915 aboard SS Invicta.

On 3 August 1916, the battalion moved to relieve the 1/6th Northumberland Fusiliers on the front line. On 4th August, the enemy opened fire on their positions with trench mortars. Fire was exchanged throughout the next two days, until the Northumberlands were relieved by the Royal Irish Rifles. The battalion war diary reported one killed and three wounded during their two-day stint in the front line.

Comrie is listed has having died on 9th August 1916, although that may not be entirely accurate. It is possible he was one of the three reported wounded who died as a result of those wounds, or he may have been the soldier reported killed during the two days in the trenches. Sadly, we will probably never know as he has no known grave.

George Kennedy

George Kennedy appeared for Lincoln 42 times over two seasons having arrived from Maxwelltown Volunteers of the Dumfries area. Turn of the century Lincoln City erred towards players from north of the border, perhaps due to the influence of manager David Calderhead. He played 25 times in 1906/07 as City finished second from bottom of Division Two, although he did feature in the FA Cup 1st Round win against Chelsea. The following season injury ruled him out of the early season exchanges, by the time he returned City were already doomed. The Imps finished bottom and were relegated to the Midland League, Kennedy left with Calderhead for top-flight Chelsea.

He only went on to make 12 appearances for the London club, including a couple in the FA Cup. In 1910, he left Stamford Bridge and signed for Southern League side Brentford, where he would spend the following three seasons. He returned to Scotland in 1913 and spent time back home in Dumfries before emigrated to Canada in June 1914.

Private 418239 Kennedy enlisted in the 42nd Battalion (Royal Highland Regiment) of the Canadian Infantry in March 1915. He was sent to France with the Canadian Expeditionary Force where he won both the Military Medal (MM) and Distinguished Conduct Medal (DCM) for gallantry. He rose to the rank of Company Sergeant Major but was seriously wounded during the Third Battle of Ypres. He died from his injuries just over 100 years ago on 16 November 1917 and is buried at Lijssenthoek Military Cemetery, located 12km west of Ypres.

Peter Mackin

Peter Mackin, often referred to as 'Machin' in contemporary press, was another of David Calderhead's recruits. He joined from Wallsend Park Villa is May 1905 and played one season in the same team as George Kennedy.

He opened his account with City on the opening day of the 1905/06 season with a goal against Burslem Port Vale as we ran out 3-1 winners. After a slow start he found real form at the turn of the year, scoring a brace as we thrashed Burnley 5-0 and again a fortnight later as Burton United we despatched 5-1. His penchant for grabbing goal in big wins continued with a hat trick as Bradford City were beaten 5-0 at the Bank. In our penultimate home game of the season he scored twice as Manchester United beat us 3-2. We finished the season in 13th place, Bristol City, Man Utd and Chelsea making up the top 3. He scored 16 times from 33 outings.

Injury restricted him to just five goals from 21 outings the following season, two against Clapham Orient in March 1907 seeing us win 3-0. They were his final goals for City as we finished second from bottom. Machin returned to his native north-east and joined Sunderland.

Private 201049 Mackin of Northumberland Fusiliers was killed in action in Flanders on April 9th, 1917. He is buried in the Roclincourt Military Cemetery in Northern France.

William Morris

William Morris does not often appear on lists of fallen heroes who represented City as he featured only in the Midland League campaign of 1908/09. It was a season glossed over in paragraphs in Brian Halford's book and Morris represents nothing more than a footnote in the Nannestad's A-Z as a player that didn't play a League game for us.

What Morris did manage was an FA Cup tie at Liverpool, a game we lost 5-1 on January 16th, 1909. Morris scored our only goal of the game, one of 13 he bagged in 18 outings. His other matches were less than illustrious, a brace beating Denaby United 3-2, as well as goals against Bradford City reserves and Sheffield United reserves. We also contested the United Counties League Northern Division where, on April 9th, 1909, he scored twice to beat Coventry City 4-0 at Sincil Bank.

In the summer of 1909 Morris moved to Liverpool, probably on the strength of his goal against them. His career never took off though and he eventually returned to Arnold in Notts to marry Maud, where they lived at 140 Front Street.

On September 21st, 1918, Ordinary Seaman Morris was killed in action aboard the S.S Polesley. The Polesley was torpedoed and sunk by UB 88, 1-mile North of Pendeen, Cornwall. It was torpedoed without warning and sunk with 43 lives lost. She was en route from Cardiff to France with a cargo of coal.

Thomas Strong

Thomas Phillips Strong, also known as Tommy, was mostly a reserve at Sincil Bank. He spent three years with the club, appearing twice in 1913/14 and seven times the following season. He was a left-sided full back who played away at Arsenal in a 1-1 draw but never appeared on a winning league side. His last outing was April 3rd, 1915 against Grimsby Town, a game we lost 5-1.

Private 31770 Strong joined the South Staffordshire Regiment 1st Battalion but died on 15th July 1917 of injuries sustained at Flanders. He is buried at Croisilles Railway Cemetery.

May we always remember them and their sacrifice, always.

Revenge for 1990: Crewe 1-4 Imps
November 12, 2017

I wrote on Friday about how Crewe Alexandra ruined my 12th birthday by turning City over 4-1 at Sincil Bank. Yesterday, on a cold and windy day at Gresty Road, Lincoln returned the favour, ensuring my 39th birthday this coming weekend will not be ruined by the Railwaymen.

I've been told I can't use the cliché 'a game of two halves' in this blog, so I won't. However, in the first half we were (for want of a better word) lacklustre. Crewe grabbed an early lead, a weak goal from our point of view, an easy header from a set piece. That was bread and butter to us last season, but they cut through our defence easily to grab the early advantage. After that all I can really say positive is that we didn't concede again.

Crewe were poor too, the spectacle served up in those first 45 minutes barely warranted the title of 'football match'. Bostwick aside, we were out muscled, but neither side looked capable of scoring a goal. On the terraces, it was Lincoln City with a massive advantage though. Our 990 fans were in tremendous voice, barely stopping to catch breath from half an hour before kick-off. Contrast that with a sparsely populated main stand and an incessant drumming that rarely got accompanied by any home support. 'You're supposed to be at home' had never seemed so apt and in the second half, following a brief cheer from Crewe for something, they were hit with 'we forgot that you were here'. I had almost forgotten they were there such was the silence from the home support. Even at 1-0 down, we out sang them. I think we sang louder when they scored than they celebrated. If title were handed out for quality of support, we'd already be in League One.

Half-time was a somewhat sombre affair behind the away stand, not least because they'd run out of cheeseburgers and I had a barely-steak pie instead. I even made one of those dangerous half-time social media posts lamenting our side's ineffective performance. I claimed only one or two of our lads looked like they wanted it, and I stand by that. To say we were poor might be harsh, we controlled much of the possession in the first two-thirds of the pitch, but we had nothing up front, no threat, no fire and no sharpness. I had a brief discussion with a chap called Phil and his better half Rachel (I hope) who asked for a sneaky mention in my blog today. I don't usually do requests, but I'm in a good mood. I wasn't after 45 minutes though as it looked like being Wimbledon all over again, lots of possession, lots of play but no route to goal. I'm glad I made that post on Facebook because I love nothing more than being proven wrong by my team handing out a resounding thrashing.

The players had been out for around thirty seconds when it became apparent we were going to be in for something very different. Elliott strode onto the ball and looked up and instantly everything seemed to fall into place. We'd forced a corner within a minute, pouring forward from every angle against a Crewe side that looked like a pheasant caught in the cross hairs of a farmer's shotgun. Five minutes in we pulled level, finally a league goal scored by one of our own players, something of a rarity before the game. 237 minutes after Sean Raggett headed home against Swindon, Harry Anderson cut inside from the right and fired a low shot beyond Dave Richards. The away end erupted and from that moment on, only one team was going to get anything from the game.

All over the park home heads dropped, the same happened in the stands. The drummer tried to rally them as soon as the goal went in, but to no avail. You wouldn't have heard him anyway as the Dambusters rang out across the Railwaymen's home. Air beats rail, every time.

City continued to hunt Crewe down, Harry looked dangerous every time he got on the ball. He's not just a good player, he has the potential to be a great player, his raw pace combined with that bullish strength had their full back terrified. Add to that our eager full backs on the overlap and the threat was multiplied further. Sean Long, decent in the first half, raided the flank time and again. I have a suspicion Sam Habergham might have a fight on his hands getting back into the side, because at the moment I think Neal Eardley and Sean are the in-form pairing.

Elliott Whitehouse got much more joy in the second half too. Elliott is a darling of the crowd, the unassuming Yorkshire lad with the odd goal up his sleeve is easy to like. If only he'd stop wearing gloves, or at least make up some excuse about poor circulation! In the first half he struggled to have an effect on the game, but as Crewe became stretched he found time and space to make a telling contribution. It was Elliott and Sean that linked up to provide Harry with our first goal, not the last time they combined on the afternoon either.

When the second came on 67 minutes, it was no surprise it was Harry again. A whipped corner was headed goalward by Sean Raggett and despite being cleared off the line, Harry was on hand to hook the ball home. With 23 minutes left on the clock, the home end emptied. City fans didn't know whether to celebrate the goal or berate the poor home support for abandoning their side so easily. They knew there was no way back, they'd been twice as bad in the second half as we were in the first, they offered absolutely nothing at all.

Lincoln were looking ruthless by now, desperate to slam in some more goals to shake the tag of 'goal shy' and it took just three minutes. Woodyard nodded a ball to Whitehouse, he found Sean Long on the overlap yet again and his teasing cross was turned in by the hapless Michael Raynes. He'd given his side the 1-0 lead, but his next effort at goal ensured even more home fans poured out of the ground. Someone at the side of me joked that they gave the attendance early because with 20 minutes to go it had halved, he wasn't far wrong. Crewe had the look of a beaten side when they were 1-0 up, now they just looked ragged, eleven men on a field, strangers to each other and completely separated from the crowd. The last time I witnessed such separation between home support and their team was Ipswich in the FA Cup.

Anderson looked to pick up a knock and I'm sure Danny took him off as a precaution. He's vital to everything we do, without him in the side we lack the link between the midfield and forwards. However, Elliott Whitehouse's performance must also be lauded as he too provided that link, at least in the second half. When Harry went off it was Luke Waterfall who came on giving us five at the back. Danny was happy at 3-1, so were the fans. Elliott Whitehouse wanted more.

Alex Woodyard was the provider with a simply delicious pass that split the defence open like an axe through a log. Woody is such a good player when he strides forward, I'd love to see him more advanced as he has a unique skill set that I think is often underutilised. The work he does in front of the defence is terrific, but when he roams forward and plays the ball forward you get glimpses of something else, something more than the guy that does the dirty work. His pass was reminiscent of Adam Marriott in the FA Cup replay last year, threaded through the eye of a needle with precision. Elliott made the run that complimented the ball too, striding alone into the area and giving us a deserved fourth goal. In the away end, Christmas had come early. It took us over 600 minutes to score our previous four league goals, but we'd bagged four in twenty to wrap up the game. As we left, not one person mentioned the awful first half, football is a game played over 90 minutes and only the cynics and sceptics will point to that as a worrying sign.

Also, nobody could criticise the players efforts or endeavour in the second half. Even Ollie Palmer, berated by me extensively in the run up to the game, got an ovation and his own song, 'We've got Ollie Palmer, he can't win a header. we've got him on a two-year deal', might not be the most complimentary song, but at least it is some sort of recognition.

There's no doubt Harry Anderson and Elliott Whitehouse will win praise for their efforts, but Sean Long's performance must not be allowed to pass by without a tip of the hat. I thought he was excellent, one of the few that did it from first minute to last. He slipped under the radar when he signed, he's an understated player often in the shadow of others (Bradley Wood, Eardley etc) but he grows in confidence and stature with every kick. He's clearly enjoying having the experience of Neal Eardley in the side too, he's benefiting more than anyone from the former Premier League man's presence.

It wouldn't be my blog without praise for Alex Woodyard and Michael Bostwick either. I know there's some discussion as to whether we're too negative in the current set up, but those two are immense. If you recall, I said we controlled the first two-thirds of the pitch even when we weren't playing well, they're the reason why. I challenge anyone who reads this to tell me of a better midfield pairing in this division; there isn't one. Bozzie is a monster, aggressive and intimidating with presence and a fearless approach to the game. Alex is more of a thinking man's footballer, tenacious and cunning, utilising his wits and endeavour over physicality. They make a great pair, they're as much to thanks for our great defensive record as the actual defence too. I've heard calls for Bozzie to drop into centre half when Raggs goes, but I'm a big fan of him in that holding role. What we need to do is find plenty of routes to goal without separating those two.

Am I convinced of Ollie Palmer? I'm afraid not. He's quick, big and runs at defenders which scares them, but when those defenders realise he isn't running anywhere in particular and he can't win a header, the threat diminishes. He had a decent second half, but he just didn't do it for me in the first period. Josh Ginnelly didn't have a great first half either, but we know there's more to come from Josh. He had an electric start to the season but that injury has set him back a few weeks. I'm not saying anyone played badly in the second half, we were excellent, but there's always something to take from the match. I wonder if next weekend against Coventry it might be Matt Green ahead of Elliott.

Whatever happens, nobody can take away a fine 4-1 win over Crewe. I've carried the nightmare of that 1990 FA Cup defeat for too long, watching a slick and organised Crewe batter Allan Clarke's City with a second half salvo that we had no answer for. This Saturday, we did the same to them and for ninety minutes I forgot about my crumbling spine to enjoy every second of it. I'm paying for it now, but I don't care. City won 4-1 away, we're eighth in the table, level with Coventry in sixth and as yet, we're nowhere near our best.

I'd like to pay tribute to the Crewe stewards and staff whom I thought were superb. When we arrived, we got advice on pubs, the bouncers and police were friendly and helpful throughout and overall they were incredibly gracious. There are plenty of horror stories about Cheltenham stewards and bad service, Crewe are an example of how it should be done. They're a team on a downward spiral, that much is for sure, but off the field they're a very decent group of people and I respect that.

I won't be mentioning too much about the racist incident I witnessed, it's a shame that individuals amongst our own support still find that sort of behaviour acceptable. The world has moved on a lot since the early 1980's, barracking of players because of their colour are nationality is simply not okay.

Anyway, if our recruitment in January is as good as I think it'll be, we're going to be around the top seven come May. I might have to get my surgeon to put my operation back a few weeks as I'm currently due under the knife the day before we play Yeovil on the final day. If we get to Wembley, I'm going, even if I have to be carried there upright shrink-wrapped to a plywood board. On our second half form, I wouldn't bet against it.

Freck: Another rumour does the rounds
November 13, 2017

The benefit of being a so-called indie writer rather than an official reporter is the ability for me to float rumours that are circulating for discussion. Traditional media are very tied by the reporting of facts (or not in some cases) but being in my position does allow a certain freedom in writing that perhaps the Echo cannot have.

One thing I keep hearing again and again is the news that one of our January deals has already been done and tied up. This isn't 'inside information' in any way, if I knew for certain ironically I wouldn't break the club's confidence! However, the terraces are alight with the potential for a club favourite to finish his career in red and white.

I suspect there's several reasons for this. To my knowledge, his Millers contract is up at the end of the season. He signed a two-year contract in July 2016 meaning once this season is complete, he is a free agent. At 32-years old he's probably looking for one final move, one last switch to wind down his playing career and build for the next step of his life. Given his family's strong football tradition I wouldn't put it past him looking to move into coaching and management either.

Then there is his recent move back to the city. He spoke to the Echo prior to our Carabao Cup clash earlier in the season, telling how he'd recently moved back to Lincoln and how he loved the buzz around the club. Ever since he was 11-years old he wanted to play for Lincoln, his idol (quite rightly) was Peter Gain and he just wanted to break into the side. There's a degree of unfinished business here also, he told Mark Whiley he was 'disappointed' with how his Imps career ended as Peter Jackson seemed to prefer Stefan Oakes to him. He moved to a side top of League One, Oakes ended up leaving a season before we were relegated.

Some of the more astute Imps fans have also noted he hasn't played since October 7th, not long after smashing a hat trick past Walsall. He hasn't been dropped, as club captain it was unlikely anyway, but he has picked up an injury. He was withdrawn from the Miller's 1-0 win at Rochdale after just four minutes. At the time Paul Warne played the injury down, telling his local media: "I initially thought he was out for six weeks. I thought he had ripped his hammy, but the physio thought it was more aligned with his back. He has been scanned and he has got slight hamstring damage, but it's hardly anything. He has had his back treated, so hopefully he can be involved this weekend. It might be too soon, but we are evaluating it on a daily basis. He has come on in leaps and bounds."

That was on October 12th and now initial fears he could be out until December seem well-founded.

Lee Frecklington was born in Lincoln, and to some extent born to play for Lincoln as well. He made his way through our Centre of Excellence and was rewarded with a scholarship place in the summer of 2002. Under John Schofield, Frecklington's ability developed and was well noted and during his schooldays he undertook trials with both Norwich City and Leeds United.

He made rapid progress in the youth set-up, making significant strides towards the first team. He particularly impressed in a friendly against Manchester City which prompted Keith Alexander to give him his full debut in the Football League Trophy against Telford United. He continued his progression in the final season of his scholarship and made his Football League debut as a substitute in the game at Rochdale on 12 February 2005.

After a spell out on loan at Stamford he became a regular presence on the substitutes bench and in February 2006 he came on to score his first league goal in the game at Stockport. His reward was his first league start the following week at home to Torquay United. Always impressing, he made 18 league appearances in the second half of the season, though only three of these were starts.

Lee had a lot of ability and for a player so young was able to show it in and around the first team. Over the years we've seen lots of these 'bright young things' emerge and ultimately fail. Ollie Ryan, Gary King and even Connor Robinson were given chances that they didn't take. Lee Frecklington was different. In the 2006–07 season he featured heavily in a very pivotal role towards Lincoln's unsuccessful push for promotion to League One. John Schofield placed a lot of belief in his former protégé and he boasted a number of exceptional performances. He was named in the PFA League Two Team of the Year for the 2006–07 season, and he was only beaten to the Imps Player of the Year by Lee Beevers.

In January 2008 the Imps and manager Peter Jackson turned down two bids for Frecklington from Peterborough. In his programme notes around that time Jackson remarked; "I didn't think it was the right offer or the right club for Freck, and we're now in talks to keep him at the club because he's a real asset for us. There's only one or two midfielders in the division who can do what Lee does and we've come to expect it every game despite his age."

The following season as his star continued to rise he seemed increasingly less likely to remain a Lincoln player. There was some surprise when he didn't move on in the January 2009 transfer window, and even more surprise when just six days after the window closed he finally moved to Peterborough initially on loan.

After leaving Lincoln, Freck made a real name for himself at both Peterborough and Rotherham. His last action in a Lincoln shirt was scoring a last-minute equaliser as we snatched a result against Bournemouth having been 3-1 down with four minutes remaining. He departed days later, replaced (of sorts) by Michael O'Connor until the end of that season. He made seven League One appearances for Posh before the season ended but broke through to make almost 40 Championship appearances the season after, although they were relegated. Injury blighted the 2010/11 season for him, but he was back playing Championship football the season after, grabbing five goals in the process.

He played just six matches of the following season in the second tier before surprisingly dropping down to League Two to play for Steve Evans and Rotherham United. He smashed a debut goal against Aldershot and bagged eight more as Rotherham were promoted. Rather ironically, he ended the season partnering Michael O'Connor.

If he hadn't already endeared himself to Millers fans, the opening few days of 2013/14 certainly etched his name into their hearts. He grabbed a brace on the opening day as they drew at Gresty Road, including a last-minute winner. Three days later his 38th minute goal gave them a 2-1 victory in the Carling Cup against local rivals Sheffield Wednesday. 49 appearances and 13 goals later he found himself back in the Championship, partly responsible for the awful sight of Evans bounding up the Wembley touch-line after the play-off win against Leyton Orient.

In 2015 he was made Rotherham captain, a position he still holds today. At 32 he's approaching the latter stages of his career but having only played once in the fourth tier since leaving Lincoln he has shown consistent ability since we last saw him. He's a goal scoring midfielder, fitting the bill of the rumour I've heard, but his wages may be a stumbling block. The again, Danny has always said he is willing to pay a player what he is worth, what price on an emotional home-coming for one of our best youth system products? What price on an experienced attacking midfielder, a player who has 'been there, done that' in terms of our ultimate goal, Championship football?

The likelihood is that this is no more than rumour and chatter, half-truth and circumstance combining to create a fanciful titbit to spread around the terraces. However, I wouldn't rule out seeing Lee in Lincoln City colours one day and I certainly wouldn't rule out seeing him in coaching or management at the conclusion of his playing days. He's a likeable lad, Lincoln through and through and he'd be an asset to this club at any stage of his career.

Football as it should be: Imps 1-2 Coventry

November 19, 2017

It was fast-paced, enthralling and engrossing. Two good sides going toe to toe in front of a packed stadium, two sets of fans in fine voice and fine humour making more noise than a top-flight game. It was end to end, combative and frantic. In the end, we came out on the wrong side of the result, but just like away at Wimbledon I've found it hard to get too upset.

I don't like losing, I don't like us dropping crucial points in a promotion race, but it is mid-November and there's lots of time to catch up. This is a fledgling Lincoln City side, the early foundations of our League One team. The evolution since last season has been remarkable and fast, but we're nowhere near where we need to be just yet. We as fans know that, Danny and Nicky know that and for 45 minutes at least, Coventry City showed us that.

Let's not beat around the bush: they're the best side I've seen at Sincil Bank this season without a shadow of a doubt. When they really turned it on after half time, they were unplayable. We weren't bad, far from it, but they've got players of championship standard and it showed. I'm not talking Michael Bostwick-style strength and power either, I'm talking speed, precision and clarity of movement. I know we all loved to hate Jodi Jones, but what a player he is. Duckens Nazon also showed the depth in their squad and perhaps highlighted the difference between the sides. When they needed a game-changer they had an international striker on loan from Wolves. We had Ollie Palmer. No disrespect intended there, but last season our squad was our strength and this season, as we know, it is not.

However, we were certainly the better side for much of the first half. Danny got his game plan absolutely right, Matt Rhead was back to his monstrous best, agitating, winning headers and dictating play. It was a Matt Rhead of last season, the unplayable beast that defenders can't handle. Nathan Arnold had perhaps his best game of the season as well, using his body excellently and always looking lively. I wondered if Harry might have been carrying a knock because he had a quiet game.

Still, we knocked on the door a couple of times and the best defence in the league let us in. Sean Long was the provider again, his pinpoint cross swept home by an unmarked Rhead at the far post. Long had a good game again, he's growing in stature and confidence every week. I feel for Sam Habergham, but at present I don't see a route back into the side. Many are touting Eardley as a potential Player of the Season already, and Long has created something like three of our last five goals.

Once we got our goal Coventry sparked into action and we felt the full force of their potential. Clearly, they're not reaching those levels every week otherwise we'd see them winning 7-0 every so often, not Luton. They're quick on the break, they move the ball across the field succinctly and swiftly, they're simply outstanding when they slide into full gear. I've not had cause to praise opposition sides much this season, nobody had impressed me enough to say they were better than us. Coventry were.

That wasn't to say we were over-awed. Matt Green had a good opportunity to volley us into a two-goal lead but couldn't get around the ball. I know Green is coming in for some stick on social media, harsh but unfortunately increasingly likely as the games go by with a goal. Last year at this time he had eight for Mansfield, but if you look he bagged three early doors and then had a run until October without scoring. Suddenly he smashed five in four games, I'm still sure that is going to happen here. However, I understand the criticism and I can't continue to say 'the goals will come' without acknowledging this is a bad run for him.

One thing I've noticed we do that really frustrates me is pen ourselves in at corners. As early as the first half, whenever they got a corner we get all eleven men back into the box, often meaning a clearance falls straight to the feet of an opponents and brings the pressure back on. Why not leave Nathan or one of the other quicker players out on the half way line, just in case? They could at least contest any clearance and buy vital seconds for us to clear our lines. I don't think we've conceded because of it yet, but it does seem to help build opponents confidence.

At half time there was lots of positivity around me, lots of people saying it was the best game at Sincil Bank in a long while. It was, Coventry were growing in confidence and had tested Josh on several occasions. He was a well-deserved man of the match, his first half performance was excellent, his second half one bordering on ridiculous. Again, I'm a big Paul Farman fan, but he's going to find it incredibly difficult to get regular first-team football whilst Josh Vickers is filling our goal.

Last weekend I noted the immediately change in the balance of play, how we came out and almost immediately I knew we'd win the game. Yesterday within about five minutes, I thought we'd lose the game. I didn't want to be right, be we got an idea of the level you need to be at to win this league. At this moment in time, we're not there. We're not a million miles away, but we're five players and perhaps six months work outside the top three. We're still top seven material in my eyes, but it will take a push in January.

Their first goal was excellent, a beautiful cross-field ball picked out Jones and his hit deserved to win a football game all on its own. Sure, he pissed a few of your off with his celebration. You know what? That's football. Matt Rhead did it all of the time, I'd be shouting abuse and booing him if I'd seen it, but in truth it is no more or less than we do. His own fans were the other end of the pitch, he had to celebrate and he was pumped up to score a goal.

They then looked like losing grip of the match almost immediately. We worked our way up the pitch with a move that ended with a Matt Green header hitting the bar when it looked more likely to go in. Had that gone in, we wouldn't have seen the Green hating online in such abundance. The difference between hero and villain is one inch either way. Had that gone in, we would have killed their resistance I think, but it did not. From that moment on, there was only one winner and their second was a lesson in persistence. I think (and feel free to correct me) it was a save, then the crossbar and finally a well-placed shot past Vickers. They just kept pouring forward, unleashing shot after shot, eventually they were going to get their rewards. we'd dealt relatively well with the onslaught but there's only so much you can stop.

Once we changed the shape, in particular once Rheady came off, that was our threat more or less finished. Elliott is a decent player but he can't influence a game like the big man can. Coventry were happy to defend their lead and we were unable to unlock their defence. The game didn't lose any of that vibrant, pulsating appeal it had, but the battle became more about the fans than the players. A round of '2-1 and you f*cked it up' was met with 'Premiership, and you f*cked it up'. Imps then went down the leagues before Coventry decided to mock us with imitation, rather flattering us in the process. We weren't on the right end of the result, but what an afternoon to be a supporter of Lincoln City. We played well, not well enough according to many, but in my eyes we probably did enough to earn and unjustified draw (if that makes sense), but it wasn't to be. I kept saying to Ian Plenderleith, book judge and part-time referee, that I felt there was another goal in the game. He kept pointing out to me the decisions the referee was getting right.

Eventually the end came and they'd won their FA Cup. From Tottenham in 1987 to Lincoln in 2017, 30-years of decline that they're looking to halt. We came off the field a little battered, carrying a couple of injuries but a better side for having experienced a proper game of football. Not many sides have had a real go at us this season, Crawley, Cambridge, Morecambe and even Luton looked content not to get beat here. Coventry opened up and gave us a proper game and every single fan in the stadium should be happy they did.

Back in the days of John Schofield I remember us losing 3-2 to MK Dons, I came away telling my friends that I didn't mind us losing if I thought we were playing to win. I don't accept defeat, it hurts and never more so than on my birthday when I should get everything I want, but it can be forgiven if your team have given a fair account of themselves. This Lincoln City side is good, perhaps not to the standard of a team with the resources and pulling power of Coventry, but we're still better than seventeen teams in this division, I'm sure of it. We don't always show it and I'm not sure we know the best way to set up at the minute, but Danny Cowley's teams never give up, always compete and always run through walls for the paying fans. Win, lose or draw that is all we can ask.

I'm not going to insult anyone's intelligence by saying 'look where we were last season', I've tried it enough in conversations. Football moves fast and maybe we were at FGR last season, but those days have gone. We're Football League now, we competitive and we should never be complacent because we've come so far. However, Coventry have come from League One and the Championship before that, big wages, big crowds and a bigger attraction for players. We're 'little old Lincoln', on our way back but growing and evolving at an alarming rate. Yesterday's game told us what we already knew; we're not quite there as yet. Did anyone expect us to be the finished article in six months? That would be ridiculous, almost as ridiculous as telling Danny he 'needs to sign a striker' on social media. Do you think he's going to read that, turn to Nicky and say; "You know what? Billy Big Bollocks on Facebook thinks we need to sign a striker. Pick up the phone and call that 40-goal proven striker that we know is sat at home and tell him to come to Sincil Bank. If only we'd thought of that, we've been driving up and down the country five nights a week for eighteen months for no reason, this guy has the answers right here. Plus, he posts lots of really funny memes featuring face palming and Matt Green's name. If only we'd known." Of course not. He knows he needs some new faces, we all do. I still maintain Matt Green will turn his barren spell around, but my voice is becoming increasingly isolated in proclaiming it.

Now, bring on Colchester on Tuesday but perhaps more importantly, bring on New Year's Day and 'phase two' of Operation Football League. We're still in this race.

Just Falling Short: Colchester 1-0 Imps
November 21, 2017

Many of the current 5,500 season ticket holders are not used to losing two games in a row on a regular basis. Many of the keyboard warriors have been aching to get all indignant the next time we showed a chink of vulnerability or poor form. After tonight's game those newer fans will get a glimpse of what it is really like to be an Imp and the frantic tappers will be putting words like 'serious' in bold capitals to accentuate their anger.

Let's look at it objectively shall we? We conceded a sloppy goal after three minutes and spent the next 42 looking relatively lost as to how we could get back into the game. Nathan rattled the bar from a dead ball situation, but aside from that we didn't really threaten their goal. In the second half we saw a similar story to other recent matches, we came out with more intent and purpose and were perhaps the better side. We still looked very blunt in front of goal and have ended up on the wrong end of a 1-0 defeat.

I've seen people calling 'fundamental errors' the reason we're having a bad patch, crying out for the return of Terry Hawkridge and a more positive tactic, but the truth is tonight we've learned nothing we didn't already know. We're a small squad, partly due to a tough summer of recruitment and partly down to a couple of injuries. We're lacking a cutting edge up front and when it comes to shuffling the pack, we're out of options. The transfer window is meant to protect sides like us from having our best players cherry-picked, instead it condemns us to another 40-odd days of 'making do'. We know Danny has a war chest to utilise as he sees fit, even the biggest armchair supporters know where we're lacking and frankly tonight doesn't change a goddam thing.

Now to wildly contradict myself with a couple of observations about tonight. I suspect we did learn a couple of things that perhaps we've been wondering about. Some of the current players, some that have been lauded as great footballers are not cutting the cheese at this moment in time. Billy Knott is one who, not for the want of trying, simply isn't doing the business. The game plan tonight was clearly to play lots more into feet, especially with Ollie Palmer up front not winning headers. Whitehouse, Knott and Palmer are all better with the ball on the deck than they are in the air. I wonder, if Danny could have tonight again, would he perhaps start with the physical presence? I think the only times we've looked dangerous in recent weeks has been when we've gone route one with Matt Rhead on the pitch and Matt Green running off him. Palmer is something of a lone wolf, eager and willing but seemingly preferring the isolation of being a lone striker than linking up with anybody. Billy has been ineffective since his dismissal against Notts County and I'm afraid the darling of the crowd, Elliott Whitehouse, has only performed in fits and bursts.

What does that tell us? That we need an attacking midfielder and a centre forward or two? Well hold the front page that's news to me (detect the tone). We've shuffled the pack time and again, we've tried every combination you can think of and in my eyes the only one that looks even slightly dangerous is Rhead and Green. I'm not saying they look a menacing goal threat, but I believe they're the best we have. At present I don't know who then fits in the Michael Bostwick shaped hole we have, but I'm not paid to have all the answers, am I?

I also think the step up in division has robbed us of one of our 'secret' weapons, fitness. We won games late on against tiring sides last season, but this campaign is different. Everyone is fit, training full-time and ready to run 90 minutes. Most teams have bigger squads than ours and hence fresher players to bolster them late on in games. This change is the reason we're not putting teams to the sword as much, it isn't that the players we have are not as good as last season. I often see people romanticising about Jack Muldoon, Alan Power and Terry Hawkridge. These were great lads last season but losing them is not why we're struggling to find the goal in 2017/18. Living in the past helps no one but remembering how quickly we've come from nothing to mid table League Two is worth remembering.

I also have to wonder about the failure to bring in a final loan player on deadline day. Correct me if I'm wrong, but we're allowed five and we have four (Raggett, JMD, Ginnelly & Dickie). It does seem to be something of an oversight that we didn't explore that avenue, although perhaps we did and it fell through as several deals did in the summer. Mansfield brought in Kane Hemmings, well above our budget, but look at the effect he's had. At the time I suggested losing out on Akinola wasn't the end of the world, the truth is it has severely impacted our season so far. That said, we're four points outside the play-offs and we're more than one player short of where we need to be, so it wasn't the be-all and end-all. We're not bottom four, we're not locked in a relegation battle and we're not still in the National League visiting places such as Maidenhead and Solihull.

Those who are saying 'something isn't right' or 'we need drastic action' are wide of the mark. Those season ticket holders are here until May at least and when January comes we'll be dipping our toe in the water and bringing in some faces. Statements along the lines of 'crowds will drop and so will our momentum' are, in my opinion, ill-informed. We've got 40 days to wait now, last season our momentum didn't even start until Oldham in early December. This is a race rather than a sprint and at present we're in the middle of the pack with potential.

I think promotion caught us a little short off the pitch as well as on it and perhaps we didn't have the infrastructure off the field to handle to complexities of so many deals in one go. Whatever happened in the summer can't be described as all bad, we got Michael Bostwick and Harry Anderson which was a massive coup. I still maintain Matt Green was a great signing, certainly on paper. I won't shy away from the fact it isn't happening for him at the moment, but we beat several clubs to his signature which is an indication of his ability. Neal Eardley and Sean Long signed too, both stalwarts of the current side, Alex signed a new deal… it wasn't the ideal summer but it certainly wasn't a disaster. Our transfer business didn't fill all of the gaps, but it was sufficient to see us nestled in the top half. Isn't that what we expected, stay tucked in until January and go from there? That being the case, how does tonight's result truly affect our long-term aims?

Wildly critical posts on social media won't help anyone, of course there will be some criticism as we have lost two in a row, but don't lose your head for heaven's sake. This is a dip in form, not a crisis. We have the means and the ability to arrest the 'poor' form and push on. It was only a week or so ago we'd hammered Crewe 4-1 wasn't it? Positivity ebbs and flows like a river, but negativity seems to lurk below the surface like a biting current at all times. I know there are some who relish it, the doom and gloom merchants who already have Danny and Nicky leaving at the end of the season and the club subsequently imploding. I've got news for you; it isn't going to happen, certainly not after a 1-0 defeat at Colchester.

There isn't a single Lincoln fan who will be happy tonight and I understand that. Those dedicated souls who travelled will be frustrated, I get that too. A little venting is okay, but let's keep it reasonable eh? There's no point in going over old ground, no point in getting personal about players who may well see the posts and absolutely no point in winding yourselves up into a frenzy arguing with fellow Imps. It was a bad result, we're in a bit of poor form and we know exactly what it is going to take to get out of it. For the next 40 days we should just stick together, support the team and trust in Danny and Nicky to do whatever they can to see us press for the top seven in the early part of 2018.

Rheady: 100 and counting

November 23, 2017

Our 1-0 defeat against Colchester might not have been the most illustrious game Matt Rhead has played in, but on a dreary night in Essex he passed 100 league appearances for the Imps.

Including cup games he's now up to 119 outings for City across two and a half seasons, with an impressive goals tally of 40. A strike rate of 1 in 3 isn't bad at all, not for a so-called 'big man' with limited mobility.

Matt Rhead plays to his strengths and I think he works best when he's being written off. He thrives on being the focus of the opposition fans jokes, especially when he slams home a goal right in front of them. He awkward to handle, bullish and constantly irritates defenders and fans alike. He's a brute, an uncomplicated hulk of a man often used as the focal point for direct tactics.

The paragraph above is how most opponents would describe him, but occasionally Rhead pulls something out of the bag which belies all of his obvious traits. Every so often he'll pull a fifty-yard ball out of the air on one foot before cleverly switching to another to distribute it. Some of his goals are right out of the drawer marked 'top class', fewer and further between than his first season but still the potential is there. I always rated that chip against Eastleigh as his absolute best, the way he strode onto the ball, switched direction and lobbed the keeper all in one beautifully poetic movement.

Sometimes Matt Rhead has the grace of a swan, he possesses an innate technical ability which few credit him with. Far from being a Jon Parkin, just a big lump to aim at, he can be a thinking man's footballer, a visionary with the ability and inclination to spot a great pass or wonderful opportunity to score. Boreham Wood at home last season was a great example, a long ball came to him which he killed, wrong-footed a defender and calmly slotted home when it had seemed he was crowded out.

I once likened him to Matt Le Tissier, perhaps ambitiously but he does remind me of the great Southampton striker. Le Tiss was lazy, Rhead isn't he just lacks mobility. Le Tiss was perhaps more influential whenever he played, but when you've seen the wonderful technique of Rheady in action I'm sure you can understand the comparison. Admittedly Le Tiss didn't miss quite as many penalties though!

At the beginning of this season it seemed his unique talents were being used less and less, but as we've strode through autumn with a goal drought on our hands, he's reappeared. The truth is even now we're back in the Football League, there is still a place for Matt Rhead. His lack of mobility can be counteracted if we get pacey players around him. Once again, in the face of adversity, he's back and crucial to what we're doing. January will bring a new test no doubt, another player that will get ahead of him in the pecking order, but not necessarily keep him down. I expect him to be a fixture in the side until then, the first half of his 100 league outing showed that despite the new arrivals, the step up in class and the change of approach, Matt Rhead is still a key part of our attacking threat, Tuesday night proved that. Ollie Palmer doesn't cut it as a loan striker and I'm not convinced Palmer and Rhead can play together, meaning the Rhead and Green is the way forward.

100 league appearances, 119 appearances, it is all irrelevant in the grand scheme of things. What matters is the Big Man is still here, still battling for a first team place and still a handful for any defenders in the league. I look at Akinfenwa, I look at the rich lower-league career Jon Parkin had and I wonder if we're trying to be too cute up front, trying to move away from the 'long-ball' Lincoln tag too quickly. Matt Rhead can pass it more accurately with his chest than most of our forward players have done with their feet recently, he certainly wins more headers than anyone that doesn't play centre half and after Saturday he's proved he still has a goal in him. For the next 40 days, Matt Rhead is our major hope of staying in touch with the top ten.

City get the rub of the Green: Imps 3-1 Port Vale

November 25, 2017

On a bitterly cold afternoon at Sincil Bank, Lincoln City went some way to warming up their fans with a well-fought 3-1 win against a resilient and strong Port Vale side.

It's been a tough week for Danny Cowley and the boys. Defeat against Coventry was softened by the quality of the game, but defeat at Colchester was certainly not. Lots of questions were asked in the week about recruitment, about certain players and about the level we hope to be at. Whilst I acknowledge one game does not make a season, one game does not break it either. Colchester was not the end of our hopes and dreams, likewise today doesn't mean we've won anything. What it does show is our character, our ability to adapt and perhaps most importantly of all, our togetherness as a team.

The Stacey West – A Season in Blogs 2017/18

The match itself was not one for the purists. Both sides wanted to get from back to front quick, little of the play took place in the middle third. In that respect we matched fire with fire, something I championed in the week. The team selection looked like that of a man eager to impress on some players the importance of reaching their levels. It looked very harsh on Nathan Arnold and Sean Long, neither have been bad in recent weeks, in fact Sean Long has been incredibly solid. Michael Bostwick's inclusion shocked us all, Danny included by the sound of the post-match interview. What didn't shock me was the forward pairing of Matt Rhead and Matt Green. Say what you like, they're the best we have at nine and ten.

They say one swallow doesn't make a summer and one burger doesn't make a barbecue, but Matt Green's goal was important for all sorts of reasons. I'm delighted for him, I believe he'll go on a run of scoring four or five in the next seven or eight games, but aside from that it was just nice to see him enjoy it. When it finally came it was a typically well-worked Lincoln goal, a ball in from the flank and a smart header from close range. He's been close to a couple of those recently without getting the reward for his work. When the ball hit the net the relief was immense, both Dave (my mate) and I immediately started chanting his name. You won't find me going around saying 'I told you so' because he has to work at producing it most weeks, but it was a lovely moment to be one of his biggest advocates. His celebration said it all, it was far more than just our first goal of a mid-season game.

The goal didn't spark us into life, if anything we retreated and invited Port Vale onto us, as much as you can invite long balls onto your defender's heads. I'm not being critical of the style, we employ it when we need to, but you don't invite pressure against sides like them. You brace yourself for an aerial bombardment and we didn't brace ourselves well. They came more into the game as it wore on, although the game was being ruined by the man employed to officiate.

I'm not usually critical of referees if I can help it, it is such a cliché to blame the man in the middle. Even at 1-0 up today's match official had no redeeming qualities whatsoever. His decisions were completely random, at first favouring them but latterly working with us. He looked to his assistant referees for guidance and they were as much use as toilet paper in a fish tank. At one point I yelled something colourful in their direction about learning the offside rule. A father in front of me, sat with his kids, turned and I thought I'd overstepped the mark. I apologised only for him to say 'no, he needs to understand the rules'.

Here is the rule they got wrong on more than one occasion. Ball comes over the top, Harry Anderson is coming back from on offside position. He moves onside as Matt Green runs from an onside position to chase the through ball. Flag goes up offside. HOW?? How can a player running onto a through ball be offside? There was one decision where we cleared a ball and it ricocheted off their player to Tom Pope, stood in an offside position. No flag? I find it incredulous that match officials could get it so wrong, it isn't just me either as several around me commented on it. I try to give them the benefit of the doubt when I can, but that referee today seemed like he got the whistle and shirt out of a cereal packet.

I thought the final 20 minutes of the first half we were poor, I singled out Josh Ginnelly to those around me as being a virtual passenger. He hadn't had a good half, he seemed to spend his afternoon running down blind alleys or hiding in plain sight. How frustrating was it to see Neal Eardley wanting to take a throw, but having Josh behind the full back asking for the ball? He wasn't the only one unavailable, but he's never going to win it in the air, I felt he was hiding when things got tough. Harsh? Maybe. I was considerably harsher than that when his awful corner was met at the near post. To give him his due he chased back, missed three or four opportunities to tackle and they scored. Needless to say, I did my half-time tweet about how bad I felt he'd been.

In the second half we got a much better Josh and he showed some big brass balls to come out after his mistake and put it behind him. In truth, the whole side did. After two defeats in a week, surrendering a lead before half time to a physical side such as Port Vale could have spelled disaster. We went in with our heads down and I feared the worst. We came out like a side that have character and resilience. It would have been easy for Danny to take Josh off, take him out of the firing line but instead he stayed on and battled for the team. Just as we did against Crewe a fortnight ago, we came out and from minute one I believed there would only be one winner.

Nobody could say we didn't deserve the lead and once again, I credit Matt Green with making the goal. Even if some of our support don't rate him, the fact he had three defenders on him every time he got the ball demonstrates opponents know what a threat he is. He holds the ball up well and it was that strength which resulted in Michael Bostwick receiving it on the edge of the area. He's primed a few rockets to go recently and not managed to bag a nice clean strike, today was a great day to change that. At 2-1 up we were only ever going to lose the game by our own making, they weren't likely to win it of their own accord.

I thought Vale offered very little in the second half and our third really killed any lingering doubts our fans had. It was Josh Ginnelly who started the move off, he wriggled free only to be unceremoniously hacked down just inside the Port Vale half. If there's one thing we pride ourselves on it is converting dead balls into goals scored and that is exactly what happened. The fact it was Luke Waterfall on the end of it made the day seem even more cathartic than it should have been. He's the club captain, the man at the centre of our title charge last season. He's been marginalised as we look to move forward with younger, fresher players, but when the chips were down it was Luke on the end of the ball to kill the game off. With Rheady flicking it on too, it seemed almost poetic. The much-maligned striker opens the scoring, two old-hands recently cast aside completed it.

In the middle of the park it was the combination of old and new that helped us secure the points. Alex and Bozzie worked tirelessly but today especially was a game for Bozzie, the big grizzly bastard. If I were his opponent I'd be having nightmares for a week that a Game of Thrones character was stalking me all over the field, winning headers and tackles like he was taking down White Walkers (GoT reference, if you don't get it I make no apology). He wasn't the only one though, the level of commitment in the second half was, in my opinion, as good as any half of football I've seen at Sincil Bank since April. Woody surged forward on runs, Josh Ginnelly probed the space, the centre halves put their bodies on the line and Sam slotted nicely back into the swing of things.

I'm going to single three players out though, Neal Eardley has to be first. I'm not sure how we've ended up with a player of his class in our side, but he is such an asset. He's calm and collected on the ball, an organiser not afraid to dole out the advice in whatever means he sees fit, but so composed in possession. You can see he has come from a level above and today, as ever, he was superb.

Harry Anderson is a boy you'll see at a higher level later in his career. Within twelve months he'll be our 'Jodi Jones', the one that opposition fans look at and say 'he is different class'. He strong as an ox and nothing showed that more than a run at the end. Bear in mind he's put in eighty odd minutes, they're applying pressure and their midfielder looks to barge Harry off the ball. Instead he bounces out of play as Harry wins the ball and strides forward. It raised another rendition of 'Oh, Harry Harry....' and rightly so.

Finally, Rheady. I think he compliments Matt Green well, the 'big man, fast man' combo will do for me until January at least. Amusingly I don't actually think Rhead was outstanding today, but he did what he does so well. There were so many classic 'Rheady' moments today, the slow amble towards the Coop Stand when he knew he was coming off, him being fouled constantly but never getting a free-kick and of course the hilarious run around the area to lose his marker. He brings more than just his ability on the ball, he has the knack of galvanising fans, getting them wound up and cheering for him. He received a standing ovation for a six out of ten display, because that is what he does. We've missed him, his character and his unique abilities.

I had a chat with my mate Dave about what was different today. He pinpointed the fact Green was in the right areas, not chasing all over the park looking for the ball. He laid the praise at the feet of Ginnelly and Anderson doing the right running outside the full backs, not inside. I disagree, I think it was Rheady. He took care of things between the midfield and Matt Green, not by attempting slick passing or lots of running like you get from Knott or Whitehouse, but by providing the target and holding the ball up. I know I'm a Green fan but I desperately hope the two of them remain in the side for the next few league games because they're our best route to goal. Also, no player can give you what Matt Rhead does, he just has that 'je ne sais quoi' that transcends the actual game. He's a motivator, an irritant and a character and even when he's had an average game, he's the one the fans call for. At one stage we're three one up and everyone is chanting 'Rheady'.

They weren't singing 'Greeny', despite his goal, not 'Bozzie', despite being my man of the match and not Luke Waterfall for his brick heading ability. That tells you everything about Matt Rhead.

Even at 3-1 Coco the Referee showed little or no competence at all. My eyes at have deceived me, but I'm sure I saw Matt Rhead pushed over by their defender. Did I see that? He went down, play stopped and nothing happened. Dave was having kittens next to me, he was as incandescent with rage as he can be, asking complete strangers why it wasn't a booking. Still, he made sure he had his yellow card for Matt Green for kicking the ball away after he was called offside. He wasn't the first, he wasn't the last be he was the only one booked. I love a consistent ref who makes rational and fair decisions, this afternoon we didn't get that.

After the game you could tell Danny was delighted and rightly so. Many have questioned the direction we took in the summer and whether we were really the team some fans believe we are. People are entitled to their opinions and have a right to voice them. If we'd lost today, or drawn after taking the lead, those questions and doubts would spread and grow. One win doesn't stop people having the differing opinions, but it does stop the so-called rot from setting in. It shows that despite having a small squad, despite perhaps not bringing in every player we needed in the summer, this group has something. We're not a top three side at present, but we're just outside the play offs with a lot more football to play and a degree of money to be spent. Danny's sides always get better after Christmas (so I'm told) and by grinding out results as we did today we're only building better platform for ourselves.

The Stacey West – A Season in Blogs 2017/18

Pos	Team	Pld	W	D	L	GF	GA	GD	Pts
1	Luton Town	20	12	5	3	48	18	30	41
2	Notts County	20	12	5	3	35	20	15	41
3	Accrington Stanley	20	11	4	5	32	22	10	37
4	Exeter City	20	11	3	6	28	22	6	36
5	Wycombe Wanderers	20	9	6	5	38	29	9	33
6	Coventry City	20	9	5	6	21	12	9	32
7	Mansfield Town	20	8	8	4	30	23	7	32
8	Swindon Town	20	10	2	8	30	25	5	32
9	Newport County	20	8	6	6	27	22	5	30
10	Lincoln City	20	8	6	6	24	19	5	30
11	Colchester United	20	8	5	7	26	23	3	29
12	Grimsby Town	20	8	5	7	24	26	-2	29
13	Cambridge United	20	8	5	7	17	23	-6	29
14	Carlisle United	20	7	6	7	28	27	1	27
15	Stevenage	20	7	5	8	26	31	-5	26
16	Cheltenham Town	20	6	6	8	27	29	-2	24
17	Crawley Town	20	5	6	9	17	23	-6	21
18	Yeovil Town	20	5	5	10	27	38	-11	20
19	Crewe Alexandra	20	6	2	12	21	34	-13	20
20	Forest Green Rovers	20	5	5	10	23	39	-16	20
21	Morecambe	20	4	7	9	15	25	-10	19
22	Port Vale	20	5	3	12	19	31	-12	18
23	Barnet	20	4	5	11	21	29	-8	17
24	Chesterfield	20	4	5	11	23	37	-14	17

The Stacey West – A Season in Blogs 2017/18

December
Turning despair into joy: Imps 3-2 Accrington
December 6, 2017

Firstly, I'm judging nobody nor sparking debate here, but those boycotting the competition must be a little dismayed at the quality of football on display at Sincil Bank and beyond in this EFL Trophy.

We opened with a 3-1 against Mansfield, the sort of result that, had it been in the league, we'd still be crowing about now. Everton U21's are beaten by a free-kick that was as good as anything you'll see at Sincil Bank in a decade, only for Josh Ginnelly to rival that with a wonder goal of his own to put us through against County. Finally, last night we face a strong Accrington side, a side that got stronger as the match wore one, but still beat them in an end to end game that kept fans riveted for 95 minutes.

I spent the evening in the executive boxes courtesy of Chris Illsley of Running Imp. Just for the record Chris is a top guy, the hospitality is second to none and they make my Dad feel so welcome up there. Thanks to Chris, Josh and Paul for giving me some memories with my Dad that I know will last a lifetime. It makes it even more special when the team keep their half of the bargain too.

One caveat last night was we were also the Man of the Match sponsors. That brought the obvious pre-match banter about my criticism of Ollie Palmer, especially from my Dad who often gives me stick for it. "Palmer will score first," he joked. "You watch."

To be precise, Accrington scored first. We'd barely finished off the plate of chilli and wedges lovingly provided by the top rate staff at the ground before Paul Farman's net bulged. Cue derision from some in the box, from one end of the pitch to the other it looked as though Farm's might have got a hand to it. The truth? I didn't see. I was readjusting my glasses and I'm not going to condemn a man on hearsay. In the bar afterwards the general consensus seemed to be there was very little he could do, so I'll roll with that. After all, this blog and Farman go back right to the very start and I've got a soft spot for the likeable Geordie.

I don't think we played well in the first half, bar a couple of players. Alex Woodyard was full of industry as always, from a high vantage point he's like Scrappy Do, bursting all over the pitch picking fights with bigger men he looks unlikely to win. He does win them though, that is why he's such an asset to the side. Harry Anderson was full of direct running, not always getting the breaks but still willing to try. Also, and please know it delights me to say this, Ollie Palmer was having a good game. He looked a real handful, he won a couple of headers and laid the ball of once or twice too. Positionally he's not always on the ball but he wasn't playing badly.

The trouble was these performances were from individuals and as a team, it wasn't working. Accrington are clearly a good side, they indulged in a few of the dark arts too, Harry got a clattering once or twice and their big centre half, Richards-Everton, was incredibly good at knowing when to hold a player and when to let him go. I really liked him, tough and uncompromising but also aware and alert. In their midfield Sean McConville also looked a threat, he's been around the block a few times and was one of the names on the team sheet that highlighted their intention to win the game. Up front Billy Kee, another big name, was anonymous.

It wasn't a pretty first half, but not long before the break it became an even one, at least on paper. Both strikers were involved, after a Harry Anderson knock-down Matt Green helped the ball across the six-yard box to an unmarked Ollie Palmer. The striker made no mistake in bringing proceedings level with a straightforward finish. 1-1 and, despite the lack of real thrills, it was probably a fair reflection of the game. Neither side gave any indication of what was to come.

With injury time seconds away, Sean McConville embarrassed Paul Farman from all of 45-yards. It was an innocuous looking effort; the Imps' defence suspected no threat but McConville launched a rocket goal wards. From our vantage point you could see Farman back tracking, stumbling almost and then the net bulged. Again, much anger seemed directed at our keeper but replays suggest he was done by a real wonder strike.

It was so frustrating that, after being behind for so long in the first half, we gave up the lead we'd earned so well. Right before half time is a great time to score and to take a 2-1 lead into the break gave Accrington and John Coleman chance to shuffle things about, catch their breath and regroup. What Lincoln needed, what we absolutely had to do to give ourselves any impetus at all, was equalise. This time instead of a winger winning a knock-down it was a defender whipping in a cross, Sean Raggett's delicious ball over caused panic and between McConville and Matt Green, City got an equaliser. Officially McConville has been awarded the own goal as has Farman for their second, both harsh on the midfielder. Matt Green's presence scored our second even if McConville got the final touch.

City came out rejuvenated and revitalised and for twenty minutes absolutely battered Accrington. Raggs went close with a header, Ginnelly frightened their full-back into near submission and once again, Alex Woodyard did everything he needed to to keep play in their half and not ours. It was, for a period, a superb display and just after the hour we got our rewards. A great corner from Sam Habergham was met by the head of Raggs to give us a 3-2 lead. On December 5th, 2016 we beat Oldham 3-2 in a thriller at Sincil Bank, one year to the day later we were 3-2 up against Accrington. Could we hold on?

At first it was more a case of us extending our lead. Matt Green beat the keeper with an exquisite finish only to see the defender chase the ball back and clear off the line. Accrington needed to do something, something other than fall out with the Lincoln bench. In between some rather heated exchanges, John Coleman sent on Kayden Jackson and Farrend Rawson and began to turn the screws. They went from retaining the ball in the middle of the park to whacking it long at goal and it changed the game again. As the minute ticked by we went from fling raids on their goal to desperate defending in front of our own. Rob Dickie came on followed quickly by Nathan Arnold. As the minute ticked away we got further and further back, defended deeper and deeper. Accrington move the ball down one flank, launched it in and when it was cleared they simply came again. I wasn't at the Alamo, if I was I imagine I'd have felt less under threat than Paul Farman did.

Paul had a decent game, but some fans were still on his back about the goals. His kicking had been poor but as the game wore on it became more useful for clearing the lines. As the final minutes turned into injury time, he made the sort of save that should be recorded under 'goals', that is how crucial they were to keep us in the game. Here's a kicker: in the box we'd already named Alex Woodyard as Man of the Match, if it had been two minutes later we would have chosen Farman.

He made two saves from Kayden Jackson, the pick of the two coming after Accrington had hit the bar, but both we reactive and instinctive, both reminiscent of times last season when he was called into action. Josh Vickers might well be the current number one, but Farms made sure that after 90 minutes it was his saves, not the goals conceded that were talked about.

In those final few seconds Harry Anderson took the ball into the corner and finally the referee brought proceedings to a close. City 3-2 Accrington in a truly mesmerizing and engrossing game. Running Imp chose Alex Woodyard for Man of the Match, his industry and endeavour spanned both halves of the game and lasted for ninety minutes. Ollie Palmer, Harry Anderson and Sean Raggett got honourable mentions also.

I would be interested to know the thinking behind the state of the pitch, there was more sand on there than I've seen at Sincil Bank since 2003 when we played Scunthorpe. Even from behind glass we could see it spraying up like standing water during tackles or even just when the ball landed from height. Danny seemed surprised too, something that was interesting as I'm led to believe he usually controls every little thing, so to hear him discussing the pitch as though he wasn't aware of the sand did have me scratching my head a little.

John Coleman made much of the pitch, also he commented on the big crowd turning the referee's head. apparently (and this surprised me) we went out to foul them early in the game and get in the referee's ear. Now, I know my football and when their full back twice hacked Harry Anderson it wasn't anything we had planned. Coleman even went as far as to say, "they like to play it direct and it works for them, well not all the time as we're above them in the league." Saucer of milk dug out two please. I liked Coleman but his assessment of the game wasn't entirely fair. Apparently if Kayden Jackson had been more 'dishonest' they would have got a penalty and a red card at the end of the game (nope, not sure about that). Accrington are a good side, there's no doubt about that, but moaning about another team's tactics is hilarious. He admits he knows how we play, he knew exactly what to expect and yet he couldn't counter it? Their league position hints at him being a really good manager, his comments suggest perhaps not.

So, we're on to the next round and all those social media snipes about boycotts, supporters with integrity and 'you'll go to Wembley' claims can carry on for another month at least. Joy. Leicester City went some way to indicating a reason for boycotters to stay away by fielding £35m of striking talent and a 30-year old keeper as they beat Scunthorpe, something absolutely legal but perhaps not in the spirit of the competition. They've within their rights to start Ulloa and Iheanacho up front, but morally doesn't it spit on the 'ethics' of the competition. The reason the EFL have given for their controversial inclusion is that it is helping nurture and develop the youth of tomorrow, not giving a Premier League club the chance to field a couple of reserves not likely to get a game. I know I will be immensely pissed off if we draw them and they do the same, to a point where, if that happens, I will boycott next year. After the fine football we've seen so far, the battling displays and wonder goals, it would be an absolute travesty for a cash-rich top-flight club to come here with £35m of attacking talent that can't get a first team game and roll us over. Even more so if they got to Wembley.

I imagine this morning there's been a phone call made to Leicester just asking them to clam it a little bit. Whilst 3,000 fans and a brilliant 3-2 score line adds respectability to the competition, their actions take it away in equal measure and the last thing the EFL want right now is more reasons for people to stay away.

'Respectful' Imps put pressure on Way: Yeovil 0-2 Imps
December 10, 2017

It was a typical lower league winter's game. Yeovil away, 250-odd hardy souls braving the long drive and subsequently being treated to an important and hard-fought win. City now climb to 6th thanks to results elsewhere and in those results we can see exactly why this wasn't just 'routine'.

"You have to be beating sides like Yeovil" is what I'm sure many fans said privately ahead of the game. They were 18th and despite having a 14-goal partnership up front they were seen as cannon fodder for the resurgent Imps. All was not as it seemed though, they had lost just twice at home and have a similar record at Huish Park to our record at Sincil Bank. Away form has seen them plummet and for this clash, they weren't away.

Danny spoke after the game of team not being 'respectful' to Yeovil as if that was a major factor in us winning the game. It is typical Danny, always positive about our opposition, always complimentary about their endeavour and ability and yet always managing to play down our own win. Sure, he's always happy and congratulates our players but he is never over enthusiastic nor bullish about promotion chances. "Up to sixth tonight Danny", said one interviewer. "Are we, that's great for the supporters." Once again, deflecting the success and achievement elsewhere. It isn't accidental and it always removes any pressure that position or achievement try to bring on the team.

Was it us respecting Yeovil that caused the win? Not solely, but by understanding and respecting opposition you do gain an upper hand. Aside from Notts County no team has truly dominated us this season, even Coventry who were so impressive at the Bank edged a tight-fought game. Accrington are up in third but next week we face 75% of the same players we beat on Tuesday night, only we'll be back up to full-strength.

What does 'full-strength' look like for Lincoln City these days? Vickers in goal, Eardley in somewhere, Raggett, Woodyard and Bozzie with Rhead and Green up top, Anderson out wide. That's the spine, that is where the most effective play comes from and they're the players that, if they're fit, should always start for Lincoln. How you dress that up, who else you drop in and how we approach games varies, but that is the spine of the team. Accrington thought we were tough on Tuesday, Rheady was only on the bench and Bozzie wasn't even in the squad.

Back to the game and Michael Bostwick's return to the side was an important factor. Many people say we're too negative with him and Alex in the side, I say that is absolute garbage. Between them they're the most solid midfield pairing I've ever seen at Sincil Bank, defensively and in terms of winning turnovers and breaking up play. Bozzie rode a fine line between tough and nasty, something it is important the does every week. Creative players don't want to face him nor do they want to be chased all over by Alex Woodyard. I have visions of Woodyard being tethered to a post in the dressing room after the game to stop him chasing his opposite number into the car park trying to get one last tackle in. They work hard, they do lots of the dirty work and for once, they get recognition for doing so.

It'd be remiss not to mention Matt Green too. He's shown immense strength of character to keep ploughing on up front, especially when you consider he was 'rested' (Danny speak for dropped) for two games. I've said it before and I'll say it again, but he is the best striker we have at the club, I would be surprised if, even after January, he isn't still the best striker we have at the club and the best partner for him is Matt Rhead. Earlier in the season Rhead was floated as a possible reserve, I mentioned his time might have come to an end, but he's proving many of us wrong. The thing with Rheady is he's uncomplicated, he's a handful but he has that touch and twist of skill that surprises many. Both him and Green have showed real personality to fight their way back onto the team sheet and both got their rewards.

The first goal was classic Lincoln, Rheady with the touch to Green and him bearing down on goal. We've seen it way before Danny and Nicky arrived, Yeo getting a flick on maybe from McCombe and off he went. It's a well-worked and well-worn routine but we do it well. The finish came from a player regaining confidence too, six weeks ago the keeper saves that but a revitalised striker puts it in the net. Don't be surprised to see Green with at least two more before 2018 joins the party.

The second goal was classic Cowley play. Green worked the channels superbly, almost too well as he seemed to be in a blind alley. The season's unlikely success story arrives (Neal Eardley, pictured top) and from nowhere provides the sort of ball Matt Rhead dreams about at night. When writing his list for Santa, somewhere in between 'Stoke shirt' and 'place in the starting eleven' I imagine he wrote 'the sort of balls that land on you head with pace and precision'. Well, Christmas came early. You don't need to give Rheady a written invitation to put that in the back of the net and at 2-0, the game was dead. In truth, it was dead at 1-0. It was dead as soon as half time arrived and Yeovil hadn't scored. In my analysis pre-match I said they only scored in the first half, us in the second. As things went they didn't get their one.

There's a lot of pressure on Darren Way and I'd be surprised to see him in a job when were all singing Auld Lang Syne. The home fans were singing for his head and he came out with a reference to their size in his defence: "Let's make no bones about it, I see the budget I'm working with, and keeping this football club even when you're coming up against a team like Lincoln, keeping it in the Football League every year is a good achievement. I know supporters don't want to hear that, but unfortunately when you look at our budget that's where we are."

In fairness to Way I've seen no reference to us being physical, no 'you know what to expect from Lincoln' quotes although maybe I've missed them. Most managers seem to think our approach to the game is one to be shunned or frowned upon. Well, we're sixth and 18 of them are below us so make your own judgement on that.

Yeovil away might have looked like a gimme, but I'm sure Crawley away looked the same for Mansfield Town, look how that worked out for them. No, our first ever win at Huish Park was well-earned and well-executed. For this squad, short of a couple of bodies, to be sixth in the table today is a hell of an achievement. Consider that we can only get better, Danny gets his teams fitter and stronger as seasons wear on and he's going to add several new faces in January. Michael Hortinsaid it felt like an important result, he's right in a way as every game is important and as Danny said, the next game is always more important than the last. For me, Port Vale was the really important one, coming off the back of two defeats with a striker lacking in confidence, that game could have bitten us on the bum. Instead we won, gained confidence and that has led to the result. Don't get me wrong, it's a great score line and one I didn't truly expect despite my predictions, but the boys went and got the job done.

To be sixth is a real boost for everyone, especially as there has been some mutterings around social media of slight discontent. Nothing brings fans together like three wins on the spin, eight goals in those games and a clean sheet right to boot. The players are growing in confidence, the management have never lost confidence and the fans will always be buoyed by a triple pack of wins. Accrington won't relish coming to City next week, especially not after their game was cancelled yesterday. We go to Newport in a couple of weeks, they conceded three at home to Carlisle. With Stevenage and Forest Green to come too, there's no reason why we can't be seven unbeaten heading into 2018 to face Luton and Notts County.

I'm genuinely excited by the future, it isn't sycophantic pandering either, but I've seen enough with my own eyes to believe we can finish in the top seven this season. We have 90% of a promotion capable team and 70% of a promotion winning squad. With January coming up fast and a little war chest to dip into, there's no reason why those two figures shouldn't increase and, if the new faces gel and the current ones keep performing, we're as good as anyone in this division on our day, If Coventry are the best we've encountered and we're above them, that is all the proof you need.

As for Yeovil, I genuinely wish them well. I think they've got a real fight on their hands to stay in the league and the next time we face them both of our fates might already be decided. That won't be down to the level of respect we've given them either, nor will it be solely down to budgets. No, our success is attributable to a real ethos of togetherness and hard work throughout the club, something that Yeovil simply didn't display after an hour of yesterday's game.

Ask, and ye shall receive
December 15, 2017

It was what, an hour ago that I put Danny Rowe on top of my Imps Christmas wish list. Well, Santa McCarthy was clearly reading and he's let slip the midfielder is coming to Lincoln in January on loan.

There's no word from City yet, probably because good old Mick has let the cat out of the bag before the I's have been dotted and all that. He's always one to rely on to let something slip is Mick.

Rowe began his career at Stockport County in 2009, making 56 appearances in four seasons at the club either side of a brief loan spell at Northwich Victoria. He spent the 2012–13 season with Barrow, before joining Macclesfield Town in 2013. It was at Moss Rose where he began to catch the eye, especially after a dazzling April 2016 match against Danny Cowley's Braintree. He scored and ran riot as the Silkmen won 3-1. Afterwards John Askey said of Rowe: "He's brave, strong, quick, good on the ball and has a good shot on him".

Last season he was heavily linked with a January move to Sincil Bank only for Ipswich to weigh in with an offer of around £100k. He's failed to break into the first team there, making just three appearances this season.

It's the Seb Stockbridge Show: Imps 2-0 Accrington
December 16, 2017

City grabbed a vital win, a well-earned and justified win this afternoon in a fiercely contested match that sent fires raging through the hearts and minds of every freezing fan watching the game.

I'm going to jump straight in with it: the referee was absolutely appalling in every way. Up until the penalty decision he had been inconsistent, hesitant and wildly unpredictable. He seemed programmed to give Stanley every little decision but ignore the constant infringements on our forward players. I'm usually not critical of referees if I can help it, but this one has form and his mere presence made you feel something out of the ordinary was going to happen.

As it happens, it went in our favour. Matt Green was fouled in the box, his shirt was pulled from his back as he broke through on goal and the referee pointed to the spot, dismissing their player at the same time. Of course everyone was delighted, especially after the Accrington antics of the previous forty-five minutes. However, and remember I try to be as balanced as ever, for me it isn't a penalty. If it is a penalty we've been robbed in virtually every other game we've seen this season. Shirt pulling goes on at every corner, every set piece at every game in this land, why is it this afternoon it has been punished in the harshest possible manner? It worked in our favour and of course I was delighted but it would be remiss of me to claim it was a penalty when I didn't think it was. Mind you, if Matt Green was less honest like his Accrington counterparts, he could have had one not long before. Also, if that is a penalty then I saw offences at Crewe and Wimbledon that were as bad, if not worse. That inconstancy is maddening for everyone involved in the game.

All afternoon Stockbridge was a menace, it was suggested to me he sent their player off to get a handle on the game, but that didn't happen. There were ugly scenes at half time which, I'm told, were a result of one of their subs wanting to confront one of our fans, that went unpunished. I saw Rheady stood on, that went unpunished. Yes, we committed one or two tough tackles which went unpunished too, but in the main Accrington got away with most of their theatrics. How can one of their players dive to the floor whilst the ball isn't in play, suggesting to the referee our player dived, but not get spoken to? It was unsporting and yet moments later he did dive with the ball in play and got the free kick!! I'm afraid Seb Stockbridge baffled me for most of the game, despite it being in our favour.

What is disappointing is the penalty decision gave Accrington's manager somewhere to hide for what was a really poor show from them. I've seen an interview where it was called the 'turning point' of the game, but that's not strictly true. Yes, going down to ten men alters the complexion of the match as does conceding a goal, but we'd been by far the better side in the first half. Matt Green was excellent, his phenomenal work rate has now been matched with the confidence he needed and you feel he'll get something every game. Their keeper has made a wonderful save not long before the penalty and it wasn't the first either.

My Dad leaned across in the first half and said: "they knock the ball round well." I had to pull him up, Accrington played the ball sideways, backwards, sideways, backwards, but rarely forwards with any purpose in the first half. I watched one passage of so-called slick football where they advanced from the edge of their own eighteen-yard box to just in front of the centre circle twenty yards away. It took something like fifteen passes and a couple of minutes, we won the ball and within seconds it was in the channel as we attacked. Where is the beauty in passing aimlessly? Where was Billy Kee, the so-called lethal striker we've lacked? He barely saw the ball and unlike Matt Green, he didn't go looking for it either. It may have been superbly managed by us at the back, but they were well below the level I expected from them.

I must apologise because I'm starting on the ref, then the opposition before I've even come to Lincoln, but Accrington disgusted me today. Their gamesmanship was abhorrent at time, Jordan Clarke in particular stood out as a real nasty piece of work. Sure, we tackle tough. We know we tackle tough, but it is a man's game is it not? It is a hotly contested game, is it not? I didn't see too much happen outside the laws of the game, but the amount of histrionics was ridiculous. I thought we were going to see a slick passing team come and try to break us down, instead we saw a side intent on getting our players sent off and simulating fouls wherever they could. This isn't me in rose-tinted glasses, I've already said the penalty was soft, but they were a disgrace. If they're the third or fourth best team in this division, we've got no problems at all.

On to us, to a man we were excellent throughout the match. Okay there was the odd misplaced pass or poor decision, but I think the players perhaps had the ref's unpredictability in mind. I thought in the first half we let them have the ball where they couldn't hurt us but snuffed out any serious threat before it got near Josh Vickers. I think I counted two saves from Josh, both barely warranted the term 'shot on target'. Matt Green was simply brilliant, he's not doing anything different to a few weeks ago but now he does it with confidence. I did say if he got one he'd go on a run of four or five games and it has proven to be the case. Okay, a penalty is a gimme of sorts, but it takes balls to score from the spot under pressure. Their keeper was huge and yet Matt wasn't fazed. I'm delighted for him and for us, a fully firing Matt Green is as good as any striker in this division.

Obviously Matt Rhead was doing exactly what we expected of him. I'm not sure his booking was justified; the referee didn't appear to see it but pulled the card out on the advice of their keeper. After that I thought they'd maybe target him to try to add another yellow to his collection, but he didn't get involved. What he did get involved in was our second goal, a wonderful finish that even John Coleman described as 'beautifully taken'. The key point in the goal was yet another sumptuous cross from Neal Eardley, top-flight delivery from a top-class player. Eardley was superb again, but I almost get tired of typing those words. To think he was a last-minute throw of the dice after trialling four or five other players is breath-taking.

I've got to call out Alex Woodyard and Bozzie again as well, with those two in the side I feel we are as solid as at any point since I've been a fan. Bozzie is just an animal, you can feel the fear as he bears down on a player with the ball. It must be frightening to look up and see that angry mass of hair and aggression homing in on you. I wonder if the look is as much about instilling fear as it is fashion? Seriously, I talk about Eardley's arrival being breath-taking, but how on earth have we got Michael Bostwick?

You know what I love about him? How simple he makes the game. Win a tackle, pass the ball. Win a header, follow in the second ball, win it again. Get the ball, pass the ball. He never takes too many touches, sometimes he barely takes two. He's a functional footballer, he's not bags of tricks or unpredictable passing, he's simple and effective. They say every team has a player that does the unseen work, we've got two and their work in noticeable. Alex is just Alex, he's never changed since the first time he pulled on a red and white shirt at Sincil Bank. He rarely puts a foot wrong, he is always looking to spread play but is also acutely aware of keeping it simple. He works incredibly hard for his team mates at both ends of the field and is a massive asset to the team.

I heard lots of moans in the last twenty minutes about us having ten men and not taking the game to them, why would we? Why would we push men forward and risk conceding a goal? It got a bit frenetic but that was never going to favour a precise passing side like Accrington. They got drawn into the scrappy affair, even resorting to long balls forward by the end of the game. It wasn't pretty to watch, but with so many variables such as the referee and their swan-diving, why would we take any chances? It wasn't an example of the beautiful game, but when one looks back at the results at the end of the season there won't be an asterisk by the 2-0 that reads 'got scrappy in the final twenty minutes'. Nope, it'll just say Lincoln 2 Accrington 0, it won't even mention Seb Stockbridge which I imagine pains him immensely.

There's a lot of football to be played, but we're in great shape here. Last December 17th we faced Tranmere at home, similar to today really in that there was a dubious penalty at the same end of the ground and we ended up beating a promotion rival. That game was the first after Oldham and for me that was when our status went from play-off hopefuls to champions elect. Today we have gone from fringe play-off hopefuls to being right in the mix. It was a crucial win, the sort of result that can influence a season. I guarantee you for all of the respect we'll show Newport, for all of the 'they've got great players' you'll hear on the radio, they will not want Lincoln City visiting on December 23rd. Stevenage will not want to come here on Boxing Day and Forest Green most certainly won't relish the December 30th clash. Other sides will be looking through the results and ours will jump right out at them. "Bloody hell," they'll say in the Mansfield board room tonight, "Lincoln beat Accrington and yet our massive budget brought a draw against Yeovil. At home."

We're in form, we're as solid as the abs on these Strictly Come Dancing finalists and we're dark horses in this promotion race. The Danny Rowe rumours have all-but been confirmed by Danny and my spies tell me he is the first of a couple of 'wow' signings we can expect in the New Year. If 2018 dawns and we're still sixth you need to fasten your seatbelts, dust off your Neil Diamond LP (sadly) and prepare for five months of genuine excitement because we're only getting better.

Return to form, return to identity

December 22, 2017

Four wins from four, ten goals scored and three clean sheets. Those so-called dark days of struggling for goals seem a long way away now, don't they?

As we turned our attentions to the final knockings of 2017 I think the reason for the revival, if it can be called that, is clear. In the last few weeks, we've gone back to being the Lincoln City that won games for fun last season. We've been back 'on method', we've found our identity.

You'll know exactly what I mean, the big man buzzing around a live wire centre forward, wingers running at full backs and Luke Waterfall at the centre of defence. Since we turned Port Vale over at Sincil Bank we've looked a different team to the one which lost to Colchester. We've never been 'bad' as such, far from it, but something seems to have clicked recently. Newport away would have struck fear into my heart had we been the shot-shy side that drew a blank with Crawley. We're not though, Matt Green has found his purpose and confidence, Matt Rhead has found his rhythm and all over the park (bar left wing) we look a settled and comfortable side. If Nathan can find his form from last season, we won't need a January transfer window!! (Joke, we do.)

Sadly (at least for one player) the change has come about at the same time as one player's game time has dried up. It might be luck, it might be judgement, but I think our return to what we know has coincided with Billy Knott not being on the pitch.

He's not a scapegoat, let me make that clear. I believe that pre-Colchester Danny wanted to crowbar Billy into the team, somehow. We know Billy has talent, there's no denying that, but are we poorer for it when we're trying to pack it into a functional side such as ours? When Billy was on form, great. This season though he has rarely been on form and we've tried to accommodate him nonetheless. Since we've stopped pushing him into the gaps, we've looked a better side. Our tactic is based on hard work, pressing and energy and that is only possible when all eleven players are on method. Billy, for me, is a mercurial talent. when he's good, he's very good. When he's bad, he's ineffective. When your game plan is all about energy and intensity, all eleven players need to be functional.

It does genuinely hurt me to write this because I rate Billy and he's the type of player I love to see on the ball. He has a great range of passes and can strike a ball as sweet as anyone, but we just haven't seen enough of it to justify his continued inclusion. I truly believed earlier in the season he was the key, sitting him behind Green and letting the creativity happen. I wrote about it, passionately. The problem is, it didn't happen as I foresaw it. I imagined he'd get a start in the ten role and start spraying the ball around like Paul Gascoigne in his pomp, skipping past players and weighing in with goals too. Instead he sat behind the forward, misplaced a few ambitious flicks and we failed to score goals.

Our entire game plan has to chance to accommodate Billy and that was evident as we started to draw a blank in front of goal. We weren't conceding, we never will with Bozzie and Woodyard marshalling the middle of the park, but the responsibility for creating chances fell to Billy and he couldn't deliver. Again, I stress it wasn't all down to him and he did have decent games, but when you're as talented as him you need to show more than he did do. There were others not firing on all cylinders too, Matt Green was low on confidence, I get all of that. The trouble for Billy is Matt has got his confidence back, the others are on point and it's happened whilst Bill is warming the bench.

The reinvigorated Matt Rhead has been able to create chances from the ten role. He's been able to weigh in with a couple of goals too and the doubters, me included, have had to eat their words a little. I did wonder if he'd handle the pace of League Two and I wondered if we'd need to work too hard to accommodate him. Evidently that isn't the case, he has worked twice as hard to force his way into the side and we have suddenly found our flow. Neither him nor Matt Green look shot-shy anymore, we pour forward with purpose and with delivery from Mr Eardley we're a different prospect again.

So, where now for Billy? As I was asked in a recent message from reader Steve Lawson; is Billy a number ten? Is he a winger? Does Danny know? Does Billy know? If he's neither of these, where does he fit into the squad? We've found our identity and rediscovered what it was the made us successful last season, but will Billy be able to find his identity before it's too late?

The heart-breaking thing is I think Billy is as much a confidence player as anyone. It's no secret he's one of the so-called "trouble' household that Danny jokes about, the ones he stuck together in accommodation to keep them away from the sensible lads, but when you strip it back I think Billy is just a lost soul, low on confidence and struggling to find the rhythm required to get himself back on track. If he hadn't been cruelly sent off against Notts County, we would have seen a different player now. Those first 28 minutes he looked exactly like the number ten we want, full of endeavour and scheming. Then the red card came, he sat out of three games in which we accumulated seven points and he came back a shadow of that player.

Of the ten games we've won, Billy started three, 30%. Of the six we've lost, Billy started four, 66%. That may be an unfair statistic, but I do think it highlights the fact we've struggled to find a place for him in a winning side. The worst thing is it isn't through a lack of effort on his part, he works tirelessly hard. He was training right up until kick off during his suspension, alone on the astro turf. It isn't a lack of desire, but something isn't quite right and unless something out of the ordinary happens between now and January I fear for him.

Five unbeaten, three clean sheets: Newport 0-0 Imps
December 23, 2017

We'll skirt around the obvious, this afternoon City have notched up a fifth game unbeaten, kept a third clean sheet in a row and hung on to a play-off spot for Christmas.

Last season we revelled at being top come Christmas, once again Danny Cowley has taken Lincoln City to a respectable place that leaves fans at ease to enjoy festivities in good cheer. Sixth in our maiden season back in the Football league is superb at Christmas, it's actually frightening what might be achieved when the ranks get bolstered in January.

The only team news ahead of the game was the return of Nathan Arnold at the expense of Cameron Stewart. Stewart picked up an injury but many would suspect Arnold's inclusion saw us field our strongest eleven. Nathan might not have been in the side on a regular basis, but at present he's our second-best winger.

We came up against a resolute and hard-working Newport team, a side that have improved tenfold since their brush with relegation last season. It always promised to be a controversial afternoon after Robbie Wilmott's comments pre-game.

Without dwelling on the point too much, Wilmott's comments were absolutely ridiculous. He started by saying: "To be honest, they are a horrible team. They're very direct, teams call us direct but that's a different kind of direct. I saw them on television a lot last season and they are direct, and I think that's what we're going to have to deal with." He followed that up by saying: "I don't think we really care (when people call Newport long ball), if you beat teams and they come out and say that then you've obviously done a good job. I've seen a lot of managers this year saying that they've worked on a lot of things in training and haven't been able to deal with what we bring. Set-pieces are part and parcel of football and if you're not good at them you're going to ship goals." Whatever Robbie. There wasn't much he could do from the bench at Rodney Parade (pictured top).

Newport had the best of the first half, as the home team you'd expect that. Nouble, the former West Ham player, looked a real threat but ultimately they didn't create anything too worrying for City. They controlled play, they brought the game to us as you'd expect from the home team. At half time though, the score was 0-0. Both sides hit long balls, the pretty long ball side Newport and the horrible long ball side Lincoln. Referee Brett Huxtable looked very much a 'homer' as we didn't get a single decision, but we were still in the game and that was all that mattered.

At half time Luke Waterfall said in the dressing room "If that's the best they've got then we've got a chance." He was right, City came out with (using Danny's favourite words) purpose and intent but it wasn't to be.

In the second half a good game was altered by a yet another soft red card for our opposition. Newport had a guy sent off for a hard tackle on Matt Green whilst Green was heading away from goal. Huxtable immediately flashed a red card which sparked mayhem. A long break ensued during which it appears Danny was pelted with coins from the stand. They weren't pretty scenes but Danny played down the incident claiming he had "about £1.20" to go and buy a can of Coke with, following up by saying he respected the Newport fans and didn't want to get them into trouble. For the record, they will get into trouble as the referee spotted it and will report it.

The decision changed the complexion of the game completely, the atmosphere turned from frenetic to vitriolic with home fans baying for a red card at every turn. Huxtable perhaps lost control a little, to the detriment of the spectacle.

After that Newport were still organised and hard-working, City should perhaps have taken better advantage of the situation but didn't. I think that lays bare the issues with the threadbare squad we had, with the greatest of respect to both Palmer and Billy Knott, if we'd got a little bit more industry to come from the bench we might have snatched it. To be fair to Billy he looked decent after coming on, he played some nice balls and sat in the 'free role' which he'd doubtless like every week. The problem is, most weeks we play eleven players.

We got a few balls into the box but not enough to break the deadlock. Keeper Joe Day was excellent, commanding his area well and making saves when called upon. Could Nathan have scored when he went through one on one? Possibly, but it was nice to see him running in behind and creating problems. Similarly, Matt Green will have been disappointed not to have done better with his later header. Either way, a draw was a fair result in the end.

Eardley was, once again, superb. He might already be a shout for Player of the Season even at this early stage, he's such a consistent and calm figure at the back. I've no doubt his arrival has solidified our back line even more than last season, that and the arrival of Michael Bostwick.

Bozzie had a shout for man of the match today. He's just immense in the middle of the park, he's as simple as a ham sandwich, as basic as a plain cheese pizza but as effective as rat poison. He wins the ball and passes it. He receives the ball and passes it. When it comes near him, he heads it away. When it comes near someone near him, he wins it and passes it. It's Fisher Price football but done with the efficiency and aggression all fans like to see. His booking was ridiculous, he rose high to win a header and got booked for it. Brett Huxtable was probably looking to even things up and was just totting up a few yellows to give himself a chance.

Both centre halves played well too, I'm delighted for Luke getting back into the squad, but also for Raggs who is giving his all right through to the end. There's no doubt he'll be a massive loss, but what price on him signing off with a late header against Luton? His story is a fairy tale and his work rate and aggression are excellent. Him and Luke look as strong as at any point last season and it will be a crying shame to see them broken up in January.

As it goes, we didn't get the win. It's a real testament to the side that a 0-0 draw at Newport feels like a defeat after 90 minutes. It shouldn't, if they play like that every week at home they'll be top ten come May and by that rationale it's a good result. We're five matches unbeaten now, each of these runs keeps us at the right end of the table, each defeat is now being put to bed with a good unbeaten run. We'll lose matches during the season, but if we go on unbeaten runs after we do, we'll be fine. Similarly we've now kept three clean sheets in a row, something else which good sides are built upon. We may have slipped to sixth but in reality, what is the difference between fourth and seventh? All four spots will see us in the end of season lottery. What is really frustrating is a win would have seen us finish the day in third!

Luton and Notts County have put some daylight between them and the rest, but Accrington and Exeter have found themselves in the chasing pack now. Five points separate Exeter in third and Newport in eleventh, but in ten days' time each side will have played three more games. By the second day of 2018 I predict the gap between 11th and 4th will be bigger, the chasing pack will slowly be whittled down and we need to make sure we stay in it. We just need to cling on to this position until the Luton / Notts County double-header, after that, who knows? Would you bet against City at the moment? I wouldn't and I can tell you this: nobody wants to play us at the minute. Not Newport, not Accrington and not even Notts County.

As for Danny, I hope he enjoys his can of Coke on the way home, doubtless Newport won't enjoy the referee's report landing on the FA's doorstep. I suspect the FA will be more intent on trying to force non-league clubs into bankruptcy rather than punishing actual misdemeanours, so they might be alright.

Boxing Day Bonanza: Imps 3-0 Stevenage

December 26, 2017

Danny Cowley's teams get better after Christmas apparently. I believed him, but I didn't think it would be so soon after Christmas that we were going to look so utterly rampant.

Firstly, we weren't playing a relegation threatened side today. Stevenage are a really well-organised and effective unit; their players were strong and they all knew their roles. I thought for the first fifteen minutes or so they looked on top in truth. Their front two are class, both Newton and Godden would grace the squad of any side and early doors I wondered if we might be lamenting their endeavour as they probed for a way through. We weren't being outplayed but I thought they edged the opening exchanges.

They certainly had the best chance in the first quarter of an hour, Josh Vickers demonstrating once again how he managed to usurp Paul Farman as the number one with a wonderful save from Newton. Not long after it was Godden causing him to make a stop, albeit a tame effort. With that the Imps looked to move through the gear quickly.

I'm not sure how Joe Fryer stopped us taking a 30th minute lead though, it was perhaps the best save I've ever seen with my own eyes. Matt Green, who I'll wax lyrical about shortly, set up Raggs for a point-blank volley. Raggs, eight yards out at most, smashed the ball towards goal but from nowhere Fryer appeared to make the save. It was super hero stuff, in the stands I wondered if maybe that was our chance. As things went, it was only our first knock at the door. Four minutes later, we got let in.

Rhead and Green combined wonderfully to set up Harry Anderson, but to at the merely combined doesn't do justice to either player's role. Rhead executed a wonderful ball for Green to charge on to, much as he did for the goal at Yeovil. Green gleefully strode away and got a shot off, Fryer once again the hero. He parried but only into the path of Harry Anderson who nodded into an empty net. Once we'd got the foot in the door, we never really looked like throwing the game away.

All over the park we looked assured and organised. Michael Bostwick was again excellent in midfield, not allowing their players time to create a thing. Neal Eardley was outstanding too, but I barely need to type that anymore do I? When did you see Eardley have a bad game? I'll answer for you: never. He's mobile, he thinks one step ahead of his opponent and he's strong in the air. I lost count of the number of times he watched a ball come towards him, took a step back from his opponent and won a header without leaving the floor. Both him and Bostwick have brought experience to our ranks. Along with Matt Green of course.

We went in 1-0 up at half time and the general consensus around me in Upper Three was that we were good value for the lead. Stevenage were no mugs, they came to have a go with three up front and they hadn't look fazed by us taking the lead. This wasn't about having a go though, it was simply a good side being beaten by a better one. All over the park we refused to give an inch, Harry Anderson and Nathan Arnold were having good games on either flank. They're such different wingers too, Nathan is all about speed and guile whereas Harry is a bull (a bloody swift one) in a china shop. In the middle of the first period their full back tried to bump into the back of Harry, usually a soft winger would go down but Harry remained steadfast and cemented to the spot. Their player went down in a heap, no foul, but minutes later play was brought back for fear of a head injury. It was typical Harry, quick as a Ferrari but as brutish and strong as a monster truck.

After the break we looked like running riot as Stevenage showed their first fifteen minutes was as good as it was going to get. Nathan had a header saved when, had he realised he'd got more time, he might have chosen to volley it at goal. I was pleased for him though, he worked tremendously hard all game and as it wore on he became more influential. Everyone reading this knows I've got a soft spot for Nathan, but I'm also a 'pundit' of sorts and I wouldn't pull punches if they were warranted. However, Nathan is our first choice on the left flank at present and today he showed why. Again.

Just after the hour we killed the game off. Up until Matt Green grabbed his seventh of the season the game was in the balance, a quick break could have seen them get a foothold in the game. Sometimes they say 2-0 is a dangerous score, sure in matches against Chesterfield and Barnet maybe, but today the second goal merely inflicted another mortal wound on the dying carcass of Stevenage's Boxing Day hopes. Another wonderful Neal Eardley cross was finished in style by Matt Green. His volley gave Fryer no chance and it came from a player oozing confidence and class. Isn't it funny, just six weeks ago some were calling for Green to be dropped, claiming he didn't look like a centre forward. Now, everyone is singing his name, and rightly so.

I don't think his resurgence has been by accident, I think it has been through perseverance and through the return of Matt Rhead. Those two just work so well together and we've found a pattern that allows for the Big Un's lack of mobility. He might not have bene involved in the goal, but he was involved in everything else we did going forward. More often than not it wasn't even a flick on either, he held the ball up on the ground, sprayed passes all over like Matt Le Tissier used to do and generally conducted the play from just behind Matt Green. That left Green free to work the channels and Stevenage's desire to attack us meant the space was there for Green to exploit. That said, his strike to put us 2-0 up was one that you can't train, it was a finish that you're either born with the ability to do, or not.

At that point I thought we might score five, we genuinely looked that commanding. Green got free again and squared for Harry Anderson who scuffed his shot badly, but he'd run fifty yards to offer green an out. I've heard it described as one of the misses of the season and that wouldn't be an unfair assessment, but Danny judge's players on being in positions to miss. Harry had no right to be stood six yards from goal with the ball at his feet, but his tireless running allowed him to miss badly. Besides, we don't want 'Anderson (2)' or even 'Anderson (3)' appearing in newspapers this close to January.

After the goals came the game management, Elliott came on and did really well in my opinion. I've been critical of Elliott, never his work rate but often where he fits in to the set up, but his introduction added some steel to the middle of the park at the expense of width. Then we brought on Josh, adding width in place of the steel brought by Rhead. It was game management of the highest order and both of them did well after coming on. Ollie Palmer also had a role to play and, despite still not winning a header, he also did well. Stevenage looked out of ideas, never out of desire and belief, but there was no clear route to goal. Our centre-halves both had good games, Raggett in particular was immense. I'm afraid to say if Norwich were watching today, he isn't coming back because they're going to want to keep him, whether they won 2-0 against Birmingham or not. He gave a master class in the art of central defending, one I'm sure Steve Thompson was watching in admiration.

Two subs, both subject of criticism from some, were able to wrap things up with ten minutes left. Ollie Palmer broke free and had his effort saved, but Josh Ginnelly finished smartly from the rebound. It's nice that these players are able to come on when the game is in hand and express themselves, Josh in particular impressed me. He got a lot of grief for that goal against Port Vale, mostly undeserved and his delight at scoring was plain to see. He made for Block Seven and gave a one-man celebration right in front of the 'signing section'. It means a lot to Josh, he's a nice lad and someone whom I believe will go far in the game as he develops.

Winning 3-0 at home against Stevenage is a good result, finding yourselves third in the table on the way out of the ground is even better. There's a long way to go, but my Dad always said to me that where you are around Christmas is a good indication of where you'll be at the end of the season. Well, we're in the automatic promotion spots and if we apply ourselves correctly on Saturday against Cooperman and his deflated troops, we'll be welcoming in 2018 as a top three League Two side.

Can you imagine having to choose a Man of the Match today? You could ask eight people and get eight different answers. Both centre halves were excellent, Sam and Neal worked the flanks brilliantly, Neal perhaps edged it but Sam was definitely more than a steady seven. The midfield functioned well, out wide were offered lots of threat and the top two carried out their job descriptions to a tee. If pushed I would have said Matt Green as my choice, I just know you'll have someone different in mind.

Crowd: brilliant. Over 9,000 home fans came along today which was great, although on the radio it was suggested Boxing Day wasn't a popular fixture. I always thought Boxing Day saw slightly larger crowds as people come back from Uni or visit family and get down to see the team. That said, 9,000 home fans? Wow. That's almost as many as we took to Arsenal, before you know it all of those day trippers will have been converted! Seriously though, I hope this support is here to stay because if it is we can comfortably hold our own financially at this level and maybe the one above.

Finally, a word about referee Carl Boyeson. I just had to look his name up because I'd forgotten who was in charge, mainly because the game was about the two teams and not him. Sure, he punished Bostwick for a hard challenge when it looked harsh but if that is all we have to gripe about, the odd harsh booking, then I'm happy. If all of our officials were as competent as Boyeson we wouldn't have any problems at all.

Let me just remind you, we're now third in the table, ahead of Wycombe on goal difference courtesy of today's triple and we host the bottom side on Saturday. We're looking organised, tough to break down and a threat going forwards. We've got bodies to come in over the next thirty-five days, bodies that will only improve the overall output of the team. If Danny had any question marks over player's heads, everybody answered him positively today.

I'm not saying we'll be top three come May, but I am saying that Danny's sides rarely rise and then fall again. We started in the middle of the pack, we hung on to the edge of the play-off race and now we've not only cracked the top seven, but we've rose to the top of the hopefuls. Catching County and Luton won't be easy, but with both sides to play in the next couple of weeks I would rule it out.

There's not one team in the League who won't be looking at our rise and hoping we're not up next for them. We're improving every week just through hard work and having a clear game plan. Stevenage couldn't cope with us when we found our rhythm and I'm not sure any team in this division can, on our day. The key is to remain focused, not get downhearted if we do fall back into the chasing pack and to keep believing in the possibilities.

I'm loving supporting my club at the moment, I can't wait to see what we conjure up next.

Drama, Tension and I missed it all: Imps 2-1 FGR
December 31, 2017

City grabbed another vital win in the quest for back to back promotions, overcoming old foes Forest Green in a tense 2-1 victory at the Bank today.

I'm afraid I can't give you my usual summary of the game, I wasn't there and I wasn't near a radio either. It would be remiss of me to try to 'wing' it too, I wouldn't insult you or mislead you by trying to analyse a game that the majority of you saw and I did not.

What I do know it a 3rd v 24th match was a close affair and that in itself tells you everything you need to know about how close this league is. From what I understand we were the better side, but we didn't blow them away. Oddly, we have now beaten Barnet, Chesterfield and this lot 2-1 at home when supporters perhaps expected a bigger score. Doesn't really matter does it? 2-1 or 6-0, three points is all we get and neither Notts County nor Luton got three today, so we continue to reel them in. The next two league games are top of the table six-point clashes, not bad considering we've only been in the league six months.

The big man continued his electric form in front of goal with a brace and, knowing the type of person he is, I bet he bloody loved it. Let's face it, there's no love lost between us and that lot and today certainly won't have built any bridges either. The return to form of Matt Rhead is a pure delight, it is one in the eye for everyone who wrote him off, to an extent that includes me. He's such a massive asset and I'm happy for him. Every goal he scores, every assist he makes and every celebration is one step further into the stuff of Imps legend for him. My Dad told me about Percy Freeman and although I don't have kids, when I'm sixty I'll be finding random children to tell them all about the Big 'Un.

I do know they had the ball in the net and it was disallowed, sadly that will probably take away from the tremendous save by Josh Vickers just moments earlier. Of course, Cooperman has stated that the ref couldn't wait to disallow it because Danny told him to, the usual ridiculous bile that comes out of that man's mouth. I've been told of unsightly scenes at the final whistle too, again probably centred around the manager who we've now done the double over in consecutive seasons.

I really wish I'd been there, it is hard to describe how it felt to miss my first home game in eighteen months. I would have loved to give Sean a good send off and I would have thoroughly enjoyed singing 'you're getting sacked in the morning' to a repulsive man too. I'm sorry, you know I despise FGR and not being there as we hammer another nail in their coffin pains me immensely.

I did spend my time constantly refreshing BBC sport, Twitter and Facebook, several people graciously messaged me including Dad and Ric Stephens. I didn't see a ball kicked but I got a real flavour of the game. We could have scored ten, we looked a bit susceptible at the back and we went a bit deep for the final ten, hanging on for dear life. Is that a fair assessment? You'll have to tell me!!

Was it any surprise that Christian Doidge got their goal? He is a player that oozes quality, he's a diamond in a pile of manure, the once Malteser sweet left amongst a Celebrations tin full of Bounty bars. He's a poacher, a natural in front of goal who deserves to be watched by more fans every week. If he rocked up in the red and white of City I'd be overjoyed. I'm told Reece Brown had a decent game too, but outside of that FGR don't have the quality to do anything other than battle relegation. They certainly don't have the manager to get them out of trouble. Promotion to League One easy is it Vince? Pull the other one, it's got bells on.

Once again though, the result on the pitch has been overshadowed by that repugnant outfit and their abhorrent behaviour. In September it was their keeper spitting at Sean Raggett, a crime for which he was cleared by the FA. I think it is worth pointing out, being cleared does not mean he didn't do it. I've seen the video and the evidence isn't conclusive, therefore the FA had no option but to clear him. It doesn't mean he didn't do it, in my opinion he did and I'm not always pro-Lincoln. I didn't think Accrington should have gone down to ten men a fortnight ago, I'm not just seeing the world through rose-tinted glasses. However, in my opinion, Raggett was spat at.

Anyway, that was then, surely FGR couldn't stoop any lower could they? Yes apparently, significantly lower. I've gleaned what I can from the incident and we haven't heard the last of it. FGR claim their coach was attacked, but this incident took place whilst it was stationary and surrounded by security. Attacked? Not on your nelly. No, there seems to be a misconception by FGR that mobile phones don't have cameras on them in Lincoln, but they do and the incident has been caught. I'm afraid the eco-friendly tree-huggers, the fairy tale rise of the little man against all odds, are being let down by incomprehensible behaviour by players and staff.

The Lincoln fans involved in the incident will most likely be talking to authorities and therefore won't be able to talk too openly. The Gloucestershire media have read a few biased tweets and formed a news story that is wide of the mark, thankfully our own media have not yet followed suit.

My understanding is that Cooperman verbally abused an Imps fan after being told to enjoy the National League next season. I believe that verbal abuse included swearing and our fan banged on the side of the bus – it wasn't 'attacked' in the strictest sense. That prompted a large group of Forest Green players and staff to alight the bus, grab our fan by the neck and punch him. This fan, I believe, had his children with him. The scene got uglier as they then got involved in arguments with other Imps fans, eventually the bus driver (of all people) had to drag them back onto the bus. Professional footballers, football managers and paid staff were involved in an incident which saw a Lincoln City fan punched in the face. When it came to be broken up it wasn't their manager that did it, but the bloody bus driver.

Football fans give out a bit of banter, bit this hardly sounds like Eric Cantona style abuse does it? Players simply cannot attack fans, no matter what is said, especially not when it is a younger fan. It's beyond comprehension really, they're supposed to be professional people.

What more can we say? Once again events off the field overshadow a fine Lincoln win. I'm not sure how Mark Cooper has got to be such a vile human being, nor can I imagine how much lower Forest Green can go in their overall behaviour. I will say this: they've no place amongst football's elite and right now, I'd rather Dover were a Football League club. How dare a footballer get off a coach at our ground and hit one of our fans. How dare Cooperman keep attacking us verbally when he can't figure out a way to even get a draw from a game. They are a repugnant and vile group of people and I sincerely hope the FA or the police act against them because it is long overdue.

That aside, we now welcome 2018 in 3rd place. We're beginning to open up a small gap between us and the chasing pack (and a much bigger one between us and this lot) although matches against Notts County and Luton will truly test our resilience. If we could somehow find a way to take three points from the next two games, I'd believe we might just be in the hunt for automatic promotion. This season is panning out much like the last, start with aspirations, exceed these within five months and instil a belief that we can do it right the way through until May. On Boxing Day we won pretty, today we battled to a win. This side is looking much like Lincoln of last season, organised, dangerous and most of all, they refuse to lose.

I believe we can go to Kenilworth Road and get at least a point. I believe on our own ground, we can beat Notts County. I believe in Danny and Nicky Cowley, I believe in Lincoln City. Forget all the pantomime surrounding today's game, Forest Green will get what is coming to them eventually, but we're Lincoln City and I believe we're better than all of that.

Pos	Team	Pld	W	D	L	GF	GA	GD	Pts
1	Luton Town	25	15	6	4	58	23	35	51
2	Notts County	25	13	8	4	43	26	17	47
3	Lincoln City	25	12	7	6	33	20	13	43
4	Exeter City	24	13	3	8	34	30	4	42
5	Coventry City	25	12	5	8	27	18	9	41
6	Wycombe Wanderers	25	11	7	7	44	34	10	40
7	Accrington Stanley	24	12	4	8	38	30	8	40
8	Colchester United	25	11	7	7	35	27	8	40
9	Mansfield Town	25	10	10	5	35	28	7	40
10	Swindon Town	24	12	2	10	36	33	3	38
11	Newport County	25	9	9	7	33	29	4	36
12	Cambridge United	25	10	6	9	25	31	-6	36
13	Carlisle United	25	9	7	9	36	34	2	34
14	Grimsby Town	25	9	7	9	26	32	-6	34
15	Cheltenham Town	25	8	7	10	32	34	-2	31
16	Port Vale	25	9	4	12	29	33	-4	31
17	Stevenage	25	8	6	11	32	38	-6	30
18	Crawley Town	25	8	6	11	23	30	-7	30
19	Yeovil Town	25	7	6	12	35	45	-10	27
20	Crewe Alexandra	25	8	2	15	27	41	-14	26
21	Morecambe	25	6	7	12	24	36	-12	25
22	Chesterfield	25	5	6	14	26	46	-20	21
23	Barnet	25	5	5	15	25	37	-12	20
24	Forest Green Rovers	24	5	5	14	24	45	-21	20

January

That's the benchmark: Luton 4-2 Imps

January 1, 2018

The Christmas period has been incredibly kind to Lincoln City but today was the exception. Today we got to see the real benchmark for success in this division. Coventry might have looked good against us, but Luton showed the character and determination needed to grab a result. Coupled with the undoubted class that runs through their team, they're nailed on champions in my eyes.

I don't think we disgraced ourselves either, not one bit. I suppose when a player is sent off after four minutes you're never going to get a true barometer of how far we've come, or even how far we need to go. I think Danny would like to have seen how his eleven coped with Luton's eleven, but Alan Sheehan's unique method of dealing with Rheady put paid to that. Two punches later it's ten against eleven and, thanks to Michael Bostwick's low drive, one nil to City. Had all of this gone off after 60 minutes and we'd gone 1-0 up we would have been in a great position to win the game, but with 84 minutes left to play all it guaranteed was a thrilling afternoon.

Lots of people have said Luton players were out of order trying to get ours booked and sent off, but the truth is they're just good at what they do. Danny Hylton, that odious man who revelled in our relegation, is a really good footballer and equally as good at niggling the opposition. He's basically a slim Matt Rhead and despite my disdain for him, he's a superb footballer. His hard work gave them the leveller just past the hour and it wasn't even against the run of play. Luton looked as good with ten as any side we've played with eleven, they work hard and make the pitch big. They also demonstrated the power of a partisan home crowd too, something we have in our favour at the Bank. I've seen it described a beyond hostile, even Steve Thompson was getting verbal in the commentary box! As a football fan I have to admire that I'm afraid, I'd rather be in a stadium packed with people and vitriol than a half empty wooden box in a village in Gloucestershire listening out for pins dropping (or managers being sent off).

Their goal sparked a mad fifteen minutes which really defined the game. Matt Green immediately gave us an unlikely lead, demonstrating the character we have in our squad, but then just as we needed composure to see out the first half, Harry got sent off. I've seen the decision and I'm going to have to disagree with Danny. For me, it's a straight red all day long, irrespective of his earlier booking. It was a bit of naivety on Harry's part maybe, but you won't get me calling the lad out for showing passion and commitment. He's young and learning the ropes, you wouldn't have seen a seasoned campaigner such as Bozzie make the challenge, but I'd rather that than him withering under the pressure. He'll learn.

Seven minutes later and a scintillating first half was ended with a superb deflected drive for the home side. In my heart, I knew that was it. With 45 minutes left I didn't think we'd get back into the game, not without the likes of Neal Eardley in the side. I'd been worried pre-match that his exclusion put us in a weakened position, but to be ten against ten facing a side that use the pitch like Luton, I didn't give us a hope in hell in the second half.

Cue me eating my words for the first 25 minutes of the second half as we tore into the best side in the league. I'm surprised the referee told Danny that another tackle by Matt Rhead and he was off, but Danny seemed to indicate that was usual behaviour. If I were Nathan Jones, Luton manager, I'd be a bit hacked off we were being given the heads up, especially as his replacement, Josh Ginnelly, seemed to spark a revival in us. For a portion of the second half we looked every inch as good as them, but when we needed quality from the bench we perhaps didn't have it, not in the same measure they do. When they took the lead after 72 minutes, the game was well and truly up.

Was 4-2 a fair reflection of the match? They had 15 efforts compared to our 8, they had 56% possession compared to our 44% so maybe so. When they added a fourth it perhaps flattered them on the balance of play, but certainly they were better than us when it really mattered. What is crucial is we weren't thrashed, we battled hard and I bet they'll know tonight they were in a game. There was no 5-0, no humiliating outcome that put us in our place, just a little demonstration of what a top side does. It's left us fifth and whilst in the National League fifth was virtually nowhere, in this league it is good enough for me.

Remember, we've played four games in just over a week, taken seven points from a possible twelve and cemented our place at the right end of the table. Our players have suffered from fatigue and a bug has ripped through the squad too. We would perhaps have preferred to face one of the lower placed sides, not Luton Town. Instead of having a gentle finish to the hectic period we faced the best side in the division immediately after they'd been hammered away from home. They were like a tiger licking its wounds, able to draw on a bigger squad of players and with the massive home support behind them. I think we did extremely well against all odds.

We've now got twelve days off from league action, something that is a real bonus. There's the Checkatrade game against Rochdale which will be welcomed by the time it arrives, but we've got enough time to get some bodies in. Danny Rowe is confirmed, we knew that a while ago, but our issues lie at the back as well. Losing Raggs is massive and potentially losing Dickie is even worse. However, when Rob Dickie signed it was touted as a 'six-month loan with a view to making it permanent', and I'm hoping that it is made permanent soon. We have to move on from Raggs, but in Rob Dickie there's a centre half that could potentially fill his boots. Nobody will replace him, but we do need to work in the defence. We can't afford to host Notts County with an uncertain centre half pairing, although that game will be won and lost in the middle of the park, especially with Liam Noble joining Jorge Grant, Lewis Alessandra and Terry Hawkridge.

Jordan Maguire-Drew is going back to Brighton and it is fair to say his spell was a flop. It wasn't a lack of ability in the lad, but for me his tactical awareness was a little short of where Danny needs it to be. On the other hand, Danny Rowe is an experienced footballer and he'll be able to carry out the instructions far more succinctly than JMD. I don't want to be too critical of JMD, we just didn't see the best of him. I wouldn't be surprised to see him rock up on loan somewhere like Barnet for the remainder of the season.

I would expect us to have another forward in by the time we host County too. My spies might be wide of the mark, but they're suggesting a fresh move for Akinola is very much on the cards. It's no secret the lad wants to join up with Danny and Nicky, they know he's the right type of player too so it seems a no-brainer. I think any hold up will be caused by ill-feeling from the summer debacle. He's not getting much game time at Underhill, criminal really when they're bottom two, but one man's trash is another man's treasure. I'd be delighted to see Sim in red and white, eighteen months after I first expected him to join!

I had to chuckle ahead of the game when Neal Eardley was missing from the squad, the ripples of concern started on social media. "He's off to the Stags," was the cry, despite him committing to us until the end of the season. Maybe they've wedged a bid for him, it wouldn't surprise me if Steve fancied a couple of our players, but Danny won't want to sell. The same goes for Alex Woodyard, lots of talk is around him going to Luton, but personally I can't see him jumping ship now, just as we're on the cusp of great things. Maybe I'm an optimist, but I don't see any of our key players departing this window, unless numbers such as £400,000 start being thrown around. Even in that instance, expect Danny to have a few tricks up his sleeve.

Back to today, we saw the champions elect grinding out a result against a resilient and determined challenger. That's a fair reflection of proceedings and I don't think we can complain about the referee, their approach or anything like that. We are both decent teams, coached well and packed with talent but they are at a level higher than us. Danny said we're a couple of years behind Luton, I think we're twelve months behind them, but maybe that is the optimist in me again.

Despite this acceptance the result still hurts because I believe on any given day we can beat anyone and, had Harry not been sent off, we could have won this game to. He was, it was the right call and we got beat. Sometimes football deals those hands and you just get on with it. I think we all feel a bit disappointed tonight because Danny Cowley's Lincoln City instil belief in us all. We went to Luton half expecting to get a result, when has that ever really been the case? Most of my Lincoln City supporting life has been spent hoping we get a result, very rarely believing. I still believe we'll be top seven, at least, come May.

Expect the focus to now be on the transfer news, people spotting Ricky Miller at the ground, hearing on the grapevine Alex is going or having seen Danny and Nicky in a service station near Nottingham talking to people in Forest tracksuits. It will be exciting, frustrating and frightening in equal measure. I'm not entirely sure I can stomach any more of Martin Wardell's banter posts about his best mate Ricky Miller, but if the noises coming out of Cambridge are accurate, I might not have to after tomorrow.

Goodbye Sean Raggett: Thanks for the memories
January 1, 2018

The trip to Luton marked the final Lincoln appearance of Sean Raggett. despite there being a slim chance of him returning to the club, it does appear very unlikely as he is destined for bigger and better things.

When we initially signed Sean from Dover ahead of last season it was a real coup. Barrow were after his signature and a last-minute phone call diverted him to Lincoln for a look around. The story goes that young Sean was driving up north with his agent, and a Lincoln City representative got wind of the situation. I understand a call was made to 'come and have a chat' on his way up the A1, and history shows his journey never progressed further than Newark. The lack of training ground didn't put him off and for once the official club reveal beat social media to breaking the news.

He was a cornerstone of our success last season, an integral part of a tight defence but also of our threat from set pieces. He rapidly became a City hero, a player who could always be relied upon to perform to a high standard. One thing that always struck me about Sean was how much it mattered to him. I remember how crestfallen he looked after being sent off against Wrexham, he was genuinely upset at having let the team down. Of course letting Lincoln City down was not something Sean Raggett did very often at all.

As the season wore on, everyone at Sincil Bank knew what capability the youngster had. When Dover visited shortly after we turned Ipswich over, their fans were full of bile before the game. I spoke to some Dover fans who claimed he'd let them and his team mates down by moving on. He hadn't, he could have got out of Crabble much earlier than he did, but he stayed until he simply became too big for them. In truth, he was probably too big for us too, how a Football league club didn't take a punt on him I'll never know.

Before long, the cat was out of the bag and his reputation spread beyond Lincoln. I suppose it helped him heading in a last-minute winner against Premier League Burnley, making history by sending City to an FA Cup quarter-final. Suddenly his name was all over the papers, not just nationally but internationally. With that comes interest from scouts but I'm told Norwich had been watching him since we'd beaten Ipswich. Even then, we all knew Sean Raggett would move on at some point.

When the summer came the speculation intensified and eventually Norwich did make their move. However, instead of being swept away to their reserve side, he came back for another six months to help propel us to 3rd in the League Two table at New Year. His goal scoring threat never subsided, grabbing the winner at Swindon and against Accrington in the Checkatrade Trophy proved that. No, Sean Raggett simply got better, effortlessly stepping up from marshalling part-time centre forwards to looking after seasoned professionals.

As January loomed we all hoped he'd stay until the end of the season, but I think a return is highly unlikely now. He posted on social media 'goodbye Lincoln' and Norwich manager Daniel Farkas has spoken of 'working with Sean' upon his return. Bradford City have sniffed around too, they'd love him to help them in League One, but all of the interest effectively makes it very hard for Lincoln City to compete.

Sean owes us nothing and if he ends up on loan at Bradford, fair play to him. He need regular football for sure, but he's good enough for League One. I think he's perhaps not ready for Championship football just yet, but he'll only improve by playing at a higher level than ours. I know many will disagree, but I'm afraid it is the truth. No, Sean Raggett's journey has led him away from Sincil Bank and he now needs to take the next step on his journey.

History will remember Sean for a number of reasons, Burnley, Forest Green, even Swindon this season. Each of us will have a favourite Sean Raggett moment, inevitably his winner at the New Lawn of at Turf Moor, but he's been so much more than a target at set pieces. He reads the game superbly, he tackles ferociously and he has the potential to grow into a fine centre half. Comparisons with Trevor Peake are inevitable, joining us from non-league before making a move further up the league and whilst many will say he's not as good as Peake, others might consider him to be takin a similar path.

The world is at Sean Raggett's feet, with hard work and a little bit of luck he'll be playing top-flight football in the next couple of seasons. We should feel honoured to have been part of that journey and proud that we were able to aid his development sufficiently for him to return this season and help us. Someone said on social media that they've rarely seen a player leave with such an enormous amount of goodwill and I'm inclined to agree with that. Then again, when you've headed home a winner in an FA Cup Fifth Round tie to send a non-league club to a quarter-final, you do tend to build up a bit of goodwill.

All the best Sean, good luck in your career. You're a great defender and an even better personality and I'm sure you'll be a roaring success wherever you play your football.

Jordan Maguire-Drew: What went wrong?
January 4, 2018

Jordan Maguire-Drew returned to Brighton officially this week, no sooner had he done so than he rocked up as a Jodi Jones replacement at Coventry City. He's joined them on a six-month loan and, according to Mark Robins, they've been after him a while.

"We targeted Jordan during the summer and unfortunately missed out, so we are very pleased to be able to bring him in now," said Robins. "He has great technical ability and quality, and is a scorer of goals, so we are delighted to get him through the door and for him to start with us. Having got into the top three of the league on Monday, Jordan will supplement our squad very well as we look to establish our position."

Before we look any further at what happened to him at City, it is worth noting the first line of Robins' quote there; 'we targeted Jordan during the summer'. That means Lincoln City were his preferred choice over a side with a bigger profile, better facilities and a former Premier League player in charge. That's something we should bear in mind when we're lamenting losing out to other teams, we're a big draw at this level and getting JMD in the summer proved that.

After a stupendous goal on the pre-season tour of Portugal, Maguire-Drew found himself starting regularly for the Imps. Aside from our opening day trip to Wycombe, he started every game in August, but he didn't catch the eye of Imps fans. All too often I read (and wrote) words such as 'has great potential, hopefully we'll get to see it'. On the ball he showed good technical ability, but that was as far as being impressed went.

Without the ball I thought he was incredibly naïve, almost to a point where he looked clueless at times. That might sound harsh, but even my friend and sounding board Pete, a Manchester United season ticket holder who dips into Sincil Bank without prejudice, remarked how he looked like a little boy lost on the wing. When we had possession he made aimless runs, pointless runs and often no runs. Sure, he asked for the ball but we could all run around asking for the ball couldn't we? Kevin Gall made a career out of it once his goals dried up.

When he did get the ball he may have been technically gifted, but he was clever with it. He seemed to have one thought every time; run towards goal. If he beat a player and got into a crossing position he was more inclined to drop back and beat the player again than to deliver a cross. It is fair to say by the time Swindon away came around, few were upset at his lack of game time.

He landed a wonderful corner on Raggett's head that evening and gave us all a glimpse of the talent he possesses in his left foot. A week later he bagged a brace against Everton's kids to leave us on the cusp of qualifying for the next round of the Checkatrade Trophy, one of the goal a precise free-kick of top flight quality. His celebration said it all, he looked as though he'd been on a journey and finally found redemption. Indeed, he was back in the first team for the game against Crawley, a lacklustre and timid affair in which he barely had a kick. He came off with twenty minutes left for Billy Knott having failed to deliver once again.

Little did we know, but that was that. He picked up an injury and went back to Brighton for rehab and, despite allegedly coming back here in December, wasn't seen again. Few shed a tear when it was announced he'd joined Coventry this week, most interestingly Danny never mentioned a desire to keep the player at the club beyond his loan spell.

Was it just a lack of consistency that led to him failing at the club? From the outside looking in possibly so. As a fan I didn't think he looked to like the tracking back and defending and perhaps he fell into the trap of wanting to stand out too much. I suppose loan players get noticed when their name appears in the 'goals scored' column which could have made him a little more single-minded than most.

Whatever the reason, the player who promised so much when he arrived delivered very little when it mattered. He's still got lots of quality and maybe a different system will get more out of him.

And then there were two....
January 4, 2018

Centre halves that is. In a surprise move this afternoon, Rob Dickie has signed for Oxford United on a two and a half-year deal.

I'll admit, it's taken me completely by surprise. I'd heard Dickie had an issue with his lack of game time recently, but I assumed Sean Raggett leaving would placate him enough to return here for the rest of the season. Instead, he's moved up a division to League One with alarming speed. As I understand it, he's barely been back home two days.

I am disappointed, I'm not going to change my tune and proclaim he wasn't any good anyway. I've spoken to a few people and some were convinced by him, other not so much. I thought he had potential and in truth a move to League One is a decent result for him. I doubt very much he would have been offered such a long deal here, certainly not on his outings this season. He's played well and shown potential, but I'm not sure he was worth such a long deal.

To be fair, you can't really blame the lad can you? Oxford are battling for a play-off spot in League One and are much closer to home for him too. It's a no-brainer, especially with the added security of a long deal. Best of luck to him.

I guess it's a good thing we don't have a game this week as we're back to the bare bones. Much has been made of Michael Bostwick allegedly moving her because he wants to play central midfield, I'm fairly sure that is a fallacy and nothing more. Bostwick is a no-nonsense professional and I can't see him acting like a prima donna and dictating where he plays.

We also have Callum Howe to return. He's been impressing at Eastleigh having played 24 games for them this season. He signed off in style on December 30th by grabbing a last-minute equaliser as they drew with Woking in a mid-table clash. Eastleigh are currently 18th so Howe has been busy, but he's certainly done well there. He may well be crucial, especially now Dickie has done a bunk.

Luke's experienced a renaissance recently, perhaps that is what has prompted Dickie's move. His return to form and to the match day squad saw the Reading loanee dropped to the bench. At least with Luke you know you're getting consistency and, after a shaky start, he's looked every inch the title-winning captain of last season.

Thus far, as they say in Forest Green, that's shallot. Two defenders and Michael Bostwick currently members of our promotion chasing squad. I'd appeal for calm, I've already seen rumblings of discontent on social media, although part of me is glad it isn't Supporters Board working group backlash. I don't think our manager will let us down, not at all. It isn't about us, it's about him and Nicky. They haven't spent the past decade dragging themselves up through the leagues to naively sit on their hands in January as everyone signs players except us. No, I'm still confident that we'll bring in a centre half or two.

It is quite amusing, in a dark way, to think that our problem area is now at the back. Although we do need a new striker, the form of our Matt Attack has made it difficult to justify spending upwards of £200k on Ricky Miller when we're so short in defence.

I'm hearing whispers of a move for Fraser Franks, but then I've been hearing those for as long as I can remember. Maybe I just need to sit in a darkened room and ignore the voice in my head incessantly repeating player's names over and over again.

Anyway, for now keep calm and believe in the Cowley's magic. After all, when have they ever let us down?

Imps on the Wembley trail: Rochdale 0-1 City
January 9, 2018

It wasn't the prettiest of spectacles, a battle fought by two committed teams on a field of sand will never serve up a feast of flowing football, but after 90 minutes City emerged victorious and progressed in the Checkatrade Trophy.

This is a good result for City, depleted during a period of transition and down to the bare bones. On paper it looks even more impressive that we've beaten a League One side, but the harsh truth is Rochdale and City are at the same level technically and tactically. Whether that speaks well for us or poorly for them, time will tell.

It wasn't really a surprise that Danny Cowley named a strong side, he didn't really have a lot of choice with a squad of 16. Nonetheless new loan signing Danny Rowe got a run out, our double-headed Matt Attack started as well as Bozzie in the middle of defence. It wasn't a new-look City as such, but it had a different feel about it.

It wasn't really a match for the neutrals though, scrappy at times and punctuated by the referee's whistle. Ben Toner didn't have a bad game, just a picky one and coupled with the atrocious playing surface it made the game look more like our mid-90's league tussles than a 2018 match. City were well organised though, it took Bozzie perhaps ten minutes to settle before we looked solid, but with Neal Eardley around we're always going to have an air of confidence at the back.

On a personal note, I was delighted to see Farms in goal even though he barely had a save to make. I've always been a Paul Farman fan, his attitude has been impeccable throughout his spell at City and even though he's not the number one, he's still a competent keeper and great squad member. His chances might be limited, but he's slowly adding clean sheets and starts to his tally.

I didn't think Rochdale looked particularly bad, they just didn't look good either. Both sides threatened to break but more often than not resolute defending kept the scores at 0-0. They were restricted to half chances, Alex Woodyard looked industrious in the centre of the park which certainly helped the new-look defence. Imagine, if we could sign a midfielder in the Lee Frecklington mould to partner him, Bozzie could remain at centre half and we'd look every bit as solid as we have the last six months.

At half time it seemed likely we'd be getting penalties, it felt like that type of game. Both Matts had worked hard as had Danny and Harry on the flanks, but the pitch simply wasn't facilitating good football. For those who didn't go or watch it on iFollow, think Sincil Bank, May 2003. I'm not sure what style of football it would suit and, although it was the same for both teams, it was a major influence in the quality of the product.

City made a couple of changes and I thought they injected fresh impetus in City's play. As the minutes ticked by we looked more dangerous, Ollie Palmer added another dimension after his introduction but the real catalyst was Nathan Arnold (pictured top courtesy of Graham Burrell). He's still a handful, he's no different to last season just without the starts under his belt. Whenever he got on the ball you felt there was a chance for City, especially as Billy Knott's introduction changed Rochdale's shape too. They looked to be confused as to how they should set up and we began to pour forward.

Still, with just two minutes back I was ready to go and put the kettle on in readiness for penalties. Just as I stood up, Nathan Arnold whipped the right-back's pants down, slapped his arse and squared for Palmer. One thing you have to say about Ollie is he gets into the right places and he had to keep his head to slot home. Awkward pitch, lots of pressure but he slotted home and City are into the last eight of the tie.

After the game there was an air of relief in the voice of Danny Cowley, his first comments were about the pitch which underlines how important it was. He never comments on things he can't control, but his opening gambit was praising our ability to play beach football. After that he compared the game to Solihull Moors last season, a hard-fought win in a game overshadowed by the transfer window. Rob Makepeace made a joke about Theo Robinson being at the game and Danny, albeit briefly, seemed flustered. It was a split second, but is that an indication that recent speculation linking us with a move for Theo is right? Maybe, maybe not.

Ollie Palmer had a chance to speak too and he underlined his commitment to Lincoln City. He said something along the lines of 'I'm here, even if you don't want me to be I'm sticking around'. It wasn't quite as 'poor me' as I've just written, it was very much tongue in cheek at speculation linking him with a move away. I've always said Ollie offers something to the squad if not the starting eleven and I stand by that. He's a great weapon late on, people see the big man and think it's going to be lumped up to him, but the opposite happens because he's worse at headers than Dean Keates. Instead he works hard, probes greedily and looks for goals. Tonight, that paid off and credit to him.

We now look to Thursday's draw where Yeovil, Fleetwood and Peterborough wait amongst others. At this stage of the competition it really doesn't matter who you draw, although a home tie against Yeovil would be preferable to Chelsea U21's away. Either way City are two rounds from Wembley, three games as the semi-finals are two-legged. Can we finally break our Wembley hoodoo?

I'm also impressed with both sides of the boycott argument too. Neither side niggled at each other this time around, whether everyone is sick of it or whether transfer talk kept it on the back burner I'm not sure, but it was nice to play a Checkatrade Trophy game without battle lines being drawn on social media. For once all Imps got along which is how it should be.

Now, where the Freck are these new signings?

Freck and Ellis in terrific Thursday double header
January 11, 2018

Of course, you all know the big news by now. Lincoln City have not only signed Lee Frecklington, darling of the Rotherham fans, but also tied the future star Ellis Chapman to a three-year deal.

There was something very poetic about this evening, the master himself, the last grand export from our youth system, returning on the same evening the baton is passed to another great hope. Seeing Freck there, a veteran of 32, made me feel old. I remember when he was just a quiet, unassuming young man embarking on his football career. Now, he's back and we've got another quiet, unassuming young man looking to take on the world.

There's not a lot I can add really. The rumours of Freck coming back have been around for a while, first floated by me back at the beginning of November and fuelled by his public appearance promoting the Imps book just before Christmas. despite this, did anyone truly think it could happen? Did any Lincoln City fan sit in the New York Stadium in August, see Freck in a Rotherham shirt and think 'he'll be ours by January?' Of course not. I could barely believe it myself, even though I knew he was coming back. When he walked around that corner, the same Lincoln lad that left us almost a decade ago, I could have wept with joy. Genuinely, that is how much something like this means to me and I'm sure to many of you. Footballers always say that it is a game without sentiment, you try telling that to Lincoln fans tonight.

As if to make himself even more of a hero, Lee then comes out with the following quote: "If you're asking me would I rather go to Mansfield Town or Lincoln City, the obvious choice is here. I'm here now and not there, so I'm really excited." Burned Steve, burned.

I'll do a separate piece on them and him later, this article isn't about petty vendettas or negativity, it is about this football club and what we've achieved today. Lee Frecklington is one of our own, he's now a definite Imps legend, a player who excelled here once and has the ingredients to do so again. If you take all of that away though, his roots and his history, we've signed the captain of a League One side. That means we've now got Peterborough's captain from last season as well as

Rotherham's. Last year Lee Frecklington led his side against Newcastle, Michael Bostwick led his against Sheffield United and Luke Waterfall led us out against Boreham Wood. Today, less than a calendar year later, all three are on the pitch for Lincoln City. Wow.

Look, this isn't all about Lee either. There's such a buzz around young Ellis and at just seventeen, there's so much to come from him it is unreal. I know how highly he is rated and how much our management think he can achieve. He struck me as a grounded young man, humble and respectful of where he'd been. When he spoke of his time at Leicester and how he just wanted to play for Lincoln, he did come across like a young Lee Frecklington. If he goes on to achieve the things Lee has in the game, and there's every indication he can do, then he'll be a credit to our youth set up.

Finally, back to Lee and Danny. Listening to them oozing respect for his former club filled me with pride. We really do have a club to be proud of right now, a club that respects its fans, its opponents and itself. There's no mudslinging, no taunting and no gloating. The evening was conducted with respect for Rotherham as well as, rightly or wrongly, Evans. Danny didn't name the team that tried to scupper the bid late, he didn't need to.

So, we've got two local boys tied down to good contracts, one with the world at his feet, the other who's been there, done it and is ready to share his knowledge and experience with those who need it.

Finally, Lee was asked to give Ellis some advice on signing his first pro contract and everyone in the room got a brief glimpse of exactly what we can expect from Freck off the pitch. He turned to Ellis and addressed him properly, not as an answer to a question, but immediately slipping into mentor mode.

"Take this in, this is a big day. Make sure you don't let it get the best of you. Keep training, keep working hard and good things will come."

I'm sure a young Mr Chapman couldn't fail to be impressed by the role model sat next to him. There wasn't a person in the room who wasn't impressed by the end of the session. Lee Frecklington has come back home and we're all the richer for it.

He's Knott coming back

January 11, 2018

The world of puns lost a match made in heaven this evening as Billy Knott left the club, on loan to Rochdale.

Whilst this may not be the end of our dealings with Rochdale this transfer window, for now it's one in and one out. Freck arrives and out the back door goes billy, a tainted genius whom the Cowley's couldn't get the best out of. It's is with regret I'm sure, but sadly Billy looks destined to leave his potential unfulfilled.

The 25-year old summer signing from Gillingham instantly gave City a little dig too, sadly lacking the class shown by Freck in his press conference, happening simultaneously. Knott said; "I've seen the way the gaffer plays football, his style of play, and it suits me. I trained today and really enjoyed it. The boys are full of confidence and it was a really good standard. It was nice and enjoyable. My last few moves probably haven't been to passing teams, so I'm like a little kid again and I can't wait to get passing the ball, moving it quickly and making movements off the ball. I'm looking forward to it."

His assessment of City's style is both harsh and fair in equal measure. We do play a quick back to front style at times, but when Billy has been given the ball to feet, he's failed to deliver this range of passes we keep hearing about. Without being bitter, I think perhaps Billy tried too hard when he was in the team, always looking for the spectacular. He struck me like the talented kid in the playground, the one who had a bit about him but spent more time trying to demonstrate it than getting the basics right. I wish him all the best, especially trying to play his neat passing game on that pitch.

Genuinely, I hope he settle in at Rochdale and reaches his potential. I know there's a great footballer in there, but if Danny and Nicky Cowley don't know how to get it out of him, I'm not sure anyone will. Keith Hill does have a good record with signing players, although former Imps target Jordan Williams hasn't been the hit expected at Spotland.

Billy Knott made 22 starts for City, 12 more as a sub and scored three goals, one against Bromley last season, one against Lee Frecklington's Rotherham this season and the pick of the bunch as we cruised to a win against Carlisle. The writing was on the wall for Billy when he liked this tweet the other night. No doubt the new arrival pushing him further down the pecking order was a major catalyst in him going. All the best for the future Billy.

Welcome to Sincil Bank: James Wilson
January 12, 2018

City have today signed free agent James Wilson, a player recently released by Sheffield United after spending the first half of the season on loan at Walsall.

Wilson is a centre back, all six-foot two of him. He's experienced too, he's represented Wales once as well as having plied his trade at Oldham and Brentford. He came through the ranks at Bristol City, playing in the Championship for them early in his career, but after a loan spell at Cheltenham he moved to Oldham and it is at Boundary Park where he played the majority of his football.

His one Welsh cap came in 2013 when he lined up against Eden Hazard, Kevin De Bruyne and Romelu Lukaku in Wales' fine 1-1 draw. Since then he hasn't been back on the international scene, but he's played almost exclusively in League One. Make no mistake, for a League Two side this is a super signing. He started last season at the heart of the Blades defence, but an injury away at Gillingham forced him out of the first team. Once fit, he struggled to regain his place which came as a blow to a defender who played 93 games over two seasons for Oldham.

He's been on loan at Jon Whitney's Walsall this season, he originally signed on a year-long loan but, like most of these season-long deals, it had a clause in which he could be recalled. Sheffield United activated that clause and then freed Wilson from his contract, making him a free agent. Doubtless this was done with a view to him arriving at our door, which he subsequently has.

A statement from Walsall said: "Walsall Football Club can confirm that James Wilson has been recalled from his loan spell by parent club Sheffield United. The 28-year-old defender scored once in 20 appearances for The Saddlers after joining on loan from The Blades. The loan deal was for the whole season but contained a break clause in January, which Sheffield United have activated to bring him back to Bramall Lane. We would like to thank James for his efforts in the first half of the season and wish him the best going forward."

The Express & Star, the local paper covering Walsall, have described him as 'an integral part' of Walsall's season and defined his departure as a 'blow' for the League One side. He becomes the fourth player to arrive from a higher level so far this transfer window, something I'm sure will be catching the eye of managers up and down the country.

There's no doubt at all, Wilson has been signed to drop straight into the first team. There's going to be no qualms whatsoever here, Wilson will play every single game in which he is fit. He's a custom-made replacement for Sean Raggett, at a different stage in his career having achieved different things, but an out-and-out centre half, solid as a brick wall and good in both boxes. He's tall, physical and considerably experienced. To get him in as a free agent is incredibly astute business and yet another indication of the trajectory this football club is on.

This signing excites me somewhat, just as all the others have. Danny said to me once he wanted a January which got pulses racing. Well Danny, you're doing a fine job so far.

Welcome to Sincil Bank: Jordan Williams
January 12, 2018

Finally, I get to type that title, albeit a couple of months later than expected. Today, City have secured the services of Jordan Williams after an unsuccessful summer pursuit of the player. He joins from Rochdale and will remain at Sincil Bank on loan until June.

Williams is a winger / centre forward who attracted Danny's attention in the summer. He played his football at Barrow last season and really shone out at Holker Street. He joined them from Northwich Victoria two seasons ago, and made 67 starts for Barrow, with just three from the bench. He scored 20 goals for the Bluebirds during his year and a half with the club and he attracted interest last summer as well as in the January window. In our clash at Sincil Bank it was a Williams cross that lead to Byron Harrison scoring the late winner, which all seems a lifetime ago now!

He was linked with a six-figure transfer in the summer but it all got a bit rich for our blood and he ended up at Rochdale. Keith Hill was delighted with his acquisition at the time, but the move hasn't gone well for him. He earned himself man of the match on his debut against Bury back in August, but since then his chances have been limited. He's turned out 19 times for Rochdale, but only six of those have been League One starts. Most recently he came on in the 71st minute of our Checkatrade Trophy clash, rather ironic given that Billy Knott came on in the 70th minute for City. Now, the two have swapped clubs, at least for a six-month spell. Williams is contracted to Keith Hill's side until June 2019.

Williams said of the move; "Danny has spoken to me and I know the interest has been there for a while. He spoke about how he wants to use me and the direction the club is going in and it's great. The atmosphere here is great and I'm really looking forward to getting out and playing in front of them."

Doubtless Williams is here to battle for a place in the first team, that goes without saying. I expect we'll see him from the bench initially though, Nathan has been returning to form and with both Danny Rowe and Harry Anderson also in the frame for a starting place it leaves us with lots of competition out wide. Jordan can play through the centre which offers more options, but one wonders if this perhaps spells the end for either Cameron Stewart or Josh Ginnelly. Time will tell.

Jordan will almost certainly go straight into the squad for tomorrow's clash with Notts County, he started December 23rd and December 26th for Rochdale and has come on as a sub in every game since. That means he is match-fit and raring to go. It might be six months later than expected, but finally Danny gets his man.

Imps held in thriller: City 2-2 Notts County
January 13, 2018

These are the games we live for. These are the games we would dream about whilst sat in half-empty stadiums playing Welling or Dartford. Packed terraces, two good, combative teams and enough noise to wake the dead. In the end it was honours even, but the fact it felt like a defeat is testament to how well City played.

Firstly, the line-up. It was refreshing, if not surprising, to see Luke Waterfall at the back. I thought Wilson would partner Bozzie, but other than that the team looked as I'd expect it to look. With Harry out it paved the way for both new wingers to get a first league start and Lee Frecklington was always going straight into the first team. Josh Vickers' injury meant an appearance for Paul Farman, a safe set of hands in the sticks. I was delighted for Farms, he's a cracking lad and I know how much his first team outings mean to him.

First 25 minutes I thought we looked off the pace. County are a good side, they wouldn't be second if they weren't. They've got good players across the park; Jon Stead is a real menace but the bank of midfielders is frightening. It's almost pointless to write 'I like Jorge Grant', frankly he's the best player I've seen line up against us this season. We've seen him twice now and he's a class act, far better than League Two. I do fear for County if he goes because they look decidedly average in other areas of the pitch.

They move the ball around nicely in triangles when they can, but today they just smashed it up top every time they got a chance, mirroring our own approach at times. I'm not saying either side are long ball, both have game plan which revolves around hitting the channels and having good players on the edge of the final third picking up the seconds. It isn't John Beck style long ball, it isn't really even Keith Alexander style, but it is, to a degree, long ball. They played it, we played it and the game was pretty exciting for the neutral.

It turned for me on 27 minutes. County had a corner and looked in the ascendancy. We hooked it clear and it fell to Danny Rowe. He sprinted the length of the pitch, diagonally towards the corner drawing players with him and allowing our lads to get up the field. It was incredibly intelligent play, we forced a corner from it and from that point on, we were the better side. The run didn't come to anything, but his single-minded surge lifted everyone, the crowd and the players. We started to apply the pressure, only for County to take the lead.

The was nothing Farman could do about the goal, it was well worked despite a clear foul on Sam Habergham in the build-up. That said, we've had our breaks of luck this season and it would be hard to point to that as a deciding factor in the game. Ross Joyce, the referee, chose to send Danny to the stands for his protestations. I didn't hear what Danny said, I won't comment on whether it was correct or not.

It was as if the goal and sending off didn't happen just a minute later. Superb work from Danny Rowe (a sentence I'll be typing regularly over the next few months) resulted in a cross being nodded down by Jordan Williams and our home-coming hero smashed the ball home. It was written in the stars for Freck to score and he put the icing on before even baking the cake by opening his account. I'm reliably informed that's two in two for him now as he scored on his last Imps appearance, eight years ago as we drew 3-3 with Bournemouth.

After that I thought County were done as an attacking force. Sure, they looked capable of getting forward but we defended resolutely and often on the front foot. The only moment of note for them came on the stroke of half time when Jon Stead, a constant threat, broke one on one with Paul Farman, who then pulled off a superb stop to keep us level at half time.

Within seconds of the restart we should have been 2-1 up, Matt Rhead turned smartly in the area but fired wide. He looked to have far more time than he realised and whilst everyone thought 'smash it', he tried to be cute and put it well out of the keeper's reach. That set the tone for thirty minutes of constant City pressure. Matt Green, tirelessly running all afternoon, hooked an overhead kick at the keeper then headed at Fitzsimmons from six-yards out. County looked dead on their feet as we poured forward and took an inevitable lead.

It was excellent work by Danny Rowe (again) that freed Green and he finished smartly and succinctly. That's the thing with Matt Green, he misses a few chances but if you give him three, he'll score one. He's into double figures now for the season and, as we continue to drive forward with panache and style, he's only going to get more.

Danny Rowe, who I may have mentioned was excellent, looked on course to add a third as he sliced through County like a hot knife through wax moments later, only to be cynically hauled back. It was his last action of the game but he left the pitch to rapturous applause and rightly so. If he plays like that every week, we're going to be pushing the top three. That's a guarantee.

City looked likely to add a third at any moment, the blue shirts were getting deeper and there looked to be no way back into the game for the visitors. Only, there was. County scored, against the run of play, to make it 2-2 on 77 minutes. That's the difference between them and the likes of Barnet, they're a good side with class players and none more so than Jorge Grant. He's got two in two against us and despite a defensive mix-up leading to the chance, he made no mistake. Nothing Farms could do, he was let down slightly by two players going for the same ball, but ninety-nine times out of a hundred that mistake goes unpunished. In this division there's only Grant and Doidge with the foresight to turn it into a goal.

After that they clung on for dear life. Usually we see City retreat, hanging on to the tiniest of threads as the opposition lay siege to our goal, but instead we kept the pressure on right to the last. Green was excellent, Palmer played alright when he came on and the subs put in a good shift too. Time and again we pressed on, winning corner after corner. Then, in the final minute, we finally got the winning goal. A ball forward caught the defence napping, Green turned his man well and Palmer stroked the ball home. 3-2, and City move up to....

Oh no, wait. That's right, I forgotten about the other element haven't I? I've forgotten about the main player, the most noticeable player on the park. How remiss of me to get 1,000 words into my assessment of proceedings and not mention Ross effing Joyce.

Joyce, the referee, was an absolute shambles of a man, inept to the point where he defines the word rather than being described by it. He's clearly out of his depth, this match was high pressure, lots of noise and two teams who know every trick in the book. It wasn't dirty but it was competitive, yet he's seen fit to book seven players. He lost control sometime around the first minute of the game, then aimlessly ambled around the pitch looking increasingly forlorn and at a loss. His decision to take the ball off their keeper, only to drop it back into his hands after two-minute deliberation was hilarious, if only it had been done ironically and not for real.

Also, how did he not send their lad off for pushing Freck over? HE WAS RIGHT THERE. He was stood next to the action, he saw it and pulled a yellow card. If he sees the offence, it is a red. There's no debating, yes it would be a soft red but within the laws of the game, it is a sending off. Bizarrely, after awarding the free-kick, he then immediately saw a yellow-card worthy foul from Luke Waterfall and booked him too. I've seen referees even up the red cards, but never a yellow.

Moving onto the disallowed goal, the linesman didn't flag (that I could see) and replays show there was no foul committed at all. Yet he, Ross Joyce of Super Referee fame, saw an infringement. In truth, had the whistle not been blown (for the millionth time) then I think Fitzsimmons probably saves Palmer's effort. I'm not blaming Ross Joyce for us drawing, we drew a tough game against a good side. I'm blaming him for causing it to be less of a spectacle than it should have been by being weak, indecisive and utterly incompetent.

I'm genuinely going to write to the Fa, as a fan, and ask how much longer we must suffer good games of football being potentially ruined by the officials. Both games against County were spoiled, although oddly Seb Stocksbridge would probably have sent off three players this afternoon, as well as award at least two of the blatant penalty shouts. Instead we got Ross Joyce, a man convinced he should punish the small things and turn a blind eye to any serious indiscretions. He didn't affect the result, but that is only by pure chance. Some might say, had he spotted the foul in the build up to their first, we would have won the game. Maybe, but officials miss the odd thing. Ross Joyce missed 90 minutes of action, occasionally waking from his slumber to blow his whistle, point indiscriminately one way or the other before shutting off.

It's not fair on fans, neither County's nor ours. I got a bit of stick from a Notts County blogger earlier for apparently having the same narrative as last time we played them, that's because it's the same issues. 9,600 of us sat in a stadium today to watch two teams battle it out for a promotion spot, instead we were all watching one guy we'd never heard off for fear of what he might do next. 90 minutes of nerves based around what level of pure idiocy the so-called official might reach. As it was, we still got a spectacle today, but what of next week? Or the week after? We get one good ref, two crap ones and somewhere it has to stop. Somewhere down the line, someone has to be held accountable for the awful standard of referees such as Joyce, Stocksbridge and Huxtable.

1,000 words on the game, 700 on the referee, I ought to have some for the 617 and associated volunteers. I respect the guys but as you know, I'm not a serial panderer. I believe the atmosphere is all our responsibility, not just a core group and although I respect what they do you'll never find me massaging anyone's ego without good reason. However, the display was all them, they organised it, they asked for volunteers, they designed it and they ensured it was implemented. I didn't see the design until afterwards, obviously, and I was proud to be involved in such a wonderful undertaking. The band of hardy souls that put that together deserve respect, it is what sets us as a fan base apart from other teams. Other League Two sides would love the numbers we get, but they'd love a group such as the 617 who work so hard at improving the atmosphere. When have you ever seen something like that at a Football League ground before? Well played guys, respect.

So, the dust is settling and as it happens, we drew 2-2 against a top side whom we should have beaten, Lee Frecklington got his 'Roy of the Rovers' moment, of sorts, and we were all treated to another afternoon of passion, pride and (thanks to Joyce) a little bit of prejudice too. I suppose this is what football is all about, right? Thrills, spills and the ultimate knowledge that whatever you do, the pr*ck in the middle can get away with murder right in front of your eyes. Rest assured he'll be getting a little telling off from the assessor but he'll never have to explain his actions, the FA won't hear a word against him and next week, he'll be at another League Two ground ruining an afternoon's football for another set of fans. At least it won't be us.

Next up at Sincil Bank, Peterborough. See you next Tuesday, Joyce.

Is this the greatest time to be a Lincoln City fan?
January 15, 2018

Football is a fast-moving game, I'll grant you that. Last season Exeter City were in a 'relegation battle' in October and at Wembley in the play-off final at the end of the season. Players come and go with alarming regularity, rules change, managers change, everything changes. However, I think as Imps we need to pause just for a moment and appreciate the speed at which things move at Lincoln City, not just in two years, but in just under four months.

I don't want anyone to think this is a criticism of Chris Moyses by the way, not when I draw parallels between then and now. Chris did a fantastic job at this football club at a very tough time and his early role in building foundations should not be forgotten. However, the change over 24 months is so frightening it is beyond belief.

In January 2018 we've signed Lee Frecklington and James Wilson amongst others. Whilst all five of our signings are excellent, those two do stand out having essentially been second and third tier players for most of their careers. This transfer window is shaping up to be as exciting as the summer, perhaps the two most significant and ground-breaking transfer windows in Lincoln City's history. Signing Michael Bostwick and Matt Green in the summer was exciting enough, but now we're pushing the boundaries even further.

In January 2016, Chris Moyses was making enquiries into quality players. He'd spoken to Scunthorpe about Andrew Boyce and to West Brom about Samir Nabi. Now, those names might not be mouth-watering in 2018, but for the level we were at they'd have been quite a coup. Chris couldn't convince them Lincoln City was the place to be though, so we ended up with Patrick Brough, James Caton and George Maris. They were underwhelming at the time, Caton perhaps the pick of the three and the only one not currently playing league football. Yes, finances play a part, but after Clive's investment in December 2015, we weren't poor, not 'selling-club' poor anyway. Lincoln City was a hard sell and Chris, despite sound transfer targets, found that out. He did bring Jamie McCombe in though, maybe the very first time in ages we saw a higher-level player recognise the potential in the Imps.

Two years ago, Lee Frecklington was out injured, but on his return he scored in a 1-0 win against Premier League hopefuls Middlesbrough. James Wilson played centre half for Oldham against Millwall and Bradford. We lost to Wrexham, Forest Green and Dover.

This isn't intended to pour scorn on the side of 2015/16, we lived within our means and in the early part of the season battled really well against most sides. For a while we looked like play-off candidates in the National League, but although it seems a lifetime ago, it isn't. It's two years and the movement we've enjoyed in that time is frightening.

Whilst we may not think two years is lightning quick time, how about four months? That is how long since we went to Meadow Lane and faced that same Notts County side, getting beaten 4-1. Yes, we were done by dodgy decisions that day, but the truth is they looked better than us for periods. They moved the ball around well and, despite us pressing hard, we only ever looked like grabbing something from the game, not earning it throughout. Fast-forward to this weekend and you see us completely control three-quarters of a game against essentially the same County side. Our squad, reshaped and reshuffled, looked infinitely better than one from just sixteen weeks ago. The new signings certainly impressed, but those old hands looked much-improved too. Matt Green had one of his best matches in a City shirt, despite some calling him wasteful in front of goal. He could perhaps have done better with his header, but other than that I thought he looked sharp. His goal was well-taken, his overhead quick was instinctive, accurate and saved well. He ran for ninety minutes without ever stopping. That's a confident and complete Matt Green, back in September he was only just bedding in.

We might 'only' have drawn against the team in second on Saturday and thanks to the referee it might have felt like a defeat, but for me the change in our side since September and even October has been massive. Danny's sides do always get better, he tells us that every week and we've seen it ourselves, but the speed with which it has happened has caught me a little by surprise. Maybe it shouldn't, last season it was the October 1st game against Braintree in which Danny said, 'we've begun to find our method'. I think it took six weeks longer this season, until November 25th against Port Vale, but it has happened again. We've hit a benchmark match and seemingly, everything has clicked.

I'm finding it staggering how quickly we're moving, but only when I pause to take stock of the situation. Often as football fans we spend a lot of time looking ahead to the next game, the next place above us in the division or the next new signing. Doubtless, I'll soon be blogging about centre forwards I believe we should bring in, almost moving on from the amazing week of recruitment we've just experienced. When you pause for a second and realise what is happening here, it really is an amazing time.

Right now, this very second, I believe it is as exciting to be a Lincoln City fan as at any time before in history. Again, I'm not taking away from Bill Anderson, Graham Taylor or Colin Murphy, nor from Keith Alexander. Those guys achieved much for the club, working in their own ways and with their own methods, but there was always something hindering their progress. Often it was money, perhaps not with Graham, but certainly the others. Right now, that isn't an issue. Don't for one second believe we're a rich club, don't think we've got limitless reserves of cash to spend as we see fit, that isn't the case. What we do have is a stable football club, organically evolving and growing to fit the new world of the EFL. However, never before have we attracted players from a higher level with such alarming regularity. Never before has that come hand in hand with a growing and passionate fan base, exciting and vibrant young managers with respect and integrity. Just look at the display, instigated by the 617 and performed by the whole Coop stand. I've never known a Sincil Bank like this, not in my 30 years of following the club. It is astounding where we are and what we now stand for. I'm not sure about the #impsasone personally, but we do exude unity and togetherness like never before.

The most comparable time has to be Graham Taylor's era, there's no question about that. I think Graham's teams existed in a simpler time when it perhaps was all about football and bums on seats rather than all the other stuff a modern-day side gets bogged down in. The 21st century brings an awful lot of additional complications to a football club, but the rewards are much richer. Football moves quickly and right now, nobody in football is moving quicker than Lincoln City FC.

Enjoy it, cherish it and never forget how it feels each and every day to support our club right now. This is what all football fans strive for, this is what Morecambe, Grimsby, Accrington and all the other League Two sides aspire too. For once, we are the envy of the Football League, the National League and (dare I say) half of League One also.

Poor Afternoon All Round: Barnet 1-1 Imps

January 20, 2018

It's not been one to write home about has it? We've seen 45 minutes of the worst football from Danny Cowley's Lincoln, combined with some of the poorest stewarding I've ever witnessed at a League Two ground. Now we have to travel home disappointed with a 1-1 draw.

The day started fairly well, Barnet's away facilities are superb, Imps fans congregated in the bar in relatively high spirits. We took our place in the ground hoping that the performance would match our superb support. It didn't.

At half time I would have taken a draw, no doubt at all. We were, in all honesty, bloody awful in the first half. It's been a long time since I've seen a Lincoln City performance as toothless and devoid of ideas as that. I'm not going to pull any punches, we looked terrible. Barnet were average at best, in Akinde they have a real threat but they were nothing special. That didn't matter though, we were shocking.

It wasn't just on the pitch that things went awry. From fifteen minutes in there appeared to be disorder in the stands, heavy-handed stewarding resulted in lots of flash points behind the stands. There's little for me to analyse from the on-pitch performance, all I could say is perhaps we lacked Bozzie in the midfield which led to a complete breakdown between defence and everyone else.

I can comment on the actions under the stands though because I went to the loo and witnessed some fairly horrible stewarding. As I came out of the toilet, five stewards piled into a lad of about seventeen. He was on his way to the loo, nothing more as far as I could see. Five grown men laid into him, punches were thrown and he ended up being ejected. from what I saw, he did very little. Something must have been said, but his treatment bordered on assault. Stewards were agitating for a fight, not all of them, but a small portion were desperate to throw fans out.

We had a drink at half time and lamented our complete inadequacy on the field. Over 1900 Imps fans travelled, even though the official figure was lower than that, but overall they were let down. Spirits were low, morale was rock bottom and tempers were frayed.

I missed the equaliser, sadly. Another incident seemed to spark stewards to storm in again, fans were ejected and police were involved. City scored whilst fifty or sixty fans argued vehemently with the authorities, but when the goal went in the trouble dispersed. Suddenly, City were back in the game. One of the Metropolitan Police actually apologised to me as I filmed proceedings, remarking "we know there's two sides to the story, we will investigate both the fan and the stewards." Fair enough, I guess. As I turned away a steward said; "that's it, now you've scored you can f*ck off." Nice.

The rest of the second half saw a below-par City fight harder than in the first 45, but it still wasn't great. Both Harry Anderson and James Wilson looked decent, Freck began to get into the game, but it still didn't inspire confidence. Barnet looked poor, we looked at their level. When the final whistle finally went it was a merciful act that relieved paying fans of their misery. Neither side covered themselves in glory, the only comfort is we know we're much better than that, they're not.

I'll blog properly when I get home, but as you can probably sense, I'm not entirely happy. It was a bad day at the office all round, a sub-standard performance from City combined with shocking stewarding.

Boycott on for some, but are we missing a point?
January 23, 2018

Firstly, I shall not be sharing this on the usual banter sites due to the provocative nature of the subject. However, Danny laid down a challenge to the 617 to suspend the boycott and they have voted not to do so. It's a story and therefore I shall offer some input on the site. Please, if you don't want to read this article, don't. If you can't read it without getting angry, don't. I'm merely responding to events.

I laid in bed wondering about the situation last night and something struck me. All the talk is about the 617 boycotting the Checkatrade Trophy, but it seems we're forgetting something, certainly those of us in the media, alternative media and suchlike. The 617 are a group of around 70 fans, the difference in attendance between the two Accrington home matches was 4,670. Whilst I know there are other reasons for not attending, that actually makes the 617 around 1.5% of the stay-away fans. With that in mind, does their decision not to attend the game mean Danny's statement was futile, or has it reached fans who perhaps do not align themselves with the 1.5% whose voice has been focused on?

That isn't a slur on the 617, but they're not the only fans boycotting, nor are they the official voice of those that have. I appreciate they are a focus and, because of their efforts at raising the atmosphere at games, they're focused on as a conduit to reach the boycotting fans, but 68 cannot possibly speak for 4,670. I know you could easily dispute those numbers, I know Block 7 holds far more and the people in that block are influenced by the fans around them, but it is a fair point to raise. Who knows if Danny's cry for help has galvanised other stay-away fans to come back to the games?

I'm of the opinion it was wise for the 617 not to suspend their boycott, irrespective of how much the club needs them. I know 6,000 or so in Sincil Bank can make enough noise to power the team on, whilst the 617 lads do a great job they the spark that lights the bonfire, but the raging inferno of noise is produced by each and every single fan. Simply put, others must step up this evening, be it in block seven, six or five, and lead chants. Not one of the boycotting fans wants to see us lose, but had they chosen to suspend their boycott I believe everything they claim to stand for would have been belittled.

Everyone who argued against a boycott has said "you'll come back if we get to Wembley," and this week the club opened the door a little to allow for a climb down. I'd bet the vote was close, I don't know but I would imagine some within their organisation want to come back, especially given the club stance. I would hope those people are free to attend if they so desire. Let's face it, how many of the 617 do you know? I'd identify six or seven members in a line up, nothing more. Many of the fringe elements could come to the game and not even be recognised. The real 'faces', the prominent members, are the ones who have to stay away for their own dignity, no matter what the club say. To come back through the door now we're doing well in the competition would be an affront to their arguments prior to Danny's press conference.

It was masterful PR by the club though and although it was done with the correct intentions, if it were a game of chess it was almost 'checkmate'. To indulge not only in dialogue with some boycotting fans, but to also then state publicly which way it would vote in the event of a B team vote was exemplary behaviour. Over at Blunder Park the 'B' team debate has caused divide and debate between the board and the club, but that isn't going to happen here. In fact, the board have been able to remain quiet whilst Danny has put his neck on the line with his comments. He was very clear on his own personal stance and whilst I believe the club feel the same way, they could never come out and say it, certainly not when we're in the quarter finals of the trophy and new-boys to the Football League.

The 617 really couldn't win, there move will be met with criticism no matter what happens. There is an element of fans who don't believe the praise they get is entirely justified. The display in the stand was superb, but I've heard it argued lots of non-617 members helped set it up. Again, they're the fire-lighter, but the roaring open fire is an example of everyone coming together. We must never forget the input the group had when we were on our arse in the National League, when many of those feeding negative comments back were sat at home listening to the results, telling their friends "I used to go and watch Lincoln once."

This will be my last word on the boycott, there is enough division and ill-feeling between fans as it is without adding more. I just felt it important to wrap up the story and now move on from it. I just hope whoever does come along tonight finds the courage to start chants, the fortitude to join in and the longevity to continue them even if we are losing the game. The boycotting fans are making their point by not being there, those who chose not to can make their point by being loud, proud and helping City get to Wembley.

Simply Outstanding: Imps 4-2 Peterborough

January 24, 2018

It's hard to know where to start with matches like this. I had the pleasure of being invited into Running Imp's box and on 90 minutes I stood looking out across Sincil Bank in awe. Once upon a time my football club never surprised me, now they rarely fail to. With just one game stood between us and Wembley, we're once again on the cusp of history.

It wasn't like the other cup-ties though, there was no weakened team to use as an excuse. Peterborough wheeled out the full plethora of attacking talent they had. Jack Marriott was named but it seems perhaps injured in the warm up. His replacement was former Imp Danny Lloyd, a young man who has developed into quite a footballer. All in all, this wasn't a match I expected us to win, but one I wanted us to compete in to act as yet another barometer. We'd lost at Wimbledon and won at Rochdale, it does seem as if we're facing tests for next season at intervals this campaign. This was by the far the sternest.

Let's not take anything away from Posh, they're a really good side. There's no doubt they're the best side we've seen this season, they move the ball across the field at speed. In Danny Lloyd they have a player who is oozing Football League ability, full of intelligent runs and always looking to find an opening. I really liked the big lump at the back too, Ryan Tafazolli. He was mopping up almost anything in the air in the early exchanges and looked a threat from set pieces too.

In fairness we almost opened the scoring through Lee Frecklington, a player I thought looked far happier dealing with Peterborough than Barnet. After that, our visitors pushed forward and caused Farms to make a couple of saves. It was end to end stuff, a proper old school cup tie. Although they looked vibrant and dangerous, we didn't retreat looking to stop their threat.

Within the space of two minutes, both keepers made great saves too. Firstly, Jonathan Bond clawed away a Luke Waterfall header, but not being outdone Farms made an even better stop before quarter of an hour had passed. It was a close-range header from a whipped cross that he somehow pushed around the post. It was a save that was as good as a goal, but heartbreakingly it only delayed Posh by 60 seconds. The corner was half cleared and Neil Eardley sliced an attempted clearance into the back of the net.

City's heads didn't drop though, not one bit. In days gone by, that would have been your lot. A bright start would have been dampened down by the early goal and the higher-level opposition would have closed the game down. Not on Danny and Nicky's watch. We saw a clever free kick straight from the phantom training ground almost catch Posh out and we saw Matt Green covering every blade of grass, twice. He has an unbelievable engine and when you have a willing runner like him, you always have a chance.

Whilst Peterborough always looked dangerous, we weren't just acquitting ourselves well, we were taking the game to the side chasing promotion to the Championship. Green stood out, but every single player had a part to play. From out wide we offered direct running and a potent attacking threat. In Lee Frecklington we had a calming presence in the middle of the park. Elliott Whitehouse worked hard, if I'm honest I think he struggled at times, but it wasn't through a lack of desire. The visitors didn't capitalise on their lead, more of a testament to our fortitude than anything they did wrong.

When we got back into the game it was thanks to a superb strike from loanee Danny Rowe. A Championship player produced a strike that wouldn't have been out of place in the top flight, sending the 5,600 home fans into delirium. This competition has produced some of the finest goals I've seen at the Bank in years and his wonderful curling effort from the right was right up there with the best of them. Quite deservedly, City went in level at the break.

Neither set of fans could be disappointed though, both sides had set out to win the game and both had chances. Junior Morais impressed me in the centre for Posh, but as I've mentioned Danny Lloyd looked (to coin a phrase) different gravy. Within five minutes of the restart he perhaps bettered Rowe's strike with a stunning 25-yard drive that caught Farman unawares. It seemed as though our brave resistance had been shattered by a former Imp.

Or not. I recall the mantra 'refuse to lose' last season and once again, it was clear City weren't going down without a fight. It took five minutes to draw level, once again showing a resilience that we've become familiar with. Eardley, Green, Rowe and Harry Anderson contrived to land a ball at the feet of the Big 'Un at the far post and, after what seemed like an age, he smashed the ball into the top of the net. 2-2, game on. Again.

From there we had 35 goal less minutes, but not a period without thrills and spills. Paul Farman put his body on the line with a couple of saves that ended with him colliding with the post. The side that had battled so bravely for an hour began to break up. Lee Frecklington came off for Sean Long, pushing Neal Eardley into midfield. Ollie Palmer did his customary swap with Rheady to leave us looking a tad understrength. It mattered not, a fine Neal Eardley drive almost put us 3-2 up, it beat the keeper but was cleared on the line one way or another. Even with a full back in midfield, we still looked capable of winning the game. Finally, Danny Rowe, a man of the match contender, came off for the lesser-spotted Cameron Stewart.

For a short while I thought we lost our shape having been on top. Danny Lloyd took advantage of a weak foul but fired a free kick over the bar. Just as quickly as we lost our shape, we found yet another gear. From 75 minutes in, there was only going to be one winner. Palmer and

Green seemed to panic a Posh defender into running almost into his own goal, but the keeper cleared ta last-minute. Luke Waterfall had a clear header easily saved and Matt Green had the ball in the net only to be harshly adjudged to have fouled his marker. As if to remind us they're quality though, Danny Lloyd's effort almost beat Farman with six minutes left. It was a pulsating cup tie, end to end with enough sass and attitude to fill sixty episodes of any reality TV show. It was real, live thrills and spills, a game nobody wanted to end. The most merciful conclusion would have been extra time, but perhaps the threat of penalties helped to conjure up the fantastic finale.

With four minutes left, it seemed Elliott Whitehouse had missed the best chance to put the Imps in front. Sam Habergham's whipped corner found him completely unmarked just outside the six-yard area. All he needed was a firm contact and City took a 3-2 lead. Instead, it awkwardly skewed off his head at an angle leaving everyone in red and white cursing under their breath. That was it, that was our chance of the Checkatrade Trophy semi-final. Arses.

The board went up, a rather tight four minutes. If we're meant to have thirty seconds per sub and thirty per goal, that was three minutes in itself. It seemed cruel to curtail such a wonderful contest any earlier than needed. However, if that is the only criticism of the referee, you can tell he had a good game. The ground braced itself for penalties, Harry Anderson braced himself for his big moment.

The goal that effectively settled the tie was created by two of the substitutes. Ollie Palmer held the ball up in the area before sliding it out to Cameron Stewart. He fired a cross over and there was Harry Anderson, former Posh player, to smash the ball past Jonathan Bond. Roy of the Rovers, Jossie's Giants and Striker's Nick Jarvis all rolled into one. It was comic book stuff, fiction that writes itself and a real-life, modern-day fairy tale. He wheeled away in absolute ecstasy having got the goal he so desperately wanted. Some Posh fans began to head to the exit, but with three minutes left anything could happen and sure enough, it did.

Peterborough pushed forward in search of the equaliser, but it left a huge gap at the back. Matt Green showed the sort of energy reserves we saw from Nathan Arnold last season against Ipswich to chase down Neal Eardley's ball forward. Holding off his marker he strode into the area before coolly slotting home to make it 4-2 on the night. Game over, those Posh fans that departed early were joined by 990 more blue-shirted individuals with sad looks on their faces. Safe journey home chaps.

Last night was an example of a referee letting a robust contest flow freely without interruption. It was an example of the quality expected in the upper echelons of League One, but most of all it was a display of togetherness and belief from our heroes in red and white. The game itself was a joy to behold, shifting from one end to another so organically it could almost have been choreographed. The atmosphere was very good, both sets of fans berating each other time and again, the balance of noise bouncing from onset of jubilant supporters to the other. It was a cup tie that had almost everything except needless controversy, a spectacle for both the neutral as well as the two participating sides. Most of all though, it was a Lincoln City win.

Coming away from the ground the only real downside I could picture was the thought of Chelsea U21's in the next round. At this late stage I'd hope all of the kids' teams would be eliminated, but alas that isn't the case. You know what though? There's not a 21-year old alive who wouldn't shit himself at having Bozzie charging in for a challenge or having to mark Matt Rhead. There isn't a 21-year old in blue who has the experience and guile of Neal Eardley and I guarantee you there isn't a single kid at Chelsea that could display the character our boys showed last night. Part of me wants to have the kids at Sincil Bank so we can strike a blow for all that is good about lower league football. After all, we've done bloody well so far, have we not?

Aside from the fact it was the Checkatrade Trophy, last night was perhaps one of the finest games of football I've seen at Sincil Bank in many, many years. In terms of the quality, the chances and the effort it bettered almost every match from last season. We were on it from the 1st minute to the 94th. Taking away the controversy, we beat a full-strength League One side without one of our key players (Alex Woodyard) and losing another on the hour mark. To that end, it was a remarkable achievement by a team I didn't think I would ever find more pride for. I was wrong.

Where is the journey actually taking us? I'm scared to contemplate what the future holds for Lincoln City at present.

Alex Woodyard bid rejected
January 25, 2018

Luton Town's well-documented £120,000 bid for Alex Woodyard has been rejected this evening by Lincoln City manager Danny Cowley.

Danny has revealed that the bid has been expected for a while now, it finally arrived this afternoon. Someone also alerted Sky Sports who ran the story on their news show. £120k is derisory for a player of Woodyard's quality, but the interest did make a few fans a little nervous.

However, speaking to Michael Hortin this evening Danny says that the offer has been rejected and he has the backing of the board in doing so. He has no plans to sell Alex, saying "for Alex, myself and Nicky we have a unique relationship and we've been together a long time. I don't think it would feel like one of my teams without him playing in the midfield."

The bid has been coming, whispers have been heard since before Christmas, but Danny is very definite in his rebuke. Alex Woodyard is going nowhere.

Danny also spoke of still looking to add 'one or two' to the group, perhaps one of the first times he's acknowledged that there may be more than one arrival. Whilst the next few days could be exciting, don't expect Alex Woodyard to leave.

Lincoln City: Fighting all that is wrong in football
January 26, 2018

I'll confess, the Checkatrade Trophy draw was the one I didn't want. I had no problem with the other three teams, but I'd hoped ever since round one that academy teams would be eliminated from the competition by now.

Look, I don't agree with them being in the competition but I've supported it anyway. I can see the benefits and I can see the pitfalls. I just didn't want to face up to the fact a youth team could make the final. If they do, it completely devalues the arguments in favour of it. The 'little club route to Wembley' doesn't hold up when some of the best young players in the world eliminated said little club with one game to go.

Some are saying our draw against Chelsea kids is a win / win situation. If we win the game, we've struck a blow for all that is good in our lower league set-up. If we lose, we're just another victim of the cancer trying to kill our game. Only we're not, are we? We've embraced the competition, most of us have, and therefore if we lose there's no crying foul or spitting our dummies out. Live by the sword, die by the sword. We've supported this trophy and now we have to accept the consequences of that.

This isn't another post debating the rights and wrongs of what has gone before, but in drawing Chelsea U21s we are indeed all that stands between proving one argument or the other, to a degree. Of course, nobody wants to see a youth team at Wembley in this trophy, it goes against everything we believe in. I've seen City fall at this stage before, 2-0 on aggregate to Port Vale, but there was no shame in seeing Vale go forward to the final, none at all. However, lose this and the showcase event is an academy team against, let's say, Fleetwood. Brilliant, a group of talented and privileged kids against the plucky lower league side. Okay, if it was Fleetwood it would be a heavily bank-rolled lower league side that have thrived not only by out spending their rivals, but also on the back of the FA-sanctioned demise of local rivals Blackpool, but a lower league side nonetheless. Let's hope Yeovil or Shrewsbury get there instead, shall we?

I've seen Chelsea have played the likes of Batshuayi in earlier rounds, but something tells me that won't happen again. The FA need this competition to work, they need the buy in from lower league clubs and seeing a £32m striker run riot in the semi-final is not what they want. We've won six games on the spin to get where we are, we've seen some thrilling matches, some hard-fought matches and some breath-taking goals. Players such as Elliott Whitehouse (pictured top) have kept fresh because of those matches. In truth, it has been a superb cup run and yet Chelsea could play four first-team players in the semi-final and simply blow us out of the water. Will they? No, but fundamentally that has got to be wrong.

Last season League One and Two clubs were fined for putting out a weakened side, those rules were changed. I believe strongly that when it is up for discussion again, U21 teams must mean exactly that. The trophy is meant to stimulate the growth of our young players and whilst I'm sure having an 'English quota' would contravene European rights, having an upper age limit would not. For me, if you're playing an U21 team you expect to find 11 players who are aged 20 or less. It's simple, right? If you buy a packet of white toilet rolls, you expect to find white toilet rolls within, not ten whites toilet rolls and an industrial strength blue roll. That might bring some parity to proceedings.

As I've said, I can't see Chelsea playing anything other than a youth squad, they played the youngsters against Oxford and thrashed them. Remember though, this is an Oxford United on its arse with no manager. It was on Oxford side that have won just two in their last ten, lost 7-0 at home to Wigan and made three or four changes to their starting line-up also. It's also a Chelsea side that failed to beat either Plymouth or Yeovil in the group stages, they lost both games on penalties and only qualified courtesy of a 3-1 win against a weakened Exeter side. The one game that sticks out, the 4-0 hammering of MK Dons, is the one that causes everyone issues. That is when Batshuayi and Musonda both played, dealing a real thrashing to Franchise FC. There's an irony in there isn't there? Suddenly we're talking about MK Dons losing as a travesty to the fairness of football…. hang on, weren't they the team that stole an identity and a Football League place? Excuse me if I don't shed a tear at them being hammered. If anything, I'm pleased it was them and not us, Yeovil or Exeter who Chelsea rolled out the big guns against.

On February 6th, Lincoln City stand up for football's integrity. I know we've got our knockers across the football world for supporting the trophy and, should we lose, I know many of those fans will say we deserved it. However, very few will actually want Chelsea to beat us, nor will other football teams and deep down, nor will the FA. This competition has to have two lower league clubs at Wembley, it simply has to if it is going to retain the tiny particles of respect it has left within the game. If Chelsea win, then the last crumbling bricks of the competition's integrity finally turn into dust and blow away. I believe strongly in the Mickey Mouse cup, AWS, LDV, FRT, JPT or Checkatrade Trophy, whatever ridiculous guise it goes under. I believe in the viable route to Wembley for League One and Two teams. I believe in it as a vehicle for fringe players to get a run out, I believe in it as a pointless exercise until you can smell the Wembley arch. I firmly believe in it and I always have but it will be hard to retain that belief if the showcase event is Chelsea U21s against anybody at all.

A week on Tuesday, the red and white shirts of Lincoln City have a chance not just to be my heroes, not just to be heroes to a packed Sincil Bank, but to strike a blow for all of the little clubs who Chelsea have eliminated or indeed any kids team have eliminated (not you MK Dons, you can get to feck). If we win, we're off to Wembley and best of all in doing so, we're standing up for all of the teams in League One and Two at the same time (again, not you MK Dons).

I've been proud of my football club for a while now, but that will increase tenfold if we're victorious a week on Tuesday.

Woodyard stays despite near record bid
January 28, 2018

The Alex Woodyard story reached a conclusion this weekend, but not the one many thought it might.

Social media has been alight with talk of a Luton move since well before the transfer market and a £120,000 bid was rejected in the week. This morning the club revealed his buyout clause has been met, a figure which would have been one of the highest the Imps had received for a player. Despite this and despite scurrilous social media posts, last season's Player of the Year is going nowhere.

More on all that in a moment, but first a few words from the player himself, courtesy of the club website.

"I signed a new contract in the summer to stay with the club. I have been overwhelmed with the level of support I have had since I joined. It is a privilege to play in front of the best supporters in lower league football. We've done well so far in League Two and everyone can see what the club is trying to do. I've worked with the manager and Nicky for quite some time now and we are good for each other. They know how to get the best out of me. I'm ambitious and want to play at the highest level, but I believe I can do that here at Lincoln City. We all want to build something that will live on long in the memory and we can all be proud of. I don't want to just be remembered for what we did last season. That has just created a platform to continue to progress even further in the Football League. I remain firmly committed to this cause and I am going to do all I can to continue to drive this club forward."

So, Alex Woodyard is staying which is great news, also I've highlighted a passage for special attention. His industry and endeavour has been vital to everything we've done as a club since Danny arrived and, as Danny said last week, would it really be one of his teams without Alex in midfield? I think not.

Now to the conjecture. One assumes it is Luton Town who came in with the second bid. Talk of £120,000 is all well and good, but surely that is not the bid that is being talked about as (and I quote the clubs statement here) 'if successful would have been amongst the highest ever fee received for a player by Lincoln City'. If memory serves me right, we got £750k for Jack Hobbs, around £500k for Gareth Ainsworth and around £250k for Matt Dickens. One assumes that the bid was somewhere in the region of that, representing profit if not entirely great business. How much is Alex Woodyard worth in real terms? Not financially, but as a component of our promotion bid?

The news does give fans another positive in the transfer window. Many ne'er sayers have had him down for a move for a long while, there's an element of our fans that I believe want things to go wrong so they can moan again, but once again that hasn't happened. Alex Woodyard has remained loyal to Lincoln City despite talk of having his head turned, talk of cash-hungry agents and a desire to move closer to home. Given that I still expect a departure this window, I'm delighted Alex isn't part of a mass exodus.

Like Alex said though, why would he be? Why would a player want to leave Lincoln, certainly if he's getting regular football? Yes, Alex has a good career ahead of him, but Danny and Nicky have proved they know how to handle him. His star has risen incessantly since he's been with them and I think he'd be mad to jump ship now. It's nice to know the player feels the same.

We'll never be sure of the amount we were offered but I'd probably put it around the 200k mark at a guess. It isn't them money that is important though, it is the message it sends out. We're promotion candidates and although Luton (assuming it was them) are a bigger club, were on a journey to the same place as them. Once upon a time Alex would have gone, or rather players such as Alex would have gone. Every player has a price, every club bar perhaps two in the world is a selling club, but we've moved higher up the food chain. Sean Raggett is proof we don't hold players back, Alex Woodyard is proof the move has to be right.

Every Lincoln City fan should afford themselves a wry smile this morning, this is good news indeed to wake up to. Cheers Alex, you've made my Sunday.

Three-asy does it as City get back on track: Imps 3-1 Newport

January 31, 2018

It's been three league games without a win, but this evening at Sincil Bank, three of the best ensured that City put three more points on the season's tally. Newport were swept aside in a comprehensive Imps display which, aside from twenty first half minutes, was organised and dominant.

I had the pleasure of accompanying Stigs, Karen and a selection of competition winners in the big box, number 9, for the evening. Beef rolls, roast potatoes and the best seats in the house which I am incredibly grateful for. I got to meet our number nine too, the big man came down for a pre-match chat with us. I snuck a photo in too, he's one I haven't managed to get my ginger face in a picture with yet, so that was pleasing.

It was Rheady who wrote the story of the night, but not before we'd come out of the blocks like a greyhound on speed. We attacked with a verve and tenacity not seen since the early stages of last season, looking to put the tired legs of Newport to the sword early. Half of them looked as though they were still hungover from their draw with Spurs as the first exchanges firmly belonged to us. Harry could have put us 1-0 up in the first two minutes, by the time we got to fifteen, Rheady had. The goal was pure class from front to back, Eardley sold Nouble a dummy that resulted in their big man having more egg on his face than I have on a full English. The ball was then played down the channel to Green, some might call it a long punt, but it was with precision and accuracy that would have made Mr Beckham proud. Green, a centre forward, winger and striker all rolled into one, worked a superb cross into the Rhead and he did what he does best. 1-0 City, in all seriousness I wondered if we might go on and grab six.

For some reason an early goal often throws us off our stride and it did just that. The booking for Neal Eardley didn't help, a yellow card that was incredibly fortunate in some respects. Depending on your angle it was either a booking or a straight red and from my angle, there was no doubt. He stretched for the ball, studs up and straight into their lad. He must have bullets in his boots though because I thought their player had been shot through the heart. The referee didn't buy it, probably his only really bad decision of the night. Neal Eardley was lucky he wasn't sent off, we were perhaps more so as he went on to give another masterclass in football.

I thought we retreated a little until half time, Newport are a good side and they began to play a bit of football. Nouble might have been sent to school by Eardley, but he's a good player and held the ball up well. They played some nice football too, across the final third. They're a bit long ball to get there, but we're living in a glass house so I won't throw any stones. In Amond they have a player who will always get a goal if given a chance and so it came to pass. Could Paul Farman have done better with the initial shot? His doubters will say yes, I say he saved it so that is job done.

After the quick-fire start I felt a bit flat at the break, but only is as much as I thought we were the better side. We played some nice football tonight, we go to the channels quickly but not incessantly. Matt Green manages to work both, as well as the eighteen-yard area and nobody should under-estimate his contribution this evening. The two wide players were a constant threat too, Freck almost bagged a header from a corner but it hit Green on the line. That would draw some comments from Green's doubters too, but it was just one of those things. Green can do no wrong in my eyes, he's a complete centre forward, not a natural goal scorer but as close as you'll ever get. I would be very, very surprised in any moves in tomorrow are for a big name who wants regular first team football, because Matt Green is a top player and should start every game he is fit.

After the break, he proved it pretty quickly. After he supplied Rhead in the first half, the favour was returned with a typical Rhead ball through. Green went one on one and did what any confident striker enjoying his football will do. I do remember saying something like 'if he gets one, he'll bag a hatful' in October. Since then, he's got eight in twelve. Not a bad return that.

The second period belonged entirely to us, whether it was solid defending or asking questions at the other end. Many were surprised when James Wilson came on, but it showed the sort of fluidity to our formation you should expect to see more of. Danny once said people get too hung up on formations and this evening proved that. Rhead came off and we went to a five-man midfield, two wide players and a diamond of sorts in the centre of the park. The one area we'd been a little overrun was in front of the back four, but by switching it around it gave us a more solid feel but took a little away from our attack. I suspect Danny hoped to keep it at 2-1 and take the points.

One thing I'll say about James Wilson is this: he'll be a big part of Lincoln City history. I've seen him play for around seventy minutes so far, in the depressing draw at Barnet and again tonight, and I see something very able in that lad. Danny said it would be hard to replace Sean Raggett, but I suspect it might have been easier than he thought. Wilson is incredibly mobile, he reads the game superbly and with Bozzie either aside him or in front of him we're going to be incredibly tough to break down. Luke keeps his place for now, he's done nothing wrong to warrant being dropped, but James Wilson will make the starting eleven and, when he does, he won't lose his spot again.

I'm going to confess, when we made our next change I winced a little. Ollie Palmer came on for Matt Green and I stated, quite loudly, that was the end of our goal scoring threat. I was still talking about his ungainly manner, likening him to a long-necked zoo animal, when he fired a delicious ball through the crowd and into the net to put the game to bed. It's a good job the lights were dimmed, because I had more egg on my face than Franck Nouble after Eardley mugged him off for the first goal. In fact, I'm not sure who'll be washing it off longer, me or him. I'm ecstatic to be proven wrong, nothing pleases me more than Lincoln scoring and if it's a player I'm not sold on, more fool me. Palmer brings something to the party whenever he turns up, but you never know what it is. He's the guy who knocks on your door with a crate of lager, but when you let him in he opens it up and he's actually concealing eight bags of quavers and a bottle of mad dog 20/20 instead. You can't predict him, he doesn't always have what you want, but in the end it is worth having him along.

As a person, I really quite like Ollie. His post-match interview, the one where he dedicates his goal to his cousin Frankie, eleven years old and suffering from cancer, was very heart felt. I follow his Instagram and he comes across as a devoted family man and even his post-match interview the other week where he said, "I'm staying whether you like me or not," showed the no-nonsense spirit and attitude I really like in a player. When he comes on, I'm not confident, but he proves me wrong so many times. He's a great squad player and I'll happily eat my words when he plays well.

After that we showed some superb game management. Paul Farman pulled off another class save to ensure we didn't have twitchy bums in the last ten minutes and, thanks to the Sky TV in the boxes, we were able to laugh at Grimsby for a bit. For the record, losing 3-0 at Yeovil and having two men sent off is surely the straw that breaks Russell Slade's tenure as manager. One player, Osbourne, was booked for fighting with his teammate and later dismissed for two yellows. We think it is bad drawing at Barnet, spare a thought for that lot up the road.

So, there you have it. Back to winning ways, two points from third with a huge clash coming up against Swindon on Saturday. They won at Stevenage tonight and have a cracking away record, but how many have we lost at the Bank in the last year? Two? Besides, do not under estimate the magnitude of tonight's result either, Newport are a very good side and we not only contained them, we dominated them for long periods.

It was also a nice night for reunions so I hear. Jack Muldoon, Terry Hawkridge and Billy Knott were all spotted in the stands watching on, as was an unnamed midfielder from another League Two club. He was only spotted if you know what he looks like though and thankfully, I do.

Finally we've got the bloody football over and done with so we can concentrate on the stuff we all love, transfer gossip. Tomorrow is crazy season, moves in and out expected on a day which could define the next four months for Lincoln City. Three in, maybe two out? Possible, who knows? One thing is for sure, I'm gutted as I won't be near a computer until 1pm at the earliest. Rest assured though, once I am I will be striving to bring you the usual speculation, coverage and pretending I didn't know what was happening that I save for every deadline day.

Tom Pett is first deadline day signing
January 31, 2018

Winger Tom Pett, as predicted here this morning, has become the first deadline day signing at Sincil Bank.

Pett was a rumoured target in the summer after turning down a new Stevenage deal, but they kept him at the Lamex for the first six months of the season. He's primarily a winger, something we know Danny places a lot of value in, but he can operate through the centre if required.

Speaking to redimps.com, Pett said: "I can't wait, I saw the game last night, it gave me a taste of what's to come. I can't wait to get to the training ground, meet all the lads and kick on this Saturday with three points. The crowd are not quiet, which is massive for a player, it's one of the main things when I heard Lincoln were interested in me. I remember coming here around Christmas time and the crowd were loud and worked as the twelfth man, I know it's a cliché but it really does (make a difference). That was massive in my decision in coming here, I want to play in front of big crowds here and the followings when we go away from home."

Pett is a good signing, a player who Stevenage were very keen to keep hold of. He arrives for the now-standard 'undisclosed fee' and will go straight into the squad for Saturday's match with Swindon, having played 34 times for Stevenage already this season, scoring 7 goals. He's had a stellar season so far, a brace on New Year's Day saw Stevenage beat Cheltenham 4-1. He's one of the more highly-rated player in this division and normally his arrival would be seen as incredibly impressive. With the number of wingers we've got and the quality we've already added, it might seem to be underwhelming, but that isn't the case. When Danny Rowe and Jordan Williams return to their clubs in May, Pett will still be an Imp.

What this means for Nathan Arnold, one can only speculate, as it currently leaves us with more wingers than anything. The next Imps move is awaited with baited breath.

First one out – Callum Howe joins Port Vale

January 31, 2018

Callum Howe's stuttering Imps career finally came to an end today as he signed for Port Vale for an undisclosed fee.

Highly-rated Howe has been incredibly unlucky at Sincil Bank, two superb loan spells at Southport and Eastleigh haven't been enough to force him into contention. Since his return to the Bank earlier this month he hasn't featured and now he's got a Football league move that he craves.

It is likely to be a nominal undisclosed fee and his departure will doubtless cause many discussions amongst fans. There is a large section of support who feel he hasn't been given ample opportunity at Sincil Bank, but with James Wilson and Michael Bostwick both fighting Luke Waterfall for a centre half spot, it just seems as though there isn't room at the table for a fourth defender.

Howe is the first departure of deadline day, although one more is expected before 11pm. Activity is likely to pick up in the next hour or two as Danny finalises his squad for the second half of the season.Best of luck at Port Vale Callum, you're a class act and I have no doubt you'll go on to achieve plenty in the Football League.

Another one in – Scott Wharton from Blackburn

January 31, 2018

Scott Wharton has replaced Callum Howe at Sincil Bank, joining on loan until the end of the season.Wharton is a left-sided centre back and a youth of just 20-years old. He's made a handful of appearances for the Ewood Park outfit, as well as appearing in their U23 set up. Last season he had a spell on loan at Cambridge where he scored once in nine appearances.

It would appear that Wharton has come in as back up, his first team chances will be limited due to the arrival of James Wilson and of course the presence of Bozzie and Luke Waterfall. Danny did say he only adds to a group if it makes it significantly stronger, but I'm not sure this is the case.

It will vex fans to see our own promising defender, Callum Howe, leave and another youngster come in, but I implicitly trust Danny's judgement. Perhaps there's a chance Wharton will be available in the summer and Danny wants to run is eye over a League One quality player, whereas perhaps he feels Callum is League Two quality.

Blackburn fans certainly rate our new arrival, there's been an outpouring of love for him on Twitter already.

I've already had an angry message from a fan who claims that Callum Howe is a better defender than Luke and he would have liked to have seen him given a chance. well, that isn't going to happen I'm afraid. Callum Howe is the past and Scott Wharton, for now, is part of the future.

Deadline Day – One Hour to Go and We've Got a Keeper
January 31, 2018

So we have one hour left of deadline day and for the second transfer window running, our hunt for a striker goes down to the wire.

Firstly, we've brought a keeper in on loan. Ryan Allsop joins on loan from Bournemouth. For those who haven't heard the news, Josh Vickers has sustained an injury that could rule is out for a while, so Allsop was needed as back up. It's a bit like the Ross Etheridge move, only Ross hadn't played much football whilst Allsop does have Premier League experience, albeit two matches. He hasn't won a friend in the Twitter user below though.

On the striker front, those hoping to see Ricky Miller become an Imp look set to be upset. He's agreed a loan deal with Mansfield, cleverly releasing the news on his own Twitter account before hastily withdrawing it just as quickly. It's now been officially released with Evans at the centre of it, 'fighting off' interest from other clubs. Yeah, that sounds about right given that his chairman couldn't give him away two nights ago.

It isn't a major surprise to see him move to Field Mill, but I suspect it will be a bad move for him. Evans isn't known for loyalty to his players, nor does he seem to have patience with them either. Ricky Miller is a cracking player, I won't change my opinion because he's not coming here, but he is troubled and needed a stable environment to work in. With the financial clouds allegedly forming over Mansfield chairman John Radford, one wonders what the future might hold.

Pos	Team	Pld	W	D	L	GF	GA	GD	Pts
1	Luton Town	34	20	8	6	74	34	40	68
2	Accrington Stanley	34	20	5	9	58	38	20	65
3	Wycombe Wanderers	35	18	8	9	67	51	16	62
4	Notts County	35	17	10	8	56	36	20	61
5	Mansfield Town	34	16	12	6	53	35	18	60
6	Exeter City	33	18	4	11	44	37	7	58
7	Swindon Town	35	18	3	14	55	51	4	57
8	Coventry City	34	16	6	12	38	28	10	54
9	Lincoln City	34	14	11	9	46	37	9	53
10	Carlisle United	35	14	9	12	50	45	5	51
11	Crawley Town	35	15	6	14	41	43	-2	51
12	Colchester United	35	13	11	11	45	41	4	50
13	Newport County	34	12	12	10	41	43	-2	48
14	Cambridge United	35	13	9	13	35	45	-10	48
15	Stevenage	35	11	9	15	46	51	-5	42
16	Cheltenham Town	35	10	10	15	48	52	-4	40
17	Yeovil Town	34	10	8	16	46	55	-9	38
18	Crewe Alexandra	35	11	3	21	41	57	-16	36
19	Forest Green Rovers	34	10	6	18	39	56	-17	36
20	Grimsby Town	35	9	9	17	30	51	-21	36
21	Morecambe	33	8	11	14	34	44	-10	35
22	Port Vale	34	9	8	17	37	49	-12	35
23	Chesterfield	34	8	6	20	35	61	-26	30
24	Barnet	35	7	8	20	33	52	-19	29

February

Deadline Day Latest: What??

February 1, 2018

That's it folks, that's your lot. The transfer window has shut and Michael Hortin has spoken. The business has been done.

Only it hasn't, has it? We've not actually brought in the striker we believed was coming in, have we? For the second window in a row, it appears something has gone wrong. Everyone was certain we were bringing in another forward, even those close to the club. Remember, Michael tweeted earlier that the reason for the delay would 'all become clear'. Well, it is as clear as mud right not.

I'm not going to moan, we've done some super business this window and brought in some top-quality players, but we haven't added that elusive fourth striker, again. With one defeat in fourteen matches it would be remiss to start wailing 'woe is us', but if Matt Green picks up a knock or a suspension, to put it politely, we're up the brown creek without a paddle. Ollie Palmer has his attributes, playing ninety minutes as part of an effective team is not one of them. He's an impact player, not a starter. Rheady isn't mobile enough to lead the line himself, so then what?

I'm surprised, very surprised, at the lack of activity on the striker front. Have we been done over at last-minute again? Were we one of the Ricky Miller clubs, or were we waiting on a deal that didn't happen? Barnet's business went through late again, was Akinola part of that and we lost out? Has Evans done us over with a promise of Lee Angol, only to withdraw it at last-minute?

Knowing Danny, he will be as honest with us as he can be, but clearly something has not gone to plan. Maybe there's been some paperwork sent off and we'll hear news in the morning, that is a possibility. After all, several deals get announced the day after so perhaps we're one of them.

Deadline Day Extra: Questions Must Be Asked

February 1, 2018

I'm still here, plugging away at my well-worn keyboard. After thirteen hours of following proceedings I'll admit, I felt a bit cheated at 11pm. I'm not alone either, am I? There's a lot of you out there wondering what exactly has happened. After thrashing some poor kid on FIFA 18 and having a nice up of tea I've settled down and composed myself.

Disclaimer: at the end of this article there is some bad language. If you're easily offended, don't read the last line. Cheers.

There are questions that have to be asked and I feel, having followed this transfer window and reported on it for you, I should be the one to start asking. Are you ready?

Why do some fans feel that we need a 20-goal striker? Matt Green has eight in twelve, we've failed to score once in 13 games and scored twice or more on ten occasions in that run. We're hardly stuck for goals are we? Where our rivals have a fifteen-goal striker, we've got goals from all over. Those people looking at the stats saying our rival's strikers score more, have you factored our wingers goal in against theirs? No? thought not.

Why is our entire transfer window being judged on not bringing in one player? Okay, so we've not fulfilled all of our targets, but it could be worse, we could be Grimsby or someone like that. You know why they've been so tragic this season, aside from John Fenty? Because managers have been allowed to bring in average players who subsequently clog up the budget. You know, the exact thing Danny is wanting to avoid. Do you think there is a single team in League Two who has ticked all of their boxes in this window? No. Do you think there is a single team in League Two that wouldn't take our business over theirs? We signed a League One captain in Lee Frecklington, a Championship quality defender in James Wilson and the same in midfield in the form of Danny Rowe. We've taken one of our rival's star players in Tom Pett and resisted having the same done to us by Luton. We've undoubtedly strengthened and improved since the window opened, hanging on to all of our best players and bringing in far better than we had, bar perhaps Raggs.

Those people crying on social media about a lack of goals, consider this: we've scored more than two of the sides currently in the play-off spots. We've scored as many or more than every single team below us in the table. To suggest we're being held back by the lack of striker is madness. Yes, if Matt Green gets injured we're going to look a little light on the ground, but we're not being held back because we haven't brought in Ricky Miller. Any neutral observers wouldn't glance at the table and go 'if only Lincoln could score more goals', because we're comparable with those teams around us. So Padraig Amond has got more than Matt Green, we're still above Newport and have scored the same amount overall.

In fact, where do some supporters get the nerve to moan about our dealings in the transfer window? Two weeks ago Danny was the messiah for bringing Freck home and then securing Jordan Williams and James Wilson the next day. This window has been superb and I have utter belief in the manager. If he couldn't get value for money, I trust that he's done the best for our club and walked away from deals. Can you tell me the one time he hasn't done the best for us? Can you tell me one time he's frittered away our money on a whim? Never. Can you tell me a time over the last eighteen months where his win percentage has dropped below that of any Lincoln City manager in history? I'll give you a clue: it's never. Why then, do some feel justified to sit behind a keyboard and call him naïve in the transfer market? 'Danny's got to learn how the big-league works' I saw last night. Has he really? He's got a 60%-win percentage as Lincoln manager, Graham Taylor had 44%. Danny has brought us Michael Bostwick, Lee Frecklington, Matt Green, James Wilson and a host of other superb players. He's barely put a foot wrong in the market since he arrived and in the space of twelve months we've reached two semi-finals, an FA Cup quarter final and won a League Title. We're now one win from automatic promotion in League Two and in serious danger of achieving back to back promotions for the first time in the club's history. I think he understands the so-called big league very well.

Yet still, some fans moan. Sure, I felt disappointed when the clock struck eleven and a striker was nowhere to be seen but seeing as the man responsible for the transfer policy has taken us on an unprecedented run and completely rebuilt a shattered team, got an entire City to love the club again and given us all belief we can reach the Championship, I'll trust his judgement. If the players he wanted to sign weren't value for money, then I'll trust him implicitly when he doesn't sign them. How do we know Tom Pett, a wonderful player by all accounts, won't drop into the centre and bag a few goals? Jordan Williams is rumoured to have played centre forward too, how do we know he won't do it again? Because he's a winger on FIFA? Sure, that must be a better way of judging, rather than trusting the manager who works with the players day in, day out and is dedicating every single second of his life to pushing our club forward.

You know what? I won't entertain it any longer. I won't have the negativity and bad vibes. You're entitled to an opinion and I respect that, but no longer will I indulge in arguing my point. Danny Cowley does not deserve to be questioned incessantly on social media, his record speaks for itself. He is on an upward trajectory and his actions are completely in line with the actions that have brought him and Nicky to this point. I am not saying he is beyond reproach, nobody is at any level of the game, but I will not indulge the doom and gloom merchants when we're as good as we've been in my lifetime.

Let us not lose sight of who we are, where we are and what we're achieving. Lincoln City haven't been to Wembley in 133 years, yet within 12 months we've been within one game thrice. It hasn't happened by accident either, one of those semi-finals, due to take place next week, has been achieved with 'just' three recognised strikers. Who the hell do we think we are as fans to start calling out a man who has done the things for our club which Danny Cowley has? I feel disappointed with myself for doubting him at 11pm last night, but I'll leave the article up to remind myself of what posting rash blogs achieves. Nothing.

If Danny didn't do business for a striker, there will be good reason. Until we're in the bottom two (FGR), spending beyond our means (Mansfield) or have only scored three in ten games (Grimsby), perhaps we should trust in the man who has led us for the last year and a half? Perhaps we should rally behind the excellent squad we do have and stop wanting more and more all the time.

The transfer window and football in general has turned fans into gluttonous fools, desperate to add more names to a squad list when in truth, we're not doing too badly at all. Our clamour for more news was like a spoiled kid at Christmas, no sooner had one announcement been made than we wanted the next, disregarding the new signing we'd just witnessed in an incessant hunger for more, more, MORE. More presents Mummy, more players Danny, MORE!

Right, my deadline day is now over, it is 1.38am and I want to be by the radio at 8.50am to listen to what Danny has to say. When he talks, he's earned the right to have us listen and believe. In the meantime, if you're raging about us not getting a striker in time, go and have a flick through our last six years of history and get some fucking perspective.

One gained, or two lost? Imps 2-2 Swindon
February 3, 2018

Football comes with so many clichés attached to it. It's a game of two halves, it's a real six-pointer, you have to play to the end and a whole host of others. Whilst they may be clichés, this afternoon all three of those are perhaps apt.

Also, football is all about opinions and what I am about to write will not match everyone's opinion, even though we spent 90 minutes watching exactly the same match. I often wonder how opinions differ so greatly, especially when you consider we're all Lincoln fans, we all want to win, we all hurt if we don't and we all watch the same game. How is it then, that people with exactly the same intentions watching exactly the same game can come away with such contrasting opinions?

Today's match was always going to be tough and although Danny wouldn't accept it, I would perhaps have settled for four points from the last two matches. After all, we've now taken four points from Swindon and four from Newport, both rivals in the play-off race. With 15 minutes gone of today's game a draw would have been a poor result. With 1 minute of normal time left, a draw seemed a great result. Perspective.

I'm always wary of setting up differently at home in order to accommodate the visiting team, but it seems as though that may have been the case today. It has been well documented that Swindon play 3-5-2 and we struggle against sides employing those tactics with our 4-4-2. Many were surprised Rheady was on the bench and many express their belief that we didn't utilise Harry Anderson enough. The truth is, neither of those players are entirely comfortable playing against a 3-5-2. Harry can't get in behind the full back because although they're advanced, there's an extra centre back to squeeze our wide players out of the game. We should know all about that, Keith used it to great effect in 2003-06.

Before we start with today's game, here's why Rheady was dropped. Firstly, we've got one eye on Tuesday's game. There's a few hard core out there who consider it to be a nothing game, I am not one and neither is Danny. The chance to get to Wembley is one we must not throw away because we don't value the opposition. Chelsea kids, to coin a phrase, will not like it up 'em, and Matt Rhead is the man to stick it up 'em, so to speak. He's a completely different threat to anything they've dealt with so far and so he must be fit. Of course, Danny would prioritise the league points, but when you consider the problem with Rheady playing from the off in a 3-5-2, his exclusion makes sense.

We play a lot of diagonal balls into Rheady and playing against four men means just two centre backs. Therefore, whenever the balls come into him in a normal situation he's challenged perhaps by one centre back and one full back. His options are then two-fold, he can look to nod down to Matt Green occupying the other centre back, or flick over his head to the onrushing winger. That gives the full back a problem, does he double up on Rheady or track the winger? That is why the diagonal ball is so effective, but against a 3-5-2 the conundrum is taken away, because two central defenders can double up on Rheady whilst the full back / wing back handles the winger and any spare men are mopped up by the third central defender. That, ladies and gentlemen, is why Matt Rhead didn't start today's game.

Danny knows Swindon have a great away record because they flood the middle areas of the pitch and, with us having three of the finest midfield players in the division, he thought we could win the battle by overloading them. The first fifteen minutes suggested perhaps that might be the case, it was nip and tuck with neither side really getting a break. Then they had a man sent off and that actually worked to our detriment.

I know we scored the penalty and they went to ten men, but they shuffled the pack immediately and we did not. The penalty was a dead cert, Matt Green played for it and even admitted afterwards he 'felt contact' and went down. I'm not sure that sits too comfortably with me, but we were calling Green at Wimbledon and Crawley for not going down when he was fouled, this time he did despite it being soft and got a reward. It was a penalty, to the letter of the law it is a red card and City were 1-0 up. I hoped given the man advantage we'd kick on.

We remained 4-3-3, a formation we didn't look entirely comfortable with, which meant we didn't capitalise on the extra man. After the goal and for the rest of the first half I thought we were poor all over the pitch. Matt Green worked hard, but not one player showed any real composure on the ball. Our wingers ran down dead-end streets, the midfield three blocked each other out more than Swindon and at the back we looked uncertain.

Swindon's equaliser wasn't pretty viewing and I know Paul Farman will be sat at home beating himself up about it. As a keeper you're always told if you can't hold it, parry it away from danger, but for the second time in a week his initial save led to a goal. I didn't think he was to blame on Tuesday, but the shot this afternoon didn't seem to have the same venom to it. He saved the initial shot, they bagged the rebound and once again sections of our support have a scapegoat.

It wasn't long before a resurgent Swindon got their second, I actually missed it but I've seen it back and again, it isn't directly attributable to the keeper. Yes, he could have done better with it, but he wasn't offered the level of protection ahead of the shot that we have come to expect from the Imps defence. They backed off sufficiently to allow Ollie Banks to crack a shot off which perhaps could have been dealt with better. Once again, fuel got poured on the scapegoat fire.

I despair when I read comments such as 'take him off now' at half time. What on earth is that going to achieve? Paul Farman is not a bad goal keeper, in the past few weeks he has pulled off some super saves. At the moment, a weakness in his game is dealing with long-range efforts and that has snowballed since the Accrington cup game. Other teams have done their video analysis and spotted he was beaten from range by Sean McConville, since then every side visiting the Bank have cracked shots off from distance.

People are entitled to an opinion and I won't be shouting anyone down either way on social media. What I will say is this: I saw one comment saying Allsopp deserves his chance, I ask why? Has he been working tirelessly in training for the last few weeks, eagerly chomping at the bit? No. Have you seen him play? No. Please, have your opinions on Paul Farman if you must, but don't lose sight of the fact he isn't the only factor that cost us a win today. We've lost one in fourteen, yet we still want a scapegoat to blame when we concede. I fail to understand the mentality of someone who relishes it when our keeper makes an error, or is perceived to be at fault for something, but each to their own. By the way, last time we were in a semi-final we dropped Paul Farman and played Ross Etheridge. He let in two weak goals and we blew our chance of Wembley. I hope history doesn't repeat itself.

Anyway, from one to eleven I thought we were average at best and poor at worst in the first half. Swindon earned a lot of praise, maybe because their ten men went ahead against our eleven, rightly so I suppose. Having the man extra isn't always the advantage it seems, we proved that at Stevenage and Swindon proved it today. By the time half time came I was actually thankful they hadn't added to their tally, Ollie Banks in particular looked decent, but it was more a case of us being bad than them being good.

It was a game of two halves, as I alluded to in the opening gambit. After the break I thought we were the better side, not least because I think Danny had a few choice words for them in the interval. How many times have we seen Lincoln come out first for the second half? I can't ever recall it happening if I'm honest. We came out with an increased tempo and intensity, but things still didn't really go our way.

Swindon retreated and although I've heard lots of plaudits from Lincoln fans, I actually thought they were alright, no more. They defended like ten-men, lots of bodies behind the ball and offering very little as an attacking threat. They had their lead and they looked like they just wanted to defend it and go home with three points. They're clearly good at it and they invited us to break them down. Despite the array of creative players we had, we didn't really look like scoring.

Rheady came on and shook things up a bit, the free kick for time-wasting was earned by his mere presence. He's a fan favourite and rightly so, but it wasn't his physicality that changed things, nor his actual impact. He played ok, not brilliant, but he did enough by coming on and asking questions to free other players up. Despite this, we loaded balls into the box but didn't look like converting any of them. As the game pressed on, Swindon hit the bar, but that was a rare foray into our half. They were happy with a 2-1 win and by the time 89 minutes turned to 90, they looked to have done enough to earn it. We had much more possession but it was an afternoon where we lacked composure, cohesion and a cutting edge.

Scoring deep into injury time meant many fans felt in high spirits on the way out. Danny always says if you get the ball into the danger areas, eventually something will happen and that proved to be the case. Nobody seems sure who got the goal, whether it was Bozzie, their keeper or even Ollie Palmer, but it ended up in the net and that is all I need to know. On the balance of play, I think it was a deserved draw and even though we weren't on it, we still earned a point. On 89 minutes it was a point gained, but after fifteen it was two points lost. Call it what you will, we'll only know on May 5th which it was.

It's another game unbeaten, another reason for fans to tear each other to shreds on social media and another fine display of character, if not ability, from the Imps. We huffed, we puffed and eventually, somehow, we blew the Swindon house down, or at least blew the front door open and nicked a point from the cupboard when they weren't looking. Other teams would have lost that 2-1, other managers would have hung individuals out to dry but we're not other teams and Danny is not other managers. Managers calling out players doesn't help anyone, fans making their own players scapegoats doesn't help either. If you were in the ground today and you ironically cheered Paul Farman when he cleared a ball after Swindon's goals, you really do need to take a long hard look at yourself. Have an opinion, by all means, but when the game is in progress get behind the lad, yeah?

It wasn't a good day at the office, but we took a point. I think we're expecting the new players to settle in very quickly and it actually takes time. Rome wasn't built in a day and what we're creating here is exciting, but those new faces need time to adjust and understand the Cowley Method. It is happening, we are evolving and we're still showing character and fight even though today it didn't quite work. You can't win them all they say. You win some, you lose some they say also. Well, we've lost one in 14 and that was to the runaway leaders on New Year's Day. It's not all bad, is it?

A battle for Wembley, a battle for integrity, a battle for all of football

February 6, 2018

Tonight Lincoln City go into battle, perhaps one of the oddest and most controversial battles of our 133-year history. The lure of a first Wembley appearance alone is enough to whet the appetite, but the stakes are much higher than a simple prize for our club. We're fighting for everything that is right in football, the beleaguered competition's last modicum of integrity and perhaps for football itself.

I'll be frank, despite attending games as I have, I don't like the youth team's presence. I don't find it insulting particularly, I just think they epitomise what is wrong with our game at the highest level. You want to know why our national team is, for want of a better word, crap? Because all the best young players stay stuck in an academy before slowly filtering down the league system, broken and poorer for it. Whilst potential future England players such as Jacob Mellis and Billy Knott fester in the lower leagues, players such as Jamie Vardy who played proper football from a young age, litter the national side.

I appreciate there are counter arguments each way, but nobody can argue soundly that our philosophy of protecting young players in under 23 leagues or sending them out on a hundred short-term loan deals, is aiding their development. They need competitive football, they need to be part of a team that achieves something. Turning up for three or four games in the Checkatrade Trophy won't help, it is arrogant to think it will. The rise of these academy teams is killing our talent, pure and simple.

I've always believed in the Football league Trophy though, whether it is to give Lee Frecklington his first run out in a Lincoln shirt, or to provide a viable route to Wembley for a club that otherwise might not get there. I couldn't boycott the tournament as my principles were not as strong as my love for the club. We spent too many seasons competing against the likes of Ebbsfleet to pass up the chance to watch a match against Notts County or Peterborough, no matter what the circumstances. We've actually been brilliant in the trophy, we've seen some wonderful games of football, some superb goals and we're now just 90 minutes from a first ever Wembley final.

People might think a team not having been to Wembley in 133 years must be a bit rubbish, but we've been desperately unlucky. Okay, up until around 1980 we didn't have a sniff, but many other sides didn't either. It has only been since the inception of the play offs and the FLT that lower league teams have had a real chance. We've not got a bad record in both, but circumstance and fate kept us away from our national stadium.

In 1983 a rather wonderful Colin Murphy side battled bravely through to the final of this competition, or an early version of it, and came up against Millwall. It had been a turbulent season, one in which we'd beaten Leicester and narrowly lost to West Ham in the League Cup, one in which we'd looked like being promoted to the Second Division (now the Championship) before board room troubles halted our progress. Harry Redknapp's first game in management ended in a 9-0 defeat at Sincil Bank, Millwall were also defeated at the Bank with Sam Allardyce in their defence.

By the time we made the Football League Trophy final later in the season, we'd slipped out of the promotion race. We had still managed impressive wins against the likes of Norwich in the quarter-final, the Canaries a Division One side at the time. We were eager to win it once we made the final stages, Grimsby had been the first team to lift the trophy the season before but they were eliminated at the group stage by us. Chester fell in the semi-final after extra time meaning we were through to the showpiece final. Sadly, it took place at Sincil Bank, not Wembley.

In 2003 we bounced back from administration to finish in the play-offs for the first time in our history. Keith Alexander's brave collections of cast-offs and non-league players proved the whole of the fourth tier wrong with battling displays of bravery and courage. Once again, near neighbours were beaten en route, Scunthorpe defeated 6-3 on aggregate in a wonderful two-legged semi-final. This time, the showpiece event was at a National Stadium, only Wembley was under renovation so we went to Cardiff instead. When we repeated the feat two-years later, we were back in Wales.

So, Lincoln City could have been to Wembley three times in our history, we could have been three times in the past year too! We were only one dodgy penalty kick away from an FA Trophy final, 90 minutes away from the FA Cup semi-final and earlier this season we would have drawn Spurs in the third round had we progressed. Again, it didn't happen. Tonight we're just 90 minutes away from going, again with it in our hands and the odds stacked against us.

Standing in our way are, arguably, some of the most talented kids in the world today. Chelsea have a fine academy of players who you'll doubtless see turning out for Barnet in eight years' time, but right now they're on top of their game. They're young, hungry and being coached by the finest staff money can buy. Their facilities will be infinitely better than ours, they have more staff, more resources and more ability. It is the haves against the have nots, no matter how well we do, we cannot be compared to the pampered princes of football that will arrive this evening.

One thing money can't buy, one thing that cannot be coached into you is attitude. Another is a viciously partisan home crowd. They're our two 'secret' weapons tomorrow, something that tactically you can't prepare for. These kids might be special and all that, but will they ever have played under such hostile conditions? Even when they beat Portsmouth for instance, was the atmosphere cranked right up? I doubt it. I did notice they beat MK Dons earlier in the tournament too, if there was ever a game that lacked soul that must have been it. I've been called a cab for going to the city games, what on earth does that make the Franchise FC fans?

We won't win on ability alone, we won't win on attitude alone, but our secret weapon won't even step onto the pitch. There's two of them, they're both called Cowley and they will have prepared for this game as though it is their last. They want Wembley just as much as we do, they want a legacy at Sincil Bank, they want to be remembered in fifty years' time as the managers that changed everything. Two of our greatest managers of the last 37 years took us into games which should have been played at Wembley, they want to go one better. If that means getting Matt Rhead to introduce himself early, or asking Michael Bostwick to get in an early reducer, they'll do it. If it means churning up an already well-worn pitch, they'll do it. Whatever it takes to win, they'll do it.

How will the kids cope with that? Our previous brush with an u21 side saw a match that was pretty much men against boys take place. It was a narrow margin, but if we'd gone at it with a full squad we should have won by a bigger margin. Will that be the case tonight?

I'll tell you one thing, there will be a lot of suits and ties up in the FA headquarters with very nippy bum holes this evening. They never imagined their experiment would backfire like this. They will have hoped the kids got through to the quarter finals at the most, not all the way to Wembley. With Chelsea having fielded Batshuayi and Musonda early doors too, they really defecated over the so-called aims of the Checkatrade Trophy. If Chelsea were to get to the final it would cause even more uproar than anything that has gone before. This is a lower league competition, not one for Premier League clubs to field £32m strikers when they feel like it. They'll want us to win almost as much as we want it ourselves.

If someone had said to me, would you take defeat against Swindon and a win against Chelsea kids, I would have said yes. I've never felt like this about a cup competition, not even Arsenal in the FA cup last season. I've always prioritised the league, but tonight is different. Tonight feels important for so many reasons and I believe come May, our fate won't be decided by a solitary point. We'll either be two or three outside or inside whatever we're aiming for, history won't care whether we beat Swindon or not. However, history will be made no matter what happens tonight, either the evil corporate scum that control the upper echelons of our game break up another fine tradition, the mickey mouse trophy being a route to Wembley, or knights in shining red and white armour strike a blow for all that is good and great about football in League One and League Two.

I hope we win, I hope we go back to being vilified for (in the main) supporting the competition because if we watch our team run out at Wembley against Shrewsbury or Fleetwood, it will all be worth it. We will have stopped the cancerous u21 teams from succeeding, for now. We will have flown the flag for League Two in the final and, most importantly of all, we will have written another chapter in the history of Lincoln City.

Those players tonight have the chance to etch their names on this club for eternity and in doing so, can show English football that all is not lost just yet. Up the Imps.

Lincoln City are Wembley Bound
February 7, 2018

It's 11.24pm and I've just walked in from a truly unique evening in our club's history. The result is that for the first time in 133 years of trying, Lincoln City are going to Wembley.

I'll do an article tomorrow talking about the game, the incidents and the outcome, but right now it is hard to formulate the words that will do how I feel justice. I know there are thousands of you out there who feel exactly the same.

I know this is a tainted competition, I know there's plenty of controversy surrounding it, but nobody complained when they made the JPT final, certainly not our friends up the A46 whenever they got to Wembley in it. No, whatever your feelings we've reached a Wembley final on merit.

Not only that, but we struck a blow for lower league football, we put the rich kids in their place, blame the pitch, our tactics, whatever, but in the end we wanted that and we went out and took it. Chelsea kids were a good side, they have some very special footballers who will go on to play at the very highest level. They won't be playing at Wembley in April though, we made sure of that.

History was made at Sincil Bank tonight and I'm honoured to have been there to witness it. Countless Imps fans have lived and died without ever knowing what it was like to reach a cup final, but I'm fortunate enough to have found out. On April 8th, I won't care that Swansea kids took part, nor Chelsea kids, nor any of the academy sides. Some might find it an insult we had to face them at all, but we beat everyone put in our way, we beat kids, we beat League Two teams and we beat League One teams. Now, for the first time ever, we will walk down Wembley Way in our red and white striped shirts, proud to be Lincoln City fans.

I didn't cry at the final whistle, I guess I save the emotion for league titles, but by god I was proud. Our players have performed superbly throughout the season, tonight each and every one stood up to be counted. Whether it was Elliott Whitehouse with his commanding display, Ollie Palmer putting emotion under his hat to remain calm during penalties, Bozzie and Rhead doing exactly what they needed to in order to leave an impression on the kids, or even Lee Frecklington's one touch of the evening. To a man, they were superb.

Last season, we wrote National history as well as our own, but this evening we stopped debatable history being written as well as adding another page to our own. We stopped the kids reaching the final, not MK Dons, not Portsmouth, not Oxford, us. Lincoln City. We did it.

It hasn't really sunk in just yet if I'm honest. I need a night's sleep and a bit of perspective before I can write coherently about the game, but just as I did against Burnley and Ipswich, I had to write something. I had to get some of the whirlwind of emotions onto a page and up for people to read and identify with.

Lincoln City are going to Wembley. I am one of the first people to ever write that in an internet article and it makes me proud with every inch of my being. 133 years of history, rewritten.

Danny, Nicky and the players; I thank you as a fan, as a lifelong supporter of this sometimes-downtrodden football club. If there was ever any doubt that you were amongst our greatest managers ever, tonight has surely dispelled that. Thank you.

Down to the wire: Imps 1-1 Chelsea Kids (4-2 on pens)
February 7, 2018

The headlines will read "Lincoln City go to Wembley", but behind that there are a million stories all converging together. There are tales of personal joy, tales from fans, players and staff and the story of a football match steeped in controversy.

The story of my semi-final started in a dome atop of the Lincoln Tap House and Kitchen with two bottles of champagne and strawberries (very Made in Chelsea) and my Dad (definitely Made in Lincoln). We'd been invited as guests of my significant advertiser to enjoy pre-match drinks. It meant starting a Lincoln match amongst more new faces, something that has come to define this season. Every week I seem to be with different people, hearing different stories and getting contrasting opinions on all things Lincoln City.

Oddly, very few of the assembled fans poke of the actual game. There wasn't any excited chatter about our line-up, about possible trips to London or how Danny might approach the game. Everything seemed apprehensive, almost mooted to a point where we didn't want to consider the fact we were attending a match. For those not driving the bubbles and nibbles helped.

I think the stunted excitement was two-fold. I think we all knew the game wasn't the stereotypical semi-final. Deep down, we would have loved to be facing Swindon or Port Vale, not Chelsea U21s. I won't pretend I backed their inclusion, not one bit, but when you're presented with an opponent you have to beat them. This competition has provided a viable route to Wembley for many other sides at our level, why must we feel inadequate because we've got through when the kids are involved too? From 2001 to 2006 non-league teams were involved, did that diminish the finalists achievement? No. These kids, rightly or wrongly, are far better quality than the FGR or Halifax were in 2005 yet somehow we all felt a bit dirty at acknowledging this as a real game.

Secondly, we were scared of losing. It wasn't just Wembley at stake, if Chelsea kids had won through the competition would have been degraded further, perhaps more pertinently our achievements in it this season would have been for nothing. That 4-2 win against Peterborough was superb, as was the 3-2 victory over Accrington. Those games should not have been in vain, not spectacles deemed worthless because some pampered kids rocked up and turned us over.

The game itself was well supported, that didn't surprise me one bit. It was a semi-final, people turn up to semi-finals. Whether you support the FLT or not, last night it meant a lot to an awful lot of people. Many fans see beyond the B-team threat and just want to see Lincoln City at Wembley.

On the pitch I thought we were excellent. If it had been a league game we would have commented how they looked a threat on the break, but in truth they didn't seem to be able to find a way out of their own half. Ampadu, the lad they signed from Exeter, is a proper talent though, he wasn't fazed by Rheady although he didn't win many headers either. I saw an article from a Chelsea programme where they mentioned this game would provide a good warm for their Premiership B matches. Don't be fooled into thinking the U21 teams are giving this competition respect, many don't want to be involved (so I'm led to believe). That said, those kids wanted that game last night. We didn't let them have it.

Elliott Whitehouse, at home in these games as he came through the Sheffield United ranks, had one of his best games in a Lincoln shirt, but Michael Bostwick was absolutely superb. He clearly had a remit: tackle hard and tackle often. He flew into everything, fighting for every loose ball, every free header and every single kick he could get. The kids up top did not like it one bit and whilst they looked a force at the back, going forward they offered nothing at all.

Ryan Allsop came in for Farms, a big call but one many felt needed to be made. I didn't, I was worried because in my eyes, Ross Etheridge perhaps cost us the first semi-final against York last season. History has a habit of repeating itself and I could see it happening all over again. I need not have worried, Allsop didn't have a save to make in the first 45 minutes. He did have a big part to play later on though.

We poured forward, at times it seemed as though we laid siege to their goal. There was a clear threat from set pieces, our best chances inevitably came from corners or diagonals into the box. I'm told after twenty minutes we'd had something like 70% of possession and by half time the ball had been in the final two-thirds of the pitch for 80% of the time. World class youngsters? Whatever.

We pressed and harassed superbly, their keeper didn't enjoy kicking and you could see we'd done our homework. Obviously, in the Premier League B or whatever it is called, they can roll the ball to the edge of the area and go from there. against Lincoln City, or in the real world, you can't.

In the second period they did have some more of the play, but I'm not sure they ever threatened to run riot, or even really threatened to score. That isn't down to them being a bad side, it is because we worked tremendously hard. Everton might be above them in their little league, but this Chelsea side was far better than the Everton one we beat earlier in the season. However, going forward we made a significant point about our own football. As Lee Frecklington said in his interview with me the other week, there's no particular way you should play football, you win games and that is what we did, we tried to win the game.

I didn't realise our goal had gone in, I thought it had caught the side netting and everyone around me was cheering for no reason. Genuinely, it took five second or so to convince me we'd scored. I was pleased for Luke, he's had a tough season and I envisage it being tougher over the next few months, but to get the goal that helped us to Wembley was a big thing for the skipper. Neal Eardley was instrumental too, another player who had a fine night.

Had Danny Rowe laid the ball off to his left rather than shoot we would have been two up moments later. It wasn't an easy night for the wingers, they peddle the style of football Chelsea are used to, playing on the deck and beating players, so their threat looked less significant than most.

Only when we scored did Chelsea look like they wanted it and sure enough, they were quickly level. I'm sure Danny will say it was a bad goal from a defensive point of view, it rolled across the goal and past three defenders before they picked it up at the back stick. When the shot comes in, Allsop has three players in front of him. It was tough on City, really tough.

From there Chelsea looked happy to go to penalties, odd for a side that had already lost twice on spot kicks in the group stages. Maybe they knew we hadn't won a shoot-out in 17 years, maybe not. Let's face it, we've not seen many penalty shoot outs at Lincoln, the odd county cup perhaps but that is about it. It was the first I've ever seen in the flesh, to be honest I almost walked out. The pessimist in me had convinced the rest of me that the story had been written and we'd go out. I was even preparing the humble 'we supported the trophy, now we must accept our fate' blog. When Sam scored his spot kick but the officials didn't give it, I felt even more certain. Luke's hand ball last season, Wembley being closed when we earned our last two visits and now a dodgy decision from a penalty. The Wembley curse strikes again.

Ethan Ampadu, by far Chelsea's best player and a product of the Exeter City youth system, missed his penalty. It was harsh on the centre back because he will go on to be one of the very best footballer sin the Welsh side, there's no doubt about that. Elliott Whitehouse and Ollie Palmer are two players I've been known to criticise, constructively of course but I've often asked whether they offer anything other than a brief impact from the bench. Both stroked home confident and assured penalty kicks, then our new keeper gave himself an instant reputation amongst fans with a wonderful save, before the ever-dependable Matt Green bagged his. I thought Green had a tough evening, he was shackled well and didn't really get a sniff of goal, but he never gave up working and always offered a run. From twelve yards, I never doubted him.

I suppose for someone who has a passing belief in fate, in fairy tales and stories which write themselves, as soon as Freck stepped up the job was done. Ironically I'd spoken to Freck last week about penalties and he told me he'd only ever missed one, in the Wembley play off final for Steve Evans. Those notes appeared in the Swindon programme where he scored his penalty and then he bangs home the final spot kick to seal our own Wembley performance. He always envisaged his career ending with a spell at City, I'm not sure he dared imagine he'd score a spot kick with his only touch of the game to secure our trip there.

Of course, that sparked scenes of delirium. In that moment, nobody cared how we'd won, nobody cared about who we'd beaten. Lincoln City were in a cup final and, quite rightly, that emotion overrode all of the others. I'm sure those who choose not to attend the games will have afforded themselves a smile at home. We didn't just beat kid's teams, we beat local rivals, we beat League One sides and we did it convincingly at times. Oddly, when I listened back to the highlights of the tournament, Billy Knott set up a goal in the first match, JMD grabbed tow in the second and Josh Ginnelly put the third group game to bed. Sean Raggett scored late against Accrington, Nathan Arnold provided the cross that beat Rochdale, all players who have left or are likely to not play for us again. Danny was right, this Wembley final has taken a great effort from an awful lot of people.

Without sounding too much like a cliché, we must now park Wembley and pretend it isn't even happening. There's an awful lot of football to be played between now and April 8th, football that is far more important than the Checkatrade Trophy final. There's 11 games, 33 points up for grabs in a quest to secure our second appearance in two months at the national stadium. The benefits of getting there though are immense, financially it is good for the club, on a day when we announced such a superb financial situation it just added to the good news. There's also a psychological benefit too. If we do get to the play offs and if we do get to Wembley again, our players will know what it is all about. They will experience the big event; the noise of the crowd and they will have had their 'day out'. When we played in Cardiff the first time it felt like a day out, a great experience for the club, but the second time felt like proper business. On April 8th we get our day out, we get our day after 133 Wembley-free years. At the end of May, let's hope at the very least we go there with the serious business of promotion.

Just a word on that 133-year wait, it technically isn't correct is it? The stadium opened in 1923, so we've actually endured 95 Wembley free years. If you take away the five years it wasn't open, that is just 90 years. See, it isn't all that bad after all, is it?

As for the Checkatrade Trophy, in my eyes it is now the competition which brings us our first ever national stadium final. It is a very much maligned and misunderstood trophy with lots of positive and negatives, but in beating the kids last night we at least retained the slim sliver of integrity it does have left. I know I won't worry about under 21 sides, B team or anything like that when the red and white striped shirts grace the hallowed turf in April and deep down, wherever you choose to be and whatever your principles are, I know there will be a little bit of pride in almost all Lincoln City fans that day. Genuinely, I don't say this to be provocative, but if you don't even feel a tiny bit of pride at City reaching a Wembley final, winning six games on the spin and then despatching the pantomime villains in the semi-final, I'm not sure you're actually an Imp at all.

Perspective: Cambridge 0-0 Imps

February 10, 2018

Football is a game that provokes so much opinion, from such a wide spectrum of people, that it is bound to spark conflict. Last night Lincoln City drew 0-0 with mid-table Cambridge, that is fact. From there, opinion takes over.

Did a tired team, who have played five matches in fifteen days, grind out a good result against a Cambridge side that are strong at home? Or did an Imps team tumbling out of the promotion frame drop two points against a club in turmoil, a club who effectively sacked their manager straight after the game?

Did City play well, creating a couple of chances against a strong side, or was it a toothless display? Were Cambridge a good side, perhaps in a false league position given the quality at their disposal, or was it a mediocre team that were waiting to be beaten but we couldn't press home an advantage? Has our recent transfer business been shrewd, or have we recruited too many wingers and not enough strikers?

It is all opinion and how we express that opinion can often be misconstrued too. If I were to write "last night wasn't good enough," what does that imply to you? I could mean it in the context of not being good enough to win the game, but it could be read as me having a pop at the manager and players as a collective and in the wider context of the season. Five words, a thousand interpretations.

Last week, after the transfer window shut, I got a phone call from a certain Danny Cowley. I didn't write about it, we just chatted about the window, his targets and what the current situation was. I respect Danny, obviously because I get kept in the loop, but because he is candid, up front and will always be honest. There's a mutual respect I hope, there must be otherwise I'm sure I wouldn't be entrusted with such frank conversation. One thing he did say was, when challenged on team selection by fans, "I work with the players every day and I know what they can and can't do, or what condition they're in."

Remember that, please, when criticising team selection and tactics. Last night, Danny Rowe's exclusion raised a few eyebrows. I say his exclusion rather than Tom Pett's inclusion, but they're effectively the same thing. Don't for one minute think Danny sticks a pin in a list of names when picking a team, he agonises over it, analyses the opposition and evaluates his own squad. We, as fans, watch ninety minutes of football and throwaway a comment such as "if Danny Rowe had started we'd have won that game." If only it was that easy.

As the game became stretched late on, both Matt Green and Ollie Palmer missed chances. I'm told by some of the armchair pundits that a new striker, a 20-goal striker, would have buried those. It's costing us, not signing a new forward in the transfer window. That's what I hear, our failure to bring in a fourth forward, a starter at that, is going to cost us promotion.

Is it? It is detrimental to this season by Danny's own admission, but he has players he can utilise up front if required. From our chat, I know he worked tirelessly on bringing players in, but not just any players. We're building a squad for now and the future, we're managing finances carefully to ensure longevity and the right faces are adding value in the right places. Danny and I spoke about the forward situation and the sound bites in popular media were absolutely on the ball. he did chase targets, plenty of them and good quality ones too. They eluded us for one reason or another, mainly either location or League One sides moving for the players we wanted.

Look, it's no secret we wanted Alex Revell who went to Stevenage, that's been reported in the media and therefore I'm not breaching Danny's trust. Alex and his family are based far enough away to make Stevenage a viable option. League Two clubs do not pay life-changing wages, not those with a firm understanding of fiscal matters. Mansfield might, that's why they have an out of shape Ricky Miller in their squad and Lee Angol rotting on the bench, but we don't. Believe me, we haven't just lost out on strikers due to naivety or bad planning.

On to last night's game and let us be totally honest, we didn't look at it. Mind you, we did play against some of the country's finest young players 72 hours before, and it was our fourth game in ten days. One or two of the lads did look to tire, perhaps that should be expected. You know what though? We're still unbeaten in eight games. Cambridge were no mugs and they perhaps demonstrated something we couldn't do when bringing off Waters for the big lump. They could change their approach mid game. We can to a degree, just not so much up front. It didn't do them any favours though, did it? We still got a draw, we still kept a clean sheet.

For once we went to a ground where there were a few home fans making a bit of noise and played a team who have lost once at home since November 8th. They were organised, have good players who have been mismanaged and I thought they showed that, in patches. We showed our quality, in patches, but neither side got into a rhythm or pressed for long periods of time. Sure, it opened up in the last fifteen minutes, but I have to disagree with Thommo who said it was exciting. It was engrossing, in spells, but it wasn't keeping fans on their feet. Even in the terraces I wanted to sit down for a bit!

There's not a lot that can be written about an unremarkable game, but our response as fans is important. If you're suggesting we're in some sort of trouble, I think you're perhaps being melodramatic. Danny Cowley is here for the long-term, he wants to finish a job and I believe that job is third tier football. Lincoln City have never achieved back to back promotions, so disappointment at not doing it this season is basically being disappointed that we haven't achieved something that has literally never, ever happened. Of course the squad isn't as strong as it could be, when has any Lincoln squad been as strong as it could be. I feel from back right the way through to the attacking midfield roles we've got depth and options. We lack up front, nobody is making any bones about that, but we don't lack quality elsewhere. We as fans should be content that we're building too.

I don't buy us derailing our league campaign for the Wembley appearance and I take issue with those sneering at the final appearance. By all means sneer at the competition, but a cup final appearance means a hell of a lot to the people of Lincoln. I'd argue it means more to some then the four points we've failed to pick up either side of it, financially to the club it means a lot too. Also, for prospective signings next season, an appearance in a cup final makes the club that little bit more of a draw. At the beginning of this season most fans would have been happy with a tenth placed finish, so a tenth placed finish and a Wembley appearance is dreamland. It is important not to lose focus, I wasn't one of the odd few who were singing "we're the famous Lincoln City and we're going to Wembley" last night. We park it and we focus on the league, but genuinely (and I know I'll be criticised here) I'd take the Wembley appearance over the four points we've not won this week. I make no apologies for that statement, I don't care about the reputation of the tournament either. I'm going to see my team in a cup final at Wembley and that, in itself, is a measure of success whether you like the FLT or not.

Last night was an average performance against a half decent side with a good home record. It wasn't a defeat, it was a clean sheet and it certainly isn't the end of the world. It is a real barometer how far we've come when draws against Swindon and Cambridge are regarded as below-average results. Swindon were two divisions above us last season, Cambridge away has always been a tough prospect and yet taking points from both has disappointed fans? It can't be all bad.

So it's a blank Saturday now, so depending on the status of your glass you can either be happy that the teams around us are playing each other and dropping points or lament the fact we haven't capitalised on that as much as you'd like. Me? Now I've warmed up and chilled out I'm easy with last night's result for two reasons. One, the clean sheet and the point and two, when it became clear on fifteen minutes that neither side were likely to score I stuck some a quid on below 0.5 goals. It hasn't made me rich, but it means that my match ticket was paid for, so all I lost was a couple of hours of my time. I'd call that a 0-0 draw of my very own.

Nathan Arnold: Farewell, but not goodbye.

February 10, 2018

The news has now broken that Nathan Arnold has joined Salford on loan until the end of the season. It is perhaps little surprise that he's gone, but more so that he's in the National League North. Let's make no mistake about it, on form Nathan Arnold is League Two quality.

On the face of it, this isn't a move about football. Nathan isn't your typical footballer, he isn't mercenary and he isn't someone who would make a choice lightly. I don't for one second think he's gone to Salford to resurrect his career. I don't think he's gone there to play minutes and force his way back into Danny's plans. No, this move isn't one born out of any of the usual reasons for a transfer.

Nathan will be a revelation at Salford. He has incredible talent as we saw when he dumped the Rochdale full back on his arse in the Checkatrade Trophy game. He's far better than National League North and to think he'll be up against Gainsborough and Boston is a travesty. It is also his choice and therefore it is to be respected.

I know Nathan scored against Gateshead, a superb goal, but I'm not sure he's been the same player since that wonderful goal against Ipswich. I appreciate it must have been tough to cap that, but the joy on his face after the Gateshead goal told you all you needed to know about his motivation. I hope there's no negativity around this move and I hope the ridiculous rumours of refusing to train get left where they are. We owe Nathan Arnold our cup run last year, it is as simple as that. If the lad had chosen to go back to Grimsby, he would have done so with my blessing whether I chat to him on a personal level or not.

I feel a little sad sat here typing these words if I'm honest, because a real icon of our National League win has gone. Yes, our squad is changing rapidly and improving all the time, but with Raggs and now Nathan gone we've lost two absolutely integral parts of last year's triumph. I know football moves fast and I know there's no sentiment in football, but for fans I think there is. For a player it is a job, for us it's more than that.

If I had to give an honest assessment of the situation, I'd say Nathan is falling out of love with the game. He'll always give his best and he'll be a huge asset to Salford, but I think the pensive and softly spoken man who opened up his soul this summer is thinking beyond his playing days. As I alluded to earlier, Nathan isn't a typical footballer, not one bit. He'd never be in the card school on an away trip, never seen in town after a game or throwing insults at other players on the pitch. He is respectful, self-aware and philomathic. He's eager to better himself and equally as keen to use his experiences to help others. I don't think that means coaching or managing, not one bit.

We might see Nathan back as yet, he might go to Salford and find a new-found desire to come back and excel as I know he can. However, I think Nathan Arnold has climbed his mountain here and if that is the case, I wish him all the best for whatever he does in the future. People spoke about Terry's goals when he left last season, Nathan's might not have secured the league on the day, but his overall contribution was pivotal to everyone we achieved. We wouldn't be where we are today without Nathan Arnold, that is absolute fact.

Grinding and grafting: Imps 1-0 Cheltenham

February 14, 2018

Some you win pretty, some you win easy and some you win by fighting and scraping even when things are not flowing for you. Tonight, we won via the latter method.

It wasn't a great game, we were certainly better than we were at Cambridge but there was still enough to draw groans from those less easily pleased fans around me. Wild balls into the channels, missed headers and such like. Who cares?

Cheltenham are a decent side, they go quick up top just as we do and they packed the centre of the park. It was a battle, a scrap, a proper lower-league encounter with all the ingredients for a disaster. We could easily have lost that game, especially after failing to get the early goal our first fifteen minutes deserved.

I thought, to coin a Danny phrase, we attacked with a real intensity and purpose early doors. It was high-octane stuff, Cheltenham looked awful as we pushed forward. When we failed to capitalise early, the complexion of the game changed. If anything, we looked nervy that we hadn't gone ahead after our hard work, the visitors looked big, strong but barely capable of scoring themselves. I can see why Mo Eisa has 15 goals, I can also see why he doesn't have more. They go long, direct and are physical but he is the polar opposite. He sniffs around looking for a chance, but he isn't one you'd go long into. I guess they were looking for Adebayo but he was marshalled superbly.

We got our first look at Scott Wharton and he looked decent in the first half. I did see him misplace a header and miss a pass, that had me groaning a little bit. I'm not usually quick to judge a player and as he settled he looked quite composed alongside Luke. They dealt well with any first half threats, having Bozzie just in front must help immensely.

I thought if we were going to get any joy it would be from Matt Green. That man works so hard throughout the game, he is phenomenal. He draws criticism for not being clinical enough but I'll tell you something; I've never seen a centre forward work as hard at Lincoln City as he does. He chased every ball whether it was long, short or completely hopeless. It is a real bonus for us because even if we're not on method, he's still providing an outlet. Some of the wayward balls he chased this evening were lost causes before they left the passer's foot, but he still chased them down.

Overall, it wasn't a great half of football, it was very much like the first half of the Cambridge game. However, Neal Eardley decided enough was enough, the paying fans needed something to cheer and he conjured up a goal from nothing. Bozzie played a great ball through, Neal fired a thunderbolt through a gap and into the net. It was the perfect shot, it raised approximately two feet off the ground and stayed parallel to the turf until it nestled in the net. I like the word sumptuous, I use it quite often, but I think when Oxford are looking at defining in their new dictionary, they should just use a YouTube clip of Neal's hit. To clarify, for those who need telling twice, it was a bloody super goal.

From there, I hoped we'd come out and blow away the opposition, after all they were alright, but not great. Half time was spent smirking when Alan Long introduced Tony Battersby as a 'the legend that is, Tony Battersby'. He was a good player, when he turned up, but if he's a legend then someone better get on the blower to Paul Connor or Gavin McCallum, ask them if they're free for the 24th against Crewe. Once that had passed I remarked to my mate Dave how the goal just before half time would kill off Cheltenham and we'd kick on and win by two or three.

Instead, they mixed it up and brought on Danny Wright, a proper horrible bastard of a centre forward. I like him. He does the things Rheady does, just without Rheady's finesse but with a bit more mobility. For ten or fifteen minutes of the second half I feared we'd have them score. It is easy to see how they bagged five on Saturday, if they're allowed to play their game then they are a real threat. It's testament to our excellent defensive players (Bozzie and Alex included) that they only looked average. when they did get through, Ryan Allsop had the answers.

I'm a Paul Farman fan. you know it, I've not tried to hide it and I never will. However, Ryan Allsop has looked excellent since coming in. He commands his area superbly, he has a knack of maximising his time on the ball when we need the game slowing down, but also distributing it quick when we need an out. His shot stopping looks good too, I'm not really sure what the Blackpool fans were moaning about when we signed him. I worried about a loan keeper coming in, on the evidence of the last 180 minutes of football, I need not have bothered.

Danny tweaked it fairly early too. I thought Rheady coming off after 59 minutes was a bit premature. After all, we know Ollie's strengths and weaknesses and he's not one to give you an extra dimension with thirty minutes to go, normally. I actually thought this evening he was excellent, his introduction helped swing the game back into our favour. Most of our second half chances came after he entered the fray and I didn't see him lose a header. He worked tremendously hard too, bit hard not too when Matt Green is leading by example, but he clearly frustrated the Cheltenham defence.

I'd like to give a special mention to Tom Pett too, I really like the look of him. He ran down a few blind alley's tonight and was out-muscled on occasion, but our conditioning and sports science guys will put hairs on his chest, that is for sure. He looks to be a 'footballer', a player with a bit of panache and an eye for a pass. I think he's got a big future at the club, once he leaves balls to bounce out for a throw instead of standing under it!

Usually when we're 1-0 up at home we endure fifteen minutes of pressure at the end, but as Cheltenham chased the game we had the better chances. Ryan Allsop pulled of a great save from Eisa with ten minutes or so to go and that was effectively their last threat. as the minute ran down I didn't think they would score, usually I'm fearful but we marshalled them so well. Wharton got increasingly more comfortable as the game progressed and it is clear he isn't here to make up the numbers.

After the game Danny was quite critical of the pitch, but it has seen an awful lot of action recently. Nobody is too blame, the harsh fact is grass doesn't grow in the winter, so the more games that get played, the worse it is going to get. The ground staff must be delighted when the clocks go forward because it is likely the grass will be growing by then and we can start seeing improvements in the playing surface. Reports of it being deliberately churned up for the Chelsea game are not correct, the staff try really hard to get it playable. we get the ball down in the final third and play some nice stuff, we often work the ball down the flanks on the floor too, so it doesn't exactly suit us in the current condition.

We end the day in the play-off spots but that means nothing. Sure, it might be a psychological boost, but I'll get excited if we're still there in May, not before. What does please me is a win, a clean sheet (again) and a spirited performance at the sharper end of five matches in just over two weeks. Our players are jaded, it has been high tempo, high pressure and high risk but we've come through the period relatively unscathed. Once Crawley is out of the way we have a full week of to recover and focus on the 14 matches that now stand between us and League One.

As for tonight; job done. It wasn't a classic but at this stage of the season, who needs classics? We got three points, a clean sheet and a moment of magic that will forever be the one memory of an average game of football.

Imps Financials

February 15, 2018

Football is a business, we must never lose sight of that. Sure, for you and I it is much more, it is a passion and a lifestyle, but at the very sharp end it is a business. It must make enough money to keep putting on matches in order to survive, pure and simple.

Throughout history, we've been poor. There's been a little spike here and there, a big player sale or a little cup run, but never enough to keep the wolves from the door for very long. We've skated through 133 years of financial struggle and hardship, never quite sure if the next decade is safely in the bank. Even in my life time, I've gone to bed at night fearing for the existence of my club, not just once either.

Welcome to 2018, the year everything is different. Now, instead of keeping the wolves from the door, we've built a big fence around our property, a fence that is eight feet high and covered in a paint that poisons wolves bringing financial hardship. It'll take some time for the buggers to get through that.

I'm sure you've all read the annual financial statement by now, it makes great reading for anyone who is used to the usual narrative. Gone are the positive messages glossing over financial losses. Gone is the dependence on selling players to make ends meet. This time, arguably for the first time in our history, the money men are talking a language we can all feel comfortable with.

How about a pre-tax profit of £1.3m? Remember, merely reading the words profit is unusual there, let alone knowing there a seven-figure sum behind it. The historic FA Cup run brought us almost £2m, after costs. It was a great season, not just on the pitch but in the board room as well. How Bob Dorrian must be feeling right now is hard to put into words, he was on the cusp of becoming vilified within the city like Gilbert Blades two decades before. Bob believed in the club though and, with a little bit of help, he's come through the other side. If he walked away now, his legacy would be positive and very few chairmen from history can ever say that. John Reames legacy is positive, but at the time of his departure it can't have felt like it.

Here's the big one: historic debts cleared. You can talk about one off seasons all you want, but the clearing of debt is something we should all raise a glass to. For years we've been running from the spectre of debt, hoping for the cup run that could chip away at it, cultivating good players not to rise up the leagues, but to sell on for profit. Nearly all football clubs are in some form of debt or another, but Lincoln City have moved their historic debt, ploughed through it and made it a thing of the past. Last year Notts County were losing £1.6m a year, Forest Green have lost £4.5m over two years. At our level, there's almost a belief that a club has to lose money, how on earth is football sustainable in League Two? Well, we've shown a decent cup run helps. However, where we go now is crucial.

There has been a 96% rise in expenditure, not just on playing staff but also back room people, office staff and infrastructure. The club is unrecognisable from 12 months ago with apps for tickets, a CEO who I'm told personally calls some fans in other countries to answer complaints and increasing numbers of support staff for Danny and Nicky. The media team has grown and evolved, everything is changing at an ever-increasing rate too. I know some fans will comment that money should be ploughed into playing staff, not suits and ties, but that is both short sighted and false economy. We couldn't have signed the players we did in January if we hadn't put certain people in place behind the scenes, that is fact. No, spending will increase but as a fan base we should be happy to see it being kept on a budget. I love hearing Danny saying things like "we must spend sensibly," or "I'll only pay what I think a player is worth." Damn right, that money has been 133 years in the pipeline, I wouldn't want some joker throwing £300K of it on an overweight centre forward who has barely scored in the Football League.

It was nice to see the contribution from both the Fan's Player's Scheme and the Red Imps Travel Section, amongst others. The FPS is something I believe strongly in, I'm not a member now as a season ticket holder, but last season I enjoyed some of the rewards for putting all of the DF money into it. Paul Dawson and Andrew Helegsen started it up expecting to raise a few grand I imagine, but £72k over two seasons? No, I don't imagine that crossed their minds. Helgy is the current driving force, a man so focused on raising money I've forgotten what he actually does for a proper living. He's relentless, single-minded and has certainly driven the FPS to these phenomenal levels.

I was pleased to see £16k from the travel section too, Chris Ashton is a lovely bloke, not to everyone's tastes but he's a man I personally have a great amount of respect for. His passion for our club is evident for all to see and to see £15k come from them last season was also nice. I thought the club breaking down the different contributions from fan's groups was a nice touch to the report, not all our money comes from doing well on the pitch. It also goes to show that fund raisers are still as important as ever, even when we're perceived to be in good shape. We must never stop pushing for more, not out of greed but out of love for the club.

We've done our bit, not on the same level but much of our work is for the Future Imps Fund, whether it was a percentage of the second books sales, or dedicating time to the recent Impvasion book. The most recent effort, Imperfect Focus, didn't generate an awful lot of income but we're hoping to pass some copies to the club to sell for pure profit over the coming weeks.

Considering the year before we lost £418k, the turnaround has been magnificent. We knew it though, didn't we? We knew things were on the up. I hope for some the release of the financials is a bit of a wakeup call, we don't have 'millions' in the bank to play with. We're not FGR, bank rolled well beyond our means. The numbers show we have a healthy football club, but not one that can spend what they like, when they like. No, the current custodians of the club have a huge responsibility right now, they've got our club in their hands. It is as financially sturdy as it has ever been, but they must juggle on pitch success with off field stability.

Everything starts with Danny and Nicky, right there are our two assets, our two talismans that will always draw fans to the club, players to the club and garner media attention. Once the sun is shining on us, the rest of the staff have got to be out harvesting those fields, toiling away in all hours to reap the benefits of our current success. Together, we have come so far. Together, we might just go a hell of a lot further.

Tough day down south: Crawley 3-1 Imps

February 17, 2018

For a moment, albeit brief, Lincoln City looked like they'd take all three points today. Trailing to an early goal Jimmy Smith goal for most of the first half, they looked anything but promotion contenders.

It all got worse on half time after Danny Cowley received his third red card of the season, sent to the stands by Trevor Kettle. I'm not going to comment on Mr Kettle, do a search. Type

"Trevor Kettle" and "awful" into Google, draw your own conclusions. However bad he might have been, we weren't 1-0 down because of him.

No, we were 1-0 down because our Achilles heel, first halves away from home, had seen us barely in the game. One half chance perhaps, nothing more. Crawley on the other hand looked slick going forward, well organised and efficient. Boldewijn and Ahearne-Grant had some real movement in them both. I have it on relatively good authority that Ahearne-Grant was one we were in for in January, but location (along with Karl Robinson's relationship with Harry Kewell) scuppered the move.

It really has been an issue at times, our inability to turn in a decent first half performance on the road. Usually we do what we did this afternoon, then come out all guns blazing, which is exactly what happened. Within seven minutes of the restart Tom Pett had hit the bar and Matt Green equalised for City with a typically well taken finish from a tight angle. From there on, only one winner. City shifted a gear against a tired and beaten looking Crawley. After all, you go 1-0 against City you need to hang on to that lead because once we get a foot hold, we don't let go.

Well, we don't let go normally, but a twist of fate ensured this afternoon wasn't one we were going to find fruitful. A simple long ball over the top beat Scott Wharton and, as he tried to recover, he pulled down Boldewijn. I was critical of the forward man before the season started, questioning whether a lower league Dutch player could cut it in League Two. He can, he did Wharton and they got a penalty because of it. Was Trevor Kettle to blame? No, Scott Wharton was. 100% stonewall penalty which Ryan Allsopp couldn't keep out.

The goal changed the complexion of the game immediately and the remaining 22 minutes belonged to the hosts. They dusted themselves down from the spell of Imps pressure and within five minutes added a third. It was poorly defended again, a simple free kick whipped in to the far post and headed past the keeper.

That prompted a raft of changes, Ollie Palmer and Jordan Williams coming on, as well as Elliott Whitehouse, but sadly we know two of those are game holders, not game changers. Our bench has good quality on it, but not up the top of the pitch. There wasn't a way back for City via those three, perhaps Pett or Anderson might have sparked something, but it was folly to believe we could find two goals. In the end, we were beaten by a good side in a game that turned on a penalty.

Let us be honest shall we? We weren't good enough in the first half against an in-form side. We came out in the second and did well, but naivety has cost us at the back. Scott Wharton had a decent game on Tuesday night, but he didn't look comfortable this afternoon. That's the call the gaffer makes, but with Frecklington injured, Bostwick can't play centre half and central midfield. With Wilson injured, Wharton plays. We're beginning to feel the pinch of injuries through the small squad, but even that isn't to blame. No, today a decent side beat us. 3-1 flatters them, but it was a more just result than us taking anything away.

For the record, this defeat has nothing to do with our Wembley final. I've already seen the smug comments from 'fans' opposed to the Checkatrade Trophy that the push to Wembley has cost us the play-offs. Why do these people need to rear their head every time a result doesn't go our way? Why must the Chelsea game have cost us points against a Cambridge side with a super home record and Swindon who are chasing the play-offs themselves? I wish some fans would reel it in a little bit when a bad result comes away, some seem to revel in things going against us if it proves a point for them.

There's not a great amount I can say, bar fifteen minutes after the break we were poor this afternoon, but it is the end of our Saturday / Tuesday run of matches that has put pressure on our small squad. I know the moaners will be out in force peddling the 'weak January' rhetoric or the narrative I've mentioned in the first paragraph. Football, sadly, is a game of ups and downs and today was a down. I feel most for the 750-odd fans who made the journey down the country to witness a 3-1 defeat. After such an intense run of games, they deserve more.

That said, it is our first defeat in 48 days, so it isn't all bad is it? We're still seventh also, so I do hope the doomsday peddlers keep their vitriol to a bare minimum.

Just a word on Danny's sending off too, I am a big one for passionate managers, I even like to see him admonish referees from time to time, but you have to do your research. Kettle likes a card, he takes no prisoners and there wasn't an incident, that I could see at least, in which we were cost a goal or they should have had a player sent off. Pick your battles Danny, you're a massive influence on the touchline and a motivation for the players and you're no use to them or us up in the stands. When it's critical, give 'em hell. When it's half time of a game we clearly still had a chance of winning, maybe send Jimmy Walker over instead. He's expendable, surely?

Is this signing more imperative than a striker?
February 22, 2018

The news coming out of today's press conference is incredibly encouraging for Imps fans; Neal Eardley is in discussions over a new deal.

Since his arrival in the summer, Eardley has proven himself to be possibly the player of the season. He came in as cover at left back, Sam's injury ruled him out and we desperately needed someone to fill the role. Bob Harris tried out, Matthew Briggs had a couple of games as did Brandon Ormund-Ottiwell. We were also led to believe by some that Noah Chesmain was close to a loan deal. None came off.

Instead, just days before the season started, Neal Eardley joined the team photo shoot, with Danny later confirming he'd signed a six-month deal. Eardley had suffered three years of injury hell, falling from Premier League star to a failed trial at Port Vale. Danny saw something though, to be fair in his friendly outings I think we all did too.

Neal is, without wanting to mince my words, bloody brilliant. He's calm and assured, he gets up and down the line like nobody before and he's got an air of class whenever he's on the ball. He rarely gets caught defensively, he's always a willing runner and as we saw against Cheltenham, he's got a shot on him too.

Neal is a super right back, he's keeping the solid and dependable Sean Long on the bench yet he can easily switch to the left if Sam picks up an injury. He's practically got it all, certainly for this level and everyone at the club was delighted when he triggered his contract extension. Had it not been for his injuries, I confidently predict he'd be in Ryan Giggs' mind for the international team. I honestly believe if he'd stayed in the top two divisions he would still be a Welsh international.

In January, several people messaged me with sensationalist rumours about Eardley going to Mansfield. Yeah, Evans wishes. Not having him on a long-term deal was a worry, but I never imagined for one second he'd jump ship, certainly not just for money. Neal Eardley doesn't strike me as a mercenary. After today, that belief has been reinforced.

In the press conference, Eardley spoke glowingly of the Imps and his willingness to remain here beyond his current deal: "I'm really enjoying my football here and if that was to be prolonged, I would be delighted. There's been conversations between myself and the manager and they seem to be going quite well at the minute."

Exciting? Absolutely. Eardley has earned his stars here; Lincoln fans don't warm to players for no reason and one bad game can often leave you with a mountain to climb in terms of popularity. Look at Jordan Maguire-Drew, he started badly and despite some stunning EFL Trophy goals, never won the fans back. Ditto Tom Champion, albeit with the goals. Ditto Billy Knott. We might have great fans, but as a group we're very expectant of our players. Neal Eardley has never put a foot wrong. He's committed but disciplined, a role model for kids and a leader on the pitch. Even in his interviews he's measured, he never walks into traps laid by tricky questions. When asked about the training ground he remain diplomatic and thoughtful.

So, is his signature the most important of the summer? We need a striker and that will clearly be addressed, but no matter which division we're in, Neal Eardley will be a huge part of everything we're trying to achieve. If we're in League Two, he would continue to be a cut above the rest. In League One we step up to a level more befitting of his abilities and we have no worries about our defence.

I'm not going to put a silly poll asking which is more important, football is all relative and the one we don't get will be the one we lament. If we signed a great striker but Neal ended up somewhere else, we'd be gutted at him going. If he stays but we don't bring in a striker, we'd be exactly where we are now. Football fans always seem to focus on the things we don't have, not the things we do

Awful outing, but keep your heads: Imps 1-4 Crewe
February 24, 2018

I'm not going to write a lot tonight. It is my Mum's 60th and I'm due out in a short while. It isn't reflective of the fact we got hammered, I'm not fair weather nor do I shy away from the facts.

We were bloody awful today. There was no clear game plan, no cohesion, no urgency and genuinely nothing to cheer. From start to finish there was a flat atmosphere, everything about the afternoon screamed 'dead rubber'. It wasn't a dead rubber, there was lots to play for and yet we didn't appear to be interested at all.

That's not to say we weren't interested, something went wrong today, something fundamental. I'm not going to say there's an ongoing problem, I'm not going to say, 'it needs sorting', I'm not going to lose my head. Don't get me wrong, I'm gutted at today's game. I've never seen such a dismal outing from a Cowley side. I dare wager the manager has never presided over such a shambles.

We're still eighth, albeit a few more points outside the play off places now. We're not tumbling down the league like Grimsby, we're not marooned in obscurity and we're not collapsing. For some to claim the wheels have come off is absurd, we all called tenth as a good finish at the start of the season and we're still exceeding that. Please, keep some perspective.

What does worry me immensely is this competition we seem to have going on amongst the fans, the constant one-upmanship and berating of each other. You'd think we were relegation fodder the way we're always at each other's throats. I won't be on social media tonight, but I logged on just before writing this and the same doom and gloom merchants are revelling in the defeat, the same arguments are firing across the keyboards. I find it desperately sad that the first sign of defeat some people believe their vitriol is justified.

That said, to see fans streaming out when Crewe scored their fourth was incredibly disappointing. We're eighth, why on earth do some feel the need to abandon hope at such an early stage? I've left early once, when we lost 6-0 to Rotherham. By early I mean twenty minutes or so, to leave today was really poor by a large portion of fans. However, if you pay your money I suppose you have the right to go when you want, but it really isn't a nice sight for the players, manager or fans. Sure, we could argue that the players didn't do anything to keep fans there, but come on, leaving with 20 minutes to go when we're still in the play-off hunt?

I get criticised because I often exude double standards and I suppose I'm doing it a bit today. On one hand I'm saying we should be united, on the other I'm calling out those who left early. I left with a minute to go, but with it being Mum's party we had to in order to get a jump on the traffic. You know what? I felt awful about it.

I'm really upset that the Checkatrade Trophy final is being cited as a negative aspect to the season as well. Whatever your politics, making the final of a competition is wonderful for the club and should be cherished. It has no relevance today, we were awful but it was a one off.

I don't have time to dissect the game, sadly. I will say I thought Matt Green had a decent game, Bozzie had a good first half and that was about it. In almost every other area we were second best, passes went astray, there was no movement, no fluidity to our game and nothing to cheer. I even felt the response to our goal was muted, as soon as it went in fans streamed off to do their half time bits, ten minutes left on the clock. Something felt wrong today, hopefully we can just put it behind us.

Next weekend is huge now, we need a result at Coventry to keep us in the frame, but if we don't get it we must retain some perspective. This club is on a journey and all journeys have their ups and downs. We've conceded seven in two games, coming on the back of some stellar defensive performances. It isn't time to panic, we'll be a league club next season and we're building for the future. If it doesn't happen this season we must remember how far we've come and the potential we have.

I haven't seen City lose 4-1 at home for an awful long time, once upon a time it was regular. It hurts right now, it is a stark reminder of what things used to be like. This isn't the norm, even if we fall short this season we are not in a spiral going down the plug like our friends up the A46.

Please before you get embroiled in heated arguments tonight, think. before you type out your statuses berating other fans, January transfer windows or the like, think. Instead of turning the computer on, maybe have a beer and just wallow in the misery of defeat. We've not lost like that at home for a long while but Danny will be putting it right. It hurts, but we just have to swallow it and move on. I won't say 'we go again' because it is a cliché that really gets under my skin, but we have to accept this afternoon as a one off.

It doesn't make it easy to deal with, but nothing is going to be corrected by arguing with each other in the stands, on social media or even in the pub.

Pos	Team	Pld	W	D	L	GF	GA	GD	Pts
1	Luton Town	34	20	8	6	74	34	40	68
2	Accrington Stanley	34	20	5	9	58	38	20	65
3	Wycombe Wanderers	35	18	8	9	67	51	16	62
4	Notts County	35	17	10	8	56	36	20	61
5	Mansfield Town	34	16	12	6	53	35	18	60
6	Exeter City	33	18	4	11	44	37	7	58
7	Swindon Town	35	18	3	14	55	51	4	57
8	Coventry City	34	16	6	12	38	28	10	54
9	Lincoln City	34	14	11	9	46	37	9	53
10	Carlisle United	35	14	9	12	50	45	5	51
11	Crawley Town	35	15	6	14	41	43	-2	51
12	Colchester United	35	13	11	11	45	41	4	50
13	Newport County	34	12	12	10	41	43	-2	48
14	Cambridge United	35	13	9	13	35	45	-10	48
15	Stevenage	35	11	9	15	46	51	-5	42
16	Cheltenham Town	35	10	10	15	48	52	-4	40
17	Yeovil Town	34	10	8	16	46	55	-9	38
18	Crewe Alexandra	35	11	3	21	41	57	-16	36
19	Forest Green Rovers	34	10	6	18	39	56	-17	36
20	Grimsby Town	35	9	9	17	30	51	-21	36
21	Morecambe	33	8	11	14	34	44	-10	35
22	Port Vale	34	9	8	17	37	49	-12	35
23	Chesterfield	34	8	6	20	35	61	-26	30
24	Barnet	35	7	8	20	33	52	-19	29

March

Coventry game off: but was it done too late?
March 3, 2018

It hardly surprised me to hear today's game had been called off. I had a ticket but, as of 2am this morning, it became clear travelling wasn't an option for me. There hasn't been a car down our road in four days and yesterday a tractor had a go at moving the six-foot drifts from either end of the road.

My belief, my absolute 100% personal belief, is that Lincoln City wanted this game reviewed far earlier. Heated pitch or not, any game of football due to be played this weekend was going to be in doubt. It's all well and good saying the motorway is a man thoroughfare in and therefore there was no problem, but that is wholly irrelevant. People don't park on a motorway do they?

This isn't an example of me being part of the so-called 'snowflake' generation either, demanding our country grinds to a standstill thanks to a few inches of snow, it is simply adhering to current advice regarding travel across the whole country. Everybody is on alert, nobody is advised to travel unless necessary and for Coventry to steadfastly insists the game was going to be on without any consideration of another outcome was, in my opinion, selfish.

Before any directs any criticism at Lincoln City, please read this statement carefully. Phrases such as "At this time, the game is set to go ahead despite the freezing temperatures and impact of Storm Emma around the country," or "Everyone at Lincoln City Football Club values your support and appreciates your efforts to back the team across the length and breadth of the country, but we would urge you only do so if it is safe to do so," suggest to me that people at our football club felt, from a travelling point of view, it was safer for people not to go. Remember, national advice is only travel where necessary and yet Coventry City were not considering our supporters safety.

I know many of you are reporting roads are clear and if I'm honest, I wouldn't know. I've not left my house since Tuesday, not due to being unsociable but thanks to adverse conditions. Not all Imps fans come from Lincoln and sadly, with weather forecast to deteriorate in Coventry overnight too, I feel the Sky Blues have not considered supporters at all.

Furthermore, I'm given to understand that conversations between Lincoln City and Coventry City have been just that, two-way conversations. Remember, Coventry don't own their ground, the Ricoh Arena is a third-party. It is my further understanding that the Ricoh Arena's first involvement in a three-way call was this morning, just before the game was called off. I feel this is an incredibly important piece of information, that the actual owners of the ground and the area around it were not involved in talks during the week. Surely, any conversations about whether the game was playable should have taken place between all interested parties?

Lincoln City did not want this game called off from a football point of view, Coventry played midweek and I'm sure Danny believed we would have had an edge in that respect. This is about supporter safety and whilst I know we'd soldier on twenty years ago, sliding over on terraces and the like, that doesn't happen now. I'm sorry if you don't like it, but in this day and age football clubs value their supporters and have to put their safety first. That is paramount.

In the end, the outcome is best for me personally as I can still get to see my team at the Ricoh, but for all of the other fans who set off or travelled overnight, it is a poor decision. I've seen lots of messages blasting the decision, but as far as I can see it Lincoln City are only able to tell you what Coventry tell them. Do I think that the game would have been called off earlier if we were the home club? Absolutely.

Imps must take points to stay in the play-off hunt
March 6, 2018

City travel to Mansfield this evening in a game which will make or break our play off ambitions. A failure to bring home any points at all would open up a gap between us and the top seven which would be incredibly tough to close over the next two months.

The Stags have been rocked by the departure of 'larger than life' manager Steve Evans, but with new manager David Flitcroft already embroiled in the hunt for a top seven finish, the impact may be lessened significantly.

City have no new injury worries; January signing James Wilson is still out injured whilst keeper Josh Vickers remains a long-term absentee. Scott Wharton, Luke Waterfall and Michael Bostwick will all by vying for a place in the centre of defence, although the latter is perhaps better employed in a midfield role.

Flitcroft already knows some of the squad having had Jacob Mellis and Danny Rose at Bury and it will be Rose likely to lead the attack for the Imps visit. He sat on the bench for our clash earlier in the season but emerged from the dugout to score the only goal of a tightly-knit game. Rose has 17 for the season, five from the last eight matches and he'll be the one to stop if City are to come away with anything at all.

In truth, Mansfield are finally beginning to ascend to the heights expected for a majority of the season. They've clearly outspent most, if not all of the League Two promotion hopefuls, so it is rather ironic that their star man was already at the club prior to Evans arriving.

Midfielder Alex McDonald is another significant threat, he leads the Stags assist charts with six, but his all-round game is about much more than just creating goals. He's their midfield livewire, he created the goal that earned them a 1-1 draw against Coventry last time out and again, he's one City must look to stop.

The most likely outcome, according to Footstats prediction model, is a 1-0 win for the home side, followed closely by a 1-1 draw. Whilst a draw would be a satisfactory result, City could really do with a win to edge closer to the top seven. For the first time in a long while, we can't end the night in a play-off spot, but we can do our hopes the world of good by finding a result.

One thing a prediction model cannot factor in is the personal motivation of players and between Matt Green and Matt Rhead, there's plenty of motivation to succeed. Green was bombed out of Field Mill by Evans, despite his never-ending hard work and constant goal threat. He'll want to score against his old club almost as much as Rhead. It was Rheady, back in 2012, who scored the goal against City to earn an FA Cup replay, where the winner ultimately got a tie against Liverpool. Green scored in that game too and tonight we hope they'll both be on the mark in City colours.

Expect a tight game, despite the home advantage for the Stags. They average 13 shots per home match whilst we usually manage nine away, meaning there is very little to separate the sides. In terms of corners they average 5.41 at home, us 4..88 away. Our set pieces were once our most favourable route to goal and that may be the case again tonight. We tend to commit more foul, 15 on average per away game whilst they concede 11 on average at home.

Danny Cowley was dismissed during our last encounter at Field Mill, the 3-1 win in our opening Checkatrade Trophy game. Ollie Palmer, another former Mansfield player, scored that evening and he'll be hoping for the same again. Danny, unprovoked by the pantomime of Raynor and Evans, will be hoping to remain on the touchline and avoid a fourth sending off of the campaign.

The referee is Graham Salisbury, he's sent of five players in his last six matches and dismissed ten for the season from 31 games. He took charge of our win against Everton in the Checkatrade but hasn't officiated an Imps league game since 2011 when we lost 2-1 at home to Wycombe Wanderers. He's been on the circuit for eighteen years and in 2002 he sent off Carlisle's Darren Kelly as we lost 2-1 in the FA Cup first round. Rather ironically, Ben Futcher scored for City that afternoon and will be in the Mansfield dugout tonight after moving with Flitcroft. Salisbury was the referee that also sent off Leon Mettam ten minutes after coming on as a sub as we lost 4-1 at home to Hereford in 2007.

Tonight's match isn't easy, not by any stretch of the imagination, but it is one Lincoln need to turn up for. Two defeats on the spin have made it as close to a 'must win' as you can get when you're comfortable in mid table, but if we aspire of anything bigger than consolidation then tonight is the time to stand up and be counted.

Palmer silences Stags: Mansfield 1-1 Imps:
March 6, 2018

I asked prior to kick off if a draw would be a satisfactory result from tonight's clash. After 85 minutes of the game, despite turning in a solid performance, it looked as though City were going to be disappointed.

Cometh the hour, cometh the man and we had plenty of former Stags looking to step forward and make their mark. Matt Green, for all his hard work, wasn't able to find the goal. Matt Rhead, unplayable throughout in a text-book 'big man' performance, couldn't find the goal. Enter Ollie Palmer, booed and chastised as he took to the field by the natives, still angry at some perceived injustice committed since he's left them.

To be fair, Ollie hasn't had an easy ride from some of our fans, me included, yet he just keeps popping up with crucial goals. Could tonight's have been the most crucial of all? 1-0 down to promotion hopefuls, four points outside the play offs and about to throw a game in hand up against the wall, but with one touch he kept our league season alive. Talk of Wembley is all well and good, but the league is something everyone can enjoy and breaking into the top seven could have been a huge ask.

What's more, it stemmed a run of back to back defeats, meaning Danny and Nicky still haven't lost three on the bounce as City managers. It might not be a win, but I would have taken it at kick off and I'll damn sure take it now.

Before I move on, I have to mention the man of the moment, Ollie Palmer. I've been highly critical of him and I'm still not sure he's the answer to our striker issue, but by god he's giving it a damn good go. His attitude seems excellent and most of all, he comes across as such a down to earth guy. I think he'll be something of a cult hero at the Bank in time, another Phil 'derby' Daley character who has impact, however fleeting, but never gets a proper first team run.

What I like about Ollie is his honesty in interviews. He had no qualms about calling Grimsby a huge club in his interview, but in a complimentary way to Lincoln. the passion with which he said his goal had shut up the Mansfield fans wasn't just likeable, it was endearing and made me splutter Pepsi down my hoodie. He's raw is Ollie, unorthodox on the pitch and down to earth off it. I think his openness and personal pain which he shared recently also showed him as far more than just the gangly striker who can't head a ball. Fans like to identify with players and I really identify with Ollie Palmer. I can't head a ball either.

Overall it was a good team performance and the change to 4-3-3 certainly helped. I have a theory on tactics changes, I think they're necessary to stay one step ahead. These days with the video analysis and constant internet chatter, a team can easily be dissected by opponents. To have something new in the locker is important and we showed that tonight. It doesn't always work, I've not seen us switch formations as effectively, but if your opponent puts a lot of work into stopping you playing a certain way, a sure-fire method to beat that is play another way.

I was pleased to see Jordan Williams get a start, Danny must read the blog. He looked a decent prospect playing off the big man and a viable option for the weeks ahead. He's clearly a winger, he wanted to get on the ball and beat his players, but he seemed to adapt to the change quite quickly. His signing is an odd one, we've got a lot of wide players currently and he's not really had a chance. If he was permanent and we were breaking him in gently I could understand it, but I wonder if he might be a prospect for the summer. He's got a way to go yet, but he showed perhaps why he was brought in this evening.

I can't comment too much on Luke's sending off, it sounds foolish, even if the bottle was thrown at him you just can't throw it back into the crowd. I hope that it isn't the case, but I suspect he's dropped a bollock in the heat of the moment and his anger afterwards was as much at himself as it was anywhere else. I know Luke, having chatted to him on a few occasions I don't believe he would have thrown it back in anger. Rheady? Sure, I can see the big man doing it, but not Luke. If evidence shows he has, it isn't something I could defend. We're now going to either hope James Wilson is close to fitness or drop 4-3-3 before we've truly settled into it.

To be honest, considering they're one of the top teams in this division, I thought we were excellent tonight. We matched them, if not bettered them on their own lawn and on another day should have taken all three points. I concede that we're a striker short and maybe, just maybe a more clinical striker would have gotten us all three points. However, I trust implicitly in the bigger picture and if Danny says the right man wasn't available then I bow to his better judgement. This isn't the time to go over old ground though, merely a time to dig over some fresh turf. Tonight, we looked as if we wanted it. Tonight, we almost put Crewe to bed once and for all and tonight, we actually looked top seven material.

A quick message for Caroline Radford too: you say your fans are the best in the league, we brought well over 1600 tonight (pictured top) and they were the only ones I could hear singing until your goal. You might have good fans, granted but you don't have the best. Could you sell out the away end on a Tuesday night? Could you sell over 20,000 tickets for Wembley in five days? Would your fans join in with respectful applause at an away ground after fifty minutes of football to honour a lifelong fan of the club? Our fans travel in numbers, they're respectful, they sing until the end and, if we don't play, they'll just represent anywhere they can. It's not a competition, but if it was, we'd win.

The hard work has just finished, but it starts again really quickly. We must beat Chesterfield and Grimsby if we're serious about the play offs, there is no question whatsoever about that. We've stumbled and faltered but we haven't fallen yet. 72 points will probably be the bench mark for promotion so we need six wins, arguably, to ensure our play off place. The world would be a much better place if we only needed four wins from our last nine games, in theory. These numbers aren't set in stone, the key is winning football matches, something we've not been good at recently. On the form we've shown tonight, we might be about to rediscover that 'refuse to lose' mentality.

I go to bed a happy man, not a delighted one but with a fresh outlook on the previously stagnated play off assault. Not for the first time this season, Ollie Palmer has proven me wrong and every time he does, I get a little kick out of it. He unorthodox, he's hard to defend against because, in the words of many people, even he doesn't know what's going to happen when he gets the ball, so defenders have no clue. He runs hot and cold, he's single-minded to the point of outright selfishness and he belies his big man billing by not being an aerial threat. Despite all of that, he scores goals, he's committed and honest and I like him.

There. I said it. I like Ollie Palmer. Not just for his goal, but because he's proven me wrong and at the same time, he's doing well for the football club I love. Good on you Ollie, now prove me wrong again, get to double figures and bring home that silverware you spoke about in the interview.

Back in the top seven: Chesterfield 1-3 Imps

March 10, 2018

The Stacey West would like to send our best wishes to the victim of the incident this afternoon that resulted in the air ambulance attendance. we hope you have a speedy recovery.

On a rather strange afternoon, City have emerged as 3-1 victors to force a place back into the top seven. Ahead of Tuesday's game we looked to be floundering, losing a grip on the play-off race. Now, just a few days later, we're back in mix and looking forward to the visit of an out of sorts Grimsby side. It won't be easy, but at the moment would you bet against us?

After the broken opening to the game, both teams could be forgiven for making first half mistakes. 25 dominant minutes for City were broken up by a medical emergency that put football into perspective. The long delay for the air ambulance to arrive broke up the rhythm of the game but after, Chesterfield found their stride much quicker than we did. They scored from a looping header, it was a weak goal to concede, but we conceded it and there's no point crying over spilt milk. To go a goal down in the first half usually means we go in down at the break. City don't typically score in the first half, but luckily Michael Bostwick had other ideas, levelling before half time to become the first player to score in an away game first half for City since Matt Green against Luton on New Year's Day.

I didn't think we ever looked bad to be honest, I've seen some criticism on social media but I thought we looked decent. I like us in a 4-3-3, it won't be the case all of the time as we have lots of wingers, but for now it gives us a different feel. Elliott thrived in his rare start too, whilst we're switching to the narrower set up he might get more chances. He showed some great work rate today and whilst I'm not sure has the pass to unlock a game, he certainly has enough endeavour to make him a cult hero, of sorts.

After the break the disruption was put behind us and we'd taken stock at the break, there was only ever going to be one winner. Scott Wharton might only be a youngster, a footnote to the transfer deadline day during which we hoped for a striker, but he popped up with a bullet header that I'm not sure any striker could have bettered. Scott had a superb afternoon, he's strong and quick and has a huge career ahead of him. Danny talks with as much passion about his future as he did Sean Raggett's, so who knows what might happen. I know one thing, there was never any doubt what the outcome was going to be once he'd scored.

I thought we looked far more threatening once the pressure of the result was taken away as well. Matt Green worked hard but didn't get a lot of joy, which will only fuel those demands from fans to play Ollie Palmer from the start. Of course, Palmer did himself the world of good coming off the bench (again) and scoring (again). Fair play to Ollie, that's two in two now and he's probably had no more than half an hour on the pitch.

I worry for the Spireites. I don't want to see them go down, they're a team close to us and always a big draw for the fans, but I can't see a way back for them. They don't have a threat up front, they looked terrified of set pieces all afternoon and quite how they beat Swindon I don't know. Incidentally, Swindon were thumped again today, they look to be collapsing after the manager merry-go-round, perhaps we ought to write Evans a letter of thanks.

Special mention to the big man Matt Rhead again, not always getting the run of the green today, but he's such a handful. So many fans felt he'd struggle to get up to speed in the Football League, he's proven everybody wrong. Again. I'm surprised that we've seen two defences in five days that don't seem able to deal with him. They know what is coming, but with us going 4-3-3 it makes it hard to double up. If a team does, they need to pull both full backs in and it narrows their play too. It's a conundrum and one of the reasons we might have swapped.

Back to that 4-3-3, another reason we've tried to switch formation could be in order to accommodate Lee Frecklington, a player who perhaps didn't stand out again today but we know is high quality. If that is the reason, a side product is that teams don't know exactly how to prepare for us at the minute. Most of the video evidence will show us playing two wingers, so to go without is a real shock to most. It relies a lot on our full backs often handling two men, especially when facing a 4-4-2, but Neal Eardley has no problems with that at all. Sam looks comfortable in the role too, I'm also delighted for Sam to lay on two of the goals, his set pieces haven't been great recently so that'll be a big boost too.

We've got a small squad, but some of the fringe players are showing they've got far more value than some might believe. Scott Wharton was superb, Elliott came in and did well, Jordan Williams has turned in two decent shifts and obviously Ollie Palmer is a case point.

I've kept it a little brief tonight, I've got to head out for a nice meal in Belchford, but I do so with a huge smile on my face. I'm sensing a Wembley double, a little dress rehearsal in front of 25,000+ before the main event, 30,000 down in London at the end of May kicking Mansfield Town all over Wembley and back up the M1.

Keep the faith, up the Imps.

Alex the Centurion

March 11, 2018

Alex Woodyard hit 100 outings for Lincoln City yesterday, a superb achievement in just under 20 months of football at Sincil Bank.

In that time he's had a couple of new contracts, plenty of interest from opposition and a somewhat odd goal scoring record of three goals, two of which came in one game against Carlisle. What he has also done is turn in confident and busy performances virtually every week.

What I like about Alex is, as Luke Waterfall once described it, his 'ratting around' in midfield. He won't settle, battling and contesting every single ball. He's got a decent pass on him too, often backwards or sideways helping to build our possession and pressure. I wouldn't say he's one to thread a thirty yard through ball or create something from nothing, he's a worker bee, doing the breaking up and laying up that helps both defence and attack but doesn't truly belong to either.

It's often called the unseen work, but with Alex much of what he does has to be seen because your eyes follow the ball and so does he. He's got his own song too, something that is a sign of true endearment (or a sign that your name fits nicely into a song).

I'm also impressed with the way he's bounced back from the January speculation linking him with Luton. His girlfriend works down in London and a move to Kenilworth Road would have brought more money and convenience, but instead he chose to remain at city and with his mentors, Danny and Nicky.

His relationship with Danny is something I'm told he's given quite a bit of stick for, being the 'gaffers son' and there's certainly a deep mutual respect between the two, or three if you count Nicky too. That relationship has been critical to him making 100 appearances, will it be the same in 100 more?

Alex started as a trainee at Charlton Athletic before moving on to Southend. A loan spell at Braintree led to a permanent move to Dartford, but it looked as though the youngster was going to drop out of the game, especially after being deployed as a right winger. Concord Rangers, managed by Danny Cowley, came knocking and you could say the rest is history.

He's been one of the integral parts of our success in the last 20-odd months, in all of the memories we've had Woodyard in the middle, working away. He might not get the goals, he might not be the threat at set-pieces but he is absolutely crucial to everything we do. From the Stacey West, congratulations on the 100 Alex, here's to 100 more.

The Redemption of Ollie Palmer
March 11, 2018

"Woo-oo we've got Ollie Palmer, woo-oo he can't win a header, woo-oo we've got him on a two-year deal."

The song rang out around Gresty Road after a lacklustre first half display by City. Ollie Palmer was starting his third game in a row, but he was without a goal in ten games. As a team, we were struggling to find a shot on target, let alone a goal having drawn blanks against Crawley and Wimbledon. Another 45 shot-shy minutes had done nothing to appease the fans.

The second half was the stuff of dreams, four goals completely blew away any notion we couldn't score. Crewe were beaten 4-1, Palmer went off without a goal on 74 minutes. Two games later Ollie lasted just 45 minutes of a woeful first half against Colchester. He's not started a league game since.

Rewind to June or July, I forget which. I'm at Sincil Bank judging the Impvasion book on the same day a raft of new signings are announced. The first comes into the room we're working in, a huge lad called Ollie Palmer. He stoops to get in the door and there's not a single ounce of excess fat on him anywhere. Danny describes him as a fine physical specimen and I wouldn't argue. I sure as hell wouldn't argue with Ollie.

He made a debut of sorts in the match against Lincoln United and didn't impress me with a lack of aerial ability. surely, for a big man, he should be dominant? I think we got off on the wrong foot, me and Ollie. Luckily, he didn't know it otherwise I might have been in trouble. Anyone with a huge tattoo on his upper thigh is going to be a concern to me, if he kicks off.

Let's head back to Gresty Road and I'm belting out the rather derogatory song with the rest of the crowd. It isn't abusive to the player, it's a bit of fun. I didn't have a problem with Ollie's work rate, but he wasn't for me. When he got on the ball it was head down and run at goal, no thought of team whatsoever. That's all well and good if you're Messi, but not when you're a six-foot four striker in League Two. All too often it led to nothing. I was still carrying a bit of anger from the Chesterfield game at home, where Palmer could have squared for one of my favourite players, Matt

Green, for a tap in. Instead he wriggled around a bit, lost the ball and Green's goal drought continued.

In the last issue of A City United I ran an open apology to Ollie, I held my hand up that he wasn't the player I'd hoped he might be because of his size, but his strengths were evident and I'd perhaps overlooked them. He's certainly a handful from the bench, an impact player impossible to defend against. He has a knack of getting into the right place at the right time, Rochdale being a case point. It might have been a tap in he scored to win the game, but he had to be there to tap it in. By then I'd warmed a little to Ollie, I didn't hold him as a scapegoat for other failings. For my sins, I think I made Ollie accountable for our goal drought, thoroughly unfair on my part.

After scoring a wonderful finish with the outside of his boot at Chesterfield, the fans called his name in an altogether different way to earlier in the season. He's gone full circle, from a figure of fun to a serious fan favourite. That tends to happen when you score late goals against two local teams in succession, especially when one of them is a great strike and the other snatches a draw from the jaws of defeat. His passionate celebration earned him a yellow card, perhaps foolish but if he's fined it is one that each and every one of us would happily chip in to cover. Yesterday, Ollie Palmer arrived.

Some argue he's been that way all season, I know I'm not alone in my belief he's been walking a road to redemption, I know plenty who suggested he might leave in January. He put paid to that with a warm and relatable interview early in the month, stating he was staying put whether we wanted him or not. In truth, whenever he's got a microphone in front of him he comes across as a decent bloke, grounded and humble.

I've felt bad that I seem to have been labelled as an Ollie hater, hate is such a strong word and one I don't like to use anymore and I never label a player and stick by that decision. Football is a fluid game, always changing and that gives scope for changing of opinions. Anyone who keeps the same opinion about everything to do with the game, all of the time, isn't a proper scholar of football. I love to be proved wrong and should I see something that changes my mind, I'll always do so and hold my hands up. I did that in the magazine last month and I'm underlining it right now.

I don't believe Ollie has the same impact from the start of the game, much as he won't want to be labelled as a 'super-sub' I really believe that is what he is. When he gets thirty minutes at the end of a game, the unpredictable nature of his approach makes things lively and interesting. You never quite know what he's going to do or how he'll impact proceedings, but as the days roll by he's becoming more effective. Yesterday's goal, in context of the game, meant very little. We would have won 2-1, in theory, but it settled the lads down, it gave us a nice cushion and secured the final period. It was also incredibly well taken, showed nice posture and poise as well as a predatory instinct.

I get it now. I get Ollie Palmer. I identify with him, I see the human side, a decent man with proper family values and a desire to play football. He seems committed and passionate, not the best footballer we have at the club, but effective and worthy of wearing the shirt. When he used to come on for the final ten minutes I'd turn to my Dad and shake my head, once even likening him to Drewe Broughton. I was wrong. Now, when I hear he's coming on I perk up, wondering which Ollie we'll get, wondering exactly what he's going to do. I imagine he's wondering the same thing, such is his approach to the game.

Thank you Ollie, the red and white suits you and long may you continue surprising fans, opposition players and perhaps sometimes even yourself.

Derby day delight: Imps 3-1 Grimsby

March 18, 2018

In the end, the words of caution and apprehension were simply the best left unheard ramblings of a pessimist, a man brought up on a diet of failure and derby disappointment.

The truth was, for all of the posturing in town, the fear of new managers and new signings, it was evidentthat a team at the top end of the table were playing a team at the bottom.

The game wasn't a bad spectacle, it had a surreal ambience with driving snow switching with bright sunshine every ten minutes or so. One constant, at least for sixty minutes, was the swirling wind which made James McKeown's distribution look like something you'd see on FIFA from a six-year old with a broken controller. Perhaps the wind eased in the second period, because Ryan Allsop was definite and precise with his delivery.

The game opened tentatively and neither side truly stood out. City started well, the first twenty minutes we got plenty into the box but weren't able to create anything meaningful. The Cods got a bit of a foothold and could have taken a surprise lead although it would have been against the run of play. It was an unremarkable clash between two sides struggling to adapt to the conditions or live up to the billing of the so-called big game.

Then we had eight wondrous minutes which I'm sure will live long in the memory of all City fans. A three-goal salvo that could have been more resulting in the end of the game as a contest. Once we smelled blood it was ruthless and effective, like a bird of prey having a go at a mouse, seeing it's distress and just going again and again.

The build-up was very familiar for the first, a corner that the conditions rendered more of a pinball game, but Lee Frecklington gave us a demonstration of what he can do, firing an unnervingly calm volley through a crowd of players and past the stranded keeper. Was it a miss-hit? Possibly a bit, but in the conditions and given the limited time he had on the ball, it was an achievement to get the shot on target away.

Grimsby suddenly looked like a side on the ropes and persistence created the second. Freck was involved again, Elliott Whitehouse did superbly to get a ball cross and Matt Green added to his tally for the season. I have to say, I was delighted for all involved. After the game it was revealed Freck has been going through a tough time personally, so to turn in arguably his best display since his return was testament to his character. You could see in his celebration how much his opener meant, the same went for Green with the second. He's taking some stick from some supporters, calls for him to be dropped for Palmer have been loud, but he's such an asset and proved it by being in the right place, at the right time.

As for Elliott Whitehouse, it was his best display in a City shirt by a mile. He was energetic, tenacious and willing not just to get on the ball, but to create with it too. The second goal summed up his entire performance, dogged and determined but also calm and collected. He's one I've had doubts about all season, but recently he's been given a chance and I think he's done really well.

The third goal was another set piece that worked its way to the man of the moment, Scott Wharton. He rifled home to end the game and again, you could see what it meant to him. I can't see us being in with a sniff of bringing him here permanently next season, he's got 'Championship' written all over him and his displays will be a delight for Tony Mowbray. He came here as cover, I can see him keeping his place for the rest of the season, such is his impact.

It could have been five, we missed a couple of great chances, one that could have earned Elliott a goal had Green got out of the way in time. We looked rampant, likely to score again and again until the entire Stacey West was empty. Instead, they got their break. It was another set play, this time the handball could be seen from the other end of the pitch. Elliott claimed a push, that may be, but the official didn't have any choice to award the spot kick. Ben Davies converted it, although Allsop made himself huge and almost stopped it.

That set us up for an interesting second period, Grimsby had the wind in their favour and should have pressed that advantage home some more. They didn't, either weren't able to physically or lack the quality to unlock defences, but we held firm. It wasn't a pretty second half by any means, it was efficient and effective from City though. We had more threat after Rheady came off, the swirling winds might have worked for him in the first but he was never going to get a sniff in the second. Harry added some width when he came on, Ollie frightens everyone at times, Imps and opponents, but he too had a positive effect on the game.

Elliott Whitehouse was my man of the match, Scott Wharton played well but I thought Elliott stood out. He really suits the 4-3-3 and I think he could play off the striker as well as advancing from midfield. He will have caused Danny a real headache for Luke's return too.

Other notable mentions have to go to Jordan Williams, Alex Woodyard and Bozzie. For Rheady and Bozzie to comet through a local derby without a card is testament not only to their own restraint, but also the referee's performance. Sure, there was the odd decision I disagreed with but I thought he was excellent throughout. What was there, two cards all game? Both were deserved and a weaker ref might have been throwing them about early and making a rod for his own back. Mind you, someone ought to tell a few of those Grimsby players it was a derby match, because with half an hour to go there were three or four who didn't look like they wanted to throw themselves about at all.

Jordan Williams) had an effective game, he is another who thrives in the 4-3-3 and whilst he doesn't have a goal to show, he made some lovely runs into the channels and always offered an out ball too. I can see why Danny wanted him last summer and I wouldn't be surprised if he doesn't go back for him this time around. The player clearly loves it here and he's already spoken a couple of times about not enjoying his Rochdale experience. Besides, we might be swapping places soon.

Alex Woodyard was brilliant again too. He's looking back to his pre-Christmas best, he never gives the opposition midfield time to breath. In a high-press game such as ours you must have one midfielder with a non-stop engine and that is Alex all over. It surprised me to find out Dartford had been playing him as a right winger in his time there, to the point where I chuckled away to myself, thinking of them having this Championship quality central midfielder out on the right wing in the National League.

Depending on your outlook results either did or didn't go our way. We're in the top seven, so that is a positive but it is Exeter who slipped up, ominously away at Morecambe which is where we go next week. I have relatives who are Grecians fans and they've got a tough March, ending in the visit to us. I expect them to drop more points, although Coventry are hitting form. They'll brush the Cods aside next week, but it might not matter. Mansfield's manager change hasn't done them any good and there's going to be lots more changes before the season ends. The important thing is we've put our blip behind us now and we've got players creeping back into the squad.

James Wilson coming on at the end was huge for us, more important than a fourth or fifth goal. Imps haven't seen him yet, but in my mind he's Sean Raggett in three years' time, having played Championship football. It's been a horrible start for him, scoring with his first imps touch and then suffering injuries, but if he is fit and ready to return, it opens the options up again for us. Clearly, Danny see's 4-3-3 as an effective approach at the moment, if we have Wilson and Wharton at the back, Bozzie, Freck and Alex can all be accommodated in the centre of the park. We know Freck will manage 70% of the games but won't play every week which is why Elliott's performance was massive positive for us.

Up front the new formation works too, Matt Green hasn't looked as isolated and Jordan Williams has really seized his chance. It's harsh on Harry though, he's probably our best player when he's on form but the new set up doesn't accommodate him, nor on-loan Danny Rowe who we know has a touch of genius about him. They do give us the option to switch to a 4-4-2 though with relative ease during a game and I'm a firm believer in that being an effective weapon. If you can change formations fluidly in an instant and be effective in both, the opposition must adjust at short notice and perhaps against any previous plans they have. It will be interesting to see how the next couple of games pan out.

The play-offs loom large on the horizon and only a fool would bet against us right now. I know Grimsby and Chesterfield are not the toughest sides in the division, on paper neither are Morecambe, but you have to win these games to give yourselves a chance. If we could take six points from our next two games (Morecambe and Exeter) we'd leave ourselves in an excellent place to feature in the end of season lottery. Two weeks ago it hardly looked likely after a poor run of form, but seven from nine has restored hope, as has our stumbling opponents.

As for Grimsby, I can safely say that is the worst side I've seen them put out at Sincil Bank since they were relegated in 2009/10. Michael Jolley has his work cut out, especially if those eleven players are the best he can find in their expansive squad. If Chesterfield find some form then the Cods are in serious trouble because they looked much like Lincoln City of 2011 yesterday. We'd threaten goals back then, maybe hit a post before utterly collapsing for ten minutes, then 'bravely' battling to get back in the game. Brave battling doesn't win you points, goals do and I can't see where they're coming from for Jolley.

Do you realise if we go up and they go down, it would be the first time in history we'd been two divisions clear of them? A new era dawning indeed. If I'm honest I don't think it will happen, to be promoted from the play offs would be a huge achievement and still one I find unlikely and I suspect the other teams in the relegation battle will be poor enough to save the Cods skin. Will they be back at Sincil Bank next season? Very possibly, but I hope for their sake there's a serious improvement before then.

Stalemate: Morecambe 0-0 Imps

March 24, 2018

The match was, I'm told, forgettable. I write to you from a youth hostel in London so I'm afraid there's no analysis, no report and nothing truly interesting from the game from me.

What I have deduced is that a couple of our promotion rivals are stumbling and whilst we're not winning, we're not losing either. Is a draw enough? Given that we're a point closer to Mansfield, yes it is.

What is frustrating for some is that had we not lost to Crewe and had we beaten Morecambe today, we'd be in a prime position not for the play offs but for automatic promotion, However, should we lament what we could have had, or should we focus on what we do have?

We have a side that have not lost away in four matches. Morecambe might be 'lowly', but the only games they have lost in 2018 have been against Luton, Accrington and Mansfield. Okay, you could say that we aspire to be those clubs and should beat Morecambe, or you could say they've beat Wycombe and Exeter in the last five games, two sides we also consider ourselves level with. I'd rather have a point and a clean sheet than nothing at all.

Mansfield, Notts County, Luton and Coventry all play sides in the bottom four this weekend and so far, one of those have lost. Again, look at the positives, we didn't lose the game and we're still in touch with the top seven. Had we lost at Mansfield, the gap would be significantly wider right now. It's easy to look at where we could be, perhaps our recent success has left us greedy.

Maybe we're not League One quality right now, maybe we should be beating 'teams like Morecambe', but you have to define what 'teams like Morecambe' is. We said when we came up the standard in this league was better than we thought and yet we're still top eight.

I tell you what though, next Friday really is do or die. We must win against Exeter to keep the season alive, keep those chasing us in their place and hopefully reel in those teams stumbling. Mansfield Town are in real danger of dropping out of the play-off race and it wouldn't be the first time a rival has dropped the ball and handed us a top seven finish. In 2005/06 we barely deserved seventh place, but Peterborough's manager change ended up giving us it anyway. Maybe, just maybe we'll stay in touch of the top seven not because we're ready, but because Mansfield are not.

There's a lot to play for between now and May and each game passed is a step closer to the end of the season. Each game sees another side concede their play off ambitions have faded for another year, but for all the moaning I expect to see tonight, we're still fighting for promotion, we're still right up there and I suspect we will be right until the death.

Today was a point earned. It might have been two dropped if you're a pessimist, but when it comes to Danny and Nicky, I've learned to be an optimist. Why not, for one night only, try doing the same?

Good point, bad point. Good run, bad run.

March 25, 2018

Having been away for the weekend, I felt I ought to build on yesterday's match reaction. I've tried to take a measured approach to this piece, genuinely looking in from the view of others and considering whether yesterday was a point gained, or two lost. The truth is, nobody knows. Not me, not you and not Mr Keyboard Warrior tapping angrily away calling everyone who argues against him names.

I've committed the cardinal sin and looked at social media where, surprise surprise, people have a differing opinion. I've no problem with that, but some don't seem to be able to either accept other think differently or respect the opposite argument. Shame, some people with good ideas fail to do themselves justice by considering what their opposites think, some use very aggressive language when dismissing others and some, naming no names, shouldn't be allowed near a keyboard as a punishment for crimes against the English language.

I can fully understand the points being made that Morecambe is not a good point, we didn't create chances and should be beating 'teams like them'. The problem I have is when those holding those opinions pay absolutely no attention to the fact they beat Exeter last week, or that in the form table over the last four matches, they're above Mansfield and Luton. I despair for anyone who becomes so blinkered to their own views that they fail to at least recognise those that other people also have. I try, very hard, not to shoot down anyone with a differing opinion to mine. I will also change my opinion if I feel it prudent. That isn't a sign of weakness, true strength comes from admitting when you are not correct, or when you have been proven wrong.

16 teams in the division have scored fewer goals than us, including Notts County, Exeter, Accrington and Coventry. Only four teams have taken more points from their last six games than we have, with three of those sides above us. That means there is four sides above us who are not performing as well as we are.

Last night I read a couple of posts claiming Danny and Nicky needed to 'look at themselves' for trying to force certain players into the first team picture. Someone (and I genuinely forget who, so this isn't personal), used language along the lines of 'maybe the messiah should be open to criticism'. Now, I value opinion and I respect people having one, but Danny Cowley has taken us from a nothing National league side to promotion contenders in League Two inside two years. We've a cup final coming up, no matter what you think about the competition we had to get through eight games against decent teams to earn that final. I'm utterly gob-smacked that people are filled with such desire to pick holes in what we're doing. Tell me, those of you who think Freck has disrupted the team, how has he trained recently? What's is his fitness like? How do Morecambe set up, 4-3-3, 4-4-2, 5-2-3? I dare say you can't tell me the answer to that question, because you're paid to build computers, fix cars or sell meat, not manage the team. Danny sees these players every single day, he works with them on intimate levels and yet some people think they know better.

As for whether yesterday was a good point or not, you don't know and neither do I. I think it was a decent point, not a brilliant one but certainly not a terrible one either. The fact is, until 46 games have been played we won't know so please, don't go shooting others down and telling them they're wrong, you don't know and neither do I. I know this, if we're one point outside the play-off race come May, I won't look at Morecambe and say, 'it was lost right there', I'll look at Crewe at home or Colchester away and point to those matches.

Please, express and opinion but for heaven's sake, don't make out like you know better than Danny. You don't, that isn't even opinion, that is fact. If you did, Scunthorpe would be coming to you to save their season (fifth and they need saving? Jesus).

However, I also concede there's a counter argument. We've lost the same as Wycombe who are in the automatic promotion spots, so maybe it is our inability to convert draws into wins. Again, I'd look to draws against Morecambe at home or maybe Cambridge as games we should be winning. A promotion chasing team looks to win at home, draw away. If you do that you average two points a game and inevitably, you go up. Over two games with Morecambe we have two points, not four. If one of those games is to 'blame' (which I don't believe it is), then surely it is the home match where we had 125 shots on goal (approx.) and scored once.

This is the stage of the season where the teams that have been bad suddenly get that fighting mentality, when the so-called easy games become challenging. Look at County today, hammered 3-1 at Chesterfield yet, just a couple of weeks ago, I read an Imps fan saying we should have won by more there. Look at Mansfailed (deliberate) too, didn't we win at FGR? The point is anyone can beat anyone in this league, we've known that from the off and yet here we are, just over a month or so left and we're still in the mix.

Is this the first REAL threat to our current success?
March 29, 2018

Grimsby, Notts County even Nottingham Forest, none of those teams worried me when they lost their manager. Same with Oxford, Peterborough or Southend. I couldn't see Danny Cowley getting in the car with Nicky riding shotgun and travelling away from Sincil Bank for good.

Now, I can. That isn't to say I think it will happen, that isn't to say they're going, but this is a job I could see them taking. It's their neck of the woods, it gives a natural transition to West Ham and it's another great challenge, just like we were.

Firstly, the news. Mick McCarthy, Ipswich manager of six years, is leaving at the end of the season. It's very amicable, both parties have agreed it and he's not being booted out right now. His entire spell there has been handled the right way by Marcus Evans, no knee-jerk sacking, no public courting of other managers and a chance to walk away at the end of the season with both heads held high. It is almost sickeningly mutual, the sort of respectful departure you'd expect from a club with values.

Danny has said a hundred times that he and Nicky always finish a job that they start, on TV the other week he even said that if Barcelona came knocking, he wouldn't jump ship. It is easy to say these things, but tougher to actually live through them. I'm not saying Danny isn't true to his word, but I've lived apart from my partner before, journeyed up and down the A1 and A14 incessantly and I know what that can do to a person.

The big questions are these: Would Ipswich risk the club's future in the hands of so-called untested managers? Is the journey Danny says we're on something he plots season by season, or is it a bigger picture which he won't be swayed from? The answers to those questions are going to be the key to us retaining our gaffer's services.

I can't see why Ipswich wouldn't want Danny and Nicky. They've seen first-hand how effective their football is, we've dealt with Ipswich over Danny Rowe too so they'll be well-known to the owners there. They're from that neck of the woods and will have a growing reputation that is hard to stifle, so much depends on the owner's leanings. Having checked the odds I see Steve McClaren, Mark Warburton and Tony Mowbray are amongst the other front-runners. McClaren would be a similar appointment to McCarthy, Warburton failed at Forest but perhaps has unfinished business and Mowbray is doing a great job at Blackburn. Remember, Mowbray also played for Ipswich and has managed Celtic.

My gut feeling is they'll go for Mowbray, a manager proven at the level, a manager with extensive contacts and someone with an affinity to the club. Danny will get due consideration, but I'm not sure he'll be the one.

The bookies will tell you otherwise, I've already been tweeted by a guy who follows me with a statement that Danny is down from 16/1 to 4/1. He's only reporting where the money is going, but people get early money on outside bets in hope of a big win.

The bookies will look to drive this as much as possible and Danny is perfect for taking punters cash. The links between him and the South East are extensive and he's been talked about before in this context, but will Ipswich Town, a side hoping for a Premier League return, lump everything on a manager who, as yet, hasn't won anything in the Football League? That's not detrimental to Danny, but take emotion out of it, we're outside the League Two play offs. For us, it is good, but is it enough for a potentially huge side to gamble on? Or, will they see Tony Mowbray, top of League One and with Celtic under his belt and break the bank?

Danny and Nicky don't leave a team during the season, they act with integrity and grace and I feel that Ipswich would be a decent fit, but is the time right? They never start a job they don't intend to finish, so is that simply season by season, or is it the bigger picture. Remember, they're so wrapped up in this club it is unreal, they don't just manage the side but they're helping shape the training ground, they're building for the future and they seemingly love the city.

I've heard (and I've not written it before) that the families are looking at moving up here too, houses have been viewed (allegedly) and plans are in place.

The Ipswich job is one that would obviously attract the managers, but there are too many variables at this stage. It wouldn't surprise me if Marcus Evans didn't chat to Danny and Nicky, but with less than a year in the Football League I think it has come a year or two early. The transfer window showed a degree of hesitancy and that alone has been a learning curve for our management team. We know it wasn't ideal, they do too and they're developing from that.

They're building a good squad here, one for promotion this season or next and I firmly believe they'll stay here and finish the job. The training ground is their baby, they'll be responsible for so much that perhaps they won't at Ipswich. We've seen how much this place means to them and vice versa and whilst football doesn't come laden with sentiment, these guys do. Just today I received a message where they'd hand-written a letter back to a fan thanking him for writing to them. it's personal, it's warm and it shows a different type of character to Steve Evans, or Dean Keates who is prepared to jump up divisions without winning things.

Maybe it is wishful thinking on my part, but I'm told Steve McClaren has been lined up, if Tony Mowbray can't be prised from Blackburn. Danny was always going to be mentioned, the FA Cup tie last season made that inevitable and betting companies will drive that forward too. even sites I write for such as Football League World will bring stories of him being linked, it is good material for people to read. We all love a success story and Danny is just that, what better story than from PE Teacher to Portman Road in two years?

My advice to Imps fans is this: don't panic, not until McClaren rocks up somewhere else and Mowbray distances himself too. Outside of those two, maybe Danny will be in with a shout. If he was, I wouldn't begrudge him it either, but I truly believe he'll be with us next season. Have faith.

Cowley issues resounding statement on Ipswich job
March 29, 2018

Danny Cowley has just issued his thoughts on the speculation linking him with Ipswich, by underlining the commitment him and Nicky have to Lincoln City.

BBC Radio Lincolnshire's James Williams asked for his reaction and Danny reiterated the previous rhetoric about leaving the club: "Our focus, as always, remains wholeheartedly here at Lincoln City," he said: "We're always eternally thankful for the opportunity here, we've been shown a lot of loyalty by the people of Lincoln, when we're shown loyalty we like to reciprocate."

Strong words indeed, but only the same message as when Colin Murray jokingly asked about the Barcelona job. He continued: "For us the total focus is here. We worked hard, day in, day out from the end of last season to put us in this position. It would be crazy to think of anything other than Lincoln City."

Danny has emerged as the bookies favourite in the hours after news of Mick McCarthy's departure, along with former England manager Steve McClaren. Twitter seems to suggest McClaren has already been approached, but Ipswich fans do seem keen to see Danny in the frame.

Resilient City back in the top seven: Imps 3-2 Exeter
March 30, 2018

Being a football fan isn't all about the big matches or the pay off. It's often tough going, it's 0-0 draws at Cambridge or Morecambe, it's labouring to home wins in the middle of the season against Cheltenham. Being a football fan is an investment, you pour you time, your heart and your soul into something hoping that maybe, one day it will be your time.

We didn't win anything other than three points today, but it is days like these we fight for, it's days like these we want to enjoy as a fan. Huge six-point promotion clashes in front of a packed crowd is what we all want to experience, there's nowhere in the world I'd rather have been today than Sincil Bank.

Let us leap straight into the bit you probably won't agree with, I thought we were loads better than Exeter in the first half. They sat back and soaked up our pressure and granted, we didn't convert chances, but we created plenty. I've heard loads of moans about the first 45 minutes but from my vantage point we just didn't quite get the bounce. Their goal wasn't good defensively, my uncle and Exeter fan Keith said before the game 'keep it at his feet, he won't score'. Ten minutes in, it's on his head.

Our forwards get loads of stick but if anything is letting us down at present, it is across the back. The goal was their first attack, it was a poor one to concede and from there, they barely had a kick. I was glad to hear Danny agreeing with me on the radio that we controlled possession well and had a decent first half. Elliott Whitehouse was superb, yet again, the 4-3-3 really suits him and he's thriving. I'm baffled at the game some were watching, I know I occasionally have the rose-tinted glasses on, but some fans could do with taking their doom visors off (mentioning no names, Craig). Anyone labelling that first half performance woeful, in my opinion, is blind to the intricacies of the game. We worked tremendously hard, Exeter defended really well and I felt I was watching an engrossing game not unlike a chess match. I said at half time we were still in it, all we needed was to keep knocking on the door and eventually we'd be let in.

If I did have a gripe it'd be towards the back four who looked uncertain throughout, whenever Exeter broke I thought there might be a goal. Ryan Allsop, not one to command his area at the best of times, pulled of a heroes save from the free kick, but at the other end our smart set piece almost caught them out. Fool me once, shame on you, fool me twice shame on me. More on that later.

We had a let off before half time, again from a situation that should have been defended better, but overall I wasn't unduly worried. Genuinely, I'm surprised at people ripping the first half to shreds, I thought we showed endeavour in our approach, I thought we showed character in not letting our heads drop and I thought we stuck to the game plan when the bounce wasn't going our way. I like to think I know a bit about Lincoln City and if we're not good I say it, but we weren't bad at all.

Then came the blistering festival of football that was the second 45 minutes. Whilst it was rarely pretty, it served us up a feast of excitement that couldn't be predicted using stats, figures or algorithms. Exeter shouldn't have scored two away from home, we're not usually ones to blitz the goals either and all indications pointed to under 2.5 goals. Instead, the stats were flushed away in an avalanche of excitement.

Those two quick-fire goals changed everything, just like the Grimsby game we turned the game on its head quickly. They didn't happen against the run of play either, we set about the second half with (in the words of some bloke from Essex) a real intensity and purpose. It was only the same as we showed in the first 45, only it began to pay off. Perhaps Exeter took their eye off the ball, perhaps we just got the bounce for a change, but before we scored we had one cleared off the line and another saved by Pym.

Then young Mr Whitehouse had a shot saved which Danny Rowe nodded home and the tide shifted. When that ball hit the back of the net, the tension subsided immediately. It wasn't unlike last Good Friday when Harry Anderson equalised for us, we got one and immediately you felt we could get another. That is exactly how it panned out, this time that smart free kick paid dividends and Matt Green added to his growing tally. Once again, a side from Devon came on Good Friday and surrendered a 1-0 lead to two quick fire goals. History repeating itself?

Kind of, this time there was plenty of the game left in which to see further action and our goals fired Exeter into action. I thought our worst spell of the game came in the ten or fifteen minutes after scoring. We retreated looking hesitant, almost panicked and they saw that. Their equaliser was poor defensively, their forwards were alive as three of our back four switched off. I tweeted immediately after that it was a poor goal to defend and when Danny spoke about 'bit and pieces to work on', he will have meant that. It wasn't the first time we shut off in that left-hand channel either, they'd hit the bar not long before from the same sort of range.

Still, cometh the hour (mark) cometh the man, Ollie Palmeiras never disappoints. I didn't think I'd write that about our new cult hero, but by god that man has won me over. He's unique is our Ollie, ungainly, unorthodox and bloody effective. I keep repeating it, but how can you defend against a player who doesn't know what he's going to do when he has the ball? Pretty soon after they scored he knew exactly what to do, he smashed in a goal, with his head I hasten to add, and set about running a marathon to celebrate it. Tom Nield robbed him of the goal, unfairly, by making a fairly odd decision, but Ollie didn't get the message. He's clocked up more on his GPS getting down the line than he had since coming on, but the score remained at 2-2. Still, he wasn't done.

After their goal, the balance swung back in our direction, the switch probably helped somewhat because it gave us a new shape and asked Exeter questions. Suddenly, from being on the front foot, they retreated and we looked like scoring. One effort had apparently crossed the line by some distance, but again the officials didn't give us the decision. I'm not going to criticise the ref, it's too easy and he was equally as bad for both sides, but Paul Tisdale and Danny have both alluded to being as unhappy as each other. It's easy to be pragmatic when you've won.

Win we did, courtesy of our very own super sub, the faux-Brazilian Ollie Palmer, the man who has gone from zero to hero, the name on everyone's lips after an hour of a game. I've apologised enough for slating him earlier in the season, I won't do it again. He's proven his worth, just like Elliott has and once again it was he who smashed home the winner. This time there was no flag, no killjoy referee spotting fouls that weren't there, just the big old lump charging up the line, whipping his shirt off and getting another booking. I might start chucking a fiver on him to get a yellow because he's good for it whenever he scores.

From there the game went end to end, they pushed and created chances, we broke and could have added a fourth. The game pulsated back and forth, rippling with excitement and breaking only for the ball to cross the half way line in either direction. It's why we come and watch football, it's why we endure those 0-0 draws because one day, you get a 3-2 that could have been 6-6. We were the better side, not by much but we were. I was a relieved man when the final whistle went though because Exeter definitely had another goal in them if we had another ten minutes. We did too.

You don't qualify for the play offs by being seventh in March, but you do give the side renewed hope. That win was earned, it was carved out of a tough game by a dedicated, hard-working bunch of players who stuck to their jobs despite losing the early goal. It was wrestled from the arms of a very good Exeter side, a side we may yet have to face again in May. It showed character, not so much from coming back after the early goal, but for finding more reserves of energy after they levelled. It was League Two at its best, sometimes lacking in quality but always threatening to break out into a goal fest. I tell you something else, it was contested fairly between two robust but honest teams.

After today, I have a lot of respect for Exeter City. I like Paul Tisdale, he's a manager who cuts away excuses and bluster and tells honest stories about what he's seen. For 400, their fans made more noise than some much bigger crowds and they kept singing throughout. I don't often gush about our opponents, but if we did have to pick a side to be in the end of season lottery with us, I'd rather them than Mansfailed or Notts County. Respect where it is due and all that. Mind you, it's easy to be nice about a side when you've beaten them, isn't it?

So we go on to Carlisle needing another three points if we can get it. Last Easter Monday we travelled up north, albeit to the east rather than the west, but the parallels are there to be seen. Today, a side from Devon ended up having a lead overturned and we scored late, just like Torquay. Now we're going to a side we beat by a three-goal margin in August (as we did Gateshead), who play in a stadium far too big for their current fan base (like Gateshead), needing a win to help our promotion push. They say lightening doesn't strike twice. we'll see.

The Stacey West – A Season in Blogs 2017/18

Pos	Team	Pld	W	D	L	GF	GA	GD	Pts
1	Accrington Stanley	38	24	5	9	65	40	25	77
2	Luton Town	40	21	11	8	82	42	40	74
3	Wycombe Wanderers	40	20	11	9	73	54	19	71
4	Notts County	40	18	13	9	61	42	19	67
5	Exeter City	39	20	6	13	52	44	8	66
6	Coventry City	39	19	8	12	48	32	16	65
7	Lincoln City	39	17	13	9	56	42	14	64
8	Mansfield Town	39	16	15	8	56	41	15	63
9	Swindon Town	39	19	4	16	60	59	1	61
10	Carlisle United	40	16	12	12	57	49	8	60
11	Colchester United	40	15	13	12	49	44	5	58
12	Newport County	39	13	15	11	49	50	-1	54
13	Cambridge United	40	14	12	14	42	52	-10	54
14	Crawley Town	40	15	8	17	50	57	-7	53
15	Cheltenham Town	40	12	12	16	58	58	0	48
16	Stevenage	39	11	12	16	50	56	-6	45
17	Crewe Alexandra	40	13	4	23	50	65	-15	43
18	Yeovil Town	37	11	9	17	47	57	-10	42
19	Morecambe	39	9	15	15	38	48	-10	42
20	Port Vale	40	10	12	18	43	55	-12	42
21	Forest Green Rovers	39	11	7	21	47	67	-20	40
22	Grimsby Town	40	9	11	20	32	61	-29	38
23	Chesterfield	38	9	7	22	41	68	-27	34
24	Barnet	40	8	9	23	36	59	-23	33

April

We like Easter: Carlisle 0-1 Imps
April 2, 2018

Phew, another double-header of action that could define the Imps season. Less than nine days ago I sat reading doom and gloom after a draw with Morecambe, but on reflection, that's proven to be an incredibly useful point.

Away from being proven right, this afternoon was a display of resilience, a result born out of strong characters, absolute togetherness and hard work. Carlisle aren't too unlike us, they work hard too and the early exchanges pointed to a somewhat dour game. Both sides wanted the win, but neither looked to have the quality to snatch it.

It was an unchanged City side, as expected, and as the game wore on I thought we looked more likely to score. It ebbed and flowed nicely, at onepoint flitting from end to end in almost thrilling fashion. It was 'League Two' end to end though, frantic but perhaps lacking that quality to finish the move off. Our forwards perhaps contrasted theirs, our worked tirelessly but didn't get the bounce, Ritchie Bennett on the other hand just looked a little lost. I thought he'd be a huge threat, but he appears to be struggling with league football.

The goal came from one of our star players, a man who can finish with aplomb at times but also prone to missing a sitter. I've been a huge Matt Green (pictured top) fan ever since he signed and his last two goals have been executed succinctly. It was a wonderfully calm finish to a well-worked training ground move, a carbon copy of the second against Exeter. I know Michael Hortin was asking if Carlisle actually scouted City, but it wasn't a lack of awareness it was simply switching off at a crucial time. Also we must not let them lapsing concentration take away from the quality of the goal, the confidence to try it a second time this afternoon and a fourth time in four days. It shows our players believe in the training they're undertaking and have absolute confidence in executing training ground plans.

Maybe that lapse in concentration is the difference between the top three and the rest of the pack because at times, it has certainly cost Carlisle. We've been known to switch off too, especially a couple of times on Friday, but that seemed to be eradicated today. The second half demanded a concise and organised performance, at times it needed to be dogged but there was no quarter given and nobody shirking their responsibility. We saw the odd lapse, oddly from Neal Eardley once or twice, but it was never going to cost us a goal, especially not with Bennett in such poor form.

This afternoon didn't give us an outright man of the match, there wasn't a single person who stood head and shoulders above the rest. It was a team effort, a hard-fought victory but one which came from sensible game management too. I'd hate to play us, winding the clocks down and running for the corners with ten minutes left. We are able to effectively kill a game, even when we make a sub they always seem to be the opposite side to the dugout. That management is ingrained in the player's psyche and although it isn't popular with opposition fans, it is effective.

One aspect that absolutely defines us as a football club are the fans and to take over 600 to Carlisle, two days after Good Friday and just a few days before Wembley was a huge amount. I know there will be plenty on their high horse saying it should have been a thousand, but that fact is Carlisle is a long drive and people simply don't have deep pockets. Personally, I'm staggered we've sold 26,000 tickets for Wembley, equally such that we took such a strong contingent up north too. I had to listen on the radio (and definitely not watch on a snide iFollow feed) and all I could hear was City fans. In fact, the only time I felt we weren't the home side was the disputed penalty.

Now, I know the referee will get a bit of stick for his afternoon, but I'm going to heap praise on him. The penalty incident had us all clenching our bum cheeks and holding our breath, especially when he awarded a penalty. I was hoping Ryan Allsop might make a save, I was comforting myself we might be okay with a draw, but the referee took his time and had the strength of character to overturn the opposition. It was the right decision, but it took some minerals to do it in front of a partisan home crowd. Moments like that define a season, it has certainly defined Carlisle's. They needed a win today, that penalty might have given them hope. Instead, they were full of anger at a failed campaign. They were play off semi-finalists last season, this season they look like falling short. The king is dead, long live the king.

We move on now, Wembley awaits and for a week the city will lose a little focus as Shrewsbury await in the nation's capital. Whatever the results next weekend, when we kick off in the Football league again we'll be in the top seven and that is just the cushion we needed to be able to fully enjoy next weekend. I know some of you can't, I genuinely feel for you because it will be an incredibly proud moment for all Imps next weekend. However, the league is our mountain (as Danny says) and we're steadily climbing it without letting Wembley impact it.

I'm not one to say, 'I told you so', but I am delighted that we're going into Wembley in the top seven, not just in there but now amongst the favourites to make the end of season lottery. Morecambe was a good point, proven fact. Nothing has derailed the play off push and we can be proud of our achievements in both competitions. I understand those who resent the new faces we'll see in London, I don't. I don't care if every single Lincoln resident goes along next week, some of whom couldn't name our centre halves. Nobody is missing out, everyone who wants to go can go. Therefore, why worry? Why bother? At the end of the day, a League Two club taking 26,000 fans is a wonderful achievement and a solid indication of the potential this club has. We're growing off the field and this season, we've grown on it too.

I wanted consolidation, we're in the top seven. Top ten would have been an achievement, but all of a sudden we look amongst the fore runners for the play offs and a real outside bet for the top three. It would be a huge ask, but if the aspirational target is top three with six games left, I think that is a hell of a season.

For the second year in a row, Easter has defined our season. A week after Gateshead last season, we played our 'cup final' against Macclesfield and won 2-1. This year, we have a real cup final to go to, after that we have six games to earn the club's first ever back to back promotions.

It's great being a Lincoln fan at the moment.

The award-winning Beast of Sincil Bank
April 5, 2018

Michael Bostwick was named in the League Two Team of the Year, rather odd timing with over a month of proceedings left but nonetheless an earned and just accolade for our player.

I remember where I was the minute I heard we'd signed Michael Bostwick. Normally, I get a bit of a heads up on a new player, or I've been hearing whispers of a deal for some time. with Bozzie, there was none of that. As expected, Harry Anderson was joining, but one afternoon in the summer, my phone started going mad.

I'd suggested he'd be a good signing earlier on in the summer, but never thinking he'd actually join us. Blackburn, top of League One now, were after him and the fee mentioned had been as much as £750,000. When it was suggested he was coming to Lincoln, I almost choked on my brew.

Of course, he did sign and for a short time it all seemed very surreal Peterborough's captain, a League One quality player was rocking up on our doorstep wanting to be part of the Cowley revolution. It nudged us from top ten to top seven in my aspirations and, as the season has gone on, that has proven to be correct.

Sometimes, no-nonsense is a term given to a player lacking certain qualities. Centre-halves who couldn't hit a central reservation in a Ford Capri would be classed as 'no nonsense', or perhaps more aptly 'no sense' as they stuck their face into boots and their boots into players. Bozzie is no nonsense, but not in the way I've just alluded to.

He's hard. Let's be frank. I wouldn't fight him, he's surly, he's big and he doesn't appear to feel pain. He'll throw himself in front of anybody at any time. I'm not sure he'd be too phased at tackling an ambulance if the situation arose, in fact I think he'd relish it. For me, part of our success against Chelsea U21s was him giving the kids a lesson that you can only get out in the field. However, he showed his true talents when he was poised on nine bookings, just one away from a suspension. He didn't lose his edge, but he curtailed his game to ensure he wasn't missing for crucial games. That showed to me he is far from just a midfield menace, much more than a hatchet man in the centre of the park.

He's effortlessly slipped into the defence too, he was always going to after all, it was his position at Posh. The fact he slides effortlessly between the two, showing more restraint in defence than in his midfield role, is another indication of his intelligence as a footballer.

He's an all-rounder too, anywhere in the centre of the park is his domain. We've seen him hit free kicks and 25-yard efforts, we've seen him heading towards goal from corners and away from goal at the back. I'd imagine he's a manager's dream because he offers such variety and versatility, but not in a 'average all over' way like James Milner, but in an 'equally as effective' way wherever he's needed.

Putting aside his Exeter performance, arguably his worst for City, he's been almost faultless all season. He'll never go on a fifty-yard run or beat six players, but he doesn't need to as it isn't his game. He's a player other player's love too, if they make a slip he's on hand to get them out of the sticky stuff. early in the season, him and Alex Woodyard looked wonderful in midfield and although we lacked bite going forward, we never looked shaky at the back. Personally, I prefer him in that holding midfield role, protecting the back four and defending from 25-yards, rather than in the eighteen.

I'm delighted he got the award, I'm not surprised. I am surprised one of his team mates, the lad on the right, wasn't in the side but I'm not a fan who will hand-wring at what we didn't get. Michael Bostwick has been incredible this season and whether we go up or not, he'll be a driving force behind everything we do next time out as well. He's a big game player, he's a sure-fire bet to be the first name written on the team sheet and however it happened, we're lucky to have him.

I'm going to bet that although he's in the Team of the Year, he doesn't win Player of the Year here. That isn't to his detriment though, more to the scintillating form of another experienced head we picked up in the summer. When you look back, our recruitment policy was excellent, was it not?

Congratulation Bozzie, you deserve the award. Now, go and kick a lump out of Jon Nolan on Sunday, show him what a proper midfielder is all about.

Wembley Build Up: What this means to me
April 5, 2018

I've been a little reticent with some Wembley build up, certainly before the weekend. I didn't want to agitate those proper fans who insist we focus on the league and that a cup final is a distraction.

I suppose I didn't want to see myself as one of those fan boys, the 'Wembley here we come' brigade that genuinely do forget about the league. I certainly didn't want to be the chump who got a '617 Sqd' flag printed up despite having nothing to do with the lads. Who would want to be that person?

For this article, I'm not going to think about the league or promotion though. You know why? Because Lincoln City are in a cup final and, whatever you may think about having the U21s compete alongside us, it was is a huge achievement getting to the final. Sure, I've heard it called a friendly tournament, games against reserve teams only we took seriously. After watching Accrington throw Billy Kee and Kayden Jackson into our tie, or Peterborough naming Jack Marriott, I'd beg to differ.

Once we got out of the group stages we faced strong sides and to get to the final is something we should be proud of. I won't feel ashamed or less of a fan just because fans of clubs that didn't make it think we're scabs. I bet you any amount of money Grimsby would have sold six-figures for another trip to Wembley, they loved this competition back in the days they could actually win it. Port Vale do to, I've seen today they're selling 25-year anniversary T-shirts from their Autoglass Trophy win. Don't be fooled by the hype, this isn't a gimmick or a con, it is a cup final that we have done brilliantly in so far.

I've been a Lincoln City fan for as long as I've known what football was. I first got interested in the game in 1986, the summer of the Mexico World Cup. There wasn't much football on the TV back then so when it suddenly appeared most nights, it was hard to avoid. I spent the summer kicking a ball around at Chambers Farm Woods with my mate Daniel Blackburn, him a staunch Manchester United fan through his Dad. I looked to my Dad for inspiration and I got Lincoln City. My Granddad was on the terraces before I was an itch in my father's nether regions, so it's a family thing.

Aside from the odd year of success (1988, 1998, 2003-05 ish) it has been a laborious task following Lincoln. Long drives on the M62 to lose at Rochdale. Miserable afternoons watching teletext as someone or other beat us by two or three goals. Endless headlines proclaiming our latest player was going to set the world on fire, only to discover it was Kevin Hulme. Always, you're waiting for the pay off, the moment all the time and emotion invested in your side rewards you with something. Thanks to Danny, Nicky and everyone at the club, we've been getting ours since the start of 2016/17. It's not stopping yet. after not seeing Wembley for our entire existence, we could well be going again in a couple of month.

First though, this weekend. I was trying to put together in my mind why a trip to the National Stadium is so special. Going to Cardiff twice was a brilliant experience and at the time I wouldn't hear a word against it, but it wasn't Wembley. Even without the Twin Towers, the arch is becoming just as iconic. It symbolises history, lifting the World Cup, FA cup finals that are forever seared into our consciousness. Gazza in 1996, Houchen in 1987, even Jim Montgomery's heroics in the mid-1970s. Wembley is English football and therefore it is football. We invented the game, we're crap at it now, but we brought it to the world and for almost a century the pinnacle of the English season has been the FA Cup final at Wembley. What is football without history and sentiment? What is a football club without history? Shirts change, players change, grounds change everything changes, except history. In essence my Granddad supported a completely different club to me, he wouldn't recognise the Bank now, but it was still Lincoln City and back then (as it is now) getting to Wembley was a historic event.

It's not even the stadium itself that is special, it is what it represents. Back when I was growing up in Wragby we used to play Wembley down the park, I think it was a free for all where you had to score past a hapless keeper, but the premise was the same, the winner celebrated as if he were at Wembley. twin tower, arches, whatever, Wembley is where you go when to win something in England.

I felt a certain shame we'd never been, I know fate kept us from there under Keith Alexander, but I hated being the answer to that question, which clubs have never played at Wembley. If I was asked it or had it pointed out, I'd always mentioned Millwall in 1983 when we got to the FLT final, or the play offs. I'd make excuses to defend my club, but after Sunday I won't have to.

We'll all have our stories, we'll all have loved ones who won't be there who I'm sure we'll think about on the day. My Granddad passed in 1992, he missed the Keith years too, but I'll have a thought in my mind for him when the teams run out. In my mind, we've already won whatever the outcome because we've thrown off the hoodoo. If we win the actual match, that will be beyond my comprehension. Oddly, I haven't given the game any thought at all. Perhaps that is why it's good we're going in the Checkatrade, because when we go in May it won't be an occasion, it'll be a football game.

I don't buy into the 'we've sold more tickets than you' or 'you lack integrity for going' or any of that bollocks (sorry, but it is what it is). I think about my experience, about what the day and the event means to me. Football is a shared experience but it is also a very personal thing too and I prefer to focus on what we've achieved on the field. Yeah, 26,000 is a great amount but just because the Shrews have sold 11,000 doesn't make us better in terms of support or worse in terms of integrity. By the way, anyone who think they could have sold 20,000 if it wasn't for the boycott is dreaming, they've probably lost 100 or so like we have.

I feel sorry for the hard-core Lincoln fans who are staying away and I would like to thank Nick Proctor in particular for being gracious in not trying to devalue our achievements or the final itself. There's too many good people too quick to call this trophy a gimmick or a joke, what they're doing there is bitterness at having the integrity to stay away but knowing deep down, they're missing a great day out. I'd hate to have that on my mind, that awful contradiction rattling around in my head. Fair play for not going and hopefully they'll get to join us again in May.

For now, it's little over 36 hours before I head down to check into the hotel and meet up with our good friends over from New Zealand. On Sunday my Uncle, a Lincoln fan until he left in the early 1980s for Exeter is joining us along with his boy Dan. Dave, my lifelong mate and season ticket buddy is coming too, as is Pete the Manchester United supporting Imp who's seen plenty of games this season. My Dad will be there, another fine memory to forge with him that lasts a lifetime and he's bringing Mo. I'm bringing Fe to, of course going to Wembley is a day to share with everyone and remember forever.

Whatever the score, however the game goes down, words cannot of justice the pride I will feel at watching my beloved Lincoln City take to the Wembley turf to compete in a Cup Final. I'm a little choked writing this right now and only now am I truly allowing myself to get a little bit excited.

We're the famous Lincoln City, and we're going to Wembley. Finally.

Checkatrade Trophy Win – SW's experience

April 9, 2018

"Is this the real life, or is this just fantasy?"

90% of you will recognise the lyrics, but as I laid my head on my pillow last night I couldn't help but have those words going around my head incessantly. I'm going to ignore the politics, the 'success shaming' from other club's fans and all of that. Yesterday afternoon, Lincoln City won a trophy at Wembley, something I never thought I'd see in my lifetime.

I'm going to talk about the match, the club and all of that later on, but I wanted to throw the personal bit out there first because, after all is said and done, yesterday was about more than a game of football. It was about 27,000 (okay, 9,000) personal stories of supporting the club through thick and thin, from afar or close to home. It was about individuals as much as it was the team because what is a football team if not just a collection of individuals all desperately wanting the same thing from generation to generation?

My weekend started on Saturday, we parked at Stanmore, wandered up Wembley Way and did the obligatory nose around Central London. It was very routine, ride the tube into the city, grab a bite to eat on the South Bank, bump into Casey near Blackfriars Bridge, on to St Paul's Cathedral… wait, bump into Casey? The DJ guy? Yup.

Okay, we shouldn't be surprised, but it's not every day you're walking in London and you bump into a friend of almost two decades and even though we were invading en mass, it was still a touch surreal to hear someone shouting me in the big city. As for St Paul's, it was £18 to get in. Looks alright from outside, on to the pub.

First up was the Punch and Judy where we saw Maria and Jackie of the Lady Imps, plus their entourage. Even as we had a cheeky vodka 24 hours before the game, you could see lots of Imps, sporadically cheering, waving to each other and sharing excited talk about being at Wembley.

Then it was down to Drury Lane to meet my Dad who had by then located his favourite London pub (the only one he ever goes in) and had already smashed his way through half of their Guinness reserves chilling with Mo. The media portray London as this simmering den of iniquity, where anyone with dusky skin has a knife and anyone with a shaved head wears Union Jack underpants and harbours a hatred of all things foreign. In truth, it really isn't. We got in the pub and immediately found ourselves chatting to a QPR fan who, in broadest cockney, asked us why we were in town. After three or four-minute of conversation he asked me to slow down as he couldn't understand my accent, which was a relief because I'll be buggered if I knew what he was saying. Diversity, it doesn't just come in shades of skin colour.

We left Dad in the Prince of Wales, happily watching Sky Sports news and people, whilst we went back for a shower before the first big meet of the day.

I've known Sam and Rawiri White for a while now, they grew up in Horncastle but I must confess are a little older than me. Rawiri has been watching Lincoln since the days of Sam Ellis and for a big, practical man is extremely emotional when it comes to football. Sam, who many have disagreed with on social media, is remarkably less argumentative than many take her for. They're both really nice people and Saturday was our first face to face meet in a long while.

You may or may not know, it is they who sponsor Matt Green, but they asked me if I'd like my name by the shirt. Apparently my writing helps Imps in exile feel connected and with them living 11,500 miles away, they couldn't really be in anymore exile than they are at present. They'd travelled over from New Zealand for the game, not just the final but also Exeter and Carlisle away.

We shared drinks, had some dinner and generally put the world to rights ahead of the big game. Most of the chatter was about being at Wembley and how far the team had come. It seemed a nice night with which to start the main event and, upon retiring early, a fitting way to bring our first day in London to a close.

Next day, breakfast, Fe and Mo head off to Stanmore with the bags whilst we meet Dave. Then, we all headed off to the Green Man for the festivities.

I assume many of you were in the pub at some point, a vibrant and slightly damp setting in which thousands of city fans enjoyed more than a pint or two. Not me of course, with less than a month before I become 1% robot I had volunteered to be the driver for the day. After all, a cheeky vodka and lemonade is fine, but the last six times I've drunk pints in conjunction with tramadol it's left me considerably poorly.

It did mean I got to witness much of the atmosphere without beer goggles, although at times I also felt a little isolated. Alcohol isn't needed in these circumstances, but it does help and everyone else was partaking of plenty. Once the rain really set in and the tent filled up things got very lively, plenty of songs, a bit of red smoke and a great atmosphere. I even saw Marcus Needham there, multiple times.

We were joined by Keith and Dan, the Exeter Imps, of sorts. Keith is my uncle, an Imp from many years ago who moved to Exeter as a teen. He gets up whenever he can and is famous in Devon for singing Imps songs amongst the Exeter fans whenever they're losing. He follows the Grecians too, as does his lad Dan. There's no Imps in Dan, aside from his father's influence. He's an Exeter fan through and through, but even he remarked what amazing support we had. I hope we go up automatically and they come through the play offs (or, worse case, the other way around) so we can renew that family rivalry. Keith was shocked because he bumped into some lads he used to knock around with as a young lad, before the Devon move.

The weather tried to dampen the afternoon down so we ended up in the ground earlier than imagined so we didn't drown. The concourse was full of unfamiliar faces, I suppose to be expected when you're at a Wembley final. I bumped in to a few I knew, but the usual 500 or so I recognise from the game soon get diluted amongst 27,000. I will say one thing for Wembley, the food was excellent. There was so much choice and very little in the way of queuing. It might not have been football how my Granddad remembered it, but I'm sure it has changed for the better.

Of course, it isn't like any normal ground or experience, everything is very well presented and the concourse feels like a shopping mall rather than a football ground. However, there's no view quite like the one you get walking through the doors and looking at the pitch for the first time. Here we were, little old Lincoln City, about to play on the grandest stage English football has to offer.

We settled into our padded seats acutely aware there was youngsters behind us who didn't want to watch the back of my head all game, but it was hard to stay sat for the whole experience. The teams came out and for a few minutes I watched in awe as my Lincoln City, the team I've seen lose against Welling and North Ferriby, the side whose badge I have on my arm, whose shirts I have nearly fifty of, programme well over 1000 of, that have given me memories of both joy and pain (many more of the latter) competed at Wembley.

Colin Murphy leading the team out was a wonderful touch, as was the way the entire day was about everything other than Danny and Nicky. The media love them, but they don't put themselves at the front of the club. They put Jack Notty there, they put Colin Murphy there, they do everything and anything to take the pride away from themselves. That seems to be the club ethos and whilst some long for the days when 1,000 fans huddled in one corner of the ground and felt connected, I relish the current climate in which anyone can enjoy the ride. I know that having witnessed relegation in 1999 and 2011, having marched through administration and buried my Granddad in a Lincoln City scarf, my experience on Sunday afternoon was very different to those who got on the Loco last season or the season before. I'm not saying I'm better than them, not at all, but I know when my team walked out at Wembley, it meant something very different to me.

It all seemed very surreal, sat up in the gods watching the Imps kicking a ball about. The atmosphere was odd, loud at times but also dampened by being so spread out. Complicated songs weren't ever going to take off, so we got a few 'We are Imps' out and the occasional 'Come on Lincoln'. We were there, playing at Wembley. we'd finally done it.

Then we scored.

Suddenly, in an instant we weren't just at Wembley on this wonderful day out, we weren't soaking up the atmosphere and going home with a phone full of pictures, we were winning in the Checkatrade Trophy cup final. For the first time during the whole weekend, it dawned on me we might actually win the bloody thing.

I'll cover the match later, but the next ninety minutes were, for me, just like beating Exeter the week before or losing to Aldershot in 2011. It was me watching something that matters so much unfold before my eyes with no ability to intervene. Lincoln City is a huge part of my life, aside from my home, fiancée and family probably the most important. I bleed red and white, I live it every single day. I write every single day for you now, but it goes way back, back to when I used to cut out pictures of players from magazines and put one of our players at the top with some slogan or other. It comes from standing with my Dad, eager to impress, memorising all of the 1987 relegated player's names so I sounded knowledgeable in conversation. It comes from missing a friend's wedding to be at Southport in the Conference, from crying when we went down, it comes from believing that my identity, my place in the world is with Lincoln City. Ask anyone about me and they'll probably tell you, first and foremost, I'm a Lincoln City fan. With that comes the everlasting pain of 90 minutes football, 90 minutes in which your life, your hopes and your dreams are placed in the hands of other people.

Luckily, the 'other people' in which my current life dreams are placed aren't a bad side, and it turns out we did win the trophy after all. Towards the end I could feel my pulse racing, my hands clasped together tighter and tighter with every passing second. where the referee got five minutes from I'll never know (30 seconds per sub, five made is two and a half, where were the other stoppages?). I do know they were five minutes I couldn't stand. I confess, I went to the loo. Genuinely, my nerves were shot and I spent two minutes out of sight of the game, making it back to my seat for the final sixty seconds before the whistle blew and we won our second piece of silverware inside twelve months.

What do you possibly write about the next half hour? Watching the team celebrate on the pitch, watching the away end empty before their team had even got their losers medals, then waiting as Luke Waterfall led the sides up the steps, into the Royal Box and finally lifting the trophy above his head. 134 years of waiting for the big win, almost a century of Wembley finals and finally, here we were. Sure, I got a bit teary, who didn't? My Dad did, that's for sure and why not.

Danny and Nicky Cowley now join Bill Anderson in becoming the most decorated Imps managers ever, Bill won two titles in 1947/48 and 1951/52. Colin Murphy technically has two, although perhaps the GMVC Shield isn't as illustrious as his GMVC title win the year before. Well, DC and NC now have a title and a proper cup to their name. Not bad for just under two year's work, is it?

I didn't want to leave, we stuck around and watched the celebrations on the pitch for as long as I thought we'd get away with. With each passing second it became more real, more believable. I'd never given thought to us actually beating Shrewsbury, third in League One and seemingly prepped for promotion. I truly thought Jon Nolan, the happy-go-lucky scouse, would put us to the sword with a cruel twist of irony. By the time Luke lifted that silver trophy, I forgotten the sullen little sod had even been on the pitch. Football isn't about that, not in those extreme moments.

If you're thinking about how other teams, players or even fans feel right at that moment, you're missing the point.

I got ratty as we finally came away from the ground because I didn't want to go home. I've sung the song 'don't want to go home' to the Sloop John B tune for years, but yesterday I lived it. I wanted to stay in London, I wanted to celebrate with whoever I could. It hurt even more seeing people's photos with the team and the trophy as we were stuck waiting to get out of Stanmore, over an hour after we left the ground. Getting 40,000 odd people out of London via one tube station and a couple of access roads is never going to be easy and for some reason I struggled to appreciate the win, I felt resentment we had to go. It's perhaps selfish, but I felt the same when I got an early taxi home after Macclesfield last season. Football gives you so few paybacks that when they happen, I want them to last forever.

Of course it will, sat here at my desk a day later it's beginning to sink in properly. Now the pomp and ceremony has finished, we can let it settle in with our other great memories, ferment slowly so any of the negatives are faded and all the good things made better and brighter with time. That is the beauty of a memory, especially one with such success behind it. You won't remember being cold and wet walking to the ground, paying seven quid for a burger and chips or Shrewsbury hitting the bar. Unless you're incredibly bitter, you won't remember a voice asking who our big centre forward was and seeing it came from an Imps 'fan' or being asked to sit down when we scored. You'll remember the goal, how good the expensive food tasted and how bright the fireworks were from the celebrations. You'll remember the singing in the Green Man, the look on familiar faces on the way into the ground and the tears in their eyes on the way out.

With each passing hour, day or even year, those memories will get brighter and the rain will fade. By the time DC and NC are England managers, Ethan Ampadu is the world's greatest defender and we're an established Championship club, we might even forget this competition was ever controversial in the first place.

Maybe.

IN MEMORY OF GEOFF HUTCHINSON, WE FINALLY DID IT GRANDAD x

EFL Trophy Winners: Imps 1-0 Shrewsbury Town

April 9, 2018

At the centre of it all, the whirlwind of PR, media and hype, there's a game of football. It is the same every week, whatever the angle, whatever the spin or the setting, it is all about 90 minutes of good, honest action.

I put honest in italics because if we're being truthful with ourselves, it is never like that. Football isn't an honest game, just ask the Carlisle player who handled in our area then screamed vehemently for a penalty the other week. it is a game of deception, lies and more lies. Even referees can't get it entirely right, Ollie Palmer's great goal against Exeter ruled out for a reason we'll never know. That is football.

They say these things level themselves out through a season and that was the case.

It would be remiss to focus on two key points that could have swung the game in Shrewsbury's favour though, because that would imply that on the balance of play, they deserved the win. Don't be fooled by the BBC's rather one-sided narrative, this wasn't a case of plucky Lincoln putting up a wall and kicking the ball long all the time, it was a clever and well-managed assault on the opposition's game plan, whilst also auctioning our own indomitable style on them.

Remember, Shrewsbury are in the top three of League One, we've not been able to establish ourselves in the top three of the league below. There's a huge difference between the two sides, more places in fact than lay between ourselves and Oldham when we met in the FA Cup. That was a giant killing, perhaps the same could be said for yesterday, only the giants are a club similar in size to us that have done incredibly well. They're us in a year's time, hopefully.

For the first ten minutes they looked good. They played the ball about, particularly in front of our 18-yard box, looking for the quick give and go. We seemed content to allow them to do that, it may be a result of the 4-3-3 we use now, although we saw a similar tactic backfire against Swindon earlier in the season. Our favourite worst enemy, Jon Nolan, looked to have some real class although he is terribly one-footed which dictates quite often the direction of his play. As you know, they hit the bar early on with a rasping effort which was perhaps the result of us not closing down quick enough. That didn't happen much after that.

What did happen was one of the game's major incidents, billed by some as an early Wrestlemania move in which Matt Rhead pole-axed Dean Henderson, the Shrews on-loan Manchester United keeper. At the time I cried cheat, especially when the keeper got up early. I couldn't believe he'd been given a yellow card for an accidental collision. When you look back in slow motion, it does seem as though a red would be more justified. As a Lincoln fan I could argue he was nudged and that it looks worse slowed down, but if I were a Shrews fan he'd be public enemy number one from now until we finally win a Wembley game. Remember, it was our first appearance, but the Shrews had lost three there on the spin. They wanted this too and to see their keeper floored with what amounted to a forearm smash must have been quite tough to take.

Then came a spell of play for us, followed by Elliott's goal. We soaked up their early pressure and went on the offensive ourselves, with Whitehouse winning the corner from which he scored. It was fitting captain Luke Waterfall was also involved, his scuffed effort being saved by Henderson for Elliott to slam home. It seems players I've doubted in August and September are coming good at the right time, because the goal was just one aspect of a committed and dogged display by Mr Whitehouse. Also, he scored our first ever goal at Wembley which is enough to ensure he never has to pay for a Nando's again, at least not if I'm in Nando's at the same time.

The goal knocked them quite a bit and we looked likely to get another, although there was nothing clear-cut to speak of. If the first fifteen was theirs and the second fifteen our, on 32 minutes came another of those turning points. This time the Shrews corner was headed toward goal by Beckles, with Ryan Allsop producing a truly astounding save, clawing the ball clear. Only half cleared, it came back again and the Shrews effort was turned around the post by Luke Waterfall's arm. It was, even through red and white glasses and face paint, a stone wall penalty. To their credit, only one or two of their players appealed, half-heartedly too. If it had been us, I would have cried with anger, instead I choked down tears of joy.

Paul Hurst rather magnanimously shied away from blaming the two incidents for his side's defeat, but at 1-1 with ten against eleven for the final hour, Shrewsbury surely go on to win the game. Instead it remained 1-0 to us and level in number, just the slice of luck we needed to complete the job.

The second period started much as the first one had, with Shrewsbury on top. By 56 minutes, it seemed as though it was only a matter of time before they scored. We were pinned back in our eighteen-yard area, all our players throwing themselves in front of tackles, fighting as hard as they could. We chased and harassed, battled and scrapped but still the Shrews kept coming. Then, almost at exactly the same time as a round of applause for the 56 started to ripple amongst the fans in the know, the pressure abated. Did the Shrews tire? did Messrs Stacey and West decide enough was enough and we'd proven our worth? Whatever happened, from that minute on we got ourselves back into the game and instilled belief in our fans that we might just win this bloody trophy after all. To be fair, we did save it by beating Chelsea so it was only fair we took it home once all was said and done.

Rheady could have put us two up when none other than Elliott Whitehouse turned provider, supplying the same pulled back cross he did for Matt Green against Grimsby. Instead of a tap in, Rheady had a drive to complete but instead fired just over. 2-0 would have killed the game off, instead not long after the big man came off. He got a rapturous applause and rightly so, although I don't think the big open spaces of Wembley suited his style of play.

It was clear what Danny wanted to do now, game management. There was 30 minutes on the clock when Ollie Palmer came on, 26 when Harry Anderson got his Wembley stripes, but we were going into management mode. The ball began to travel back across the defence more. Alex Woodyard turned away from play and slowed it down more too. When we're on it, and I mean really on it, we're the best in League Two at managing a game. There's fewer matches with more pressure than Wembley cup finals, but we stuck to the game plan, offering the Shrews less touches of the ball. One moment had Sam Habergham looking terrified as he slipped, potentially gifting the Shrews a run on goal. Instead, the ball cannoned off their player for a throw in.

When they did get a touch, they looked dangerous. I liked Nathan Thomas and Shaun Whalley, both players who looked to make things happen. I suppose, begrudgingly, Nolan is pretty handy too. We always knew he was a good footballer, but as the game wore on he began to let that trademark mood of his drop, eventually picking up a booking for a petulant foul. Once he got that, you knew his head had gone and he wouldn't be effective. I'm not sure he had a meaningful touch following his yellow card. Same old Nolan.

In fact, Shrewsbury didn't get on the ball much after it either. 86 minutes; Nolan booked. 95 minutes plus a few seconds; City win the Checkatrade Trophy. Those final 20 minutes or so passed without incident, bar bitten nails, clenched bums and the odd tear, and that was just Alan Long.

On reflection, yes we were lucky but we also played incredibly well against a side more used to tussling with Blackburn and Wigan than Lincoln City. Remember also, we lacked three of our first team players due to being cup tied and have Josh Vickers injured. There's little doubt one of Wharton or Wilson would have played, so we certainly lacked two first team players, if not three. That is crucial to remember, especially as Shrewsbury fielded virtually the same side that beat Oxford in the League on Easter Monday. Aside from the commentators with blue and yellow shirts on, few would be able to spot which side were League Two and which weren't.

Elliott Whitehouse was official Man of the Match and he's certainly one of a couple that could have got it. For me, it had to be Michael Bostwick for his unending bravery, his fearless leadership and fearsome tackle. Mind you, it wouldn't be easy to pick a player who didn't do well. Luke Waterfall was also excellent against some pretty tough centre forwards, Luke and Alex took the time on the ball they needed in the middle of the park but restricted the Shrews midfield wherever possible. I thought Matt Green worked really hard too, when you're as all-action as him the last thing you need is a bigger pitch, but he coped remarkably well.

What happened after the final whistle is history, as they say. I felt a bit for Nicky, the screen cut away from him holding the trophy aloft and few cheered as he raised it, only for it to come back on as he passed it to Danny. It is the latter who gets the headlines, but the former is every bit as much a part of this success as anyone.

Now we have to put the game to bed and move on, just like we did in the weeks leading up to it. At the end of the season is time for reflection, time for reliving the memories and relishing the moment. After our cup final last year against Arsenal our form suffered and we can't be letting that happen again. I must admit, I can't see that happening, because Danny and Nicky won't let it. People will keep the memories from Sunday with them forever, but I can guarantee tomorrow morning the Port Vale video will be on the screen and not one person will be thinking about Wembley.

I'm not a Checkatrade denier, but we park it and move on so that in two moth's time, we're back at the home of English football for yet another of those wonderful memories we keep creating.

Don't worry about the things you can't change, focus on the things you can affect
April 12, 2018

We're all guilty of it, worrying about something that might happen rather than enjoying what is happening. It's a typical English trait I think, worry.

We do it all the time, at least I do. As the seconds wore down at Wembley I couldn't enjoy being 1-0 up in the National Stadium, I worried we might concede a goal. When we signed Scott Wharton in January, who applauded the move? Not me, I was like most of the other fan's berating our lack of signing a striker.

Danny likened that to kids at Christmas, eager to unwrap the next present before we've savoured the one we've just been given. Now, as we head off to Port Vale, it must be actively encouraged. Drop the Trophy win, package it back up and focus on the league.

Only we can't can we, because there's something else hanging over the fans. You know, the fans who have enjoyed unrivalled success over the last two years, winning more trophies in twelve months than in the previous thirty years. Yup, there's always something hanging over us.

It's the Danny and Nicky question, the one you dare not ask out loud because it seems stupid, the one you dare not contemplate because you'll seem a fool. Nobody wants to ask them if they're going to Ipswich because they're focused on the here and now. Nobody wants to imagine they're going because it would ruin the exciting run in to the season.

It's a bit like being out with your beautiful girlfriend but suspecting she's going to break up with you. She wants it to end amicably and you're out having a nice meal enjoying each other's company. If you ask, it'll ruin it all. In your mind the meal is all about making the break up easy, but what if you're wrong? What if she wants to stay with you and your pestering convinces her to go? You don't know whether to ask or not and suddenly you're a bag of nerves, unsure as to what is happening. Now you're off your food too.

I don't want to be put off my food, or in this case the most thrilling end to a season since, um, last season. We're right in the mix talking about play offs, automatic or whatever. There's 1000 of us going to Port Vale, one in every 27 at Wembley. I'm not judging anyone, football is a tough game to follow every week and those who didn't go to Wembley have a lot more brass in their pocket than those who did. I'm doing both, not because I'm a super fan, but because I'd feel an overwhelming sense of guilt if I was at one and not the other. That, and I want to see the team I love get promoted. In fact, the latter reason is probably more important than the guilt thing. Yeah, go with that.

Tonight I get to go to the Civic Awards ceremony where Danny and Nicky are bestowed with a massive honour. For most it might mean very little, but the award signifies outstanding contribution to Lincoln, be it through industry, sport or academia. There couldn't be a more fitting pair to take the award, on behalf of the whole club, but as obvious figureheads. It'll be incredible to be there to see it as one of the people who nominated them, but even I have begun to spoil it for myself thinking about the future. Is this a swan-song? Will it be my last meeting with them?

It's all very silly, whilst studying my hypnosis diploma we were told that worry was the most pointless emotion there is. If you worry you're either focusing on something that will never happen, or something that you can't stop happening. One way or another, it is pointless. If you can't change it yourself, why expend time and energy being concerned? If it isn't going to happen anyway, you're even more of a clown. Either way, those who worry do themselves nor anyone else no favours.

Right now, Danny and Nicky Cowley are at Lincoln City, we're at the peak of our recent achievements and could surpass them all with another promotion. Lincoln City have only been third-tier once in my life time and yet next season, we could be rubbing shoulders with Sunderland, Bradford, Barnsley and Charlton as equals.

Don't focus on the things you can't affect; only worry about the things you can chance. On Saturday at Vale Park, sing loud and sing proud. If Ipswich have approached the club and if Danny and Nicky are in the frame, the only way we're going to convince them this is the place is by doing what we've done all along, supporting our club in our own unique and passionate manner.

We've got a great squad, the majority of which are contracted for next season. Why on earth are we worrying about something that has either already been decided, or won't happen at all? Live for the moment. Live for Port Vale, Wycombe and Coventry. Live for shaking Danny's hand like a star-struck teenager, in awe of a man whom, along with his brother, will forever be a part of the club's rich history and now the city's too. Live for being reigning Checkatrade champions, for the hope of a play off final and for being infinitely better than Grimsby Town. Live for being in a position to compete with Scunthorpe next season for the title 'Pride of Lincolnshire', knowing that the pride part defines and describes how I feel right now about my club. Live for being proud of your football club. Live for Lincoln City.

The Civic Award, another victory for the Cowley Brothers
April 13, 2018

It was a privilege to be invited along to the Civic Award ceremony last night, by virtue of being one of those who nominated Danny and Nicky for the honour.

For those who do not know, the award is given out yearly to anyone thought to have promoted Lincoln in a positive way. It could be a group, organisation or business, their input could be on the national stage or even something done locally. Previous winners include Rob Bradley and the 1976 Imps team, as well as Chris Illsley, Ruston (twice) and St Barnabas Hospice. It is prestigious in that it recognises those who work within our fair city to make it a better place.

With all of that in mind, how could there be anyone else winning it this year than Danny and Nicky? That's what I thought anyway, so I nominated them which earned me a place around the huge table they have in the Guildhall, situated above the Stonebow.

The question on everyone's lips isn't about the journey we've been on, it is about the one we're about to embark upon, perhaps more succinctly who is going to be coming along for the ride. More on that shortly, but first the event.

I've never been in the Guildhall, there's never really been a need for it. With a little red carpet and bouncers on the door, I felt pretty special being able to watch this great occasion, perhaps even more so when I realised I'd be sat around the main table. It was big enough to house about six Subbuteo pitches side by side, a thought which oddly stuck in my head for the twenty minutes or so I sat awkwardly around it waiting for the event to start. I'm not comfortable in situations such as those, especially not when I've left my glasses in the car and can't work out whether people are making eye contact or not!

The ceremony had all the pomp and ritual as you'd expect. We were upstanding for the mayor, a rather witty and friendly man by the name of Chris Burke. Mayor Burke, as it turns out, likes a glass of wine and has a wonderful repertoire of Lincoln stories to regale you with. He didn't do it straight away of course, there was an award to present.

After the formalities we got straight into it, Danny and Nicky wearing their Wembley suits were handed the Civic Award, a rare honour bestowed only upon those who do Lincoln a huge service. I suspect very few of us will ever get our hands on it, if any. I doubt very much whether I'll ever get to witness it being handed over again, so it was a really nice moment. It became even nicer when, after a raft of official photos, Danny and Nicky beckoned me up for a picture. I didn't get it on my phone, I was in it, but hopefully I can lay my hands on it at some point.

We were then invited into the Mayor's private chambers, the 'plotting room' at the NatWest end of the Stonebow. I met some interesting people too, Henry Ruddock whose family are almost as old as the city itself, and blog reader Charlie Partridge. It was nice, getting over the early nerves to appreciate the evening.

I caught a little bit of Danny being interviewed by several different media outlets, one of which asked about 'you-know-what'. Danny straight-batted it, played it cool, but I'm sure I heard him ask 'why do they keep asking about that?' when the microphone was down.

I'd already decided not to, it isn't my place to question another man on his career moves, even if I do have such a vested interest. This wasn't a time for such questions, it was a ceremony in which they received an honour they so richly deserved. The questions should be about their reign, about Wembley and how they went about beating League One Shrewsbury.

It was incredible looking at the 500-year old building, wondering what great conversations or slices of Lincoln history were played out within its walls. I'm really into all that, and hearing some of the Mayor's stories about Queen Victoria or the abdominal Tory MP Charles Sibthorp just enhanced the evening for me. I also met the Sheriff, Jo Rimmer, who had her own stories about Henry VIII. Here I was nibbling on rather fine food surrounded by local history, both from the past and right in the present.

I did get a nice long chat with all of them at the end, Danny and Nicky, Alan Long and Kate and Lauren. I once again saw the reasons these two guys have been such an influence in the city and on myself personally. They're not a pair of football managers, not when you're talking to them. They're humble, they play down their achievements and deflect the accomplishments on to the team. Their relationship with each other, and as a foursome, is a heart-warming and fond one. The banter that switches between all of them is just like I swap with my brother and his partner, it is just another reason we identify with them so much.

It was a pleasure to witness the human side to them, the main reason we've all fallen under their spell. I've said it before and I'll say it again; they're just like you and I. Sure, they work harder and they know a bit more about football (just a bit), but they know what it is like to be a real fan. They know what the 9-5 grind is like, they understand people far better than most of the managers we've had.

Whether it was joking that Danny reminds Lauren of Ross from Friends, talking about the set piece routines or hearing how Nicky identifies with my stories about my Dad because he recognises that 'father and son' behaviour from his own child hood, not once did I think I was talking to Lincoln managers. I never do, because they don't see themselves as special. They are unique, the way they conduct themselves is unique and it has me wondering if all this speculation about 'you-know-what' is pointless.

I eventually left far too late, a good half an hour after my NCP car park had run out, but I was thoroughly enjoying myself and couldn't bring myself to leave. It was the first time I'd met Lauren and Kate, two incredibly friendly and approachable women who clearly have to adjust an awful lot to their husbands chosen profession. They don't seem to be phased by it though, I could have been meeting two of my workmate's partners down the pub such was their warmth. Maybe I shouldn't have been surprised, there hasn't been one member of the Cowley family that I've met who hasn't been exactly like that.

I came away feeling much more relaxed than I did prior to the event. I'll confess I've been concerned about the future, but last night's article followed by the ceremony has allayed my fears somewhat. Without sounding too saccrine and pompous, Danny and Nicky will always be a part of this city now, whether they remain here for one season or fifty. They'll always be back at some point, for dinners or for ceremonies.

They might move here soon, they might not, but they're part of Lincoln right now and I suspect, they always will be. Just like Colin Murphy, just like Graham Taylor and just like Keith Alexander.

Clive Nates confirms contract talks with Danny and Nicky
April 13, 2018

Clive Nates mentioned the possibility of Danny and Nicky signing a new deal within a couple of weeks, as the fear of a move to Ipswich subsides further.

Speaking on Rob Makepeace's Friday Football, Clive confirmed that talks are ongoing and that "a lot of things keep me up at night, but keeping Danny and Nicky isn't one of those." Whilst referring to a new deal, he said there should be "good news for fans in the coming weeks".

The latest development does mean fans can breathe a sigh of relief after intense speculation that Ipswich Town might turn their heads. There's little doubt they were the Tractor Boys' number one targets, but it seems as though the dynamic duo will be remaining at the club a little longer.

It was little over a year ago they last got a new deal, one to run to 2021 which, at the time, Bob Dorrian sounded delighted with: "I am absolutely delighted that we have secured the management team of Danny and Nicky Cowley for a further three years," said chairman Bob Dorrian. We believe that this is a great day for the club in terms of continuity and echoes the ambitions that Danny and Nicky also have for Lincoln City FC."

The big question is this: if Ipswich have been rebuffed and if the Cowley's are going to sign a new deal, how far dare we dream our club can go? I think there's many of us convinced that it will take one more season at most to get third-tier status, the highest we've competed at since the early 1960's, but what price on a Championship spot?

I'd say it's early days, but is it? 22 months into their tenure and they've won as many trophies as any other Imps manager in history, they've guided us further than we've ever been in the FA Cup and taken us to a first ever Wembley final. All things considered, and I know this is a bold statement, but there could be a strong case for them being described as the greatest Lincoln City managers of all time, already.

I know what Bill Anderson achieved, he put us in the second tier for a prolonged spell, but the FA Cup quarter finals eluded us and we started in round three. Colin Murphy brought us back from the Conference as well as established us at the top of Division Three, but he didn't win as many trophies. Keith won nothing but the rise from administration under him has to be comparable to our most recent rise.

Danny and Nicky have taken elements of all those great men and mixed it up to find their own formula, if they sign a new deal, where next? League One? Win in the play-offs? Stick around in League Two for a season and win an unprecedented third trophy?

Long term, why can't a new stadium lead us to becoming the next Bournemouth or Swansea City? It is ambitious, but it is a vision built on something solid, not on sand or smoke and mirrors. There's no Goal 2010 about this, building a training ground on clay and leaving the playing squad to rot.

I'm on a high right now, I always envisaged the only clubs we might lose them to would be Ipswich or West Ham. Tonight's news has given me a new wave of optimism, something I'd had ingrained in me for 22 months until Mick walked the other night. They say you don't know what it has got until it's gone, well that is balderdash.

We know what we've got, we've got a football club that is in tune from the men at the top to the fans in the street, from keeper to centre forward, manager to physio, media manager to programme seller. It is a hell of a journey we've been on, but if we secure Danny and Nicky on a tighter contract, then we've only just set off.

Automatic set back: Port Vale 1-0 Imps

April 15, 2018

I have been preaching the top three is beyond us and I think yesterday finally put to bed those ambitions of overhauling Wycombe in third place. Anyone still thinking we're able to keep the middle of May free is, I'm afraid, delirious.

I didn't read Facebook last night, or any of the social media feedback. I slept 90% of the way home then chilled with my other half watching a film. It's all too predictable nowadays, some shooting down anyone with a negative view, others copy and pasting their usual bile from every other game we've lost this season. I don't sit on either side of the fence, I'm not one who sees no fault in the performances, nor am I overly critical when we lose.

The perspective view is this; we were poor second half, we maybe shaded the first but it wasn't something 1,000 fans should travel across the country to endure. I'm willing to put it to one side though, especially as we've had a fair few good trips this season. I'm not one who won't forgive a bad day at the office, but we're still entitled to express our opinion. Port Vale wanted it more than us.

However, I'm not going to mention the 'W' word either, because I don't believe for one second last week's heroics impacted the game. The only thing that could be said is if we'd not won last weekend, Danny could have had license to change the team.

What struck me was our midfield simply didn't exert enough control which led to us looking very disjointed. In the main, the first 45 minutes were dull, two teams cancelling each other out with little to be offered going forward. I thought Rheady might be a bit more up for a match at Port Vale, it is his stomping ground after all and I'm sure beating his hometown local rivals would have spurred him on, but I didn't really see it.

I didn't actually see a lot of fire in our bellies at all. Sadly, the man of the moment Mr Whitehouse turned in one of the games that makes you forget how effective his recent resurgence has been, along with Freck the midfield looked a bit powder puff at times. There was lots of running and panting and endeavour but nothing effective. Alex Woodyard looked better than his partners, but we were over run for large parts in the centre of the park.

Up front all of the emphasis was on Matt Green again, even when our new hero Ollie Palmer came on. Matt has taken a lot of criticism but if we were going to create anything it was going to be him. I stick by my judgement all season that we needed another centre forward, but not to replace Matt Green. One chance in the second half typified my argument, Green received the ball in the channel and whipped a dangerous ball across goal to.... nobody. It was the sort of ball Elliott Whitehouse played against Grimsby for Green to tap in, only when Green is doing the work, nobody finishes his efforts.

If we'd signed another striker, not just another fringe player, but a Matt Green type, we'd be top three. Of that I have no doubt. However, I also believe that the one we need was not available. I know Danny well and there's no chance at all he sat on his hands being too choosy. If he didn't sign them, they're not right for the side. Even Akinola was right in August but, with Matt Rhead having proven himself all over again, was not correct for January.

Anyway, there's no point looking back. It wasn't a good performance, it wasn't a good result and the travelling fans were, to some extent, let down. It might have been different if Danny Rowe hadn't got injured, he looked really dangerous and effective but didn't get enough of the ball. sadly, Harry Anderson had another poor outing. I'm a huge Harry fan, on his day he is as good as anyone in the squad, but recently he's just not been on his game. The 4-3-3 hasn't helped, but similarly he's a footballer and should be able to adapt.

Now for the perspective. That was out first defeat in seven and whilst we slipped out of the play offs, I've checked and nothing is awarded on April 15th, so we should be alright. Mansfield have replaced us but their win against Chesterfield was unconvincing to say the least and they're still likely to drop points. remember, they can only play for nine now, we still have fifteen to compete for. Our goal difference is even the same, so one win from our two games in hand will be fine if we then match their results.

Look, we have a tough run in and I said we needed nine from eighteen to be in the top seven. I still feel that is the case, so three wins from five is the aim. Colchester and Yeovil at home should be games we can win, so we need something from one of Accrington, Coventry or Wycombe. Even a draw with Wycombe, beat Coventry and lose to Accrington should suffice. It was a setback but as I said at the top of the piece, automatic was always going to be a step too far. Wycombe, Accrington and Luton have been moulding their teams over two or three years, ours is barely recognisable from the National League winning side of a year ago.

In truth, it is remarkable how far we've come in such a short space of time and I'm talking about twelve months, not the Cowley's entire tenure. They've built a top-seven side out of the triumphant National League side but have retained only two or three of the players. Only Sam, Luke, Alex, Elliott and Rheady played for us against Port Vale and started against Macclesfield.

We must keep our feet on the ground and appreciate that promotion this season isn't everything. I'm not throwing in the towel, but is it a season too early? We're at least 12 months behind the current top three, do we need to miss out this season to come back stronger? Exeter lost key players, but the experience kept the remaining squad in the hunt this time around, what could this side do in League Two next year with a few new faces?

I want to go up but, having been convinced that Danny and Nicky are here to stay, I can see the benefits of not doing also. In 1974/75 we missed out on promotion on goal difference, a distressing end to a campaign that promised so much. I'm sure the negative Neil's amongst the fan base were expressing their indignation around the open fires of Lincolnshire's pubs, how perhaps Graham Taylor lacked ambition, how we needed a creative midfield and we always had and that was why we missed out.

That summer, we signed John Fleming, kept everyone else and set a point tally that will never be beaten thanks to a chance in the points system. If we don't make it this year, keep your hats on, your keyboards untouched and your anger suppressed because with the current squad and manager we're going places and a 1-0 defeat in Burslem won't change any of that.

It seems I'm always ending my blogs with something poignant and I'm afraid this is no different. A good friend of mine, Sarah Guntripp, moved to Stoke a few years ago. Sarah used to run the Adam and Eve with her Mum in Wragby and became a close friend of mine during an incredibly tough spell in my life. We drifted apart, remaining friends on Facebook and always promising ourselves we'd get back together for 'one last party'.

I was going to message Sarah and let her know I was in her neck of the woods, but as I looked her up on Facebook, I found out she died just last week. She was only a couple of years older than me.

Never wait until tomorrow to get in touch with someone you miss today. It might be too late. Sleep tight Sarah and thank you for everything you did in 2001, even closing the pub at 8pm so we could have a twelve-hour locking in. I'll never be able to listen to that awful Blue song without a tear in my eye again.

You're not going to agree with me tonight, that is for sure: Imps 0-0 Wycombe

April 17, 2018

I've driven home from tonight's game wondering how to articulate my thoughts without being called clueless. You see, I don't really subscribe to much of the criticism being levelled at both Wycombe and the referee, a view I know might not be shared by everyone.

As I understand it, a majority of fans believe the referee was appalling all game, we should have had one goal, if not two and a penalty. Wycombe ruined the game, Gareth Ainsworth has let his hero status slide a little and we're all shocked and appalled at the way they played.

It's late and I'm in no mood for picking the bones from our team selection or other finer points of the game, so I'll wade straight into the big decisions. The first 'goal' was, apparently, ruled out incorrectly. I didn't see it properly but I'm told Rhead was not offside when he got the ball to Frecklington. The linesman on the far side disagreed and few in the ground argued the point. Fair enough, the referee can only follow his linesman, it wasn't the right decision but we all thought it was.

Rheady then pushed their defender for the second goal. Again, I didn't see it but from several reliable sources I'm told it was correctly ruled out. I was angry at the time, but I wouldn't comment further on something I didn't see clearly. It's harsh again, but do either of those chances matter if Freck hasn't skied his effort a few moments afterwards? One on one with the keeper and he went for power, not placement. The ensuing furore over the officials and Wycombe have missed the pertinent point that we should have been 1-0 up by our own means. Harry Anderson skewed his good early effort wide too when hitting the target probably brought a goal. At 2-0, does the referee's decision seem so important?

I will argue the point about Harry's penalty, it was a stonewall. I was once again in a box courtesy of Running Imp and the incident was right in front of us. I believe out of anyone in the ground, we had one of the best views and it was 100% a penalty. Yes, Harry went down too easily, but does that mean it isn't a foul? He was between the player and the ball, the player made contact, significant contact, and Harry went to ground. Correct me if I'm wrong, but contact in the box is a penalty, is it not? I won't argue he was looking for it, but it was not a dive, the defenders body moved into Harry's without a shadow of a doubt. That is a crucial moment and the referee got it wrong, but moments later he gives a free kick to them not twenty yards away for an identical incident. That was inconsistent and typical of his poor performance, but to label him on of the worst ever seen at the Bank is ignoring some pretty horrendous displays, not least from Seb Stockbridge or the clown that took charge against York City last season.

They are the three big points, but if Freck and Harry had not been wasteful they wouldn't have mattered. We got a few cheap free kicks too, it wasn't all one way. Late in the second half Elliott broke down the right, then held on to his defender for a minute before going to ground, incorrectly winning the free kick. Yes, the referee was poor but he wasn't all one-sided. He fluffed his lines, he crumbled in the face of TWO teams who use any advantage they can, on or off the ball.

As for Gareth Ainsworth, we're talking about him sullying his legend because he brings a team to Sincil Bank that, aside from playing into danger alley, do everything he did on the field that made him a legend here in the first place? Seriously? That was a softer version of Beck's Lincoln, from cultured wingers (Ainsworth / Mackail-Smith) to veteran forwards (Tyson / Stant) and back to oddly shaped players (Akinfenwa / Bos). I don't like to see football played that way, if it was football and if they were playing it, but how on earth can we sit and criticise something we used to celebrate?

The radio feedback talked about their time-wasting and game management, have a look at us in the last ten minutes of the Checkatrade final, or the final fifteen of the Exeter game and tell me if it was any different at all? Danny had the good grace to acknowledge that too, that is how Wycombe play and I'm afraid sometimes it is how we play. Maybe we're not as blatant, maybe we're not as good at it, but at times there's only a few subtle differences between us and Wycombe. If we were third, needing a point on the road, do you think we'd be significantly different to them? Yes, certain aspects might change, but on the whole that was a Lincoln-esque performance. That isn't me being critical of us or of Wycombe, but let's not sit in the stands pretending we're this free-flowing side that operate under the banner of good sportsmen all the time, eh? We're not quite as bad as they were, but we know how to kill a game when we need to.

I thought when we did play a bit of football we looked the better side. We weren't on it, but the game was entertaining if not a good advert for the sport. We had a few chances, one or two we should have taken and one or two we did well with, but the same issues that have dogged us all season sprung up. Had we another Matt Green to play with our current Matt Green up front, we win that game 2-0 tonight. No slur on Rheady or Ollie Palmer, but just as was the case on Saturday, Green found himself playing good balls across the area to nobody. Against Grimsby, Whitehouse played the same ball across the area and Matt Green finished it off. We're not hiding from the fact our squad is ever so slightly short, but let's not blame the officials or Wycombe for not winning the game. We had the chances.

I also find it amusing we (some fans and me) were sat talking before the game and everyone I spoke to told me they thought tonight would be a good point, as long as we back that up on Saturday. Just like everyone before the season started said if we were in touch of the top seven with a few games to go we'd achieved something excellent. Now we are in that position and I hear and read grumblings that we're 'not good enough'. Similarly, leaving the ground I heard moans about the draw, moans from people who before the game told me it would be a good point (yes Dad, I'm looking at you). Let me be very clear on my belief: that was a decent point. Yes, we could have won the game, but Wycombe are third and score a lot of goals, we could have lost it too. We now regain our top seven space and we still have a game in hand.

I'm concerned my assessment of tonight's game might rub few up the wrong way, but I do pride myself on telling it how I see it. I've seen worse referees, far worse. I've not seen many teams who are as direct or indulge in game management as early as the second minute, but that is what Wycombe do, we knew what to expect. Once upon a time we cheered that sort of football. Many of you reading this talk fondly to me about John Beck and his brand of 'football', so please don't criticise it now his apprentice is doing the same. At least Gareth is a gent off the field and at least he looks to gain his advantages whilst the teams are on the pitch, not with flooded changing rooms, salted tea and cold showers.

As for us, being blatantly honest I thought Freck was average, I thought Harry struggled and I thought Sam was below par too. I wouldn't have picked Matt Rhead as man of the match either, but Lincoln City Banter voted so maybe I'm in a minority. I actually thought Alex Woodyard had a good game, he looked to keep the ball on the deck and work it out wide on numerous occasions, something that made a refreshing change from diagonals into Rheady or big punts from blue shirts. Bozzie was marking Akinfenwa and the big lump didn't get a significant touch, so I'd say our own beast did well and probably deserved to be there or thereabouts in the man of the match voting. I thought Matt Green worked tirelessly again, remember he was being asked to play on the left of the striker, not the right as he usually does. I thought Scott Wharton had a good game too.

I also thought we wasted almost all of our set pieces, especially corners but also some free kicks in very good positions. For a team who are such a threat from set plays, it is criminal we didn't make a single one count tonight. I know we have numerous ways of setting up from the corners, we run different ones each time I'm told, but the only one I saw tonight was where we lift it to the back post and it gets headed away. I'm not sure what the thinking is behind it, but it didn't work.

We weren't bad, not by a long way, we were the better side for 70 minutes, but for the final thirty of those we were the lesser of two evils. We should have wrapped the game up by 40 minutes but blew two great chances without the referee's intervention, had he been a homer and given us the benefit of the doubt it should have been 4-0 at half time, with a penalty to boot in the second half. It wasn't, we didn't concede and our play-off hopes are still in our own hands.

These are the days it all makes sense: Imps 2-1 Colchester

April 21, 2018

It wasn't pretty, it wasn't entertaining and at times, it wasn't looking like it would be enough to win the game. However, with just three games left of the season the focus isn't on the football now, it's on the result.

I've seen comparisons drawn with Torquay and Gateshead last season and I'm inclined to refer to those matches myself. They were big games where the result mattered and the team who wanted it more ended up on the right side of it. Today, we ended up with three points through sheer determination, grit and a 'refuse to lose' attitude.

I'll go through the game in a moment, but at one point this afternoon I stood watching on as we laboured to a 1-1 draw, a man down with Mansfield winning against Port Vale. I looked to the sky and for a brief second, I thought 'this is it.' It crossed my mind we'd battled bravely and finishing outside the top seven wasn't the end of the world. What I'd forgotten was that Danny Cowley's teams produce the goods when it matters and once again, they did just that.

The afternoon started inauspiciously enough, despite the size of the prize. Colchester perhaps had the best of the first ten minutes, but once they'd failed to get a lead they seemed content to play nice football but not do anything with it. They've got decent players and with a good summer of recruitment they'll be a threat again, but for all their nice football, they weren't getting much off at goal, certainly nothing meaningful.

We got ourselves into the game around the twenty-minute mark, but similarly it wasn't working for us. The first half was frustrating, watching Matt Green do the job of two or three players whilst someone pretending to be Harry Anderson toiled away on the flank. I've been a big fan of Harry ever since his first outing, but he's in a real bad patch of form at present and he's been ineffective. That said, he always looks one step away from producing something special, but today he got crowded out, again.

In the centre of the park we showed lots of industry but no real panache. That middle three has yet to convince a lot of people and today I could see why. All three of those players, Freck, Alex and Elliott, are quality on their day, but today it wasn't happening. Of the three I thought Alex Woodyard had the best game, he's much the same every week again now. He's no frills, calm and strong with a tendency to get the ball backwards. That is part of our game plan and he does it superbly. The other two just weren't getting the rub of the green. Freck's taken a bit of a battering since he's been back and I can see why to a degree. He's not quite adopted our patterns yet, but he's class and it will come.

It was a drab first half really, was it not? There wasn't a lot to chat about and when people start streaming off for their half time drinks on 38 minutes you know it's been a below par half. It actually winds me up, having to stand to let people past constantly from 38 minutes on wards, why can't people just wait until half time? With the club's brilliant new initiative of having bars behind the Stacey West, queues are far fewer, so why spoil the last ten minutes for everyone else just to get a beer? Besides, we might have scored in those last few minutes, but the crowd noise dies down whilst everyone goes off to look after themselves. Do you not realise there's a football match on?

I have to be a little critical of our set pieces of late too. All of our corners have been going over the top and getting nowhere, free kicks around the box had been largely wasted and I don't get it. We've been a constant threat from those situations all season, but now with three or four games to go we've become a little wasteful.

Ollie came on in the second half and changed the complexion of our attack, his direct and unpredictable running did not do their defenders any favours. Ten minutes in and he gets a little nick as he's shooting, penalty to Lincoln. Having watched the big man trying to win one all game, it was refreshing to see us actually get one from a player trying to shoot and get on with things.

I'm not a fan of the arguing over the penalty, it's not the first time we've seen it either. didn't it happen last season, Terry Hawkridge taking (and missing) one? Seeing that hints at disharmony in the ranks and whilst it may not be the case, it was petulant and stupid. Not that it mattered when Elliott finally got his own way, his calm penalty gave us the platform upon which we should have built a fine win.

They should have been down to ten men too, the elbow from Mandron was dangerous. I conceded we might have suffered the same at Wembley, but it doesn't change the fact Scott Wharton was laid out from what looked like a cynical elbow. I'm told Mandron isn't that type of player, but the referee saw it, the linesman saw it and they gave a yellow. How can an elbow be a yellow card? At Wembley, the ref saw a collision, hence the yellow, but this was a different situation. if it's a foul, it's a red, surely? I suppose therein lies the 'beauty' of football, eh?

We then lose possession in the attacking half and concede a well-worked goal. Colchester break at speed and have some good players, but all afternoon we looked susceptible to a quick counter. Rheady got a bit muddled, a lot around me were getting mad at him but there's a lot of players between him past the half way line and the back of our net. Danny won't be happy with it though, we got caught in a game we really should have been closing down.

At 1-1, Mansfield scored and suddenly the world looked a much darker place. Clouds formed in the sky and it was there I found myself looking on 83 minutes. Colchester had missed a gifted chance to extend their lead, Ollie Palmer had struck another worldy against the underside of the bar, then Bozzie got caught in a chase. I'm not sure how that is a red card, their player is not within two steps of a goal scoring chance, Luke is covering and from where I was stood, it looked like six of one and half a dozen of the other. I've seen Matt Green impeded in the same way most weeks, but Crawley at home and Wimbledon away in particular spring to mind, both with nothing given. Danny intends to appeal, rightly so. It was a poor decision and one that could have cost us an awful lot. They say these things even themselves out, but not when you've got three games left and your closest challengers are winning.

As both games drew to a close I expected the heavens to open, the rain to fall and our season to be washed away. Instead, divine intervention. Pope Tom of Port Vale grabbed an equaliser at Field Mill, restoring some parity and giving us a chance from our game in hand. If only we could get something from a game in which we'd rarely threatened, not least from a set piece.

We'll talk about the goal for a long while to come, but remember how we got the chance from yet another tireless Matt Green run. He's been brilliant for us this season and yet again he put in a display worthy of winning man of the match. His tireless running saw him create the crossing chance. It had to be, didn't it? We'd wasted so many, but this is Danny and Nicky Cowley, this is the new Lincoln City, the ones who give us more thrills and spills than we've collectively had in a decade. I swear from my angle it looked as though Luke Waterfall jumped fifteen feet in the air to head that ball home, but once again, it was Captain Fantastic and his magic hat giving us something to cheer.

He's something odd; I celebrated that goal harder than I did Elliott's at Wembley. The whole season rested on that one cross, that one header. The outpouring of joy was fuelled by a whole season of pressure, slowly building up game after game. Just a few minutes before everything had looked gloomy, but like the threatened rain, it passed quickly and all we got was sunshine. We got the 2-1 win, we got one of those moments of unbridled joy that only a football fan can understand. Only by travelling to Port Vale and watching a turgid 1-0 defeat, only by following Mansfield' result all afternoon, by lamenting missed chances in a game last November can you truly understand that moment when the net bulges in the 95th minute of a huge game like this.

I've been out for a meal with my mate Dave (40th birthday too, old bugger) and a couple in the party said football was only a game. Anyone who says that hasn't lived one of those moments, those last-minute game changer moments. They're what I refer to as 'Danny specials', often seemingly a stroke of luck but surely happening far too often to be deemed so. Remember Ipswich at home, Adam Marriott came on a freed Nathan. Remember Torquay, Marriott again won the free kick Sam scored. Against Gateshead Danny decided not to bring Nathan off despite normally always doing so. Today, he sent on Luke with ten minutes to go and got his rewards. He might humbly call it luck, but it isn't. Those results happen through hard work, tenacity and belief. Most of all, they happen because of belief.

We weren't great today, we weren't against Gateshead, we weren't against Torquay, but those three matches will always be right up there when it comes to great memories and that, ladies and gentlemen, is why we love this f*cking game.

Three to go and never, ever bet against us. Sunderland away, opening game of the season. Believe.

Bostwick dismissal overturned: no suspension for midfielder

April 24, 2018

Whilst it hasn't been made official yet, the Stacey West has it on rock-solid authority that Michael Bostwick's red card from Saturday has been sensationally overturned and he's clear to play this evening.

Bozzie was sent off in the final ten minutes of out thrilling 2-1 win against Colchester, putting a dampener on the overall outcome of three points for City. He faced a one-match ban, tonight against Coventry City, but Danny Cowley confirmed the club were going to appeal.

There seemed little in the challenge as Bozzie wrestled with the Colchester forward, both seemingly battling in equal measure, but Darren Handley didn't agree and he dismissed the former Peterborough man.

Colchester didn't score from the resulting free-kick, instead we rallied late on and grabbed a winner.Today, news will break that Bozzie is clear to play after the FA agreed with Lincoln City's evidence proving it was NOT a sending off offence. A source from London has revealed that he will not be banned for the crucial match this evening.Finally, a common-sense decision from the FA.

This blog may seem fairly odd to include, but it sparked frenzied debate as to exactly what I should and shouldn't publish. The club did not give me this information, I found out through a contact at the FA. I was later told the club wanted to keep it a secret but one or two of our officials found out through me tweeting about it! It just seemed a fairly pertinent blog in the season and perhaps for my own purposes, I decided to include it.

Nobody wants to face us in the play-offs, if we get there: Coventry 2-4 Imps
April 24, 2018

Lincoln City FC never fail to astound me and once again, they've defied logic and reason to produce a scintillating display of football that has left fans drooling.

When I say scintillating I don't mean free-flowing passes and intricate skills, I mean a determined and dogged display of resilience, togetherness and application. We don't always play pretty, in League Two you can't, but I dare say Coventry will have us down as one of the best teams they've seen this year, simply reciprocating the honour we bestowed upon them in November.

Back then it felt like the masters teaching the newcomers a lesson, their football beat our fight and application, but tonight it was the tortoise that finally got the better of the hare. They've run out of steam recently and even a couple of well-worked goals weren't enough to stop the slow, methodical juggernaut of Lincoln City. Every week we've plough on, gaining points, climbing towards the ultimate goal of a play off place. I believe we have enough now, I don't think our points target will be beaten by Mansfailed, but to be mathematically sure we need just a single point from our last two games. I miss Yeovil at home thanks to being partly converted into a robot the day before (spinal surgery, metal rods and screws in two lumbar. Nice), but I'm pretty confident now that match won't have a bearing on our final position. I hope not, I hope the lads make it irrelevant, just for me.

A draw would have been sufficient tonight, so I stuck a fiver on one of the two teams failing to score. I thought maybe Danny would tighten it up and go there to get what we needed. How foolish am I? A Cowley team always, without fail, goes out to win a game of football. I expect Mark Robins thought that if we didn't get at them early then he'd settle for a point too. It could have had all the hallmarks of Austria and West Germany from the 1982 World Cup.

Matt Rhead weed on their chips within sixty seconds, smashing home a wonderful goal from Lee Frecklington's knock down. Within a minute of the game kicking off we'd stuck a middle finger in the air and said 'we're here for all three points'. It was a line in the sand, we puffed out our chests, let out a loud battle cry and spanked them early. The goal was almost typical Rhead, a sublime strike from nothing that has become his trademark. He's not been as prolific this season, but when he hits a ball, it stays hit. The big man was getting a lot of stick from people sat around me Saturday, next time I hear it I'll just show them a video of that goal and shake my head in a condescending manner.

That goal immediately set the tone for a frenetic half of football, delightful because we ended up on the right side of it but terrifying from a defensive point of view. Their equaliser was a swift break, knocking the ball about quickly and with ease, much as they had done at our place in November. There wasn't really anyone to blame on our side, to a man we were playing superbly, but the Sky Blues have quality in abundance and they flexed their muscles right back at us.

Enter Ollie Palmer, the myth, the legend. All season we've scratched our heads as to what our best pairing is up top, tonight Danny just shrugged his shoulders and stuck all three on. What is the worst that could happen, right? Palmer, fresh from folding his lunchtime crisps, stumbled almost accidentally through the defence, only we see it every week and that lumbering 'Paulo Wanchope' style of his is never accidental. 2-1 City, for around as long as it was 0-0.

Switch off, 2-2. There's not much else to be said is there? Coventry literally levelled as quickly as we'd opened the scoring, another good goal from them to well and truly kill off my bet and possibly Lincoln City's spirit.

As if. As if anything can kill our side's spirit when the chips are down. I'll tell you what we are right now, we're a big game team. We occasionally lose focus in the smaller games, but when we are truly needed, each and every man stands up to be counted. Coventry in November seemed like a big game, but there was nothing won and lost in November. Coventry at the end of May was a huge game and we knew exactly what was needed. In those games, we perform. Just like the last 12 games of the National League, just like Forest Green back in November 2016, just like the FA Cup matches and just like the Wembley final.

It was big Ollie Palmer who finished them off, albeit in the first half. He smashed home arguably the scrappiest goal of the evening, a close-range finish after a corner wasn't dealt with properly. I imagine at 3-2 Mark Robins slumped back in his dug out, turned to his assistant and said, "why won't they just settle for a bloody draw?"

The second half was far more measured and controlled, despite the early Sky Blue pressure. Although it felt as though something could happen at any minute, it only truly happened once more. The superb Matt Rhead, turning in one of his best performances in recent weeks, set up Lee Frecklington, the evenings Man of the Match by some distance. It was fitting Freck got the goal, he's had his detractors recently but tonight, when pushed, he rose to the occasion. That's why we signed him, he's League One quality and so are a majority of our players.

Once we'd got four goals behind us we started to do a bit of the old 'Wycombe' tactics. It's nice to see we weren't doing it from the first minute, if that had been Wycombe and Coventry I guarantee you it would have been a turgid 0-0. Anyone who says our style is anti-football ought to just bear that in mind.

Time wasting is part and parcel of the game, but tonight's result shows that last week's controversial draw with Wycombe was an excellent outcome. We've faced two very different sides, successful for their own reasons, but neither has matched us properly. Wycombe subdued us, but never looked like beating us, Coventry came at us and simply couldn't outscore us. Notts County struggled to handle us at Christmas and Exeter were simply outscored earlier this year too.

Go on, which of those do you think wants to play the Cowley's Lincoln in a play-off match? Who wants the big game team, the organised, fighting side in the end of season mix up? I'll tell you who. Nobody. That's who.

I'm confident we've got enough points to see us face the two-legged semi-final and I'm also confident we've got enough in the tank to beat anyone over two legs, certainly anyone in our division. We're organised, we're resolute and despite having a small squad, we're remarkably flexible too. The back four did very well tonight despite being 'make-shift', but then when your so-called reserve centre back is a former Welsh international who played League One for six months this season, you're not in a bad place, are you?

Massive respect to Michael Bostwick too, he's got to be pushing Neal Eardley hard for the Player of the Year. He's just an animal, a never-say-die behemoth who bullies and battles his way through every game he plays. I was delighted to see his card was rescinded, the correct decision, and I was over the moon to see him at his dominant best.

Tonight we celebrate, tomorrow we focus on Accrington. I feel like Danny Cowley saying that, but that is how I feel. Let's get to the 'best' team in the league and shove it right up them like we can do anyone on our day. It's the final away day of the season, fancy dress and huge numbers watching two of League Two's finest sides in action. Accrington can win the title, we can secure promotion and both sets of fans will probably be happy at the final whistle matter not the result. I'm pleased for Accrington in as much as they play football the right way and have defied the odds, but

I'd rather it had been us in their position. That said, we all claimed the play-offs would be a massive achievement and to all intents and purposes, that is where we are right now.

Two years ago this week we rounded off a relatively disappointing National League campaign with a 3-2 defeat at home to Woking and I'd written about green shoots of recovery, wondering what the next appointment might do for our club. If I knew then what I knew now, I'd think I was hallucinating.

4-2 at the Ricoh Arena? It's all in a day's work for Lincoln City of 2018, arguably the best Lincoln City I've seen in my 32 years of following the club.

One Hell of an Evening – Serious Intent by Lincoln City
April 26, 2018

It was another one of those off field moments where fans were either glued to screens or in attendance, another moment of pure theatre from a club that have got good at this sort of thing recently.

Aside from the packed crowd, the swish videos and the uplifting questions and answers, there was some fundamentally important things developed at our football club tonight and although a £1.3m training ground would seem like the most important, it is not. The most important thing is, and always has been, those tow likeable Essex boys who have adopted our city as their own.

They're moving up here, they've signed chunky new deals and for me, there's a lot more to be said for finding a school place than there is for signing the deals. When they spoke about Michael Bostwick's summer move they told an endearing story about Ian's staff cooking a meal for his family while negotiations were ongoing and that being something that convinced the big man Lincoln was the place for him.

It's a nice sound bite, but there's much more to it than that. It is the ethos of our staff, not just Ian and his team but the media guys, the office girls and everyone at the club. It is family orientated, Nicky has spoken about that bond between father and son resonating with him. The Cowleys get it, but we as a club have it. Danny and Nicky have brought that out and developed it, but chef Sarah, she's been one with a heart of gold for as long as she has been at the club. We've always had that family vibe bubbling away, but it's suddenly bloomed and is paying dividends.

Danny and Nicky identify with it, they know what it is like to work an eight-hour day and then pour your heart into a football club. They know what it is to support a team, they're real people. Contracts, sure they mean something to them, but when I hear their kids are going into a school here I think that's a bigger message. They might sign a deal and have their heads turned, I stress might, it is feasible. But, are these two men, fathers with young families, going to put their kids in school here if there's the slightest doubt they might be tempted away? Are they going to get their wives to commit to a move if there's an outside chance they might move on? Never. 2022, means 2022. God bless them both, in fact god bless all of them, Danny and Kate, Nicky and Lauren and the kids. They've made me one happy little ginger writer this evening, I'll tell you that.

Of course, hearing that they're getting the tools to do the job is great. I suppose if you asked Da Vinci to do your portrait in just pencils he'd make a great job of it but give him oils and a bloody great canvass and you'd have yourselves a masterpiece worth millions. This is the same, those two boys could mould a team of fighters and Championship winner by training on school pitches and RAF pitches, but what might they do with a purpose-built facility? They say it is important for development, how much more can we develop? We're currently in the most successful two-year period of our history, the only time we've lifted two pieces of silverware inside a twelve-month period and we've done it essentially with one hand tied behind our backs.

Luton Town, Coventry City, Shrewsbury, they all have these facilities and yet in fairness, we've not been that far away from them in our games. Now we're getting the edge, now we're getting the same toys and advantages they have. What can we do now?

I'm still surprised to hear managers talking about investing money in infrastructure over the playing squad, when did we ever hear that? Sutton and Jackson wanted money for players all the time, even when they got the training ground it wasn't really heralded. When has a football manager ever looked a half a million quid and said; "no, you use it on putting some foundations down and we'll stick to our budget", and done exactly that? When has sticking to a budget ever involved bringing two former Welsh internationals into the squad, a Championship captain of twelve months ago and a player as influential and dominant as Bozzie, fending off interest from bigger clubs?

I was one of those who panicked about Ipswich, I make no secret about that, but I wish I'd never doubted those two now. I'm not sure it was doubt in them, I think it was fear that this was all a bit too good to be true. Even in 1976 it all went for a Burton after the main event, all through history we've reached a peak and then lost it. Colin Murphy's great side was let down by a lack of investment, Keith's side petered out (in my eyes) due to the board room changes. We've often promised a lot but in truth, I never felt we would get to see it through.

After tonight, I'm utterly convinced we will. Long live the Cowley's, long live Lincoln City FC.We're on our way.

Down to the wire: Accrington 1-0 Imps
April 29, 2018

Some fans often feel like a 'Jonah', the term used for a sailor or passenger who brings bad luck to a ship. In football terms, a Jonah is a fan who sees his team lose a disproportionate amount of times.

This season, I've seen 62% of Lincoln's away defeats, 37% of their draws and just a solitary win. Considering we've won nine away, seeing just one is appalling. I'm not able to make any play-off semi-final, should we be there, due to the back operation I keep banging on about, but the players might just be thankful for that given my dubious record.

Not that I blame myself for the rather lacklustre defeat. We all travelled across the country in a party mood, almost certain we'd get a point and if we didn't, certain Mansfield would fluff their lines. Thanks to Lee Angol, they secured the points they needed meaning we go into the final game not knowing our fate.

There was a bit of worry spreading around social media last night, fans saying it was 'squeaky bum' time and that sort of thing. Not for me, not one bit. We're still overwhelming favourites to make the top seven, we hold a three-point cushion and need a draw against Yeovil to be certain. If the unthinkable were to happen and they were to win, anything other than a Mansfield win against Crawley would still see us qualify.

I recall playing Yeovil in consecutive seasons over a decade ago, needing nothing to secure our play-off spots. I recall losing 3-2 in the first game with a player called Aron Wilford bagging his only Imps goal, then we lost 3-0 the year after. Third time lucky for the win and momentum needed to get us into the play-offs. Here's hoping so.

The day started with a party atmosphere in the warm sunshine backed by a healthy number of traveling Imps, but it ended in a damp squib as we made our way from the ground wet, cold and looking for Mansfield's game to finish in something other than a 3-2 win. I hate Lincoln losing and for an hour or so after a match I get really down about it, but the fresh day brings a dose of reality and the realisation that three points from those last two tough away fixtures is a good haul.

As for Accrington, I'm pleased they're champions, they typify the beauty of the game, the little man triumphing with hard work and endeavour. They won't win any hospitality awards though, eight portaloos for 1,700 travelling fans is barely sufficient for a start. I was incredibly dismayed at the set up in the away end, it was dangerous that they insisted on moving fans into the packed terracing when there was no room. Various reports have come through to me about fans crushed together so tightly they were barely standing on the ground. A lady near me was told she couldn't bring her mobility scooter in, despite being disabled.

The stewards were a mix of good and bad, one or two were angrily telling fans to move away from the front of the terraces, whilst others realised the situation wasn't ideal and showed common sense. In the end a steward came to us berating his own club for selling too many tickets. I get it, they're not the richest club and they need to grab every penny while they can, but at the expense of safety? Not for me.

On the pitch our first half showing was turgid, don't shoot me down for being a moaner but it was. I'm not saying we are poor, you take the rough with the smooth, but we didn't play well. I didn't think Accrington were great either, the game barely lived up to the pre-match hype. They're meant to be a free-flowing passing side who switch play around and pose a constant menace, but aside from the bundled goal they threatened about as much as we did (very little).

The goal was avoidable but you couldn't lay the blame at anyone's feet, it happens and you must have the character to get up and get on with it. From a defensive point of view we could have done better, but football is a game in which you concede goals. That is unavoidable at times, you just have to make sure you score some. We didn't.

I've seen some criticism of the referee, wholly unjust in my eyes. It's easy to pile into the official when you're playing badly, but he wasn't to blame for the penalty we gave away. It was a penalty and Allsop was alert enough to save the oddly Southgate-esque strike from Billy Kee.

I was impressed with Scott Wharton in the first half and that continued into the second also. That lad is so talented, he dropped into the centre if he needed to cover but shows quality in carrying the ball down the flank when called upon. His passing is good, he's strong in the air and he's hungry and committed. He's an awful lot like that Norwich reserve player we all like so much, only he can play full back too.

Aside from the goal I thought we looked good across the back, it was getting forward that we struggled with, but that was a testament to Accrington as much as it is detrimental to us. Two decent side were cancelling each other out and, had the hosts read the script, it had draw written all over it. But for that one goal it was an equal contest.

Second half we looked better than we had, not with a cutting edge but certainly improved. I called for the three strikers all to start in the run up to the game and we saw the other side of it in Accrington. Against Coventry they poured forward finding space, but Accrington shut down Rheady and that nullified Green and Palmer's threat too. Both worked hard, there's never a lack of effort from Danny's sides, but it just didn't come off. I was very surprised to see Palmer come off and not Rheady, but when you've got all three strikers on the field you're not left with many options.

I did think Accrington had two lucky escapes in the second half. The first was a blatant penalty for a foul on Matt Green, a decision even the Accrington keeper agreed with. I'm no lip reader but he seemed to mouth 'that was a penalty' to our fans, not in an arrogant way but as an honest admission. Before we get angry though, let's not forget the penalty Green got at Sincil Bank in the league against them, earning their lad a red card too. That was soft and we got it, this decision should have been nailed on and we didn't.

If things even themselves out then the red card earlier in the season was cancelled out when Harry Anderson was denied a clear opportunity just outside the box towards the end. The punishment was a yellow card which I thought could have been a red. Again, you take the rough with the smooth and whilst I was mad at the time, it is just something you live with as a football fan.

We didn't trouble with the free kick, but recently we haven't really. I think our set pieces have been poor of late, I know we've made the odd one or two count but if we took a percentage I imagine it wouldn't make good reading. Corners have been less than average, we look as though we're running the same one every time, long to someone at the back post to nod across a la Burnley. Accrington got wise to it the second time and we rarely threatened. Nicky will be disappointed with those as I know they work incessantly on set pieces.

As for free kicks, since that little 'wizard' JMD left (note the tone) we've had no real threat. Bozzie drove his shot at the wall and another chance went begging. I haven't see a well-hit free kick from City for a long while now.

Matt Green, who I thought had a decent game again, could have scored late on but he just couldn't quite get his feet around the ball. Had he slammed it home we'd be laughing now, but he didn't and at the final whistle he looked visibly distraught. There's no need to be Matt, you've been excellent this season, you've worked incredibly hard and in my mind, you're the third best player we've seen during the campaign, behind Bozzie and Neal Eardley.

Before anyone jumps on me for being too negative, I'm well aware we have the upper hand and I'm happy we went away to the champions and made them look as ordinary as they made us look. It is odd how these patterns emerge in football, that is the third season in a row we've been present at the title presentation in our league, Cheltenham, us and now Accrington. This season though we weren't watching on as envious losers, we're still in the mix and have the upper hand. I wasn't watching on at all, as much as I respect what John Coleman had won I had no desire to see them celebrate when they'd just denied us confirmation of a top seven finish. Maybe I'm bitter, if we'd drawn I would have stayed, but we didn't so it would have just rubbed salt into the wounds.

We just need to keep our nerve though, I'd rather be in our shoes than the Stags. We can be proud we're in this position, in almost any other season 74 points would be enough to earn you a top seven spot, but the top eight this season have been so good that the bar has been raised.

In fact, in the last six seasons our current points total would have us in the top seven in all but one of them. Interestingly, in four of the last six years the side finishing in seventh has been promoted to League One. As things stand, we'll be in seventh. The only side to finish seventh with 75 points were Wimbledon two years ago, the side who replaced us in the Football League and were promoted via the play offs. Again, an omen? If you believe that sort of stuff maybe so.

Did you also know that our current points total, 74, is as many as we had in all of our previous five play-off campaigns? In 2003/04 and in 2006/07 we finished on 74 points, the other three we finished on less. Again, that lays bare the size of our achievement. Even more remarkable is in 1997/98, the year we were promoted automatically, we finished with just 75 points, a total we will hope to surpass this weekend.

You see, this season is as competitive as League Two has been for a long time and our record is as good as any of our fourth-tier campaigns since the early 1980s. It is proof that, despite the below-par showing, this is actually the best Lincoln City side possibly of the last 35 years. Even the 1981/82 and 1982/83 seasons brought 77 and 76 points, numbers we could finish on with a win next weekend. We could actually finish with our joint highest Football League points haul under the 3pts for a win system.

Still think we'll miss out next weekend? I'm going to be honest, I still have 100% faith we'll be there. Lincoln City don't bottle big games, not when the chips are truly down and the season is on the line. Yeovil lost to a Mansfield side that has been in freefall, they now have a suspension too and I imagine the last thing they really want is a trip to a packed Sincil Bank, a cauldron of atmosphere and passion.

It is my desperate regret that I won't be at the game, I'm not even sure how I'll listen to it or see it from my Sheffield hospital bed. It looks like one of the biggest matches in our recent history will be fed back to me through social media and friends texts. Given what is at stake, that might be the least stressful way to watch it and given my record with watching the Imps on the road this season, me staying away might just be the best thing all round. There you go, a positive to be found in spinal surgery. If we win that and any subsequent away leg I can see the club revoking my season ticket as a precaution.

So, we go down to the wire. In two years under Danny and Nicky we've had two so-called dead rubbers and even then we were pushing for 100 points. Win, lose or draw next weekend, this has been a great season and losing 1-0 might have hurt at the time, but that will fade away by the time 3pm comes on Saturday 5th May. Our destiny is in our own hands and everything we've done in the last 45 games has led us to this point.

The Stacey West – A Season in Blogs 2017/18

Pos	Team	Pld	W	D	L	GF	GA	GD	Pts
1	Accrington Stanley	45	29	6	10	76	43	33	93
2	Luton Town	45	25	12	8	94	46	48	87
3	Wycombe Wanderers	45	23	12	10	78	60	18	81
4	Exeter City	45	23	8	14	63	54	9	77
5	Notts County	45	21	13	11	71	48	23	76
6	Coventry City	45	22	8	15	64	47	17	74
7	Lincoln City	45	20	14	11	63	47	16	74
8	Mansfield Town	45	18	17	10	66	51	15	71
9	Carlisle United	45	17	15	13	61	53	8	66
10	Swindon Town	45	19	8	18	64	65	-1	65
11	Newport County	45	16	15	14	55	57	-2	63
12	Colchester United	45	16	14	15	53	51	2	62
13	Cambridge United	45	16	13	16	51	60	-9	61
14	Crawley Town	45	16	10	19	57	65	-8	58
15	Stevenage	45	14	13	18	60	64	-4	55
16	Crewe Alexandra	45	16	5	24	60	74	-14	53
17	Cheltenham Town	45	13	12	20	66	71	-5	51
18	Grimsby Town	45	12	12	21	39	66	-27	48
19	Port Vale	45	11	14	20	49	62	-13	47
20	Yeovil Town	45	12	11	22	58	74	-16	47
21	Forest Green Rovers	45	13	8	24	54	74	-20	47
22	Morecambe	45	9	18	18	41	56	-15	45
23	Barnet	45	11	10	24	43	65	-22	43
24	Chesterfield	45	10	8	27	47	80	-33	38

May

We're there: Imps 1-1 Yeovil
May 5, 2018

Cometh the hour, cometh the man. How familiar, needing a point on the last day, missed penalty drama and a late equaliser which settles things once and for all. Lincoln City are going to the play-off semi-finals.

There's not a huge amount I can say about the game, laid up in a hospital bed with Twitter for company. What I can say, safely, is that there's just as much tension when you can't see the action, even pumped full of morphine. My feed has Crawley and Mansfield on too and at various points in the afternoon I thought it might all slip away. I got to follow their game as much as ours and although it didn't matter in the end, it raised the tension immensely here.

Whilst some people will feel we've scraped in, perhaps correctly, a season is 46 games and over that season we've earned the right to be in the top seven. Suddenly, that point at Morecambe was a good point, as was the draw at Barnet. It was enough to help push us into the end of season lottery and that is now fact. It could have been better, but that is testament to how much expectation has been raised. Seventh would have been plenty in August 2017 and rightly so.

I'm delighted it was Pett who got the goal, I sang his praises pre-season, long before he became an Imp. I even defended him this week on Twitter, only to be reminded I'd done the same with Tom Champion. In my defence, Champion helped Boreham Wood to a play-off appearance (and win last night) and Pett has now done the same for City. I know it was only one goal, but he took it incredibly calmly and using phenomenal technique.

To go one down was uncharacteristic of us, to a degree. I've felt we've struggled early on this season, but then we did concede early against Macclesfield last season. We certainly like to do things the hard way. Nobody would have called Yeovil scoring first and looking like beating us, such is the stress of the final day. There was none of that over at the Ricoh was there? If I was the FA I'd be looking very closely at that game….

Watching on Twitter it sounded as though we showed endeavour, missed some half decent chances but always looked susceptible to an attack, Fair assessment? For the first time this season, you need to tell me!

I wanted to pen a few words about not being there. I've banged on about it recently as regular readers know. Thank you for all the well wishes, in the end I've had three lumbar fused which is pretty big apparently. Anyway, it has meant I'm on the periphery of the play off excitement and sadly, will be for the semi-finals too.

It's strange, having been so close to everything all season, going away to place such as Port Vale, but watching from afar as 10,000 joyously celebrate us reaching the play offs. I didn't miss a kick of 2003-2007 either, but I'll be lucky to make Wembley this time around. Sadly, I feel very distant at the moment, I'm sure that will subside but the timing of my operation couldn't have been worse.

Whether I'm there or not, we should pause briefly now and acknowledge what a truly remarkable season this has been. We've ended up with the sort of finish we would have taken happily at the start of the campaign, we've got some peripheral silverware along the way and had a day out at Wembley. If we negotiate our tricky play off tie, we'll be back and this time we'll know what to expect. If we don't, then it has still been a successful season.

Tonight, lots of Imps will celebrate, but we've won nothing. We've earned the right to compete for a place in League One, but there's a train of thought that it might be too early. Maybe we could benefit from another season in this division, but then again we're not guaranteed success. If promotion comes then it has to be the right time, if it doesn't then we continue to build as we have been doing.

One thing in my mind is certain, whatever the final outcome of the 2017/18 season, Lincoln City will become a League One club under Danny and Nicky Cowley eventually. On today's performance, we're not quite there, but then again over 46 games, we are. That's football, subjective and open to interpretation. However, in three games time there will be nothing to interpret. We'll either be in League One or we won't. Would you bet against us?

The play-offs: Sixth time lucky?
May 8, 2018

Misleading headline alert! There's no chance this will be sixth time lucky. If Lincoln City make it into League One this season, it will be anything but luck that has driven us there.

Now we've let the Yeovil dust settle we can look ahead to 180 minutes of football that will be unpredictable, exciting and for one manager, career defining. Paul Tisdale is under a lot of pressure at Exeter and is favourite for the MK Dons job. A two-legged defeat to City would put the final nail in his already-sealed coffin.

However, we don't care about Exeter, do we? We care about Lincoln and the truth is we've limped over the line somewhat, buoyed by the great win against Coventry, the low-quality win against Colchester and that final day struggle against the Glovers. We've not surged over the line in a blaze of glory, but with injuries taking their toll, we did enough.

Still, as with every Lincoln side Danny Cowley has ever put out, there is loads to be optimistic about, I'd say more than ever before. Our second leg against the Grecians is in nine or ten days' time depending on how you want to count the days, meaning the most meticulous management duo we've ever had now have more time than ever to watch videos and study players.

When we beat them earlier in the season, we had less time to study them, so the play-off set up surely benefits us. I'm not saying Exeter study any less than we do, but we have Danny and Nicky on the case. Do you believe Matt Oakley, their assistant manager, will put the same time in as Nicky? Do you believe Tisdale and Oakley, a good management pairing, will work as efficiently as two brothers who have grown up together talking about the game on the school bus, before sleeping when on holiday, playing as young men and coming up from Concord to Lincoln? In terms of preparation I believe the two-legged semi-final benefits us and, before anyone says it, York City last season came around the same time as lots of other games.

I keep hearing nobody wants to play us in the play-offs too. We're labelled as bullies, a physical side with a certain style of play, something I accept to a degree. There was little physical about Tom Pett's finish, was there? Paul Tisdale admitted in March we were the better side and psychologically that will hold some weight. The Grecians came fourth and while all that means is so-called home advantage in the second leg, it does mean over 46 games they were better than us, just.

What is notable is they changed tactics from early in the season. When they won 1-0 early in the season they played a possession game, frustrating us for long periods by dictating the pace and getting the winner through a passing move. They seem to have come full circle, now happy to launch it towards Stockley and do whatever it takes after that to pick up the pieces. The latter suits us, the former not so much, but they're unlikely to switch back now.

No, Exeter will bring the same game plan they brought in March which could result in another open game. Last season, their aggregate score against Carlisle was 6-5, they then lost to seventh-placed Blackpool in the final. I wouldn't be surprised at a high-scoring semi-final this season, I only hope the team finishing in seventh get promoted once again.

As you know I've got some close relatives who are Exeter fans and they don't paint a picture that should worry us a great amount. Paul Tisdale has been booed recently and many of their fans think it is time to go. They were, by all accounts, awful. Their last two matches have been described as uninspiring, the penultimate game against Stevenage was so bad I'm told some fans left early to go on the pop in London.

I've been interested in the one advantage they do have, the number of fans we can take to their place. It's a double-edged sword really the 350 is a pathetic number, given their current capacity is 6,087. Surely, we should be given 600? It might not seem a huge amount more, but Danny has always said our fans make a difference. They did at Coventry, that is for sure. With the FA giving Exeter special dispensation to allocate us far fewer, it gives them an advantage, however slight.

I read the calls for us to do the same, give them a similar amount. That wouldn't be fair, but as a percentage there is a call for us to maybe give them 600 and not 1000. All season clubs have done that to them, Swindon gave them something like 350 when their ground could have held several thousand. My opinion is this; we don't want to be a team seen to be spiteful. In a play-off semi-final we're supposed to give 10% and we have, even though we know we can't have the same back. They're redeveloping their ground, it hasn't been done on purpose and part of me is proud we've retained our integrity and haven't pushed to reduce their capacity. Whether they have 1000 or 600 fans at the Bank, our 9000 should create enough of an atmosphere to give us a big lift.

I actually think being at home in the first leg is an advantage for us. It was against Scunthorpe in 2003, we blew them away in the first match and left them with a job to do in the second leg. The same could happen here, City set the target and then have to stifle the Grecians on a Thursday evening. With our fans on a Saturday afternoon and hopefully a relatively full squad to choose from, I'd back us to beat Exeter, Then, with five days recovery and even more time to study their approach, I'd back us to draw there.

I'm not saying we'll win the tie overall, they're a good side with quality players such as Stockley, Boateng and Dean Moxey. They have several approaches they use and could well have been top three rather than slumming it with us in the play-offs. What I am saying is the format suits us, it suits our manager's approach and the home leg, in my opinion, gives you a chance to set the score to beat. That is psychology, like batting first in cricket. If you do your job right, you get a two-goal lead let's say, that leaves them chasing the game in the second leg, opening up and coming at us.

Then there's this 'nobody wants to play Lincoln' psychology too. We've already won the physical battle with them once recently, one of their fans has told me he feels well do the same again. There's a perception, current or not, that we're bruisers who battle and bully. If you go into a fight believing your opponent is stronger, then he's already half way there.

Whatever happens, a top seven finish has been marvellous and our work-in-progress squad has achieved significantly more than we dared dream. Now, the EFL Trophy win can be savoured because it didn't derail the promotion bid. Now, those draws against Morecambe can be considered good points because we made it anyway. Now, we face three one-off games and as I've said before, I wouldn't dare bet against Lincoln City in one-off matches.

Brave Billy faces up to his demons
May 11, 2018

It started as a trickle, one or two footballers admitting mental health issues. Now, every few weeks we hear of another brave enough to speak up about their struggles. This week it's 'one of our own', at least for now.

I think we all expected Billy Knott to tear up League Two this season, especially after forcing his way into Danny's plans at the start of the campaign. He started out wide on the left, but against Notts County came the start he craved as the number ten, playing behind Green. For 30 minutes it looked good, we matched County but then Seb Stockbridge whipped out a red card. We didn't lose Bill for three games, we potentially lost him for good.

In an interview with echo-news.co.uk, the former Chelsea trainee has opened up about his own fight with mental illness. I wasn't surprised at the words I read, but I was surprised with how candid and brave Billy was. As a football writer, I knocked him towards the end of his spell at the club but his admissions certainly coloured in some blanks, helped me make sense of his departure.

I often wondered how a young man who seemingly had the world at his feet coped with a so-called fall from grace? I imagined Billy as a jack-the-lad, but on the training day I went on he seemed more like a troubled genius, quiet and withdrawn. It's easy to forget these players are people sometimes, that they feel like you and I. Just because Billy was a talented footballer, we assumed he was wasting that talent and had been given enough chances. What we saw in those final few weeks now makes sense, a young man torn and troubled.

After the County sending off there was the very public effort to show the fans how hard he was working. I remember turning up to a night game to see him out on the 3G pitches training. He would come across to the stands and sit in the gantry to the delight of fans, behaviour which I imagine helped boost his confidence. After the sending off, suffering with depression, I would imagine he will have gone through a period of self-hatred, irrespective of whether it was the right decision, before wanting to show us, the paying fans, he still cared. Then, as we won games and his chances dwindled away, he turned to his vices for comfort.

Recently Billy Kee has been open about his fight with the 'rat' in his head, Billy has now opened up about the questions that came to him late at night and last year Nathan Arnold was candid about his own battles with anxiety. They may be lower league players but they have shown real bravery in admitting their issues.

I don't want to harp on too much, Billy will need his privacy respecting at this tough time. I've never shied away from my own battle, thankfully I've had no issues now for almost a year. I do understand though, when they say the 'rat' comes at night or the voices start to pose questions once the light goes out. We're not talking full on psychosis here, voices telling you to kill or anything, but they're thoughts that start and simply don't go away. It used to keep me up when I had a job as a manager, like Billy I'd turn my phone off before bed but then lay awake asking myself things about the day. Had I dealt with a certain situation properly? What had people thought of me? Once you start picking at a thread, there's only one outcome and I can entirely understand how things manifested themselves for young Billy.

I'm not judging him turning to drink to get away from it, people find all sorts of ways to hide from their problems. I feel desperately sad for him, that such a talented boy has found himself in the place he has, as much a victim of a ruthless profession as anyone. I think there's a bit of the 'Gazza' in there, my impression is Billy just wants to play football, but when the pitch is empty and the crowd has gone home he's alone and open to those inner demons.

Will we see Billy Knott play for City again? I'd say it is unlikely, but you never know. What I do want to see is him playing somewhere, anywhere, with a smile on his face. His newspaper interview might have crept out in Basildon under the radar, but it should be put with Billy Kee's interview and all the other players brave enough to admit they're fighting it too and splashed wherever young people can see it. Their experiences might help other young players, it might convince them that those feelings they get when the light goes out at night are not unique. Now, more than ever, young players are being stockpiled like excess equipment at big clubs, then being thrown away without ever being given a chance. We're creating a mental health time bomb within the sport, we're in the grip of a mental health epidemic in the wider world.

Suicide is the biggest killer of men under 45 years old in the UK. Mental health is a huge issue for both sexes, not a little one, not one we should shy away from, but something that we need to face up to and be honest about and tackle head on. I bet you, reading this right now, knows someone who suffers. I bet you know someone suffering right now who is hiding it too, afraid to speak up for fear of a lack of support or understanding.

I wish Billy all the best for the future, whatever it may bring for him.

Don't make me watch on Sky again, please: Imps 0-0 Exeter
May 12, 2018

"This is a battle between two styles, the direct approach of Lincoln City against League Two's slickest side, Exeter City."

That's not verbatim, I couldn't remember the exact wording, but little over thirty seconds after turning on my TV I wanted to throw something through it. Nobody had done their homework, not one person involved in bringing you this game live. It felt like a badly produced student project, from the 'studio' to the knowledge. I went on the Lincoln Uni programme earlier in the season and the production was ten times better on that than on Sky's appalling programme.

As you know, I'm forced to endure the play-offs through my TV screen and it isn't an experience I ever want to repeat. I haven't watched a live game on Sky TV for well over a decade I'd say, if not more. £12.99 a week pass to Now TV cost me, which is around the same I'd pay almost everyone involved with the programme. Combined.

You can't polish a turd and the first half was, in the main, a turd. Jayden Stockley had the best chance but as Exeter fans warned me, if it isn't near his head he's useless. So, the slickest passing side in the division teed up a cross for the striker and he completely missed the ball. The commentator, whose name I deliberately didn't catch, was gutted.

Up the other end City had two penalty shouts and a free kick waved away by Ben Toner, a referee praised for keeping his cards in his pockets. He was only doing so to prevent his arse getting splinters, he sat on the fence for so long. "It's his first play-off game and he's handling it well," the commentator gushed, moments before he bottled a blatant shove on Elliott in the area.

What he had bottled was a kick to James Wilson's face by Ryan Harley, and I'm keen to know what the rules on high boots are. Seb Stockbridge sent Billy Knott off for one which I didn't think he should have done, but Harley didn't even get a yellow as he booted Wilson in the face. Which is it? Is it a foul, a red card or nothing at all?

Then there was the shove on Elliott, a penalty all day long. I've seen them given, I've seen them waved away, but this afternoon every single comparable 'shove' outside the area was penalised. So, at what point does a shove stop being a foul? In the area, apparently. Toner is being fast-tracked up the divisions, one of the perks of not going up this season.

Seconds later Rhead was wrestled to the floor, no penalty. Toner got that right, Rhead played for it and went down far too easily. Mind you, a stopped clock is right twice a day so let's not blow too much smoke up the referee's bottom.

Anderson was then blatantly checked on the edge of the area by Dean Moxey, again nothing given. Lee Hendrie, the only pundit with an ounce of sense, claimed it was the wrong decision. Moxey watched the run and, at last minute, stepped across our player without looking at the ball. In this modern game you cannot do that. Or, apparently, you can.

We went in at 0-0, Matt Green's twist and shot our only half chance from open play and a rare free-kick on target our best from set pieces. I've griped about the referee, but it wasn't his fault we were 0-0, he was just crap. If he'd been a good ref we might have had a penalty, but we hadn't done enough to open up an organised Exeter side.

At half time Matt Taylor was asked if he felt either side did anything different to expectation. "No, not really." he replied, as insightful as I expected. He followed that up with; "Lincoln are trying to play it around in the final third though, they need to keep going long to Matt Rhead." Of course we do, we're not living up to our billing are we? No mention of the so-called passing side of Exeter going long to the sole striker Stockley, no mention of it being two sides cancelling each other out at all.

I would tell you what Stuart McCall said, but I've listened to his detritus about City before so I went to the loo. With my back and our stairs, the took ten minutes, a true blessing.

In the second half we saw fifteen minutes of the proper Lincoln City. Christy Pym was having a great game, claiming crosses which have troubled most other keepers we've seen this season, including our own. He made two great saves from Matt Green too, one resulting in Elliott tapping over with a gaping goal. Yes, the pressure was on and the Sky fools spoke about how great the saves were, but few plaudits went on the moves, slick passing that could have made it 1-0. It was all about Pym, not Matt Green.

They made much more of Rhead's crashing header a few minutes afterwards because it fitted their narrative. The big lump is great in the air, etc etc. I was so angry I considered putting it on mute and having Radio Lincolnshire on, but when I tried it my Now TV feed was four or five seconds behind the commentary. It was almost better than going back to Hendrie and his dribbling accomplice, but eventually I popped away a Tramadol and two Diazepam and sat back hoping they would sort the pain in my ears more than that in my back.

I thought we were the better side in the second half, we played better football and although Exeter looked dangerous, I thought we had things under control. I said not to bet on this being a goalless game, but after about 70 minutes I did just that. Exeter were happy with the draw, hence one up top, and we don't have the attacking nous to break down a resolute defence. I only won eight quid, but I counted it as a partial refund on my Now TV pass. It seems whatever I tip Lincoln to do, you need to bet on the opposite outcome.

Looking on social media, I'm told we should go 4-4-2 again and use the width, but with Harry off form, who else plays out wide? Cameron Stewart hasn't impressed, Jordan Williams looks better as part of a front three than an outright winger, Nathan is at Salford, frankly we don't actually have the players to play 4-4-2 anymore. 4-3-3 makes us tough to break down but relies on the opposition having to come out and attack us. When there was space behind, we found it, especially Matt Green who was excellent again today. On Thursday, Exeter should come out and get at us, which could mean another game like Coventry away. I wouldn't say we'll definitely win, us and the Grecians are as evenly matched as they come, no matter what Sky said.

Neal Eardley whipped a cross in from the flanks towards the end of the game, which the commentator referred to as "Ear-der-lee hoofs a ball to Rhead," and I immediately muted for the last ten minutes. A cross from 20 yards up the field on the flank was classed as a hoof. I suppose he hadn't had enough opportunity to say the word hoof though, so he had to get it in. Ear-der-lee apparently once played for Blackpool in the Premier League, so you'd think a commentator might be able to pronounce his name right. I just had enough.

As in many play off semi-final first-legs, neither side wanted to over commit towards the end and make a slip. I've seen some people say how disgusting it was we were playing for a draw, but we've had injuries to carry and there's 90 minutes left next week. There was no point in over committing and conceding a stupid goal, we absolutely could not give them something to defend on Thursday.

I turned the sound back up for Danny's interview, or rather two questions. I was surprised he said he'd like to see more protection for Rheady, but when the programme cut to the studio I was even more surprised to hear Stuart McCall comment negatively about it, starting with 'the manager there has said'. The manager? The manager Stuart? Did you not learn his name you disrespectful git?

Matty Taylor was then asked which manager of the two would be happier and to his credit he just said 'Paul Tisdale, obviously'. For me, it ended an excruciating 90 minutes of amateur coverage, I turned off and reached for my laptop. One particular highlight was when Matt Rhead went up for a header, the commentator said to Lee Hendrie something like 'was it like that in your day?' Hendrie, a half-decent pundit, commented back that he wasn't the most physical player due to his stature before the fawning reply came back, "yes, but you could play a bit couldn't you Lee, played top flight and Championship." Yes, he did, he also played badly for Tamworth against Lincoln which, to his credit, he mentioned.

It's half time, nobody drew first blood and the advantage surely now lays with our hosts (or at last that is what the experts think. I wasn't sure, but thankfully we have Sky to clear up these pertinent points). It's not going to be easy, apparently it's a long journey down to Exeter, although one assumes they'll be making that journey too, otherwise they'll still be in Lincoln on Thursday night.

Do I think we'll win? My thoughts haven't changed since the game kicked off. Either side could win, we're as equally matched as any side we've met this season and the game will likely be decided by one goal, one slip or one tactical mistake. Exeter could slip up, come at us early and leave gaps at the back for our pacey players to exploit. They could keep it tight, just like the first leg, meaning it will be another slow, edgy affair.

I know one thing, I might be watching it on Sky again but I will not endure anymore of their Fisher Price research or stereotypical punditry. I'd rather do my own commentary, playing the parts of failed footballer and ill-informed commentator myself. In fact, I'm quite excited about doing so.

Never under-estimate what we've achieved – whatever the outcome

May 17, 2018

Imagine, kicking off a season in August, battling against opponents, referees, weather, injuries and everything else a season throws at you.

Missing chances to win games, snatching three points in games where you barely deserve one. Players coming in, players leaving, uncertainty, speculation and transfer window madness. There's been cup distractions, heroes made and villains revealed and all of it, the whole melting pot of emotion, passion and despair comes down to one 90-minute game in the warm May evening sun.

It is both the inherent beauty of the play offs and their down fall too. They create these huge matches which in this instance only 350 of our fans can watch live, but it's such a pressure cooker atmosphere that one slip, one mistake can break a whole season. I say 'break', we never expected back to back promotions, nor a Wembley appearance, so a slip tonight doesn't break a season at all. Our season has been tremendous and tonight, the ride can be extended for one more game. If not, nobody can look back and call 2017/18 a failure and, if they do, they need to take a long hard look at themselves.

I always laugh when people say, 'what if we'd beaten Morecambe', or 'if only we'd been more clinical', or even 'if Billy hadn't been sent off at County'. Those people are the glass half empty fans and occasionally, I'm one of them. What we should be thinking is: what if Raggs hadn't met JMD's corner away at Swindon? What if Luke hadn't headed that magnificent winner against Colchester? What if Stockbridge hadn't sent Rawson off for Accrington against us in December?

The season isn't ever defined during a single one those 46 games, not when you finish top seven. However tonight, we might well have one of those questions seemingly defining our whole campaign, but if we do, it has to be taken in context of the season. If Matt Green misses a sitter, if Neal Eardley loses his winger, if the referee throws a red card at Bozzie, we have to take it in context. No one moment changes a season and we have had enough to control to finish outside the top seven and be sat at home doing nothing tonight.

There's no pre-match analysis of any value to be done. We know Exeter, this is our fourth clash and the third in two months so there's no secret weapon, no big surprises. It is two equally matched teams going at each other one last time for the right to travel to Wembley. I've said if we stop Stockley, we stop Exeter, but I think if we stop Boateng we'll be half way there. They know we'll be trying to hit Rhead and they'll try to deal with that. It could well decided by a penalty or penalties, if it is then so be it. Past meetings, shots on target, all that jazz is irrelevant. It's a cup final and the only form that matters is the form we show on the pitch tonight.

It's a tough evening for me, as you know I could have been at the Alexandra Palace as a finalist in the Football Blogging Awards. It's incredibly hard knowing I'm in the final ten once again in an event which is the 'Oscars' of the online content creation world but won't be there to see the ceremony. One-time Imps fanzine editor Darren Bugg has kindly agreed to represent me in London, he was one of the earliest Lincoln City fanzine editors when he brought out The Banker and it seems fitting that someone who started to create content thirty years ago is there this evening flying our flag. He's also the NewsHound who has put up several Imps videos this season and he'll be representing me, he'll be representing us, the Stacey West. This site isn't just me, it's all my contributors and most importantly, it is all of the readers too.

I would desperately love to win the award, either the judges award or the voted award, but just being in the final ten once again is incredible. Running this site isn't easy (especially not these last few weeks), creating content on a daily basis is challenging, especially content you want to read and interact with. I don't ever expect people to agree with what I write all the time, but I do hope to engage you, to entertain you and to get you arguing over pints in pubs or in your living rooms. Whatever the outcome, thank you for voting me to the final ten.

May 17th, 2018. A date where all of my dreams could come true, a proper national award recognising my writing and a place in the Wembley play offs, or a day that could close with us apparently achieving nothing at all. Even if it is nothing at all, you and I must remember that to even be in this position, semi-finals and finalist on the awards, is a tremendous honour and achievement. To end the day with nothing is not failure, it is not disappointment, it is the end of a chapter and the culmination of real achievement. The next chapter will start the day after and if I'm not mistaken, every chapter recently has been as good as the last. Remember that, whatever the outcome.

Now, go out and give it your all City, you've already done us proud but I would never, ever bet against you doing it again and again. Wherever you are, enjoy today. Its what life is all about.

That's all folks, thanks for coming – Exeter 3-1 Imps
May 18, 2018

That's your lot chaps, 2017/18 draws to a close with defeat in deepest Devon and the curtains come down on another remarkable season.

Putting the controversy surrounding the EFL Trophy aside, we've won silverware and competed at the right end of the table. we've made the play-offs, a great achievement for our first season back in the league, but we've come up short.

Tonight, for the first time in our four encounters, Exeter were better than us. I called Boateng earlier as the one player who we needed to keep quiet, but in truth they had three or four players on their game this evening. We had several who looked dead on their feet, victims of our 'quality over quantity' squad policy. I'm not saying Danny got that wrong, we finished in the top seven, but eventually the fact we're a work in progress cost us dearly.

There's no point in assessing the match too much is there? They scored a goal which was poor from our point, but for thirty minutes we looked like a mid-table side who found themselves in the play offs by accident. It may have been fatigue, it may have been players carrying injuries, but Exeter could have been two up.

Of course, we equalised and for a moment I thought it was on. If that had been allowed, would the game have changed? Maybe, maybe not. Rheady was pushed, he did handle it and it shouldn't have been a goal. I'll tell you what we've been punished for; Rhead going down too easily throughout the season. If it was a push it wasn't a big one and I guarantee if I squared up to him in a nightclub and gave him a push of the same force, he doesn't budge. Referees are wise to it I'm afraid. All the assistant referee has seen is a hand, all the referee has seen is the goal. We can feel hard done by, but taking off the rose-tinted glasses, just for a second, will give some perspective. If that goal is against us, we're in uproar.

The manner with which we finished the first half gave me hope we'd come out all guns blazing, but Hiram Boateng's moment of brilliance ended the game as a contest. Their third looked to add a shine to the score line they probably deserved, our late consolation at least meant we had something to cheer. Yes, there was a nailed-on penalty towards the end, just as there was at the Bank, but they weren't given. Remember, Luke handled in the first half in the area and it wasn't given either.

We've every right to be indignant about the scenes at the end, their fans attacking our players and officials is not on. I'm not convinced the 'special dispensation' they got to limit the number of fans we could take was fair either, but those factors only served to create an advantage, they still had to perform. Nobody can complain about Boateng's dominant performance or Pym's solid showing in the first leg. The end was unsavoury, but the result was, on the balance of play, entirely fair.

Right now, it hurts. I hate Lincoln losing and to lose in the play-offs for a sixth time stings almost as bad as my back does right now. Perspective is easily spoken of, I made much of it this morning, but right now I don't have the balance that I had then. I'm upset we lost, I'm upset we conceded so many goals and I could easily point to things in the season I believe were not right. How would that help? On the whole this has been a tremendous campaign, one with a Wembley final in it and a play off assault too. Yeah, we had a small squad which ultimately cost us but we're one year older and one year wiser. Danny and Nicky are going nowhere and the best players are staying put too. Recruitment in the summer is going to be crucial and there's going to be tough decisions to make, but when we look back tomorrow or in a week's time, it won't be with a feeling of anger or resentment.

I've seen lots of Grimsby fans loving the fact we are going to be in the same league as them next season, I'm delighted they can find solace from their own failings in our too seven finish not ending up as it should. That's what rivalry is all about, isn't it? It doesn't make it easier, rather petulantly I've blocked some of the worst offenders on Twitter because, when all is said and done, tonight hurts like hell. I really liked our display against them but, being truthful, I thought the shadow banner was a bit much. It's given them material to be used in the event of a resurgence on their part, something I can see happening.

Recently, I've blocked out intense pain by popping trammies and diazepam, but this stinging won't go away with a helping of drugs. It will soften with a look back at the season, the big moments like Coventry away, like Crewe away, like Grimsby at home. Once a hangover begins to shift, you can look back and enjoy the night out. Right now, I have a hangover from losing tonight's game. Tomorrow, once that subsides I'll be back to my usual self, toasting the great season we've had and understanding my own satisfaction shouldn't some from industry recognition, but from the fact you lot still read and like what I do. Roll on tomorrow morning.

Eardley Stays – Two-year deal agreed for Player of the Year
May 18, 2018

After weeks of anticipation, the club have finally announced that Player of the Year and all round great footballer Neal Eardley will remain at the club for two seasons.

After last night's defeat at Exeter there had been speculation he may have played his final matches for the club, instead from the ashes of our play off campaign rises the news of him remaining with us for the foreseeable future. Eardley has been a revelation since signing a six-month deal in the summer, triggering an extension in January after a series of displays that wouldn't have looked out of place in the Championship.

He's been a key part a defensive line that has kept 15 league clean sheets this season, with ESPN.com crediting him with 10 assists from his 54 outings. He missed just two league games, matches we conceded a total of eight goals in, against Crewe and Luton. He only missed two of our Checkatrade Trophy matches, against Accrington and Everton U21s.

Danny Cowley is understandably delighted to be able to keep the former Welsh international at Sincil Bank.

"Neal has had a brilliant season, he's brought a wealth of experience, he's technically excellent and has been such a consistent performer," Cowley said. "We're delighted to be able to extend his contract, it's something we've been really motivated to do since January. It's taken a bit of time, but there's always been a real motivation from both parties to make it happen."

The Imps boss was full of praise for Neal's hard work and dedication, but also to the supporters who he believes have made the full-back feel at home since his arrival.

"The supporters and the way that they have taken Neal to their hearts and the way they have supported him has played a big part in the extension," he added. "He's just a top, top player. He's played right at the highest level of the game, and you can see that with the way he conducts himself and works on the training pitch."

The news will go some way to softening the blow of last night's defeat at Exeter, knowing that the majority of our squad who have reached the top seven will be kept together. Eardley had perhaps been the last player with a question mark over his head, but him signing the extension now leaves us free to recruit without too much worry about the experienced players moving on.

Five things we learned from 2017/18
June 5, 2018

In pulling together the final copy for my upcoming book, I realised I hadn't done on over view of the season. Maybe the disappointment of Exeter stung hard, maybe the almost immediate contract news on Neal Eardley pushed me towards next season, but there was no overall assessment of the season.

In essence, there was no final chapter, my book would end with Exeter defeat and nothing more, something that wouldn't do justice to a good first season back. We won a Wembley final, we finished top seven and we competed with everyone we played. No side outplayed us twice, only Exeter beat us twice and they needed four goes to do it. We beat the champions twice too, proving on our day we're a match for anyone.

Does any of that matter though? After all, we're still in League Two next year, we still have to go to Grimsby and they're not really in our shadow as some sections of our support thought we could proclaim. Okay, our managers are tested and theirs is not, but we're separated by miles and not divisions this coming season.

Danny strikes me as a manager who will not sit around in his office congratulating himself on a good first season, but he will analyse, looking for points to develop. That's manager speak for criticism, I was taught it on one of those god-awful courses all managers go on at some point. We sat around the room and came up with 'developmental points' for each other, basically looking for nice ways to tell each other what they did wrong. I'm not going to tell Danny what he did wrong, I'm not qualified nor do I profess to know better than him, but instead of a season review, I thought I'd end with five things we learned last season.

5: The loan market wasn't our friend

For whatever reason, the loan market was not kind to us last season. I suppose getting Sean Raggett back made it seem as though we'd done really well, but he was the only real hit in a season of misses, not just with players but also opportunities.

Raggs, Ginnelly, Dickie and Maguire-Drew. You know what strikes me about that? There's room for one more and that point baffled me all season. We had the scope to bring in another player, we hadn't reached our limits and yet for some reason, we didn't utilise the last remaining place. The obvious position we needed to strengthen was a striker and whilst Danny says he won't bring in players who don't improve the squad, surely any striker at all would have been useful at some point?

Ginnelly would have been an Imp now in my opinion had he not suffered an early injury, but his form dipped and I suspect Burnley wanted him playing regular football. Dickie was another disappointment, clearly earmarked by Danny as the long-term successor for Raggs he showed some good form then just disappeared. Was it an injury, or was his Oxford move on the table and Danny knew not to persevere? The thinking was he joined permanently in January, I'm sure of that, but again we were let down.

Speaking of let downs, Maguire Drew. I'll say no more. Actually, I will. Maguire Drew is clearly a talented boy but it struck me had didn't have the work rate we require and I thought his positional sense was way off. He could kick a ball nicely, but so can I. Sometimes.

Danny Rowe was a coup in the loan market and he showed what a good player he was, but was he really a success? Two superb goals gave us a glimpse of what he could do, but either injury or the tactical change seemed to side line him as the season progressed. Jordan Williams was average, nothing more. Ryan Allsop and Scott Wharton both did well, but yet again we loaned four and had space for five.

I feel the loan market let us down a bit, both in quality and how we managed to play it. Maybe the players weren't available, but the truth is part of the reason we came up short at the end of the season was that some players took much of the load whilst certainly in the first half of the season, the loan players took very little.

4: Tactics

This could be a good thing or a bad thing, but through the season we played three different systems, 4-2-3-1, 4-3-3 and of course 4-4-2. The big question is, did we play any of them efficiently enough, or were we a jack of all trades, master of none?

Remember, this piece isn't me criticising the team, merely looking where things might have been better. I think we had a great season, play offs and a cup win are not to be sniffed at, but a manger's role isn't to simply praise and neither is mine.

The 4-3-3, for me, marginalised too many key players. Harry Anderson never settled in it as he's an out and out winger and it also put Danny Rowe in the shade too. We tried a few different players coming off Rheady and Green, but none shone. Jordan Williams looked good against Grimsby, but we go back to the three-striker problem. You sensed when Danny started playing all three of the forwards he'd more or less just said "fuck it, why not," and rolled with it. That is why I didn't ever feel confident in the play offs because it felt as though it all came too early. Danny found a system he liked but didn't have the players to fit it, which contradicted the early part of the season.

We started 4-4-2 and whilst we did have the players to suit that, the two central midfielders being defensive drew much criticism from the keyboard warriors. I liked Bozzie and Alex in the middle of the park, but the problem then was Rheady's mobility. The big man needed to be able to do more running to fill the gap but couldn't. That meant a reliance on the long ball, but any flick on had to be chased by Matt Green. He then played a lone striker role as the big man caught up with play, leaving us looking shot shy in games against Crawley and Cambridge. Had the wingers been up to scratch it might have worked better, but only Harry put in consistent performances out wide before the system change.

Then there was the 4-2-3-1, a way of getting the two midfield players and another creator in the mix. This eliminated Matt Rhead but meant a new approach of going in to feet and heaping reliance on the ten role. I think Billy Knott was the only player we had who could fill it, but sadly we know things didn't work out there. Three systems, all contributing to a play-off spot, but none ever without their obvious faults. Going into next season I suspect we might remain 4-3-3, but now Alex has gone, who knows? Much depends on recruitment, meaning that the players will define the system.

The positive of course is that we never mastered one approach but still had the work rate and application to win trophies. Imagine if one of these systems clicks, or if the new arrivals fill some of the roles we were missing. It could be carnage.

3: League Two wasn't better than we imagined

Possibly we all fell foul of fawning a little over the quality in the division after a tough start, but by Christmas I'd argue that we showed League Two wasn't 'all that'. After the draw with Morecambe a few journalists and the likes of myself claimed maybe it was harder than we thought but by May, there we were in the top seven.

The teams at the bottom were better than those at the bottom of the National League, granted, and the lack of part time teams meant rarely did our fitness yield us major gains in the final stages of matches, but all those sides we faced had issues, weaknesses and nobody was significantly better than us. I maintain the best side we saw were either Coventry at our place or Luton away, both teams that had spent relatively big on a striker or two. Outside of that, did anyone really stand out? Did we really feel the competition was any tougher than Boreham Wood away or Eastleigh at home? I wasn't on the pitch so maybe I'm out of order, but I think the final outcome shows we were maybe just slow out of the blocks, rather than the standard being that much better than we anticipated. After all, do you really think Danny Cowley under estimated anyone?

2: Three strikers is not enough

Whenever I think of our striker situation I cannot help but see the words 'the Fourth Man', which for me defined our season. As early as pre-season Danny was looking for that fourth striker, Ade Azeez wasn't far from signing before a ball had been kicked, but all season it eluded us. Ollie Hawkins and Simeon Akinola were two we lost in August, in January it was allegedly Karlan Ahearne-Grant as well as names such as Alex Revell and Shay McCarten. Danny knows he needed another option but he refused to compromise on value for money or quality. As it turns out, we did okay with three, but put simply, it can't be the same next year.

Matt Green's drought in the autumn cost him a 20+ goal haul which he would have fully deserved. You'll not hear me calling Green, he is by far the best striker we have at the club, an all-rounder with attributes in the channels, on the flank and out wide. He might not be a 'natural goalscorer' to most due to some of his misses, but he got into positions to score on numerous occasions. Matt Rhead is a great footballer but is labelled for his size and maybe hits the deck too often. Is he targeted and the victim, or is he the aggressor looking to con referees? It's a bit of both and at times it worked for us, at times it did not. Ollie Palmer is unconventional, a wild card that is best played towards the end of a game when even we don't know what is needed to win it. All three have useful elements to their game, but three is simply not enough for a side such as ours. How many did we have last season? Marriott, Rhead, Margetts, Bonne, Robinson, Southwell, Muldoon and that's just off the top of my head. That's almost three times as many and I'm sure if I really thought about it I could come up with one more (Alex Simmons).

We simply cannot afford to go into next season with three, but Danny has already acknowledged that. I don't think we need to be throwing £150k at a Dennis, or £100k at a Hemmings because I firmly believe that we can turn a player who doesn't appear to be prolific on paper into a good centre forward. The driving force behind our success this season was the ability to get more out of players than they were really capable of. Ollie Palmer and Elliott Whitehouse are two prime examples, both struggled early doors but you could see Danny squeezing every last drop out of them. At times he did the same with Matt Green, playing him here, there and everywhere. I don't need to see '20' in last season's 'goals for' column of a new signing, I just need to know that Danny believes he's the right man for the job. Aside from the loan deals I don't think he's made a bad move in the permanent market and perhaps that reticence is the reason. However, this season it must be put right.

1: It was a great return to the Football League

So we never found a tactic to settle on, the loan players let us down, we struggled with only three forward players and et we still won a Wembley final and got to the play-offs too. It is easy to look at things that weren't quite right, but what about the things that were? What about the attitude shown by almost all of our squad, whenever they were dropped? Luke Waterfall perhaps epitomised that more than any, lost his place twice and yet still ended up holding a trophy aloft at Wembley. Tactically we never settled, but we outfought Coventry who were eventually promoted and did the same to Exeter at our place. Our cup run pitted us against a virtually full-strength Peterborough as well as the cream of the Premier League's kids and we still came up smelling of roses.

We attracted some really good players to the club, some of whom we've not seen the best of. James Wilson and Tom Pett will both be great for the first team, Freck's return hasn't perhaps been as dominating as some hoped but he's still scored goals and settled well. Michael Bostwick came here, maybe because of location but he signed a new deal because of the set up. There's a training ground coming, that means even better players and even more time with the players for our excellent staff.

It is easy to get caught up in what didn't go right and even now, people are worrying on social media. Players leaving causes concern, the training ground progress, in fact anything there is to moan about, someone will. The fact is that we're moving forward as a club, becoming more professional by the day and that will be reflected not only in the personnel we attract but also the way we conduct our business. The Football League has changed since we were last in it and this season we've had to adapt quickly. Next time out were a year older, a year wiser and a year further on. The club I see before me today is virtually unrecognisable from the one that won the National League. Some ask if that is a good thing, if the commercial element is us losing sight of our ethos, but I argue against that. If we're going to progress we have to become smarter with the incoming, be it sponsorship, seating or prawn sandwich bars. If we want to compete with everyone in the division then we need the new training ground, bricks and mortar buildings and facilities to match.

Nobody is forgetting who we are or where we've come from, but we're progressing and even if we don't sign a player tomorrow or Wednesday, it doesn't mean we're losing ground. I've picked three fundamental issues I feel held us back last season and it was still a record breaker, the second successive season we've lifted silverware and our first trip to Wembley. We were new to the league, a little naïve to the quality early doors and we still finished seventh. Some fans got delusions of grandeur when we went third at Christmas, but when all is said and done, this was another great season. Imagine if everything suddenly clicks next season, we could be in real danger of lifting a third trophy in as many years. Now, that would be something worth writing a book about.

The Stacey West – A Season in Blogs 2017/18

Pos	Team	Pld	W	D	L	GF	GA	GD	Pts
1	Accrington Stanley	46	29	6	11	76	46	30	93
2	Luton Town	46	25	13	8	94	46	48	88
3	Wycombe Wanderers	46	24	12	10	79	60	19	84
4	Exeter City	46	24	8	14	64	54	10	80
5	Notts County	46	21	14	11	71	48	23	77
6	Coventry City	46	22	9	15	64	47	17	75
7	Lincoln City	46	20	15	11	64	48	16	75
8	Mansfield Town	46	18	18	10	67	52	15	72
9	Swindon Town	46	20	8	18	67	65	2	68
10	Carlisle United	46	17	16	13	62	54	8	67
11	Newport County	46	16	16	14	56	58	-2	64
12	Cambridge United	46	17	13	16	56	60	-4	64
13	Colchester United	46	16	14	16	53	52	1	62
14	Crawley Town	46	16	11	19	58	66	-8	59
15	Crewe Alexandra	46	17	5	24	62	75	-13	56
16	Stevenage	46	14	13	19	60	65	-5	55
17	Cheltenham Town	46	13	12	21	67	73	-6	51
18	Grimsby Town	46	13	12	21	42	66	-24	51
19	Yeovil Town	46	12	12	22	59	75	-16	48
20	Port Vale	46	11	14	21	49	67	-18	47
21	Forest Green Rovers	46	13	8	25	54	77	-23	47
22	Morecambe	46	9	19	18	41	56	-15	46
23	Barnet	46	12	10	24	46	65	-19	46
24	Chesterfield	46	10	8	28	47	83	-36	38

League Two Play-Offs

12 May 2018	Lincoln City 0-0 Exeter City
12 May 2018	Coventry City 1-1 Notts County
17 May 2018	Exeter City 3-1 Lincoln City
18 May 2018	Notts County 1-4 Coventry City
28 May 2018	Coventry City 3-1 Exeter City

The Players - Keepers

Ryan Allsop
Apps 20 Goals 0

Part of me, the nostalgic part, the little piece of e that is loyal to Paul Farman, wanted Allsop to fail. Not in a catastrophic way, not because I dislike the lad, but because I hoped Josh Vickers injury would give Farms the Football League matches he's craved for so long.

I feel bad writing that now, but I have to be honest and, as a staunch Paul Farman fan, Ryan Allsop represented something more than just a loan keeper. His debut against Chelsea offered up the chance to fail, instead he pulled off a penalty save to win us the tie. Then, away at Cambridge a clean sheet.

In fact, Ryan Allsop didn't put a foot wrong. Blackpool fans were full of bad things to say when he joined, he can't command his area, his shot stopping is poor and a host of other stuff, but as his tenure went on it proved to be incorrect. His command of the area could be better, but his shot stopping is second to none. He's pulled off several wonder saves in the sticks, not least that clawed effort at Wembley which kept us in the tie. He played two Checkatrade Trophy games but he earned his winner's medal.

Is he as influential for us as Christy Pym is for Exeter? No, but that isn't through his own fault, our defence don't let him down too often. He's not a wonder keeper, he's not been a revelation, but he's certainly come in and done the exact job we needed. I was asked in the run up to the Wembley final if Farms should play and I said 'no'. Why? Because we needed our better keeper in goal and Ryan Allsop had won me over.

He's a driven player, he wants to play higher and I don't think he'll come here next season. He's going to pass through as part of history with a reputation for saving penalties, (hopefully five more at the end of Thursday's game), but he's certainly been an astute signing, considering how quickly Danny had to bring him in.

Ryan Allsop won me over, he's not the first player this season, he won't be the last, but he's a cracking lad who I sincerely hope finds himself third-tier football next season, be it with us or someone else.

Paul Farman
Apps 18 Goals 0

I was sickened and angered by the level of abuse thrown at Farms in the middle of the season. The 2-2 draw with Swindon sticks in my mind the most, when he palmed shots away only for a striker to slam the rebound home. You know who else did that recently? Christy Pym of Exeter, only Elliott didn't slam the rebound home. The pundits gave the plaudits to Pym for the save, our fans gave Farman disgusting abuse on social media. They almost seemed happy we'd conceded as it proved their 'point'.

Everyone knows I'm a fan of Paul Farman, he's a cracking personality and someone who served this club superbly over several years. His displays last season were as good as any in the National League and for him to have Football League appearances to his name is the culmination of his dreams. I know that from speaking to him last year.

This year will have hurt Farms and to a degree it's been sad for me to watch as he's one of my favourite players, but there's little doubt that Josh Vickers is a very good keeper. Danny gave Farms a chance, but the Mansfield Town game at home didn't leave him in the best light. A keeper who commands his area should have stopped that cross before Danny Rose gave them the lead.

I didn't blame him for the Notts County goals, but he found himself dropped just a couple of days afterwards. Josh Vickers didn't really put a foot wrong, so there wasn't a chance for Farms to get back into the side. When he did, critics were quick to latch onto his errors, or perceived errors.

Look at Accrington in the Checkatrade Trophy. Sean McConville beat him with an absolute thunderbolt and the keyboard warriors were out, but few commended his tremendous double save in the dying embers to keep us in the game. For some reason our long-serving keeper had become the scapegoat for a section of support, which I find desperately unfair.

The problem Farms has now is clear. Vickers injury meant a cover keeper came in, but the fact Allsop came in and stayed between the sticks will surely be a concern for the likeable Geordie. He has a year to run on his contract, but will he be happy playing second fiddle to Josh? Will Danny be happy having a keeper on the bench whom he didn't deem suitable to play regularly in the second half of the season?

It's a big summer for Paul Farman, one I hope sees him come back determined to prove the boo boys wrong, even if that is in cup competitions and for the occasional league game.

Josh Vickers
Apps 20 Goals 0

Lots of people erroneously suggested we'd signed Josh Vickers on loan in the summer. Just to clarify, we haven't. Vickers is our player, he signed a two-year deal and when he returns to fitness, I imagine he'll be our number one.

When he signed I had visions of him being another Paul Pettinger or Simon Rayner, the guy who appears on the team sheet but never, ever gets a game. We knew Danny would give him a run out in the odd competition, but that early League Cup match at Rotherham got me thinking. Here was a player who could push Farms for the number one spot, he was all killer and no filler.

The game in which Josh Vickers came of age, in my eyes, was one we lost. Coventry turned us over 2-1 at the Bank, they were a superb side that day and had Jodi Jones remained fit or Duckens Nazon not been recalled, I think they would have been top three. However, Vickers kept the goal tally down to two with an outstanding display, commanding in the box but as quick to react to shots as any I'd seen for years.

He reminded me a little of Ian Bowling, another keeper I always held in high regard. Maybe it was my memory as a child but Bowling was an outstanding shot stopper and a keeper who commanded his area with absolute certainty. I liked Bowling a lot, I liked Vickers a lot too.

The one thing that went against him was his distribution, his kicking wasn't as good as Farman. When we look to go from back to front quickly we need a keeper with a huge kick, but Vickers didn't bring that. With hindsight, it could have been the early onset of the injury that affected him, but at the time it was an attribute he didn't bring to the table.

The 4-2 defeat at Luton saw his final action of the season, a short spell in goal curtailed by injury. Paul Farman's spell as number one ended in a four-goal blitz at Notts County, Josh Vickers lost his place after a similar mauling at Luton. He wasn't to blame that day though, it was a crazy game coming at the end of a packed period of games. Those matches took their toll and the big stopper wasn't seen again. He will be though, make no mistake about that.

I feel Josh Vickers is the best of the three we've seen this season. I think he's more confident than Ryan Allsop in the air, his shot stopping is comparable and maybe his distribution will improve with his recovery from injury. There's little doubt he is our number one though, a spot he earned by waiting for his chance and taking it when it came his way

The Players – Defenders

Michael Bostwick
Apps 54 (1) Goals 6

I didn't know whether to put Bozzie as a midfielder or a defender, but ultimately I've given him a page of his own. He's comfortable sat between the two so he's the last defender of the series and the first midfielder, of sorts.

Like Neal Eardley, he's been a stand out player this season and his new two-year deal is a sign of significant intent of behalf of the club and the player. He's a huge asset in League Two, a massive player in League One and as we're going to be in one of those divisions next season, we're lucky to have him in our side.

I used the phrase uncomplicated for Luke Waterfall and to a degree, Bozzie is the same. When he's at the back he's a mammoth, hugely effective in the air and clearly terrifying to play against.. He's an intimidating presence, not just by his looks and size, but by the way he prowls the pitch, snapping into challenges possibly best described as 'reducers'.

In the midfield he offers something a little different, an unsettling physical presence but comfortable on the ball. I couldn't see him going on a mazy run or pulling off tricks and flicks, but he's comfortable distributing the ball, winning the ball and covering the space when it arises.

He's also an organiser and an experienced head who has served us well. Is it a coincidence that the only game he missed we also lost, just like Neal Eardley? They're a pair of class players who aren't a classic pairing in terms of position or how they interact, but they do represent two vastly experienced players who have 'been there, done that'.

Bozzie is also always on the prowl for a goal and although he hasn't scored as many as he might have liked, there's always a chance with him picking the ball up on the edge of the area. I suspect our team orders are to collect bits and pieces and retain possession, whereas once in a while you just want to see him smash a thunderbolt towards goal. He's missed a few, but they won't all go high, wide and handsome.

If I had chosen a Player of the Year, I would have picked Bozzie over Neal, just. His versatility eclipses that of Neal Eardley, but he brings not just an option but a different style of play when he changes position. the no nonsense defender who reads the game well is replaced by a rampaging midfielder who wins balls and breaks up play. He's also reticent with his tackles in the face of suspensions, proving he's far more than just a long-haired warrior hacking at limbs for a living.

Rob Dickie
Apps 21 (2) Goals 0

Mr Dickie, the 'heir apparent', the man brought in to ultimately succeed Sean Raggett in our defence. He even looked like him, perhaps there was a master plan to send him off to Norwich in January instead.

The truth behind the move was that Dickie had impressed for Cheltenham in two spells and Danny hoped he was signing the new hope for us at centre half. He clearly wasn't a 'like for like' with Raggs, but he was an able and competent player. He liked to bring the ball out but didn't have the same aerial domination as our crowd favourite.

He did have one thing though, the gaffers trust, which is why he pushed Luke Waterfall onto the bench. Did Luke struggle to step up to the Football League, or did Danny feel Rob Dickie was a better player? Some felt Luke was discarded too quickly, others saw a quality in Dickie that they hoped would develop into something more.

Dickie made 21 starts in all competitions, a number that seems very high now when compared to his stand out moments. He fitted into the defence, that much is true, but writing this I can't recall a game where I came away thinking he was the best player on the park.

He was what I like to call a 'casualty of Colchester', one of three players who did not fare well in our lacklustre defeat down south. After that he started just two more games, Stevenage and Forest Green, before a surprise move to Oxford.

I do wonder if the Oxford move was something that came up a couple of months before the window opened and that led to him being used less frequently. Danny did discuss the possibility of him signing permanently in January, I could envisage those talks being approached, Dickie saying that Oxford were in for him, League One and closer to home, so we used him frugally in order to become less reliant when he did go. One thing is for sure, his rather unexpected departure at the same time as Sean Raggett left us in a bit of a hole.

After they left, we won two League games in nine. Had we converted three of those drawn games to wins, or won two that we lost, we'd be third and not even bothering about Thursday night.

As for Rob Dickie, I bear him no malice. I wouldn't say he was as good as I'd hoped when he first signed, but he settled well in a new team and left before we saw the best of him. He's gone on to establish himself in the Oxford back four which is testament to his ability, but he won't be fondly recalled by many Imps fans in the future.

Neal Eardley
Apps 53 (1) Goals 1

Seriously, what can I say about Neal Eardley that hasn't been said already? He arrived at Sincil Bank with three years of injury hell behind him, missed one league game (which we lost 4-1 at home) and secured the Player of the Season award. In terms of debut seasons, I'd say that was a good one.

Of course, Neal has an advantage over most of our players, he's played Premier League football, not just a couple of games as a kid either, but a full season for Blackpool. He's represented Wales too, giving him the sort of pedigree you don't usually find at this level.

If someone asked me his strengths I'm not sure where I'd start. His positioning is great, he reads the game superbly and he's cooler than the Fonz in December. His delivery into the box is top class, he has eleven assists this season in all competitions and even chipped in with a goal, one of the best we've seen this season, to beat Cheltenham 1-0.

He's versatile too, he can operate on the left or right, but it is the latter where he looks most at home. He rarely puts a foot wrong, is strong in the tackle and even stronger in possession. I've said before he has no business plying his trade in League Two, my fear is if we're still here next season, he might not be. Sources tell me the main issue regarding his new deal is a possible relocation, but that could be a good thing because it suggests a two-year deal is on the table.

If he plays like he did this season throughout his Imps career, I'd give him five years and be done with it. Without a doubt, one of our best players this season.

Sam Habergham
Apps 39 (1) Goals 0

He's the steady seven of the National League campaign, the improving left back that ended the season with a couple of vital free kicks and near cult status. Unfortunately, the step up to league football has not been kind to him.

I like Sam, both as a player and a person. He's very measured when you speak to him, articulate and intelligent but guarded too. He won't ever give you a controversial quote or an ambiguous answer that can be misinterpreted. He is a thinking footballer, one who will go on to be a suit and tie after the game, maybe with the PFA or the FA. That's the impression I get.

This season though, he's struggled in my opinion. He missed out on pre-season and the first few weeks of the campaign just as he did last time out, but I'm not sure he ever caught back up. Whereas Neal has all those assists, Sam has just four and not a single goal to his name. Defender's aren't measured on their attacking prowess alone, but Sam hasn't proven as adept at bombing on at this level.

Defensively he's not been bad, this review isn't intended to say he's been a poor player, but he has been a subtle seven rather than a steady seven, and whereas last season he raised to and eight or nine on occasion, this season he did not.

He signed a new deal earlier in the campaign and hopefully with a year under his belt and a full pre-season, we can start to see the real Sam Habergham once again. He hasn't been terrible this season, not at all, but there's more to come from him. I also still believe that if we were to go up, he's League One quality, despite his average showing this campaign.

Sean Long
Apps 19 (7) Goals 0

Sean Long is a good full back, he's young and learning his trade but he started the season well with Neal on the left-hand side. I wouldn't put him anywhere near as good as Neal, absolutely not, but for me he was comparable for most of the season with Sam on the left. Sean suffered because we managed to attract a Championship quality player in the position he plays. How harsh is that?

He's made 13 starts this season, most of which came in August and September. Through October he did spend some time at right back with Neal on the left, but eventually that was always going to change. I feel bad for Sean because I'm mentioning Neal Eardley as much as I'm mentioning him and this is meant to be a look at his campaign. He was given the number two shirt which tells you what the intention for him was. Football is a cruel game though and it has dealt the likeable 23-year old a rough hand this season.

Sean's a great character, always ready to entertain and interact off the pitch and growing as a footballer on it. He's had the odd cameo, his 95th minute introduction at Wembley might not have seen him make an impact, but I'm sure he'll cherish the memories nonetheless.

In a season where we've had a threadbare squad, Sean Long has been the ultimate squad player, young and hungry but having to wait for his limited chances. I don't think he's let the side down at all and I would be very surprised if he wasn't part of the side next season.

Sean Raggett
Apps 28 Goals 3

28 appearances, three goals and more goodwill than most players amass in a whole career. It seems almost unbelievable that Sean Raggett was a Lincoln player five months ago, we've been talking about his departure (or potential departure) for such a long time.

Sean's header won us the game away at Swindon, a game that had we not won we wouldn't have made the top seven. Look, I know it is easy to pinpoint any game and lay the praise at someone's feet, but that was a crucial win at a big point in the season. His goal also saw off Accrington in the Checkatrade Trophy, another crucial moment in our successful season.

Aside from that, he was the one of perhaps only two who stepped up to League football without an issue. Luke Waterfall was in and out of the side, Rheady struggled at first and Sam hasn't been himself either. Sean Raggett just fitted into the Football League, just as Alex Woodyard did. His step up was effortless, his qualities obvious for all to see which is why Norwich came in for him when they did.

Like most, I got a bit sick of the 'he's on the bench for Norwich' saga that raged all through January, but it is only a measure of how much he impacted the side, not only this season but also last. There's no doubt his departure hit us hard too, he left shortly before Josh Vickers got injured and I felt we lost some of the rear-guard resilience that we'd built our previous success on.

Will James Wilson be an adequate replacement? Yes, over time. There will never be another Sean Raggett though, just like there will never be another Trevor Peake or Gareth McAuley. He was one of those one-off players who make everything seem so easy and even though he was here for half the season, our success is as much thanks to his efforts as anyone else.

Luke Waterfall
Apps 35 (6) Goals 3

We do love our skipper and his fabled magic hat, whether it is rising highest in the Checkatrade Trophy semi-final or nodding a late winner against Colchester, he's the man you just can't knock down. It's hard to believe that he spent part of the season on the bench, kept out of the side by Rob Dickie and then almost lost his place after the water bottle incident at Mansfield.

Whatever comes Luke's way he deals with, both on and off the field. He's a straightforward character, friendly and approachable like most of the players but very down to earth. He's no nonsense, especially when he's at the heart of the defence.

Luke is also the most decorated Lincoln City captain of all time, no single club captain has lifted a trophy on two occasions, not bad for a player who has spent time in the stands as well as on the bench. In 2015/16 he watched on with the fans towards the end of the season, but a year later he lifted the National League trophy. In 2017/18 he warmed the bench as the bright young things of Dickie and Raggett marshalled the defence, but by April he was back in the royal box at Wembley with another trophy in his hand.

Luke is uncomplicated in the nicest possible way. As a defender he tackles, heads and gets rid of the ball whenever he can. He's much like Steve Thompson in that respect, an old school centre back without the frills, bells and whistles. There's certainly nothing wrong with that at all and whether he's alongside Bozzie, Scott Wharton or James Wilson, he does exactly the same.

The Mansfield water bottle incident was unfortunate and I wouldn't want to sour his season by highlighting it too much because it was a rare lapse in judgement from a man usually not fazed by emotion or pressure. As he rose to nod in against Chelsea U21s in the Checkatrade semi-final, he did so in just the same manner as any league game, yet this was a high-pressure header. One thing you can always say about Luke is, bar the odd celebration, he's never phased. Later today, as he leads the team out against Exeter with us closer to a play off final as at any time since 2005, he'll be exactly the same as he was at Wembley, or at Ashby Avenue in pre-season.

Luke won't be getting a move to Norwich or the second-tier, he's not the sort of defender those clubs want, but he is a good, solid League Two captain and one who will inevitably always be a legend at Sincil Bank. He also personifies the Chumbawumba song 'Tub Thumping', because whenever he gets knocked down he just gets back up, puts on his magic hat and writes a fresh chapter in his remarkable story.

Scott Wharton
Apps 14 (1) Goals 2

I'll happily express my thoughts on his long-term future before assessing how he did for us this season: he won't be playing League Two football in 2018/19.

If the was a successor to Sean Raggett, and I've already said there probably won't be, Scott Wharton is as close as it gets. He's proven himself to be great in the air, scoring twice in his 14 starts for the club. One was a header, the other a wells-truck effort against Grimsby which showed his class on the ball.

Why would we doubt his class with the ball at his feet? He came from Blackburn with a big reputation, billed as a potential future star for them but needing game time. When he got it, he immediately cemented himself a place in the back four and hasn't looked like losing it since. Danny built up the 'left-sided centre back' angle as if the flexibility was behind bringing Wharton in, but he was a direct replacement for Rob Dickie and a much better one at that.

That isn't me bitterly lamenting Dickie either, but Scott Wharton has looked every inch a third-tier player. If we go up, maybe he returns on loan, but he's a Blackburn boy and is surely focused on doing whatever he can to force himself into their reckoning. They've got good players and he'll do well to get regular Championship football, but there's no reason why he can't sit on the fringes there and bide his time.

Before then he has one, maybe two more matches to write himself into Imps folklore. He'll finish the season with more starts that Dickie, but the comparison should stop there. Even in dropping into left back he showed a versatility that we've perhaps missed. I'd wager Danny would love to have him in the squad for next season, he fits that 'League One quality' player our gaffer craves and his performances are always committed and resolute.

James Wilson
Apps 7 (3) Goals 1

We've not really seen much of the former Sheffield United man and to sum up his season is tough. He did get a goal with his first touch, as pictured above, but then a broken ankle against Cambridge set him back severely. His recent return to the side has been tentative and with just six starts, and a further three outings from the bench, it is hard to judge him objectively.

My firmly held belief is this; he'll be a top player for us, in League One or League Two and as he grows into our style of play and gets a pre-season under his belt, he'll be one of the first names on the team sheet. Former Welsh internationals don't spend all their life in League One or the Championship, then choose to drop down to League Two out of the kindest of their heart. He's here because he buys into what we are trying to achieve, which is promotion, for those who haven't got that.

As yet, James Wilson hasn't won over a sceptical crowd, just as Tom Pett hadn't / hasn't. Both joined permanently and as yet, Danny hasn't signed a player on a permanent deal who turned out to be a turkey dressed as a golden goose. James Wilson won't turn out to be the first, of that I'm confident.

Both Jamie McCombe and Callum Howe were registered as players, but neither made an appearance this season. Callum signed for Port Vale and of course, many lamented the fact he hadn't remained an Imp. Since his move he's barely played for them, whilst both Wharton and Wilson, signed in his place, have played plenty for us. Callum was a nice guy who will settle into a lower League Two defence, but possibly not an upper League One side, which is what Danny believes he is building.

The Players – Midfield

Harry Anderson
Apps 31 (19) Goals 7

At the beginning of the season I called Harry as one of the players who would set League Two alight. He has all the qualities you want to see as a wide player at this level, explosive pace and a bullish, rugged physicality that saw him shrugging off defenders with apparent ease.

Before Christmas I was spot on. He bagged six goals and made a significant difference whenever he came on. Crewe away sticks in my mind, 1-0 down at half time but Harry ripped them apart in the second half. Away at Forest Green he showed electrifying pace to win a dour game, running as fast as anyone we've seen in years and then finishing confidently. He looked to be growing into his role, rarely having a poor game and always poised to make a huge difference.

Then it all changed. That started with the red card at Luton, a silly dismissal which may not have cost us the game, but certainly lost us the one-man advantage that we had. We lost 4-2 and although there was no public condemnation from Danny, I bet there was a bit of a bum kicking behind the scenes. A young Harry got caught up in the moment.

Then there was the concern about Harry's inability to play against a 3-5-2, when a midfield man could track him and not give him space to run at or run into to. Harry's skill comes at pace, if he's approaching a player at speed he can drop a shoulder and beat them. If he's in behind, he'll beat anyone yard for yard. Against a 3-5-2, he's got a player on him and he drifts out of the game.

From there, he drifted out of the team. The switch to 4-3-3 towards the end of the season negated all his abilities, he looks to struggle when tucking into the 'inside left' or 'inside right' role of old. He's a winger, pure and simple.

Harry Anderson has ended the season with a lot to prove. As Hiram Boateng ran the show for Exeter, Harry looked lost for us. At the beginning of the season I could never have predicted the issues he'd face throughout the start of 2018. Next season will be massive for Harry as he must mature as a player and add some positional intelligence to his other attributes.

Nathan Arnold
Apps 16 (8) Goals 0

I find it tough writing about Nathan because he's a lovely guy and someone I truly believe could have had an impact in the second half of the season. We lacked genuine wide players and I believe we were forced into a 4-3-3 because we of that, especially after Ginnelly and JMD left and Cameron Stewart failed to impress.

I don't know what went on, I won't speculate because I class Nathan as a friend. That isn't me being sycophantic but genuinely, I don't know. I haven't pushed him and I'm not going to either.

What I do know is he started well enough, grabbing an assist in the opening game and looking dangerous right up until the Luton game. In that 0-0 draw he was cynically hacked down in the final minutes as he burst forward with a grand chance to score. That foul resulted in an injury which I feel ended his Imps campaign.

He made his way back to fitness but struggled to break into the first team, something I imagine affected him. In his interview with Alan Johnson he alluded to not wanting to be a bit-part player, something I think was taken out of context by those reading it. Nathan wanted first team football and whatever happened, he was handed the chance at Salford. I'm not commenting on that either, but as the season died down he was over in Nepal supporting Garry Goddard's excellent charity. Some lamented his absence when we may have needed him, others understood that something had gone off behind the scenes that we didn't understand.

Those who say Nathan isn't a League Two quality player are wrong. The way he skipped past the Rochdale full back in the Checkatrade win was embarrassing for the player, also he was one of the few to come out of the home tie against Coventry with plaudits. He worked tirelessly in that game and showed he's got the quality to impact a League Two side.

I hope he remains at City, I hope he comes back into the fold and shows everyone that he's not just good enough, but he's strong enough to put the past behind him and demonstrate his skills to us all. Remember, Nathan Arnold was a cod, but right now he's an Imps and whether he's my friend or not I believe he has something to offer us.

Ellis Chapman
Apps 0 (2) Goals 0

Ellis is this season's bit part player, two appearances from the bench which would barely warrant a piece here. However, he did make performances and I wanted to recognise his 'break through' of sorts.

Young Ellis is a player of huge potential, one Danny believe will be a 'special player'. We haven't seen it as yet, how could we inside two late cameo appearances? Nothing was expected of Ellis but his first professional deal in the summer was a special moment. I loved the 'old and new' symbolism between him and Lee Frecklington.

He's barely kicked a ball for the first team but rest assured, he's been developing and impressing with the group all season. It might be twelve months, it might be two years, but this boy will break through.

Lee Frecklington
Apps 19 (1) Goals 4

When Lee Frecklington arrived, everyone cheered and gasped. A Championship captain less than a year ago, him coming to Sincil Bank would surely cement our play off place. Everyone wondered where he'd fit in, what we might do to accommodate him,

On his debut he smashed a goal to sign back on, against Chelsea U21 he sent us to Wembley in a proper Roy of the Rovers storyline. In all, he grabbed four goals in 16, meaning over a full season if that average continued he'd get ten. Not a bad return, right?

So why much negativity? At times he hasn't looked as effective as we'd hoped, but this is a different level and a new challenge. Also, without probing too much off the field, he's got some personally issues to deal with too. I think he's done incredibly well to remain both fit and focused during that time.

Has he had the impact everyone had hoped? Maybe not, no. Has he been a flop? Absolutely not, no. He hasn't run the show like some had hoped, he hasn't been as consistent as even he might have hoped, but he's been far from a flop. In some games he's looked dominant and composed, but then there are matches away at Port Vale or Accrington where the ball has passed him by time and again. Remember, we play a direct game which by-passes the midfield and that doesn't help him.

He's been surging into the area late as we saw against Grimsby, giving us glimpses of what we can expect. There's much more to come from Lee is he stays fit, I hope over the summer his personal situation settles down and we get him next season able to focus on his football. However, he scored two fewer goals in the league than both Anderson and Bostwick and had six months less. He banged home that Chelsea U21 penalty too, setting up our Wembley appearance and our route to silverware.

Josh Ginnelly
Apps 11 (8) Goals 3

I was puzzled by Josh being recalled and wonder if the lack of games led to it, but I personally felt he was having a decent season. He looked rampant in the first match of the season, scoring a cracker against Wycombe on the opening day. Then he picked up an injury and in truth, he never bounced back from that.

His chances seemed limited after that, his next goal came in the EFL Trophy and what a goal it was, a curling effort from the edge of the area which was worthy of winning any game. By Christmas I thought he was getting back to his best, hence my surprise with his departure.

I think there was a little of the 'Derek Asamoah' about Josh, lots of pace that frightened the opponents, but not always an end product. Port Vale at home also hurt him a lot, his poor corner ending up in a goal for the opposition. I criticised him that day, he hadn't played well but two games later he scored against Stevenage. Then, he was gone.

He scored twice for Tranmere whilst on loan there, but he's recently been released by Burnley. Would we like to see him back? I would, I think there's a lot of quality there and a player able to play League Two football. Losing him at the same time as JMD stung us hard and I think he'd be an excellent squad player. We do need a deeper squad next season and if the right deal could be struck I'd have him back in a heartbeat.

Billy Knott
Apps 14 (7) Goals 2

Billy's admission of mental health issues has been a bit of a game changer in terms of analysis and understanding his performances. I do know that Billy's personal problems run deep and I'm not sure we're privy to everything that has happened to him both in the distant past or recent past. He's a troubled boy whom I wish well because I understand how mental health issues can affect you.

In terms of performance I thought we struggled to find a place for Billy early doors. He scored against Rotherham, the again with a cracker against Carlisle to give him two in four. At that point it looked like we were getting the real deal, the insanely talented boy who impressed at Chelsea and Sunderland, the technically gifted player who could run the midfield at will. We didn't.

Danny struggled to fit him into the 4-4-2, often playing him on the flank which wasn't the right place for him. He could sit in the middle of a 4-2-3-1, and he would have suited a 4-3-3 too, but neither of those formations appeared to be favoured as the early games passed by. Billy impressed when he did get on, but then came September 23rd and Notts County away.

It wasn't a red card, I'll get stick from County fans bothered to read this, but we now know that card shattered his confidence and lead him back down the path of depression. He played 11 more times before a move to Rochdale, one start for them was the total sum of his football. His season ended in March against Fleetwood.

Where now for Billy? I can't see Danny taking him for another season unfortunately, there's a talented player in there but to reach his potential he needs to find a level of personal peace and I don't think he will do that at Lincoln City. I heralded his arrival as a massive signing, a potential game-changer and someone with the gift of technical ability and sublime skills. I was right about the latter two points, but unfortunately we didn't see it.

Jordan Maguire-Drew
Apps 8 (6) Goals 2

Jordan Maguire-Drew angers me and maybe that's a bit too harsh, but he does. His performances for Dagenham last season set the National League alight and I felt again, we'd made a great signing. He opened his account over in Portugal with a wonderful free kick and many eyebrows were raised when he started on the flanks instead of both Harry and Nathan.

Let's be honest shall we? He was terrible. One corner that landed on Sean Raggett's head gave us a win against Swindon, a brace sent us through in the EFL Trophy but there was nothing else to mention here. His celebrations against Everton were clearly passionate but maybe also a bit petulant, as if he wanted to stick a middle finger up at the fans. He didn't, he did score a superb free kick, but two games later he was gone.

What he lacked, in my opinion, was positional sense. He looked like the kid who could run fast and beat players but has no idea of what else to do. He looked frightened to beat players, when he did he was so happy he went back and did it again without delivering balls and his tracking back was awful.

He was sent to Coventry, they loved him in the first game and then immediately saw through it. Three games later his season also ended. Two League Two sides, no impact and perhaps, just perhaps an indication of where his level is. Leyton Orient might do well to take him next season because in the National League, he's quite a player.

Tom Pett
Apps 4 (7) Goals 1

I'd championed Pett for a long time, but people also pointed out I was a fan of another Tom from last season who turned out to be a turkey. I never profess to be right all of the time, but when it comes to Tom Pett I'm certain we'll see the best of him next season.

In the early part of his Imps career he's looked lightweight, a little anonymous and has struggled to fit into the system. That's my honest opinion, it doesn't make him a bad player nor a flop, but it has taken him time to settle. My belief is that next season, with the correct recruitment, we're going to play more football on the floor and that will suit the former England C man.

I did like the way he signed off in the final match of the regular season, his goal showed such wonderful technique and calmness under pressure that it will have left fans wondering what else is to come. Had he not struck that goal then there might have been a bigger question mark over his head this summer.

I stand by what I said all along, Tom Pett is a quality footballer who wasn't brought in to take us up this season, but to be an integral part of what we do next season and beyond. The more I look at Danny's transfer policy and the contracts being signed now, the more I'm convinced that losing the play off semi-final wasn't such a bad thing. With a Cowley pre-season under his belt, this guy is going to be big for us.

Danny Rowe
Apps 13 (3) Goals 2

What a talent Danny Rowe is, a rampaging winger the like of which would have fitted beautifully in our 4-4-2 set up. He started out well too didn't he? That goal against Peterborough was excellent and his devastating runs were only ever going to bring goals and chances.

Then came the 4-1 defeat against Crewe, the day which ultimately prompted our management team to switch to a 4-3-3. With three forwards tucked in tightly, there was no room for Danny Rowe. Even worse, towards the end of the season when I think we may have reverted back to a 4-4-2, he was injured and unable to play at all.

Danny Rowe is a really good footballer who I would love to see back here permanently. However, much depends on how we set up next season as to whether it would be worth it or not. If we go with two orthodox wingers, the formation that helped us to the National League title, then he fits. even if we go to the 4-2-3-1, he fits, but that depends on the middle player of the front three being something very special. One wonders if Lee Frecklington or Tom Pett have been earmarked for that role? If we stay as we were at the end of the season, then we don't see Danny Rowe back.

Whatever happens, we will always have that wonderful goal against Posh and the similarly excellent strike against Exeter in the home league match. He's had an impact that is for sure, but I feel with Danny Cowley, loan players can't have a significant impact unless they have already played a high number of games, such are the demands on fitness and understanding the system.

Cameron Stewart
Apps 3 (3) Goals 0

Cameron Stewart was either going to be an inspired signing, a talented player who rediscovered his form at Lincoln City and set the league on fire, or he was going to look like a shadow of his former self, a player whose promise and potential had long-since deserted him. I think we got the latter.

Stewart started three games for City, two in the league and three in the Checkatrade Trophy, but his impact in all three was minimal. He did provide the delicious cross for Harry's goal against Posh in the quarter final of the cup, but that aside I can't recall one other really positive thing he did. I can't recall one cross, one rampaging run, nor one effort that the keeper tipped over or that flashed just wide.

Towards the end of the season when we flipped to 4-3-3 it meant there were even less chances for him to shine, his last outing coming against Chelsea in the EFL Cup. I'll be very surprised indeed if we see him in Imps colours again.

Elliott Whitehouse
Apps 22 (21) Goals 4

I'm sure I could write an essay about Elliott, the down to earth Yorkshire lad who seized his chance in the wake of suspensions and injuries after a stop / start campaign. There's those who love him, seeing him as a cult hero who works tremendously hard. There's also those who see him as a limited footballer, one perhaps more suited to the National League. Me? I can't make up my bloody mind.

I see the hard-working footballer, no doubt. I see the player who scored the disallowed goal against Exeter (pictured above where, by the way, none of their players are appealing). He can be instinctive in the area and he's bagged four goals this term, from 43 appearances though. He's started 22 games too, leaving him some way behind the likes of Freck and Bozzie in the goals per game ratio.

I also see the tryer, the eager and enthusiastic midfielder that just doesn't quite cut it at this level. Everyone talks about the two saves Christy Pym made from Matt Green in the play-off semi-final first leg, but few mention the miss from Elliott in the immediate aftermath of one of them. Yes, the ball fell quickly to him and yes, he had little time to react, but I'm not convinced had that been Lee Frecklington or even Ollie Palmer, we might have had a 1-0 lead.

When I say the jury is out though, I mean it. I think back to the Lincolnshire Derby where he ran the show with an outstanding display of endeavour and hard work, setting up a goal and generally impressing. Those outings are few and far between though, are they not? The more he played towards the end of the season the more I wondered if Danny was getting as many minutes into him as possible to assess the future. His contract is up soon and as yet, there's no new deal. Whereas Bozzie, Neil Eardley and the like have been tied down quickly, Elliott is forced to play the waiting game. That points to him being a 'fringe' player and we know how Danny feels about those.

Remember, he only recruits players who improve the squad and, as much as it hurts me to say it, Elliott is one area of the squad we can improve upon.

Jordan Williams
Apps 6 (5) Goals 0

When I say I feel let down by Jordan Williams, that isn't a reflection of his personal performances. I think he's worked hard whenever he's come in and he looked a home in the 4-3-3 set up as well. He's versatile, both a winger and a traditional inside left, giving Danny options but, for some reason, everything seemed to fizzle out.

He started six times for City, came on five times as a sub and I don't think he had a bad game in that time. The problem is, he didn't have a great game either. He toiled, he switched play, he got on the ball but he didn't do anything sensational. There was no Danny Rowe style thunderbolts, not even a Cameron Stewart style assist in the EFL Trophy.

That leads me to one of the things that held Williams back, being cup tied for the trophy. It may seem odd, but I think once we won at Wembley, the players who performed there had a 'free pass' if you like, certainly for the next game against Port Vale. As we impressed in each round the players who played earned the right to stay in for league matches, meaning Jordan Williams sat out. It didn't affect Scott Wharton as much, being a versatile left sided centre back he filled back in when Luke was suspended, nor did it affect James Wilson because he was either injured or coming back, but Jordan had to sit out at times when maybe, just maybe he could have been growing in stature.

The rumour is he cost Rochdale £100,000 in the summer, not a sum of money many Lincoln fans would have liked to see us pay for him. He'll go back there this term and I suspect they'll want another look at him, but with him not really cutting it in League Two I wouldn't expect Keith Hill to be playing him heavily in League One. I'd take him back on loan, there's enough there to suggest he could have an impact and he could develop, but in truth his Imps career just never quite got going.

Alex Woodyard
Apps 55 (1) Goals 2

Where I sit in the Coop Stand there's this red-faced old boy who takes up two seats. Every week he gets redder and redder every time Alex touches the ball, calling him every name under the sun. He's negative, he's useless etc etc. At one point my mate Dave, so placid he wouldn't dare tell a child off in case it answered back, got incensed and started talking really loudly about how good Alex was. Believe me, for Dave that is as confrontational as I've ever known him. He almost said it to the guys face. Almost.

I see it on social media a bit too, he's disloyal because he apparently wanted the Luton move, even though he stayed. He only ever passes backwards and is no more than a League Two player, coming from the same people who call him for almost moving to League One Luton Town. I cannot for the life of me understand which games those people have been watching because Alex Woodyard is, without a doubt, one of the best players we have.

He's absolutely not 'just League Two' standard, otherwise why would both Scunthorpe and Luton have courted him? Luton were League Two at the time but it was widely accepted they were going up and they saw Alex as part of their League One side. You know why? Because they know a good footballer when they see one.

Has it ever occurred to anyone that maybe, just maybe, the backwards and sideways passes are what he's been told to do in order to retain possession? In criticising those perhaps you're actually criticising the tactic, not the player. Most of those backward or sideways passes land at the intended player's feet by the way, so even if you think it's negative, it is accurate.

I'm addressing this as though there's a large amount of people knocking him and that is perhaps misleading. I'm sure there's far more who see exactly what he does bring to the side, the constant hard work and non-stop commitment. He breaks up play, he's a constant thorn in the side of the opposition and yes, he's defensively minded because that is his role. We looked incredibly secure in a 4-4-2 with him and Bozzie holding, but we didn't have the attacking players to make it work.

Alex Woodyard is a footballer's footballer. He's a team mate's dream, a player who does the hard work all the time. He's the midfielder who can dig a winger out of a hole if they lose the ball, he's the player dropping back on to the edge of the area to protect his defence. If a forward pass is misplaced he's the one who goes to win the ball and lay it back to the defender to try again. So what if he hasn't been threading fifty-yard balls through for Matt Green, that hasn't been his job. He looks to switch play whenever he can, if he can't he retains possession by laying the ball back.

I'm not sure we'll hold on to Alex this summer and I wouldn't begrudge him a move if it came along. Teams are watching him, teams in League One and despite what a few think, he's got the ability to play there. He's the unseen footballer, the hard worker who never comes up with a sensational goal or memorable assist, but he's integral to our side, the heartbeat of the team for two seasons now.

This season, Lincoln City played 58 matches in all competitions. Alex Woodyard played 56 of those, missing only Everton in the EFL Trophy. In that time we won the cup and finished top seven, so how on earth is he only League Two quality? For me, he's one of the best players in our squad.

The Players - Forwards

It took two fifteen pages to cover both the midfielders and the defenders, but this section is going to last no longer than two. For a whole season, Lincoln City had three out and out strikers on the books.

I refuse to talk about last season as being anything other than a success, top seven in our first season back as well as an EFL Trophy win cannot be viewed as anything else. However, what might have been achieved if we had a fourth option from the bench? What might have happened if we'd successfully brought in Ollie Hawkins, Simeon Akinola, Ade Azeez or any of the other strikers we were linked with in both the summer and the winter window?

It wasn't through lack of trying though and to be fair to the three we did have, they all have their strengths to which they work. I think I'll get widespread agreement though when I say we need to bring in at least two more forward players for the 2018/19 season

This isn't a look ahead though, it is a look back at the three strikers we did have on our books, starting with one of my favourite players in recent times.

Matt Green
Apps 52 (4) Goals 17

We desperately needed a 20-goal a season striker apparently, one who could fire us into the top three. How close were we then with 17-goal Matt Green?

I never buy into this mythical 'proven goal scorer', nor do I believe there's such a thing as a '20-goal a season' striker. Some fans cried out for Ricky Miller in pre-season and in January, he ended the campaign with a couple of goals, if that. Even looking in the Championship, £10m of Jordan Rhodes couldn't guarantee Sheffield Wednesday goals, yet he was a so-called proven scorer.

No, there's no such thing. Ten other players make a 20-goal a season striker and Matt Green is one of those players who would comfortably create goals for another striker. What we lacked all season was another Matt Green, a player the mirror image of him to partner him up front. You see, Green can work the channels, hold up the ball and get crosses in, but he can't be on the end to finish them as well. When he played as part of a 4-3-3 the goals slowed down, but that's natural as he was being asked to do the running off.

I acknowledge there was a goal drought that hampered him in autumn, 16 games without a goal was an awful run for him. As a result, the team faltered, but when he started scoring at Christmas, we started winning games. Now, if Matt Green was such a bad player, how come we relied on him so much? He might have been one of three centre forwards we had, but that means there was still two more.

Matt missed a few chances, just like he put a few away. He's not a 'natural goal scorer' in my eyes, not like Liam Hearn for instance, a player who could score from anywhere at any time. Matt Green has to work for his chances, he has to work endlessly and tirelessly and often he does. I know the goal was of little consequence, but that fourth against Peterborough underlined how much work he put in, 90 minutes on the clock and he still outpaced players for a goal.

In the play-offs against Exeter, there was only Matt Green that looked like scoring, both in the first leg and the second. I hear that other players hit the bar, but in truth Matt Green was the only player to strike shots at goal with the ball leaving his foot and us look like scoring. In my mind, he was pivotal to our success in both competitions and the third best player this season. I know there will be people disagreeing with me, I expect that and to a degree welcome it, but if in our 4-4-2 we had 'Matt Green' partnered by 'Matt Green', we'd be a League One club now.

Ollie Palmer
Apps 15 (42) Goals 11

A cult hero is defined as; a writer, musician, artist, or other public figure who is greatly admired by a relatively small audience or is influential despite limited commercial success. In my mind, Ollie Palmer became the ultimate cult hero. After all, who else could win a Player of the Month award for the entire league having barely played an hour and a half of football?

Ollie scored 11 goals from just 15 starts, but came off the bench a whopping 42 times. He desperately wanted to shed the tag of super-sub, but with stats like that I don't think it's possible.

It's well-known by those who read me regularly that I had issues with Ollie early doors. Because of his often-maverick approach to the game, his 'get my head down and think later' style, I felt he was costing us chances. He certainly didn't help Matt Green's goal drought with a selfish display against Chesterfield where he was taking shots from silly positions despite having his partner better placed.

Colchester away was the nadir of Palmer's Lincoln career, he started and was terrible as we went 1-0 down. When he came off we looked marginally better and I felt we'd perhaps seen the last of him. He was without a goal in 13 too, going through a similar drought to Green and leaving us short of goals.

After that a complete turnaround happened. He didn't get starts, but he did win us the tie against Rochdale, claiming afterwards he was settled in Lincoln and going nowhere. He seemed to get more direction on the pitch, we stopped looking for his head when he came on and gave it to feet and that confused the opposition. It's been said a million times, but how could anyone defend against Ollie Palmer when even he didn't know what he was going to do next?

Mansfield, Chesterfield, Exeter and Coventry (twice) all felt the full power of Ollie Palmer in full effect and, as the games drifted away and the season came to a close, he'd forced his way into the starting XI as part of the 4-3-3 attack. I suppose Danny threw caution to the wind, thinking that he had nothing to lose by playing all three. I'm not actually convinced it worked, but it has left Ollie with a few more starts than he felt he might get.

You know what? Part of me still isn't convinced. Part of me still thinks he should be more of a threat in the air, part of me would still like to see more impact from the start in games. Against Coventry he was excellent, but against Accrington and Yeovil he was virtually anonymous. If we could get the player that won the PFA award all the time, the unpredictable centre forward with a powerful shot and range of abilities, then we'd have a brilliant player on our hands. Instead, we have a wildly inconsistent player, one we know is capable of great goals but who sometimes doesn't show up.

When Matt Green fails to score you still notice his constant running, but in the Coventry game Palmer was dead on his feet with half an hour remaining. In pre-season, if he can begin to turn in eighty minutes at a time and if he can find a way to impact games from the start, perhaps we'll see a player worthy of a starting place. My fear is another season of minimal starts and maximum outings from the bench.

Matt Rhead
Apps 41 (9) Goals 9

He's the player everyone loves to hate, oppositions defenders, Sky TV, even some of our own crowd. He controversial, unique and I believe he shapes our entire tactical approach to games. Danny and Nicky weren't particularly known for long ball at Braintree, not to the extent they seem to be labelled by it now, but as everyone says, when you have a player like Matt Rhead it would be foolish not to use him.

What is a 'player like Matt Rhead' though? A big lump who wins flick ons and headers? A chunky guy who goes down too easily when a defender brushes past him? A victim of his own size, largely ignored by officials because of his reputation? He's all of that and, as his goal against Coventry showed, an awful lot more.

41 starts, nine goals in all competitions. Is it enough for such a big target man? I'd argue perhaps not, he's been unlucky in front of goal but he'll be disappointed with how many he's scored this season. One change has been our switch from 4-4-2, he scored eight under the old system and

just one whilst playing 4-3-3. He's the focal point of the new approach too, but he hasn't found goals hard to come by.

Remember, the big man was dropped early on too as Danny couldn't find a system that suited us, but eventually it was his pairing with Matt Green that brought us a level of success. They both bagged against Yeovil and Accrington at Christmas to set us up for a new year assault on the top seven, and of course the ultimate agitator, Green was the man who, almost single-handed, beat Forest Green just before the turn of the year. He's always going to want to score in the big games, just as he wanted to against Port Vale, as a Stoke fan.

Rhead has now scored 47 goals for City over three seasons and every time we reach the end of a campaign, the same question gets asked; how much will he feature next season? Firstly, he wasn't a Danny type of player, but he proved people wrong. Then, he couldn't hack League Two, but again he proved people wrong. What now? If we bring in forwards with the same pedigree as the likes of Michael Bostwick and Neal Eardley, will Matt Rhead be the one who falls by the way side?

Playing Devil's Advocate, would we have got a penalty in the Exeter game had it not been Matt Rhead who was pushed prior to Whitehouse's goal? Did we suffer from having the big man right at the end of the season? Maybe, maybe not. If the foul on Dean Henderson in the EFL Final hadn't been replayed again and again in slow motion, would he have got more decisions in the latter stages of the season? I'm not convinced Matt targeted Henderson in the same was Schumacher targeted Battiston in 1982, but he was treated with the same vitriol and hatred.

It's all conjecture but one thing is for certain, he's here for next season and you can never, ever rule out Matt Rhead. If other teams hate him you know it's because he's effective.